T0330219

Investment Management

Founded in 1807, John Wiley & Sons is the oldest independent publishing company in the United States. With offices in North America, Europe, Australia, and Asia, Wiley is globally committed to developing and marketing print and electronic products and services for our customers' professional and personal knowledge and understanding.

The Wiley Finance series contains books written specifically for finance and investment professionals as well as sophisticated individual investors and their financial advisors. Book topics range from portfolio management to e-commerce, risk management, financial engineering, valuation and financial instrument analysis, as well as much more.

For a list of available titles, please visit our Web site at www.Wiley Finance.com.

Investment Management

Meeting the Noble Challenges of Funding Pensions, Deficits, and Growth

WAYNE H. WAGNER
and
RALPH A. RIEVES,
Editors

WILEY

John Wiley & Sons, Inc.

Published by John Wiley & Sons, Inc., Hoboken, New Jersey.
Published simultaneously in Canada.

For general information on our other products and services or for technical support, please contact our Customer Care Department within the United States at (800) 762-2974, outside the United States at (317) 572-3993 or fax (317) 572-4002.

Wiley also publishes its books in a variety of electronic formats. Some content that appears in print may not be available in electronic books. For more information about Wiley products, visit our web site at www.wiley.com.

This development of this book was funded by Farragut, Jones & Lawrence, Inc. *FJL* underwrites the writing of reference sources for institutional investors. *FJL* also advises about best practices in fiduciary oversight.

Library of Congress Cataloging-in-Publication Data
Investment management : meeting the noble challenges of funding pensions, deficits, and growth / Wayne H. Wagner and Ralph A. Rieves, editors.
    p. cm.
  Includes index.
  ISBN 978-0-470-45594-4 (cloth)
  1. Investments–United States. 2. Business cycles–United States. I. Wagner, Wayne H.
II. Rieves, Ralph A.
HG6041.I58 2009
332.6–dc22

                                 2009005642

10 9 8 7 6 5 4 3 2 1

To Sumner and Caroline Levine, with enduring regard.

—RAR

To Larry Cuneo, for 40 years of fighting the good battles together.

—WHW

Contents

Foreword   xvii

Preface   xix

Acknowledgments   xxv

Editorial Advisory Board   xxvii

INTRODUCTION:
A Sea of Changes and Waves of Opportunity   1

Jacqueline Charnley and Christine Røstvold
*The 2008–2009 credit crisis roiled the already-turbulent
environment in which asset managers confronted their
stewardship challenges. The authors cite seven major
elements of the "pre-crisis" turbulence, and remind readers
of Darwin's dictum of survival. Proactive relationships
with all the players are the key.*

PART ONE:
The Challenges of Changes and Crises

CHAPTER 1
The Discontinuity Challenge   27

Wayne H. Wagner
*The twists and tangles of the 2008–2009 credit crunch will
long be remembered. This chapter does not address that
specific discontinuity, but discusses discontinuities in
general. From a longer time perspective, we see that these
discontinuities occur frequently, suggesting that in addition
to applying our experience and running our models in
"normal" times, we need to prepare to face the inevitable*

discontinuity environments. This is the first chapter of several in which we reflect on Taleb's Black Swan.

CHAPTER 2
The Sub-Prime Crisis as a "Predictable Surprise": Strategic
Lessons to Be Learned   44

Keith Ambachtsheer

The fallout from the events of 2008–2009 has engendered several million words of criticism, constructive and otherwise. Yet, very little relevant appraisal has come from the investment management industry. An enduring champion of pension reform describes the collective actions that can be effectively marshaled when confronted with another threat of asset erosion. Why, in this case, Bazerman and Watkins are more relevant than Taleb.

CHAPTER 3
The Solidarity Challenge   58

David G. Tittsworth, Esq.

Compared to many other laws, the statutory framework of the Investment Advisors Act of 1940 is relatively simple and straightforward. The fiduciary culture it has fostered distinguishes the advisory profession from other financial services. Now, the basic legal and regulatory structure that has governed investment advisors for decades is being debated. Well-organized and well-financed groups seek to change the laws based on the 1940 Act, charging that they are "outdated" and "losing relevance." The author suggests three actions to ensure that investment advisers work together to preserve what is good about how the advisory profession is governed.

PART TWO:
Keeping the Challenges in Perspective

CHAPTER 4
The Failure of Invariance   81

Peter L. Bernstein

When published in 1996, Against the Gods: The Remarkable Story of Risk *took its place as one of the seminal history books*

*written in the twentieth century. Here is Chapter 16
from that remarkable work. Many readers encountered
for the first time Kahneman's and Tversky's
"Prospect Theory." Investment managers who have
not read* Against the Gods *are at a competitive
disadvantage—big time.*

CHAPTER 5
Inverted Reasoning and Its Consequences   **95**

G.C. Seldon

*Not for the first time, we anthologize this excerpt
from* Psychology of the Stock Market, *first published
in 1912. Sage observations from which the author
observes, "Historical parallels are likely to be
misleading."*

CHAPTER 6
Fatal Attractions for Money Managers   **100**

Arnold S. Wood

*An experienced and innovative investment manager reflects
on "the triumph of temptation over reason," and offers a
"list of ten causes of irrational, and occasionally bizarre,
behavior" by professional investors.*

CHAPTER 7
Renzo Gracie's Brazilian Jiu Jitsu Academy   **108**

Richard Bookstaber, PhD

*An elegant analogy illustrating how innovation, endogenous
risks, and regulation should be contemplated so as to assure
a market "that is more robust and survivable." Excerpted
from the best-selling* A Demon of Our Own Design
(Hoboken: Wiley, 2007).

CHAPTER 8
Managing Outside the Box   **111**

Robert A. Jaeger, PhD

*This reflection on fads and fashion in the investment
business provides an appropriate departure for studying
Part Three of this book: The Challenges Under
Transformation.*

PART THREE

The Challenges Under Transformation

CHAPTER 9
The Evolving Challenges of Quantitative Investing   **119**

Robert L. Hagin, PhD and Kathleen T. DeRose

The authors suggest that the rapid pace of technological change affects both fundamental and quantitative investors. Despite their similarities, quantitative investors, particularly those who acknowledge the limits of technology, are better equipped to deliver on their clients' performance expectations. As investment approaches begin to incorporate insights from beyond computer science, drawing from biology and other disciplines, the debate becomes a philosophical one about the frontier between the computer and the intellect.

CHAPTER 10
EMH and the Matter at Hand   **129**

Wayne H. Wagner and Ralph A. Rieves

Do nanosecond changes in "publicly available information" and the behavioral school's challenge require a reappraisal of a fundamental postulate of investment theory? Why is Taleb relevant?

CHAPTER 11
The Attribution Challenge   **138**

Ron Surz

Performance standards focus on accurate measurements and reporting. But the most accurate measurements can be misinterpreted when compared to faulty benchmarks. Here is an extensive discussion about accurate benchmarking and rigorous attribution analysis. Tiger Woods' bowling scores are not relevant to his achievements.

CHAPTER 12
**The Academic Challenge: An Interview with Professor
Stephen Brown on Developments in Modern Finance** **154**

Harry Liem

*Some of the great questions of financial theory remain
with us. A respected academic candidly answers
some well-posed questions about "book-smart" and
"street-smart." The answers are relevant and pertinent,
regardless of occasional systemic disorder.*

CHAPTER 13
The Elusiveness of Investment Skill **171**

Robert A. Jaeger, PhD

*The author of this chapter turns from commenting on
fads and fashions to reflecting on investment skill.
Skill is elusive, but it is not illusionary. He argues that
skill is real precisely because it is elusive. "The barriers
to entry in the hedge fund business are seductively low;
the barriers to success are formidably high."*

PART FOUR

The Clients' Challenges

CHAPTER 14
The Client Challenge—Trustees as Leaders **185**

Fiduciary 360

*Recent events have generated a new challenge for
trustees. How boards are led has emerged as an even
more critical issue than it has been. The authors
remind stewards of the four characteristics of a
prudent procedure for discharging fiduciary duties:
organize, formalize, implement, and monitor.*

CHAPTER 15
The Kool-Aid® Quandary and the Enduring Lure of Outperformance **195**

Edward Siedle, Esq.

*A seasoned observer of the money management industry
reminds readers about the myth and reality of sustained*

*outperformance. Clients who can't distinguish between
myth and reality are more likely to be subject to chicanery.
The burden is on clients to make that distinction, not on
SROs or regulators. This theme is reiterated in several
chapters of this book.*

CHAPTER 16
The ESGI (née SRI) Challenge   **201**

"Dove Green"

The term socially responsible investing (SRI) *has
morphed into* environmental, social, and governance
investing (ESGI), *and is sometime referred to as*
sustainable investing. *Each of these terms has been used
by the cadres of activists to describe their persuasive
campaigns—the targets for which are now trustees,
investment managers, and corporations. Here is a
discussion about the concerns of shareholder activists
and social activists. Are ESG policies and procedures
the new intangibles? Whatever the cause, fiduciary
duty still trumps all.*

CHAPTER 17
The Marketing Challenge   **213**

Ron Gold

*Investment managers do not have to differentiate
themselves from the competition in huge ways. The
real marketing challenge is to articulate in a convincing
fashion how the differentiation "accrues to the benefit
of the client." Here are some insights and proposals
for getting more than "just a ticket on the bus."*

CHAPTER 18
The Selection and Termination of Investment
Management Firms by Plan Sponsors   **226**

Amit Goyal, PhD and Sunil Wahal, PhD, et al.

*We would have liked to have changed the title to
"Suspicions Confirmed." This chapter appeared in the
August 2008 issue of the* Journal of Finance *and is
reprinted in its entirety, including references and citations.*

A complete familiarity with this work is recommended for managers, consultants, and trustees throughout the world.

PART FIVE

The Execution Challenges

CHAPTER 19
The Market Price Challenge 281

Francis Gupta, PhD and John A. Prestbo

Are dark pools *the sell side's survival tactic, or revenge? Do the benefits of dark pools' lower trading costs outweigh diminished transparency? Over the past 20 years, volume on Nasdaq has increased over 20,000 percent. Could one argue that innovation and adaptability have been achieved at reasonable costs to investors and beneficiaries?*

CHAPTER 20
The Sell-Side Challenge 292

Steve Wunsch

Legislated order-handling rules and "shredded" algorithmic trading destroyed the longtime sell-side business model. Investments to enhance technological proficiency devour capital. Buy-side firms have more options. Is beefing up proprietary trading the best way to survive? Is there any future for the smaller sell-side firms? A veteran innovator and successful exchange officer reflects on relationships, regulation, and the cost of doing business on both sides.

CHAPTER 21
The Trading Challenge 300

Wayne H. Wagner

Our co-editor considers all the changes and reminds us that transactional basis points will always impact performance. And the clients know it.

CHAPTER 22
The Settlement Challenge   **315**

Steve Webb and Simon Bennett

The globalization of asset allocation is just one of several pressures complicating clearing and settlement processes. The pressures are significant factors in the buy-side search for frictionless trades and low transaction costs. Two acknowledged experts discuss these factors in the context of driving down the costs "to the end investor."

PART SIX

The Challenges to Management

CHAPTER 23
Investment Belief Systems: A Cultural Perspective   **333**

John R. Minahan, PhD, CFA

Beliefs permeate the investment business. They shape our decisions and our institutions. Beliefs themselves are shaped by culture, by professional training, by experience, and by deliberate attempts to clarify ambiguity and reduce uncertainty. In rapidly changing times, it is valuable to examine one's beliefs in light of theory, evidence, and alternative points of view.

CHAPTER 24
Ethical Leadership in the Investment Firm   **352**

Jim Ware, CFA and Jim Dethmer, ThM

The authors built this chapter by developing the concept of energetic integrity, which they describe as the preventive medicine against legal and ethical breaches. They conclude with a description of the key elements necessary for energetic integrity.

CHAPTER 25
The Adaptive Leader   **369**

Jim Ware, CFA

The author suggests asking 14 questions to ascertain the effectiveness of a firm's leaders. Investment management is a talent business. Bad bosses will drive out good talent.

CHAPTER 26
The Staffing Challenge   **379**

Monika Müller

The author identifies seven traits of portfolio managers. She describes a matrix composed of these characteristics, and explains how its use can enhance the recruitment and retention of consistently high performers. First, however, one should reflect on some research.

CHAPTER 27
The "Same Page" Challenge: Communicating Effectively   **398**

Jamie Goodrich Ziegler

A veteran industry executive addresses the necessity of clear communications among all the players: consultants, sponsors, sell-siders, and portfolio managers. Some practical suggestions on overcoming barriers and misconceptions.

CHAPTER 28
The Data Management Challenge   **416**

Don DeLoach

There always will be challenges to the interdependency and efficiency of information systems. Here are some recommended approaches to designing, utilizing, and monitoring the "lifeblood" of the firm.

About the Editors   **427**

About the Contributors   **429**

Index   **435**

Foreword

When the story of investing from the late 1990s to 2010 is written, students of financial history might find themselves scratching their heads and saying: *"Efficient Market What?"*

From the tech-stock bubble to the tech-stock collapse, we saw stock prices soar and collapse within a very short period. How could JDS Uniphase Corp. – a stock with modest revenues and no profits – hit a peak of $153.421 on March 7, 2000 and then lose 99 percent of its value by the end of 2002?[*] There was the matter of a $56 billion loss in 2001. So, shouldn't Mr. Market have had some idea of what was coming?

Low-interest rate policies and lax lending practices led to a credit crunch that wiped out Bear Stearns Company, Inc. and Lehman Brothers Holding, Inc and destroyed the value of previously world-beating financial stocks like Citicorp and Bank of America Corporation. How could these and the other stock values implode virtually overnight? If the market was efficiently priced all the time, or even every third day, then Jack the Ripper was a great humanitarian and Robert Mugabe should win the Nobel Peace Prize.

This has been a period when bell curves – the statistician's mainstay – were mocked, when "fat tails" became part of the common lexicon, and Nassim Nicholas Taleb became the portfolio managers' patron saint (apparently with not one of them having read any of his books.)

"Risk" is now the first word out of every advisor's and every trustee's mouth, after having been undervalued (or totally ignored) for most of this decade. A decade when the behavioral finance theorists finally gained an upper hand on the classicists: When William Sharpe moved beyond mean-variance analysis to Kenneth Arrow's state/preference theory as a way to explain the pricing of securities. And when Andrew Lo revived Herbert Simon's notion of "bounded rationality" using "satisficing heuristics" or rules of thumb to explain economic behavior.

This has been the decade when institutional investors threw out the straightjacket of style boxes and gave unfettered freedom to a new breed of hedge fund managers – and paid them a 2 percent maintenance fee and 20 percent or better of the upside for the privilege of employing their "talent." Not surprisingly, those clients are rethinking such fee structures.

I am sure some efficient market theorists will come up with an explanation of how all this fits into a universe that is rationally priced most, if not all, of the time. But I'm not sure she or he will sell as many textbooks as have been sold in the past.

Those two key questions of institutional investing still remain: Can active managers add values consistently and over time? And how effective are trustees and their consultants at picking managers?

If you are a trustee or are running a money management firm, you have to deal with all the issues I have addressed. The chapters in this book probe these issues. The authors skew many fallacies and misconceptions of the investment world. These authors don't offer any one-size-fits-all solutions. They do highlight many of the key problems that institutional investors face in any environment, not just the one that has characterized this decade.

Every money management firm, as well as every pension plan, endowment, or trust will come up with their own respective solutions. The solutions will be based on their own capabilities and needs. Moreover, the solutions should also be based on an acute mindfulness of human limitations regardless of imputed experience or "wisdom."

Again, there are no easy solutions, but this book does describe the most important challenges that every diligent manager and prudent trustee must acknowledge and address.

Joel Chernoff
Executive Editor
Pensions and Investments

Preface

Some investment managers performed relatively well during the 2008 credit crisis. They cut themselves away from the herd and adhered to their own disciplines and guidelines. These investment professionals have a heightened consciousness about their assumptions and a fierce commitment to reexamining those assumptions. Much earlier than 2008, we believed that the willingness to "think about one's thinking" was a key characteristic of a proficient money manager. And this belief was what prompted us to undertake this book.

People in the investment industry are among the most highly educated in the world; nonetheless, those associated with large investment portfolios need to stay abreast of the search for knowledge in finance. This is similar to the ongoing education of physicians, who need to stay abreast of the most recent developments in medicine. Both sets of professionals bear burdens of implicit and explicit trust.

Investment professionals face *increasing pressure* to fund the retirement of millions of workers, as well as meet the capital formation needs that sustain businesses around the world. The rate at which that pressure increases pales, however, in comparison to the rate at which changes are occurring in areas that directly impact the practice of investing. Merger activities among bourses and exchanges, plus the continued emergence of electronic trading platforms, are the obvious transforming events. However, new risk management strategies and instruments are even more impacting.

A DISAGREEABLE REALITY

Many investment professionals attempt to catch hold of the fast-moving trains of investment innovation.

The latest return-enhancing concepts are captured, refined, and implemented with the hope that one has achieved enough advantage to craft a more enduring investing modus operandi. That hope is unlikely. The competition is too fierce. There is much traction up the learning curve. The willingness to synthesize what is *known* and to analyze what is *happening* confirms that all the players in the capital markets know that they are engaged in a complex state of affairs. What aggravates that complexity is not just the constant change in venues, theories, and strategies, but also what Peter L. Bernstein characterized as a "state of disagreeable reality . . . . being wrong on occasion is inescapable."

A MAP FOR THE PLAYERS

This work is intended to assist investment managers and the attendant players (trustees, regulators, and vendors) as they meet the challenges we characterize as *noble*. The authors of the chapters in this book strove to be descriptive. The goal is to describe circumstances in a manner intended to heighten an already-sensitized awareness. The rate of changes within the milieu precludes prescribing any specific process or action. If there is prescription, it is only included to suggest means that a professional investor might consider when crafting (or re-crafting) an investment policy and a strategy. The chapters in this work are divided into five parts. Each part contains subjects that are tangential to each other.

Part One: The Challenges of Changes and Crises

The 2007-2008 credit crisis roiled the already-turbulent environment in which asset managers confronted their stewardship challenges. Jacqueline Charnley and Christine Røstvold describe the turbulence and change in the industry, and introduce the themes prevalent in this book. Wayne Wagner reminds us to take a historical perspective to ascertain the frequency of market shocks. He proposes some possible methods to address the challenges that those shocks bring. Keith Ambachtsheer recommends the collective actions that can be marshaled to avoid another asset erosion. And David Tittsworth addresses the need for industry solidarity in protecting regulations that have served and protected the advisory profession and beneficiaries since the enactment of the Investment Advisors Act of 1940.

Part Two: Keeping the Challenges in Perspective

This part presents a selection of previously published works. They are included because they are elegant discourses on some attitudinal challenges forever present. The first of these is a chapter from Peter L. Bernstein's classic book, *Against the Gods: The Remarkable Story of Risk*. He cites the research that challenges (and sometimes refutes) the assumptions held about risks and investor behavior. Bernstein's chapter is followed by revisiting

George C. Selden's work from a century ago. In this work, Selden reminds us again that "Historical parallels can be misleading." Arnold Wood's classic paper follows, in which he reflects on "the triumph of temptation over reason." Few financial books in this century have had such a conspicuous reception as Richard Bookstaber's *A Demon of Our Own Design* (Hoboken: Wiley). From that book, we have excerpted three pages of an analogy that prompts some incisive thinking about innovation and regulation. Robert Jaeger concludes Part Two with an update of his reflection on fads and fashions in the business.

Part Three: The Challenges Under Transformation

These chapters address the "town-and-gown" issues of the investment process. While the content in these chapters is likely to be overrun by events and discoveries now emerging, nevertheless, these chapters are essential for the intrepid and enterprising who utilize all of the navigational and meteorological aids in their voyages across the global markets. Quantitative managers Bob Hagin and Kathleen DeRose address the investors' challenges in the face of rapid technological change. We follow their discourse with a chapter discussing the relevance of EMH, and Ron Surz lays out the case for more informed and rigorous attribution analysis. We then share Harry Liem's insightful interview with Stephen Brown about the academic challenges. Robert Jaeger again concludes a part with a reflection on investment skill.

Part Four: The Clients' Challenges

The proper focus of investment management is on the client. Recent events and changes are more momentous from the clients' perspective than from the perspective of any particular purveyor of services or advice. The focus of the chapters in Part Four differs somewhat from the other chapters in this book. They are written so as to inform clients about some issues, as well as to heighten an investment manager's understanding about what this business is all about. The staff at fi360 and Ted Siedle each contributed chapters about trustees taking responsibility for discernment and oversight. There is a chapter addressing fiduciary duties and the future of "sustainable" investing. And Ron Gold prescribes the most effective ways of communicating with and marketing to present and prospective clients. The key feature of Part Four is the complete reprinting of the August 2008 paper by Amit Goyal and Sunil Wahal, "The Selection and Termination of Investment Management Firms by Plan Sponsors"—a paper we would like to have titled "Suspicions Confirmed."

Part Five: The Execution Challenges

These chapters describe the transactional aspects of portfolio management. Timely and cost-effective trades are critical concerns. Understanding the technology and the evolving structures within markets and venues is crucial. Again the focus is on clients and costs. Francis Gupta and John Prestbo address how much cost benefits have been achieved through technology and adaptability. Steve Wunsch discusses the impact on the sell side from recent rule changes and advances in algorithmic trading. Wayne Wagner reminds us that transactional basis points will always impact performance. And Steve Webb and Simon Bennett of CAPCO discuss the impact of globalizations on clearing and settlement processes.

Part Six: The Challenges to Management

This part includes the "best practices" chapters. Managing an investment firm is as important as managing portfolios. These chapters focus on the attributes and characteristics necessary to sustain the growth of a firm: Substantiating policy, building a professional team, and utilizing emerging technology. John Minahan talks about examining one's beliefs in light of theory, evidence, and alternative points of view. Jim Ware and Jim Dethmer address the leadership issues of ethics and of adaptability. Monika Müller provides keen insight about the challenges of staffing. Jamie Ziegler reminds readers that empathy and candor are key elements in communicating among peers, as well as with clients. Don DeLoach writes about the challenge of effective information management in the face of the increased flow of data, and the rapidity of technological change.

OUR PERSPECTIVE

Our conviction that a willingness to reexamine one's assumptions is a key characteristic of proficiency has been derived from decades of working with scores of money managers, analysts, trustees, and theorists. While our work is, for the most part, tangential to actually managing assets, it has not been conducted from a distance.

Investment professionals, trustees, and regulators agree that Wayne's work has saved investors *billions* of dollars. He was a founding partner of Wilshire Associates and designed the algorithms that governed the world's first index funds at Wells Fargo. Later, his Plexus Group validated the hidden delay and opportunity costs of trading. He is a fierce advocate for higher degrees of transparency and efficiency in trading. As the acknowledged authority on those subjects, he is invited to speak and write about them in venues around the globe. And he is the "quant's quant," as evidenced by his having been a director of the Institute for Quantitative Research in Finance for the past eight years.

As an executive editor at two book publishing enterprises, as well as being a co-founding editor of the *Journal of Financial Consulting,* Ralph has overseen the publication of over 100 books and references by the marquee players and academics in the field. Now a principal with Farragut, Jones & Lawrence, he advises emerging enterprises about the operations of capital markets, as well as assisting trustees in implementing the best practices of fiduciary oversight.

Our experience in the industry, as well as our regard and affection for it, is exceeded by those whom we invited to contribute to this book. Moreover, their contributions and achievements in meeting the noble challenges of global stewardship far exceed ours. We are blessed to have such a roster of seasoned pros.

Those readers who have joined the industry within the past five years may be bemused by the senior flavor of our list of authors and advisors. Here is our response to your bemusement: We chose our authors and advisors because, like us, they have learned to detect the industry's feedlot residue not only when they smell it, but also when they hear it or read it. Our wish is for you to acquire that same acuity, sooner rather than later.

In a time when capital flows instantly through borders, that which enhanced return this morning probably won't work after lunch. The model-building challenge, then, is *how the stewards of the world's assets should think about their thinking.* We hope that this work will assist in that enduring challenge.

Acknowledgments

This book would not exist without the critiques, encouragement, and admonishments of our editorial advisory board. It is customary to "window dress" advisory boards for books like this with names of widely acknowledged authorities. In many instances the time demands on such marquee names preclude any real involvement in the development of the book. Such is not the case with our all-star lineup.

Doug Harman and Jim Ware have been our sage sources about what really works where the rubber meets the road. Once more, how you run your business depends on *thinking about your thinking*. Jim and Doug do that all the time, so they set good examples for us. Listening and adhering to their suggestions kept this work moving in the direction to which we aspired.

Bob Hagin and Keith Ambachtsheer were involved from the inception of this project. Their advice and their contributions were invaluable. More importantly, their support and enthusiasm sustained us throughout the development of this book. That's what longtime friends are for.

Executing trades and controlling transaction costs are the most enduring of the challenges addressed in this book, and are so recognized by portfolio managers. For decades, Jay Peake and Bob Schwartz have been fierce advocates for appropriate transparency and efficiency in global financial markets. Their efforts in encouraging the education and enlightenment of investors have resulted in heightened consciousness about the necessity of sound execution decisions. Their efforts have saved investors billions of dollars. Without their advice and critiques, there would be no Part Five.

If there is a prevailing theme in this book, it is about focusing on the client. For two decades, Don Trone has been a prominent advocate for trustees and beneficiaries. His observations about their sensitivities as well as their mandated duties greatly influenced the structure of Part Four.

Doug Schmidt oversaw the compilation of all these words. Without his editorial and organizational skills, the manuscript for this work would not have been "acceptable, in all respects, to the publisher."

The theme and coverage of this book evolved from bouncing some ideas off two "downtown" friends in the spring of 2007. During the subsequent work on this book, we would recall our visits with Ed Altman and Tom Ho. Their dispassionate and informed observations were critical in maintaining theme and focus.

Not surprisingly, Peter L. Bernstein's name appears several times in this book. It is PLB who continues to ennoble the challenges of global steward-ship. He is inspiration personified. His work and writing have enriched us all.

We selected John Wiley & Sons as our publishing partner because we had been well served by them with our previous books. Emilie Herman, Kate Wood, and Michael Lisk exceeded our expectations.

During our work on this book we were frequently reminded that recre-ation and communion with our life partners would enhance our productiv-ity. Thank you, Carol and Beth. We are blessed for your loving reminders. And for the fun.

Editorial Advisory Board

The development of this book was funded by Farragut, Jones & Lawrence, Inc. *FJL* underwrites the writing of reference sources for institutional investors. *FJL* also advises about best practices in fiduciary oversight.

Keith Ambachtsheer, CFA is director of the Rotman International Centre for Pension Management at the University of Toronto, and is an adjunct professor of finance at the Rotman School of Management. He is founder and president of KPA Advisory Services in Toronto, which provides strategic advice on governance, finance, and investment matters to governments, industry associations, pension plan sponsors, foundations, and other institutional investors around the world. He is also a co-founder of CEM Benchmarking Inc., which monitors the organizational performance of pension plans around the world. He is the author of three books about pension funds and a frequent contributor to the *Financial Analysts Journal*, for which four of his articles were awarded the Graham and Dodd Award for excellence in investment writing.

Doug Harman, CFA, CPA is the president and chief compliance officer of Harman Investment Advisors Inc. He is a certified public accountant and a chartered financial analyst. He has served on the examination committee of the CFA Institute. He has also served as president and director of the CFA Society of Chicago. In addition, he has been director of the Financial Analysts Federation, as well as governor of its successor organization, the CFA Institute.

Robert L. Hagin is the CEO of Hagin Investment Management in New York, which provides quantitative asset management to institutional clients and qualified individual investors. He is a 35-year veteran of the industry, and pioneered the use of computers in investments and finance. He is the author of five books about portfolio management, the most recent of which was *Investment Management: Portfolio Diversification, Risk and Timing* (Hoboken: Wiley). He has led investment and research teams at Kidder Peabody, Miller Anderson, and Sherrerd, and was executive director at Morgan Stanley Investment Management. He has been an editorial advisor to the CFA Institute and to IMCA. He is a founding member of Q-Group, past president of the New York Society of Quantitative Analysts, and a former professor at the Wharton School. He holds a PhD from UCLA.

Junius Peake is emeritus professor of finance at the Monfort School of Business at the University of Northern Colorado. He is an acknowledged

In reality, knowledge is a very dynamic universe—and what is most valuable is not the body of knowledge but the leading edge of it.

—Bill James
Baseball Historian

Introduction

A Sea of Changes and Waves of Opportunity

Jacqueline Charnley and
Christine Røstvold

The 2008 financial crisis roiled an already-turbulent environment. The authors review major elements of that pre-crisis turmoil as fiduciaries and asset managers confront their stewardship challenges. As John Minahan of New England Pension Consultants observes in Chapter 23 of this book, "In rapidly changing times it is especially valuable to examine one's beliefs in light of theory, evidence, and alternative points of view."

The decline of capital and credit markets across the world in 2008 and 2009 profoundly changed the landscape for institutional investors, but the obligations and commitments remained the same. The magnitude of change in the institutional investment industry continues to accelerate, creating a sea of challenges and waves of opportunities for investors, consultants, and investment managers alike.

In 1980, total pension assets were less than $1 trillion. According to Watson Wyatt, the world's 300 largest pension and investment funds grew to $12 trillion as of 12/31/07. But 2008 turned the investment world upside down. Let's compare and contrast the change from December 31, 2007 to December 31, 2008.

As of December 31, 2007, at least 12 firms reported that they managed more than $1 trillion, including one firm that managed over $2 trillion. December 31, 2008 showed the severe impact of the market declines. None of us would have imagined that Bear Stearns, Lehman Brothers, American Insurance Group, or Merrill Lynch would be out of business or purchased by competitors. The $50 + billion fraud engineered by Bernard Madoff took everyone by surprise, including the Securities and Exchange Commission (SEC) and industry experts. See Exhibit I.1.

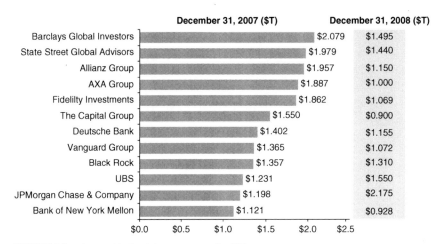

	December 31, 2007 ($T)	December 31, 2008 ($T)
Barclays Global Investors	$2.079	$1.495
State Street Global Advisors	$1.979	$1.440
Allianz Group	$1.957	$1.150
AXA Group	$1.887	$1.000
Fidelilty Investments	$1.862	$1.069
The Capital Group	$1.550	$0.900
Deutsche Bank	$1.402	$1.155
Vanguard Group	$1.365	$1.072
Black Rock	$1.357	$1.310
UBS	$1.231	$1.550
JPMorgan Chase & Company	$1.198	$2.175
Bank of New York Mellon	$1.121	$0.928

EXHIBIT I.1   Assets Under Management (in $T)
Sources: Nelson Marketplace, directly from managers, managers' websites, published articles, Watson Wyatt's The World's 500 Largest Asset Managers Year End 2007.

Institutional investors now face even more complex issues in managing their investment programs, achieving risk/return objectives, and meeting their actuarial assumptions, or payout and income needs. Investment managers face unprecedented needs to cut expenses and reduce staff, fierce competition, deeper scrutiny, and cumbersome, likely increased regulatory requirements. At the same time, investors and managers alike benefit from new asset-allocation tools, an abundance of innovative investment instruments, breakthroughs from academia, technology and mathematical science, and globalization. Debates over benefits, necessary regulations, reporting requirements, transparency, correlations, and costs abound. Opportunities are emerging from the collective efforts of governments around the world, as well as private sectors working together to resolve the 2008–09 financial crisis. We face a whole new world.

Our chapter is a random walk through seven major changes distinct from the 2008-09 financial crises that are literally transforming our industry as we write:

1. Restructuring of Investment Plans—Out with the Old; In with the New
2. Evolving Investor Skills and Preferences—The Climb to Higher Ground
3. Globalization—Broader Opportunity Set and Expanding Competition
4. Specialization in Professionals' Roles—Creating Barriers to Entry and a Stronger Foundation for Growth

5. Advances in Technologies and Systems—Penny-Wise or Pound-Foolish?
6. Proliferation of Consultants and Their Changing Roles—Gatekeeper, Competitor . . . Friend or Foe?
7. Distribution Opportunities

RESTRUCTURING OF INVESTMENT PLANS—OUT WITH THE OLD; IN WITH THE NEW

It is not the strongest of the species that survives, nor the one most intelligent, but the one most responsive to change.

—Charles Darwin

Among the most profound changes in the past decade has been the redistribution of retirement assets. The growing pool of individual retirement accounts (IRAs) and employer-sponsored defined-contribution (DC) plan assets have overtaken defined-benefit (DB) plans, which ruled the institutional investment arena for decades.

While many have predicted the demise of DB plans, a sizeable asset pool of $2.4 trillion remained as of June 2008, and some even forecast modest future growth (Exhibit I.2). Debate over the expense and appropriateness of DB versus DC continues today, with one side arguing that DB is far too expensive a commitment for public and corporate America, putting them at a disadvantage to their global counterparts. IBM froze its $48.5 billion DB plan as of January 1, 2008; assets of all future benefits will be provided through enhanced 401(k) plans. Other large, well-known companies like Verizon Communications, Lockheed-Martin, and Hewlett-Packard announced that they are also phasing out their defined-benefit plans. FundFire in December 2008 reported proposed legislation in Ohio that would freeze all five DB plans to move to a DC plan to gain cost efficiencies. Arizona State in 2006 compared costs between DB and DC plans, and concluded

EXHIBIT I.2   Projected Growth of Retirement Market Assets ($Billions)

Retirement Markets	2006	2007	2008	2009	2010	CAGR 2006-2010
IRA	$4,127	$4,530	$4,962	$5,430	$5,941	9%
Defined Contribution	$3,693	$3,951	$4,211	$4,485	$4,756	7%
Defined Benefit	$2,221	$2,334	$2,463	$2,581	$2,736	5%

Source: FRC Monitor, September 2005.

that not only were DB plans more cost efficient, but they were also better at protecting the downside. DC and IRA assets, nevertheless, are projected to win the future asset-growth race by a wide margin.[1]

It will be interesting to revisit Exhibit I.2 in light of the excruciating loss of wealth in 2008. The transition of investment decisions from DB plan sponsors to the hands of DC plan participants has led to new sets of investment solutions and challenges. With DB plans, employers make all the investment decisions—from investment policy, to asset allocation, to manager selection and termination—frequently with guidance from consultants who are expert in investment policy and manager research. Initially, oversight of the DC plan was often the responsibility of the company's HR professionals. Bundled providers who could offer plan administration, investments, and participant communications were favored. DC investment offerings commonly included company stock, "safe" capital preservation vehicles such as money market funds or stable value funds (often as defaults), and some traditional equity and fixed-income options. Little attention was paid to investment policy or specific asset allocations. Open architecture and the growth of the investment option–only business expanded the number and breadth of investment options for DC participants, which became overwhelming for participants in many cases.

As many as 30 percent of individuals who are eligible for 401(k) plans do not contribute to those plans. The 70 percent of individuals who do invest in 401(k) plans have not fared well overall because of poor asset-allocation decisions, market timing, cash flows, and lack of access to the diversity of investment opportunities available to DB plans due to the need for daily valuation and liquidity. Employers walk a fine line between educating their employees and giving advice out of fear of lawsuits if the employees fall short at retirement. Results have been murky, particularly in light of the 2008–09 financial market collapse. That is no surprise. Legislation has followed, and more is to come— again, no surprise.

The 2006 Pension Protection Act (PPA) contains provisions that affect the entire retirement system including DC, DB, hybrid plans, and IRAs. For DC plans in particular, the PPA creates a more reliable way for DC participants to accumulate retirement assets. The PPA offers 404(c) protection for qualified default investment alternatives (QDIAs) that can be used with automatic enrollment. The PPA's new criteria for QDIAs are that they must provide capital appreciation as well as capital preservation.

The new Department of Labor (DOL) guidelines for QDIAs, effective December 24, 2007, require that default options must be a target-date fund, a balanced target-risk fund, or a managed account to qualify for safe harbor protection. The new regulations provide grandfather protection for certain default investments in certain capital preservation funds (e.g., stable value) made prior to that date.

Target-risk and target-date funds, also commonly known as *lifestyle* or *lifecycle* funds, are attracting significant assets, and are the fastest-growing mutual fund category. In fact target-date funds gained $41 billion in assets in 2008, not accounting for market losses, according to *Strategic Insight*. There were 378 target-date funds available to investors at the end of 2008, with about $158 billion in assets. In 1997, these funds had only $2 billion in assets.

The new DOL guidelines are expected to generate a dramatic shift of plan assets from capital preservation funds to target-date funds, balanced funds, and managed accounts. This shift will create significant asset growth opportunities for managers with both core and specialty strategies. Many target-date funds are making greater use of specialty strategies such as emerging markets, REITs, high-yield securities, TIPS, and even hedge funds. Since these strategies are rarely used as standalone investment options in DC plans, managers of these strategies who previously stood on the sidelines can position themselves to participate in the target-date funds, embracing the diversification benefits of these strategies. In addition, new features and product innovations are increasing the demand for these products beyond 401(k) plans.

Changes at the plan and investment program level are not limited to migration from DB plans to DC plans. Public plans, endowments and foundations, sovereign wealth funds, and union plans are all undergoing enormous pressure and change. Many were forced to liquidate holdings at inopportune times just to fulfill obligations. With so little liquidity, many funds have incurred real losses. DB plan sponsors are grappling with actuarial assumptions, matching assets and liabilities, asset allocations, rebalancing, too much money chasing too few alpha opportunities, education of new board and committee members, and political pressures. Staffs have shrunk while funding levels have declined, and investment solutions have become more complex. Funded status of pensions at S&P 500 companies has dropped from 104 percent at the end of 2007 to 75 percent at year-end 2008.[2]

Questions on plan sponsors' minds include: How can I fulfill my liabilities with the existing asset base and uncertain markets? Where are the reliable opportunities given the 2008–09 collapse? Can active managers achieve their investment objectives, or should I move more to quantitative and indexing strategies to save costs and achieve consistency, predictability, and transparency? Are quantitative strategies now too closely correlated and likely to underperform collectively, as many did in the summer of 2007? Should plan sponsors move into alternatives, or is it too late, too risky? Are trustees doing the best job of allocating the investments they already have? How frequently should we be adjusting the asset allocations? How and when should I rebalance? How can assets earn better returns? Are we paying too much for beta? How do you discern a skilled manager from one that is unskilled or just plain lucky? How can all investors become better educated to make smart investment decisions, select the best managers, and successfully oversee investment programs that will fulfill their investment objectives? Keith Ambachtsheer of KPA Advisory Services, Ltd., advises ways to think about these issues in Chapter 2, "The Sub-Prime Crisis as a 'Predictable Surprise': Strategic Lessons to Be Learned."

The endowment and foundation investors, perceived by many as the leading-edge experts, fall into at least two camps—each having its own demanding challenges:

- *First camp*: High-profile mega-endowments and foundations that gained attention for their early advances into alternatives to capture high returns. But as DB plans and other institutional investors follow their lead, eleemosynary investors are pushed to find the next great waves of alpha—a feat not easily accomplished with the large assets under management at these giants. Of course, now they face enormous losses and have to review their liquidity needs against their investments. With many of the alternatives freezing redemptions and extending lockup periods, implementing desired shifts is difficult.
- *Second camp*: Hundreds of midsized and smaller endowments and foundations that were left out of their larger brethren's profitable early exploitation of alternative investment strategies. Smaller investment pools also need cost-efficient investment solutions that can reliably fulfill their needs. They may have more liquidity, but they still need growth and opportunities to offset the losses experienced from the 2008 market declines.

Other important influences at the investment program level are:

- *Adoption of the Principles for Responsible Investment (PRI)*: The PRI are designed to align institutional investment practices with the goals of the United Nations, including sustainable investing. As of January 2009, there were 458 signatories globally, including 153 asset owners, 215 investment managers, and 90 professional service partners. The geographic dispersion of signatories is shown in Exhibit I.3.

  Managers who integrate consideration of environmental, social, and governance (ESG) issues into investment decision making will have

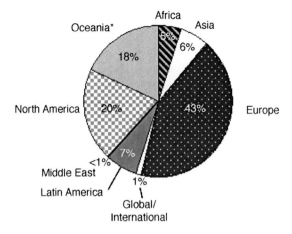

*Islands, including Australia, New Zealand

EXHIBIT I.3 Number of Signatories Has More Than Doubled Since 2007, When There Were 180 Signatories
Source: PRI Report on Progress 2008.

a distinct competitive advantage. You can learn more at the PRI website (www.unpri.org).

Sensitivity to the political environment, both for and against benefits, now and in the future, is also a charged issue. Will the public entities be able to fulfill their investment promises and obligations? Will public entities perceive the benefits programs as too enriched, a debate that is already becoming heated as states, counties, and cities suffer budget distress? Will public entities be able to confront the immigration issues associated with benefits? Do we grasp the implications of an aging population and the impact that aging will have on our society? These questions will continue to surface as major political issues, leading to unknown legislation, which in turn will cause more change.

■ *Shareholder activism*: The increase in shareholder activism coincides with the development of the corporate governance movement. Increasingly, investment managers are under pressure from investors, as well as the United Nations, to exercise their responsibilities as owners of companies and be more active. One of the impetuses of increased shareholder activism may also have been the subprime credit crisis that began in the spring of 2008.

RiskMetrics Group, a leading provider of risk management and corporate governance services to the global financial community, examined shareholder responses to the crisis in which they identified the corporate governance factors involved in the crisis and how stronger provisions might have mitigated investor risk. The group looked at the ways investors are evaluating boards' risk management and disclosure practices. A major finding was that shareholder activism and litigation have increased as a result of the credit crisis. Ineffective risk management by corporations was considered to be a cause of the losses suffered by corporations due to the subprime mortgage crisis, and a majority of investors felt that board members lacked risk management expertise. Lack of transparency and poor pay practices encouraging short-term performance were also major concerns of investors. Activist managers are tackling these types of problems when investing in a corporation.[3]

- *Continued refinements to plan structure and asset allocation, further loosening of constraints, and the departure from traditional asset allocations*: Many plans are conservative, and although an investment option may appeal on a logical basis, the unknown risks prevent many from proceeding to more innovative structures and investment options. No matter the intent of an investment program, the lack of liquidity resulting from the 2008 financial crisis is impeding many investors' abilities to adjust their asset mix.

- *Increased attention to fees and costs*: Even without the high fees of hedge funds or the layered costs of funds of funds, institutional investors and consultants are all too aware of the costs. That is evident in the debate over DB versus DC plans, and the questions surfacing on hidden costs and on mutual fund costs. Control of costs will be mandatory in a future of compressed returns, and continued high actuarial needs.

- *Greater need for education of the stewards of institutional pools of assets*: As Thomas Mackell wrote in his insightful, "call-to-action" book, *When Good Pensions Go Away*, trustees must "ratchet up their education in this volatile and complex world in order to know what kinds of reports and guidance they will need, the right questions to ask to fulfill their responsibilities, and, hopefully, preclude any dramatic implosions within their retirement systems. The well-being of the plan participants' future benefits programs is in their hands. Strong self-imposed educational programs have to become the norm."[4] The staff of Fi360 discusses this further in Chapter 14 of this book.

  Seminars, conferences, whitepapers, and timely topical papers addressing economic, political, and social events and impact on financial markets, as well as new investment theories and practices, have become victory flags for managers who provide perspective and knowledge.

- *Outsourcing of investment management, in many cases, to manager-of-managers platforms*: Providers who offer investment policy assistance, asset allocation, portfolio construction, manager selection and monitoring, risk management, as well as shared fiduciary responsibility, are a compelling solution for small to midsized plans. Even large corporate plans are choosing to outsource segments of their retirement asset oversight responsibilities.

According to a recent Casey Quirk report, assets from U.S. investors outsourcing their entire portfolios have more than doubled over the past four years, from $97 billion to $195 billion as of year-end 2008. Assets from investors with partial outsourcing agreements account for another $5 billion. Initially, outsourcing was predominantly embraced by institutions with less than $1 billion in assets. An increasing number of larger investors, however, are now outsourcing.[5]

While plan restructuring is a significant trend, what has not changed is the need for reliable, repeatable investment results at increasingly precise risk levels. It is in all our best interests to see this relentless and important need addressed in our lifetime. While much progress has been made, there are still many risks, known and unknown, impacting achievement of fund objectives. It is reassuring to see many brilliant minds focused on yet-more-refined solutions, which will no doubt fuel continued plan restructuring.

EVOLVING INVESTOR SKILLS AND PREFERENCES—THE CLIMB TO HIGHER GROUND

While defined-benefit assets were predominantly invested in traditional balanced accounts and conservative fixed-income strategies in the 1970s, ERISA ignited change—a change that seemed slow at the time, but now looking back over three decades, clearly was the spark of a wildfire. The *prudent-man rule* demanded that institutional investors evaluate opportunities and risks in an informed, in-depth manner, spawning the birth of the independent consultant community, performance measurement and portfolio analysis tools, and an ever-expanding universe of performance benchmarks.

The 1980s brought academic studies to the forefront, creating the emergence of enhanced-index funds, style investing, quantitative approaches and specialty strategies like small-cap and mid-cap equity, and closed-end real estate funds. Nontraditional investments such as emerging markets debt, private equity, and venture cap gained steam in the 1990s. Academia joined with investment practitioners to develop increasingly sophisticated and rigorous investment solutions. In the first decade of the 2000s, alternatives with leverage and ever-more esoteric securities pioneered new, innovative approaches to asset allocation and security selection.

When traditional asset returns flourished, providing double-digit returns for much of the 1980s and 1990s, most investors—institutional or otherwise—stayed true to more traditional stock/bond/cash allocations. Then along came the tech bubble, 9/11, and various other global market events. After the equity market collapse in the early 2000s, alternatives, including real estate, private equity, hedge funds, and hedge funds of funds had an almost irresistible appeal.

Hedge funds, offering prospects of more reliable and consistent alpha, absolute return, less downside risk, and low correlations to traditional assets, presented nearly heroic solutions. The result? A swoon by individual and institutional investors. Before the systemic crisis achieved headway, aggregate assets in the hedge fund industry were approaching $3 trillion.

Outflows of $512 billion in 2008 were driven by investor redemptions and hedge fund liquidations, while losses suffered by managers accounted for another $535 billion drop in assets. That left industry assets down $1.047 trillion, or 36 percent, to $1.84 trillion, for the whole year, HedgeFund net said.

Those funds that successfully navigated the second half of 2008 have attracted almost immediate attention and continued asset flows. Some experts predict that the rapid growth of hedge funds will continue despite the 2008 debacle, and foresee a multi-trillion-dollar hedge fund industry, dominated by a few large players. A Casey, Quirk & Associates/Bank of New York study projects that retirement plans will account for the majority of asset flows into hedge funds by 2010, and will represent more than 40 percent of total hedge fund assets by 2010.[6] "We are seeing signs of hedge funds evolving from entrepreneurial alpha hunters to institutional product developers." For investors, it is critical to discern the difference. "The hedge fund industry is at its core a talent pool, and talent is not scalable and cannot be cloned," says Robert Discolor, head of hedge fund strategies at AIG Global Investment Group.[7]

Alternative investments flooding the market also contributed to an evolution in asset allocation. People were willing to pay, and pay dearly, for alpha—but not for beta. Sophisticated investors separated management of the different return elements of a portfolio—alpha and beta. Indeed, the separation of alpha and beta may prove to be the defining trend for institutional investors, much as style boxes were a defining trend of the 1980s but now are cited as obsolete by some. Other experts expect large asset flows to return to traditional long growth and value equity, both large and small cap. Russell Investment Group polled 206 asset managers for its "Investment Manager Outlook" for 2009, and they were "astoundingly bullish" on four asset classes: corporate bonds, U.S. small-cap value equity, mid-cap value equity, and high-yield fixed income.[8]

Core-and-explorer investment programs using passive management coupled with skill-based management also have become popular. ETFs, appealing to investors for their flexibility, liquidity, and inexpensive sources of beta, are stealing market share from index funds, mutual funds, and traditional long-only managers. Constraints are being lifted on the quantitative side as well as on the traditional active management side. While some plans stay married to traditional programs, more are becoming better educated and more opportunistic to achieve their goals. Global products, as a result, are in greater demand. These trends will persist, particularly as academia continues to contribute, both on the practitioner level and at the college level, graduating the next generations of gatekeepers, portfolio managers, and fund sponsors.

Corporate plan sponsor concerns about matching their assets and liabilities, exacerbated by 2008, have also sparked renewed interest in liability-driven investments (LDIs). With low interest rates, however, these investments seem less attractive than they were in the 1980s, when interest rates were in the teens. An increased focus on risk management, particularly in light of the choppy markets of 2007–2008, is also contributing to fund sponsor interest in LDIs. The demand of a fiduciary role in meeting liabilities, and pressure arising from limited resources, too many constrained opportunities, and rising costs, however, are likely to lead more and more plans into LDIs in the future.

The mounting population of retired and semiretired Baby Boomers in the United States is driving an increasing need for high-income, low-risk investments. IRA rollovers, inheritances, trusts, and foundations will multiply, with current demand for "growth at controlled risk" supplanted by increased appetite for high income at minimal risk. In the high-net-worth market, generational wealth transfer and wealthy entrepreneurs have encouraged the growth of family offices and financial advisors. Financial advisors are growing in both prominence and power as the demand for investment guidance explodes. With an increasing number of retirees, expanded life expectancy, and growing rollover assets, investment solutions will be forced to evolve yet again. Tax considerations will be key. New technologies are being developed to deliver tax-sensitive solutions without relying on manager attention. New legislation to ensure effective monitoring and fee disclosure regulations are also being proposed, and will shape the future business opportunities.

GLOBALIZATION—BROADER OPPORTUNITY
SET AND EXPANDING COMPETITION

Globalization is a growing force—in both the opportunity set for asset growth and the competitive pool for institutional investment managers.

The drive for growth of assets and strong competitive positioning lured many U.S. managers to expand their sales efforts outside the United States in the early 1980s, but U.S. managers found it difficult going at first. Is it best to set up shops in Europe, Australia, or Asia, or to partner with global distribution partners? As consultants started to position themselves as "consultants without borders," sharing databases and manager research, opportunities for U.S. managers to build their presence in non-U.S. markets grew. Global consultants became influential in introducing managers in different regions of the world, both to the benefit and detriment of U.S. managers.

The easing of restrictions on allocations to domestic and nondomestic investments by countries such as Canada and Australia created additional opportunities and attracted the attention of U.S.-based asset management firms seeking to grow their businesses. The strong growth of Australian institutional assets in particular became a siren song of opportunity for many investment firms.

Sovereign wealth funds (SWFs) are another whole new wave of institutional investor. The rise in the prices of major commodities led to a rise in the wealth of exporting countries, with oil-producing countries representing nearly two-thirds of SWF assets. Although SWFs do not publicly disclose their investments, there is movement toward increased transparency, particularly as concerns arise from SWFs making major investments in troubled U.S. financial institutions or U.K. shipping companies. The question that surfaced was: "Will governments use [SWFs] simply as financial tools or will SWFs emerge as an implement of political muscle?"[9] Better regulations and definition of international standards for cross-border investments are being sought as SWF assets continue to increase.

Simultaneously, managers from outside the United States began targeting the lucrative U.S. institutional market. From Nomura Capital Management's and Phillips & Drew's successful entries in the early 1980s, to firms currently vying for market share, including Paribas, F&C Asset Management, Robeco, Degroof, and Pictet, the investment management community is truly global.

Globalization for investment firms translates into a greater need for strategic and organized marketing. An investment firm's messages need to be consistent in every market. Different markets, however, have slightly distinct needs in materials and presentations. The United States, Australasia, Europe, and the Middle East all have their own preferences. Systems help delivery and production, but personalization is still helpful to standing out in a particular market. Increasingly, global marketing teams are challenged to achieve one cohesive global message.

The impact of globalization is not limited to investment management asset gathering. The decline of U.S. economic leadership and the trend toward less constrained asset allocation are leading U.S. institutional investors to think more globally. Global equity mandates, long the norm in non-U.S. markets, but quietly ignored in the U.S. market, have gained considerable momentum. Fixed income has been a global proposition for decades, and globalization is finally influencing equities—in both passive and active mandates, and in both traditional and alternative investments. Darien, Connecticut–based money management consultant Casey, Quirk & Associates' latest institutional product review shows global equity strategies garnered $15 billion in net inflows during 2007, a sharp contrast to the $176 billion in net outflows for U.S. equity products. Emerging markets equity and international equity had negative total net flows during the same period of $8.7 and $17.6 billion, respectively.

As with equities, U.S. investors looked abroad for fixed-income opportunities. Casey, Quirk & Associates' product review shows that in 2007, global and international bonds enjoyed net inflows of $14 billion, and emerging market debt took in $7 billion. For 2008, Casey, Quirk & Associates reports net inflows for international bonds were $8 billion and net inflows for emerging markets debt were $ 10 billion.[10] Global bonds ended the year with net outflows of $23 billion. (*Sources: Casey Quirk Institutional Product Reviews 2007 and 2008*).

Nearly three-quarters of U.S. consultants will focus on core and core-plus fixed income searches in 2009, a dramatic fivefold increase over 2008. Consultants expect institutional investors to consider replacing underperforming core-plus managers. They also increasingly expect clients to consider a wider number of large core and core-plus fixed income managers, given the view that investment opportunities still exist in the fixed income markets, particularly for firms with strong credit analysis skills. A number of consultants report that they expect more investors to adopt a core-satellite approach for fixed income portolios, wrapping a large, potentially passive, core with specialized mandates in specific disciplines, including credit, duration, inflation, mortgages, distressed securities, and international fixed income. (*Casey, Quirk 2009 Consultant Search Forecast Annual Survey February 2009*).

Just as countries like Canada and Australia eased their pension plan restrictions to enhance their diversification and return benefits, so are U.S. institutional investors moving beyond their borders to the investment opportunities offering the greatest risk/reward potential. Numerous opportunities will be open to investment firms able to expand their offerings to global mandates.

SPECIALIZATION IN PROFESSIONALS' ROLES— CREATING BARRIERS TO ENTRY AND A STRONGER FOUNDATION FOR GROWTH

In the 1970s and 1980s, most of the investment companies were run by investment professionals who were also responsible for client service, presentations, finals, and in many cases, request-for-proposal (RFP) responses. Today, business leadership, client service, compliance, sales management, consultant relations, marketing expertise, operations, and administration all have developed into professions in their own right. Firms, even startups, without strong business leadership and infrastructure, and lacking expertise in any of the above areas, are at a competitive disadvantage.

Investment Management Business Leadership

One of the most challenging roles is that of business leadership. A leader who brings the right combination of vision and voice, effective alignment of resources, anagement and motivation of the firm's professionals, and strategic thinking is essential to grow an investment firm. As many founders and leaders of investment firms retire, companies are finding themselves in perilous positions. This is even more the case given the turbulent markets of 2008-09. Leadership can much more easily make or break a firm.

A client shared with us that a mark of a quality business is one where the debt ratio is neither zero nor too high. If it is zero, then management does not understand how to allocate capital to grow. Another shared that the bull markets hid management weakness. The bear markets reveal management issues. How do firms replace the original founders with leaders who have strong understanding of what is required to grow an investment management business in today's competitive environment and volatile markets? How do firms avoid business leadership that focuses more on quarterly earnings, cost controls, and compensation packages than on strategic alignment of products, effective distribution, and attraction and retention of investment talent? How do they control costs without sacrificing quality of investment results and communications?

Part Six of this book (beginning with Chapter 23) specifically addresses leadership challenges.

Client Service

When client service is strong and strategic, it can make the difference between a company's growth and stagnation. Understanding and addressing clients' changing needs, achieving investment objectives, and serving as an educational resource to fulfill needs beyond just performance, earn an investment company a reputation and role as leader in the industry. Firms that rank high in client service have teams of experts with long, successful experience in fulfilling communication and educational needs, and serving as invaluable resources to their clients. Supporting them are product specialists, client-service administrators, systems, and marketing, who address client needs as well as develop growth initiatives.

As firms grow larger, many distinguish the client-service role from sales, although this is still an area of debate among leading institutions. A firm's success in client service is frequently measured by surveys conducted by firms such as Greenwich Associates or Eager, Davis & Holmes, LLC. Best practices include proactive education and communications, strong reporting and customization, innovative solutions responding to client-specific needs, and clear awareness of and responsiveness to client concerns and issues.

Compliance

Formerly a part-time role of an administrator, compliance is now a required professional role at every registered investment advisor. Mutual fund and market-timing scandals gave rise to increased regulation and new accounting standards. As laws and regulations multiplied, intense scrutiny of performance, marketing, and client-service materials became a given. The SEC dictated the role of *chief compliance officer*. The infamous Ponzi scheme inflicted by Bernard Madoff revealed that even existing regulations were insufficient.

Hedge fund managers expect further regulations under the Obama administration. An extensive discussion of regulation can be found in Chapter 3 of this book, "The Solidarity Challenge."

Compliance officers who keep investment firms compliant with rapidly changing regulations and avoid negative headlines play an increasingly important role in the success of an investment management firm. Compliance professionals clearly either contribute to or impede the success of an investment management firm. The best compliance officers have become knowledgeable on the broader aspects of the industry, serving as strategic advisors on how a firm can best grow and serve the investment community at large. In the 2000s, for the first time, many compliance officers have become partners in investment management firms.

Sales Management and Consultant Specialists

Again, originally just part of many roles of the founding partners of investment companies, these have evolved into distinct professional roles in high demand. When DB assets were experiencing double-digit growth and firms relied on the Money Market Directory, strategic sales planning was not that necessary. Managers targeted the low-hanging fruit for direct calls, focused on a select group of consultants, and/or zeroed in with "hit list" marketing, soliciting clients of competitors who were in trouble.

Those days are over. There is no low-hanging fruit in the DB market. Managers have to take market share from other DB providers. They have to consider other institutional markets and how they will connect with those buyers. A strategic sales plan with talent and resources clearly aligned to the markets where the firm and its products will have the greatest success is essential. Today's most successful growth firms have skilled strategic management professionals leading sales forces focused on specific target markets, multiple sales teams, or specialized distribution forces, leveraging a firm's infrastructure.

Consultant firms have been a powerful force in the institutional investment industry throughout its history. Many firms have evolved from just a few consultants with focused services to large entities with sizeable staffs located across the United States or worldwide offering a broad spectrum of services. And the number of consultant firms that can impact an investment firm's growth efforts has multiplied significantly. Tiering of consultants to manage coverage is now the norm.

Surveys show that the emergence of consultant specialists has been especially well received by the consultant firms, who appreciate having one knowledgeable point of contact. The role of consultant specialist does not replace the sales professionals' relationships with consulting firms. It brings consistency in contact, clarity in messaging, and proactive communications in building relationships with the consulting firms, whether global or regional.

The consultant specialist is also typically responsible for defining the strategic plan of action for consultants. With shrinking resources, a strategic plan becomes even more critical for a manager. Which consultants are key to the firm's business? What databases are essential to the key consultants you want to cover? Which firms are not appropriate for your strategies? What level of activity and communications is appropriate for each consultant firm? What are the individual firms' preferences? Which RFPs will the firm respond to? Who are the best people to build the relationship with each consultant firm?

Marketing and Communications

In the 1970s and 1980s, portfolio managers frequently wrote their own marketing materials and presentations, completed consultant RFPs, and decided marketing strategy. Today, with multiple target markets, broad investment capabilities, and a high level of activity, the need for cohesive marketing plans, messages, and support has led to the development of strong, well-resourced, and well-structured marketing and communications departments. Ron Gold of Gold Consulting, Inc. elaborates in Chapter 17 of this book, "The Marketing Challenge." When marketing works well with business leadership, client service, sales, and investments, investment firms increase market share and earn strong reputations in the industry. Whether a global firm that needs to integrate multiple visions or a U.S. boutique, marketing becomes the ear and voice to the market, and critical to growth.

Product development, previously under the purview of portfolio managers, is paramount to fulfilling client needs and the long-term success of an investment management enterprise. Marketing serves an important role in identifying client needs that can be addressed by internal investment talent, and helping the firm develop investment solutions that will resonate in the market. Marketing is then responsible for resource management, budget, market research, database population, targeted marketing plan, materials, and new product launches. A successful product is one that aligns market demand with manager talent and ability to add value consistently and reliably.

Firms cannot afford to be complacent about their communications with clients, consultants, intermediaries, or prospects. Quality, clarity, and consistency of messages are key. Materials can be neither a shabby hodgepodge evoking past decades, nor so slick that they cost more than most clients' annual reports. Neither are desirable. Consistency of communications among a firm's professionals on key messages, asset management approach, and a firm's priorities is essential to success. Key messages must be aligned with a firm's strengths, and incorporated into all communications from introductory materials to websites to databases to final presentations to client-service materials. Seasoned marketing and communications professionals, distinct from portfolio management and sales, are assuming these responsibilities at most investment firms.

PAICR (the Professional Association for Investment Communications Resources) was founded in 1997 to provide an educational and idea-sharing forum for professionals in these roles. PAICR (www.paicr.com) is a nonprofit membership organization that empowers investment marketing and communications professionals through cutting-edge opportunities for professional development, continuing education, and networking at association events throughout the United States and Canada.

Operations and Administration Infrastructure

These are the foundation for a firm's ability to account for its clients' portfolios, effectively assimilate new accounts and assets, deliver timely communications, and achieve institutional quality across all areas to compete. Information must be well-managed with the objective of offering sophisticated clients high functionality and useful analytics. Many firms have failed to pay attention to the importance of infrastructure in achieving these objectives, and clients instantly recognize firms with growth problems. Reports are slower, inaccuracies begin to appear, trading is not competitive, and portfolio managers and client-service professionals are without tools that competitors have. In Chapter 28 of this book, "The Data Management Challenge," Don DeLoach of Aleri provides some excellent recommendations for thinking about the "life's blood" of your firm.

The infrastructures of firms offering alternatives are under especially high scrutiny. Will they be able to handle growth? Historically, a majority of the hedge fund firms that have closed have gone out of business due to operational failures, not due to performance problems.

Infrastructure also includes human resources. The need for professional development and ongoing training has become key as investment vehicles have proliferated and the ability to represent multiple solutions has become essential. McKinsey's 2008 survey of more than 90 firms says, "Higher performing asset managers who employ best practices in sales and client service are, on average, 20 percent more profitable than their peers." Best practices include ongoing training to ensure their firms and products are well represented in the market.

The evolution of investment firms as true businesses has led to this specialization of roles. These demands in turn produce higher barriers to entry. The opportunities still attract entrepreneurs, but the days of hanging up a sign with high numbers and having buyers flock to your door are over. It is the *business* of investment management that makes the difference between earning a living and achieving true success.

ADVANCES IN TECHNOLOGIES AND SYSTEMS— PENNY-WISE OR POUND-FOOLISH?

Automation of the investment industry has truly revolutionized how people work. Emergence of new or advanced technologies has changed the way investment firms invest, support client service, sales, and marketing initiatives, and communicate internally, as well as the way that managers are measured and monitored.

Communication technology has changed how managers gather and disseminate information, facilitating timely and global exchange of information. Portfolio management systems permit instant analysis of the impact of a single holding on a portfolio's risk characteristics or of the addition of a different asset class. A portfolio manager in Tokyo can see in real time what his or her counterpart is doing in London. News alerts and customized information flow are standards for analysts and portfolio managers.

In the 1970s, index cards were a marketer's CRM system. Today, relational databases are critical to the sales and client-service process. The Money Market Directory in hard paper form was the green gospel for prospect information, and detailed information on a manager's competitors was hard to come by. Today, dozens of databases and the Internet provide a plethora of information on prospects, consultants, and competitors. eVestment Alliance, PSN/Mobius, Nelson Information, Zephyr, Altura Capital, and Morningstar are just a few of the sources used by consultants, investors, and investment firms alike. To populate the databases with current data at quarter-end, or after an important event, has become a major initiative and resource demand for managers.

Global communications have become seamless with the evolution from overnight mail to fax machines to e-mail, PDAs, webinars, and videoconferencing. Managers leveraging technology have an enormous advantage, while those unwilling to invest or those who lack the vision to employ progressive technologies are at a stark disadvantage.

Performance measurement and attribution analysis have evolved simultaneously. It is no longer just about absolute and relative performance. Enhanced attribution tools present challenges to active managers. Clients are easily able to discern value-added management over time, and weed out traditional active managers just managing beta. Strong managers benefit from having tools to demonstrate their value added. The challenge is which measures are truly meaningful.

The majority of firms today use a blend of quantitative and qualitative disciplines to discover high-probability-of-success investment candidates for their portfolios. Institutional investors have followed suit, embracing similar tools to assist in their searches for high-probability-of-success managers. Today's consultants and clients can assess managers' performance against a variety of quantitative screens and metrics such as information ratio, alpha, beta, Sharpe ratio, R^2, and more. Formerly a labor-intensive process, screening managers against specific criteria can now be executed in minutes. Once you define your quantitative criteria, you simply select your database, enter your search criteria, and a list of qualified managers is at your fingertips.

Then what happens? Some clients take their lists and visit managers' websites to qualify candidates. Managers need to take these new tools seriously. Websites that are more than "brochureware" can be an effective way to leverage resources and generate new business leads. Yes, surveys commonly show that 50 percent or less of plan sponsors and consultants visit websites, but those that do, do so with purpose. More often now, knowledgeable investors are scouring databases, vetting manager candidates through websites, and contacting them directly, with no consultant involvement. Technology, on every level of our industry, is here to stay.

PROLIFERATION OF CONSULTANTS AND THEIR CHANGING ROLES—GATEKEEPER, COMPETITOR . . . FRIEND OR FOE?

As Ron Gold notes in Chapter 17, "The Marketing Challenge," "[T]he U.S. consulting industry started in the late 1960s, when three firms—A. G. Becker, Callan Associates, and Frank Russell—began providing performance measurement services to institutional investors. . . ."

The traditional consultant's business model is labor intensive and difficult to leverage. Many consultants, seeking ways to enhance the profitability of their business models, are abandoning their own proprietary databases, which are expensive to maintain, and subscribing to independent industry databases such as eVestment Alliance, PSN/Mobius, and Nelson Information.

Another profitability solution for consultants is expansion into the investment management domain, which also permits them to attract and keep their most valuable resource—their people. A number of the larger, more recognized consultants developed manager-of-managers and funds-of-funds programs and limited partnerships. These became successful business models for the consultants, and simultaneously fulfilled the needs of midsized and smaller institutional investors in particular. In a beautiful case of irony, some of these consultant firms now have consultant specialists of their own, and call on other consultants to introduce their manager-of-managers, funds-of-funds, and transition management programs.

Outsourcing, of either a portion of or the entire investment program, and sharing of fiduciary responsibility has become one of the major recent market developments. With so many investors grappling with the same issues—need for more consistent returns, less risk, more education—many consultants have risen to the occasion, some better than others. Most consultants are offering or developing outsourcing services. Moreover, as the staff of Fi360 observes in chapter 15 of this book, "The Client Challenges," the education of trustees is always a need.

At the same time, regional consultants, family offices, specialists by markets, and specialist consultants in alternatives, have gained and continue to garner market share via expert knowledge in territories neglected by the major consulting firms. In addition, many managers have started leaping into the consultants' territory, becoming more consultative in building deeper relationships with their clients, and providing them educational tools and resources. Managers with the capabilities to do so are moving into the asset-liability business.

What is the outcome? A stew of possibilities, as consultants and managers compete, as the number and type of gatekeepers proliferate, and the number of consulting and investment firms and strategies multiply like rabbits.

With consultant power continuing to ascend, and the number of consultants proliferating, how does a manager address the consultant's needs for research and insights, and achieve the manager's goal of a strong, mutually productive relationship? The answer is simple and twofold: First, those who view consultants as allies or conduits to success, and support the consultants' initiatives for education, manager research, and contact, will have greater success. That assumes one thing: that the manager is competitive—in clarity of approach, disciplines, and consistency in fulfilling investment objectives. Second is that the manager targets those consultants with the desired target client market(s). Resources need to be focused in a strategic way.

DISTRIBUTION OPPORTUNITIES

Two roads diverged in a wood, and I—
I took the one less traveled by,
And that has made all the difference.
—Robert Frost

In the early years, most managers focused their business by client type (institutional or private client), asset management style (balanced, equity, or fixed income), and perhaps geography. They concentrated on direct calls, using the Money Market Directory, and targeted a few consultants emerging as influential gatekeepers. Today, managers can leverage a variety of distribution channels, including consultants, brokers, centers of influence such as accountants or lawyers, financial advisors, subadvisory platforms, manager-of-managers and funds-of-funds platforms, and databases, and of course, there is still the good-old-fashioned approach of direct calls.

But first, a manager must determine its best target markets. Target markets have become much more specialized. The institutional market, while to some degree still generalized, has specific needs for the various segments: large public funds, small to midsized public funds, large endowments, large foundations, small to midsized endowments and foundations,

Taft-Hartley funds, corporate defined benefit, corporate defined contribution, public deferred compensation, insurance and reinsurance, hospitals, operating cash, and variations. The markets need distinct solutions and levels of service.

Managers need to establish their business focus, as well as their client-service promise for each type of client. What resources and systems will be needed to reach the target market(s) and to support that client-service promise? Market leaders serve virtually every client base, leverage multiple distribution channels, and offer a broad spectrum of investment capabilities and services around the world.

The consultant and intermediary industry has segmented as well—with plan-type specialists, global consultants, regional firms, brokerage firms, financial advisors, and others. Individuals' assets are now segmented into high-net-worth, family offices, bank clients, financial advisors, registered investment advisors (RIAs), separately managed accounts (SMAs), and brokerage firms. Subadvisory markets, manager-of-managers, and funds-of-funds all offer viable ways to grow assets under management.

With such a spectrum of distribution opportunities, the need and demand for strategic marketing explode on multiple fronts. On which markets and countries does a manager focus? Which products will be successful in which markets? How should a manager organize its resources? Will the firm participate in distribution channels that require fee discounts? If aligning with external distribution entities, who will provide the distribution needed and what requirements will that entail? Will ownership or equity be required to achieve strong distribution? Even a few years ago, it would have been unheard of for a startup alternative shop to have its first distribution partner in Japan. Today, it can well be the most advisable strategy to garner assets quickly.

Each market and distribution partner may require different levels of communication and service. When a manager makes a commitment to a distribution channel or partner, knowledge of the requirements along with a defined plan, people, resources, and systems in place are required to succeed.

SUMMARY

With rapid change on so many fronts, and unfolding risks and opportunities with virtually every change, tomorrow's investment leaders need to aspire to all of the following attributes:

- Flexibility and foresight to adapt to and serve shifting asset pools
- Innovative investment solutions and strong product development to meet changing investor needs

- Ability and resources to capitalize on global investment and distribution opportunities
- Strong, well-managed business on every level—business leadership, investments, branding and messaging, marketing, client service and sales, professional development, legal/compliance, and operations/administration
- Commitment to invest in new tools, systems, and technologies to enhance alpha generation and risk management, to achieve business efficiencies, and to lower costs
- Collaborative, proactive relationships with clients and targeted consultants and intermediaries
- Well-planned, focused, and well-managed client-service, sales, marketing, and communications efforts

For investment firms with competitive investment offerings, we believe that strategic client service, sales, and marketing will be pivotal for growth. As performance and investment management become more like commodities, strong client service and astute marketing will distinguish one firm from another. Appropriate target markets and distribution, competitive positioning, clarity and power of messages, effectiveness of communications both internal and external, experience and training of client-facing professionals—all will become the currency of the successful investment firm.

The growth leaders in our industry have a clear vision for their future courses, and are implementing their strategic plans with energy and enthusiasm. These leaders will direct their resources and talent appropriately and lead their firms, clients, and prospects through successful evolution.

As Darwin said, and we are here to echo, "Success will belong to the one most responsive to change."

NOTES

1. www.icifactbook.org, Investment Company Institute, 2008 Investment Company Fact Book, released May 2008.
2. Mercer; FundFire January 8, 2009, article, "Pensions Face Record $400B Deficit."
3. "Credit Crisis and Corporate Governance Implications," RiskMetrics Group, 2008.
4. Mackell, Thomas. 2008 *When Good Pensions Go Away*. Hoboken, NJ: John Wiley & Sons.
5. FundFire, December 9, 2008.

6. Hedgeweek.com; The Bank of New York/Casey, Quirk & Associates, October 2006, Thought Leadership Series White Paper: "Institutional Demand for Hedge Funds 2."
7. "A History Lesson for Hedge Funds," *Institutional Investor's Alpha.*
8. *Investment Management Weekly*, January 5, 2009.
9. Lee Hudson Teslik, "Sovereign Wealth Funds," Council on Foreign Relations.
10. Casey, Quirk Institutional Product Review, Fourth Quarter 2007.

The Challenges of Changes and Crises

CHAPTER 1

The Discontinuity Challenge

Wayne H. Wagner
Principal, OM◆NI

The twists and tangles of the 2008 credit crunch will long be remembered. While this chapter does not address that specific discontinuity, it does focus on discontinuities in general. From a longer time perspective, we see that discontinuities occur frequently, suggesting that in addition to applying our experience and running our models that work in "normal" times, we need to prepare to face the inevitable discontinuity environments.

THINKING ABOUT DISCONTINUITIES

Q: How's your day going?
A: Same old, same old.

Most days, things go on today as they did yesterday. A very large portion of our behavior is rooted in the *almost always correct* assumption that past experience will guide us through the next day.

Almost always correct? Yes, but what about those occasions when something crosses our path that is new and dangerous, something wholly unlike what we encountered in the past?

Exhibit 1.1 shows how these "unexpected" shocks seem to occur every few years.[1] Looking further back, we can find serious U.S. stock market/ financial panics in 1797, 1812, 1819, 1823, 1825, 1837, 1847, 1857, 1866, 1893, 1907, 1918, 1929 . . . you get the picture. As Rahl shows, these disruptive events are not the outliers we think they are, but rather common events that occur far more frequently than we recall. There are a lot of discontinuities, they always surprise many, they wreak havoc on the financially weak, and, most importantly, once the markets and the economy are sufficiently wrung out, they go away.

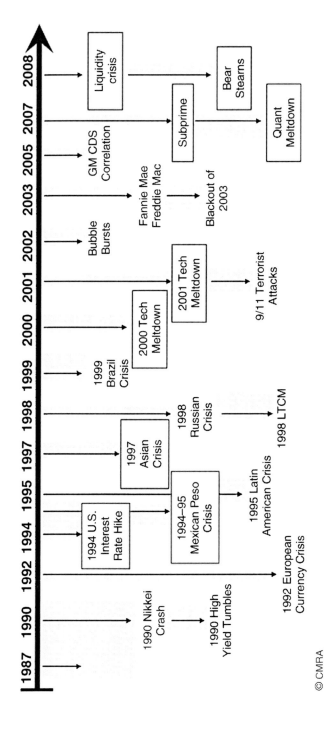

EXHIBIT 1.1 "Unexpected" Financial Shocks—Once-in-a-Lifetime Crises Seem to Occur Every Few Years
Source: Courtesy of Leslie Rahl at Capital Market Risk Advisors (http://www.cmra.com/crises.php).

© CMRA

Despite the frequency of discontinuities and the major effects they can have on the economy and our accumulated wealth, most investment thinking is based on consideration of data gathered during more normal cause-and-effect economic times. There is a very strong reason for this focus: It isn't really possible to do otherwise. We can paint scenarios of dire conditions, but we cannot usefully judge their likelihood, their timing, or their severity. Faced with our inability to deal with the unknowable, our focus naturally turns to the more intelligible.

Thus, the study of economic value necessarily focuses on the observables (i.e., history), and especially the massive data generated by the continuous unfolding of economic and market history. But out there lay broader possibilities perfectly capable of upsetting our best-laid plans. Surprise is always around the corner. H. L. Mencken put it well when he said, "Penetrating so many secrets, we cease to believe in the unknowable. But there it sits nevertheless, calmly licking its chops."

Where do these discontinuities arise? Actually, very few sources seem to account for the majority: natural disasters; large financial failures, most often arising from overextended leverage and expectations (aka greed); and the unintended consequences of political tinkering. Allan Bloom, in *The Closing of the American Mind*,[2] points out the supremacy of politics over economics:

> *The market presupposes the existence of law and the absence of war. . . . Political science is more comprehensive than economics because it studies both peace and war and their relations . . . the preservation of the polity continuously requires reasoning and deeds which are "uneconomic" or "inefficient." Political action must have primacy over economic action, no matter what the effect on the market.*

DECISION MAKING IN NORMAL TIMES

We can characterize most active investment managers as intuitive thinkers who search for significant facts that stand out from the mass of observation—that is, hidden value. The danger for the intuitive thinker is that discontinuity events overwhelm the economic thinking that must prevail during the everyday course of events. In discontinuous times, everything's an outlier, and hidden value becomes deeply and obscurely hidden.

Quantitative managers, in contrast, are systematic thinkers who focus on "normal" tendencies like orderly effects and small systemic inefficiencies, which are often obscured from the intuitors within the mass of data. But the equations don't work when we encounter the deviant outlier observations. Statisticians recognize that the importance of a data point rises with the square of its distance from the mean observation. Any statistical analysis using an observation out of the "normal" range will fit a regression line right through that deviant point. It is as though there were only two observations: the deviant point and the blob of the remaining observations, within which all normally significant relationships are insignificant by comparison.

In Exhibit 1.2, the solid line through the blob represents normal relationships, while the dotted line represents the effect of adding an extreme outlier to the regression data.

For this reason, most statistical analyses throw away obviously deviant data. But how can that be justified in the context of portfolio management? It sounds absurd to pretend that these outlier events never happen, yet our primary tools are useful only for investigating economic relationships rather than, as Bloom suggests, the realm of political events.

Well, this is embarrassing! We're damned if we include the deviant data, and damned if we don't. Unless we have some operative model, either intuitive or statistical, of how the world works in normal times, we might as well use astrology to build portfolios. So the correct course of action seems to be to set aside the impenetrable deviants, but by all means not to forget them. The danger, of course, is that once we discard the deviant data, we frequently forget or sublimate that it ever existed. And the more our "normal times" thinking makes us rich, and the longer normal times last, the more inclined we are to forget the unknowable, which is calmly licking its chops.

Keith Ambachtsheer points out in Chapter 2 that it is all too easy to get caught up in the excitement and romance of making truly serious money. It is useful here to reflect on a July 2007 quote from Charles Prince, the ex-chairman and CEO of Citigroup:

> *When the music stops, in terms of liquidity, things will get complicated. But as long as the music is playing, you've got to get up and dance. We're still dancing. . . .*[3]

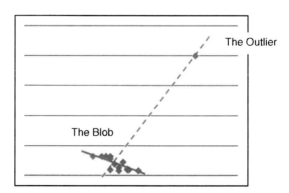

EXHIBIT 1.2 Effect of Adding an Extreme Outlier to the Regression Data

Prince seems supremely confident in his ability to know when to exit, but with everyone planning to stay as late as they can, he clearly underestimated how quickly conditions can change. Four months later, the music stopped and Mr. Prince was unceremoniously ushered out the door.

Call this temptation the financial dance of death. It's easy to string along while the money's flowing in, *but how do you know when to stop?* Those who leave the dance too early leave money on the table and initially look incompetent. However, a fully committed player like Mr. Prince finds that he can't escape when the building's on fire and everyone wants out at the same time. Envision a whole symphony hall overwhelmed with panic. Now envision the same panic in the trading rooms of Wall Street. As we've seen, hardly anybody knows how to call that timing very well.

"Haven't we been here before?" you might ask. In retrospect, all the dance steps to ruin look familiar. But each time the players are different, the lyrics sound new, and there's money to be made. We've seen junk bonds bring down the S&Ls, we've seen Russian bonds bring down Long Term Capital Management, but we've never experimented with junk mortgages before, so it looks different—at first glance. The leverage gets geared up, the duration of the assets is mismatched to the liabilities, and the comeuppance generates an illiquidity trap. In this game of musical chairs, all the chairs disappear at once while the music is still playing. "Nobody rings a bell when it's time to sell," says the wise old Wall Street adage.

It's easy to scapegoat Charles Prince as a "greedy" Wall Streeter, but all of us can be entranced by the siren's song.

The above excesses can be summed up as a slowly accumulating deficit in adult supervision, common sense, skepticism, ethical concern, and good, old-fashioned prudence. As often happens in booms, the kids, the ones who didn't live through the last debacle, shouldered the adults aside or impressed them too much. It's happened before and it will happen again.

TALEB'S BLACK SWANS

Nicholas Taleb hardly needs introduction to the readers of this book. His work focuses on discontinuities, which he identifies as "black swans." Taleb describes a *black swan* as "a highly improbable event with three principal characteristics: It is unpredictable; it carries a massive impact; and, after the fact, we concoct an explanation that makes it appear less random, and more predictable, than it was."[4]

In a recent Web article,[5] highly recommended to the reader, Taleb focuses on the problem of identifying risks when one cannot rely on conventional statistical methods.

Investment professionals are accustomed to taking risks in order to enhance expected returns. But Taleb points out that we can never correctly identify all the risks. Taleb describes risks that cannot be described by "normal" databases, and that involve higher levels of risks that cannot even be defined by standard methods. They may even involve risks that have never occurred—indeed, that based on our observable data would be considered impossible.

Taleb lays out a 2 × 2 decision table, where one axis is the decision type and the second axis characterizes two structures of variability:

Where do we get into trouble using Normal distributions?		Variability Structure	
		Quantitative	Qualitative
Decision Structure	Simple	Analyzable	Okay
	Complex	Okay	*Danger!*

Source: Taleb (see note 4).

Decisions break into two groups, which Taleb calls *simple* and *complex*. Simple decisions are true/false, win/lose on the flip of a coin or the payoffs from tossing dice. Complex decisions are situations where you care not only about the frequencies, but also the impact.

Variability structures are similarly divided into simple and complex, or very distinctly *quantitative* versus *qualitative*. The quantitative structure corresponds to "random walk"–style randomness found in statistics textbooks. Complex structures embed random jumps as well as random walk elements—the kind of distributions Mandelbrot famously brought to our attention.[6]

Taleb points out that the problems lie in the confluence of complex decisions and random jump elements. It's here that black swans bite most viciously.

Consider the dual meaning of the word *normal*. As a proper noun, capital-N, *Normal*, it specifically refers to a body of statistical knowledge developed around the delightful mathematical properties of the Gaussian distribution. But the use of the name "normal" probably comes to the statistical world from general usage, "being approximately average or within certain limits." While there are many places where *normal* experience is Normally distributed, we fool ourselves—and our clients—when we forget that much of economic life is distinctly abnormal.

Taleb points out that students of statistics approach a problem by assuming a probability structure, typically with a known probability distribution, in all likelihood a Gaussian, Normal distribution. But the critical

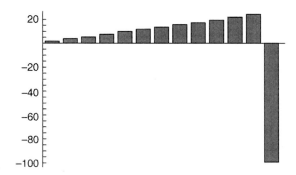

EXHIBIT 1.3 Anatomy of a Blowup
Source: Taleb (see note 4).

problem is not making computations once you know the probabilities, but finding the true distribution.

Low-probability events that carry large impacts may be difficult to compute from past data. Our empirical knowledge about the potential contribution of rare events will not, then, prepare us for black swan events. *Risk* is one word but not one number. Variance, skewness, and kurtosis (fat tails) are important. So is the application of risk-scenario analysis that illuminates survivability, best outcome, and breakeven analysis.

Exhibit 1.3 is Taleb's chart describing a blowup. In the *Edge* article, Taleb calls this his classical metaphor:

> *A turkey is fed for a 1000 days—every day confirms to its statistical department that the human race cares about its welfare "with increased statistical significance." On the 1001st day, the turkey has a surprise.*

A big problem for investors is that we can experience a long sequence of normal events before we run into these fat-tail events. We get lulled into the complacency of "a new era." Furthermore, the more our "normal times" experience makes us rich, the more inclined we are to forget that the unknowable is still out there—still calmly licking its chops.

WHERE WE GO WRONG

Lies, Damn Lies, and Statistics

Because they occur so frequently, there is an unfortunate tendency to invoke Normal distributions in situations where they may not be applicable:

"Everybody believes in the exponential law of errors: the experimenters, because they think it can be proved by mathematics; and the mathematicians, because they believe it has been established by observation."[7]

In other words, they assume that someone else is minding the other end of the store. What are we to do? Taleb describes the problem as the greatest epistemological difficulty he knows.

> *In real life we do not observe probability distributions . . . we just observe events. So we do not know the statistical properties—until, of course, after the fact. Given a set of observations, plenty of statistical distributions can correspond to the exact same realizations— each would extrapolate differently outside the set of events on which it was derived. The inverse problem is more acute when more theories, more distributions can fit a set a data.*
>
> *[This] inverse problem is compounded by the small sample properties of rare events as these will be naturally rare in a past sample. It is also acute in the presence of nonlinearities as the families of possible models . . . explode in numbers.*[8]

Let's face it: Economic data is nonnormally distributed, yet in all "normal" times, it will pass all the parametric tests for Normality. Normal thinking is unprepared and inadequate for abnormal times. In the words of Martin Leibowitz of Morgan Stanley, there are "dragon risks" akin to the ancient cartographers' depiction of the unknown as dragons inhabiting the reaches beyond the edge of the map.

Models are built on economic thinking, but noneconomic events lead to the discontinuities. It is difficult to the point of impossibility to assess the risks, gauge the likelihood of occurrence, anticipate the timing, or predict the severity.

Information Overload

Simply stated, the market is too complicated for anyone to fully comprehend. There are just too many moving parts, more than can be simultaneously comprehended by the human mind. Our minds are trained over many generations to identify the steppingstones in front of us, not taking in the whole view as a camera would. We're not built with enough mental hardware. What this means is that we can miss signals, even clear signals, because we can't distinguish them from the background noise.

Herbert Simon identified this phenomenon as bounded rationality.[9] *Bounded rationality*, stated simply, means that there is too much information for any one human being to process. In order to make a decision, we need to simplify by discarding what we believe is irrelevant or unimportant information and get to the core of the issue.

Which of these elements are the most important? Since our impressions derive from our personal life experiences, the answers differ from person to person. Thus we walk backwards into the future, with our minds anchored by the imprinted lessons of the past. And we have inadequate tools to process complex, qualitative events that extend beyond past experience.

Irrational Exuberance

The net result is that we don't play the real market; we hum along with the song the market sings in our individual heads. During Normal times the individual mental models fit well enough—at discontinuous times everyone is out of tune. However, while each participant reflects a different set of life's experiences, the market effectively processes *all* the information and choices—those that are in synch and those that are not.

Thus the market delivers its own truth. In *The Wisdom of Crowds*,[10] James Surowiecki puts it this way: ". . . a crowd's 'collective intelligence' will produce better outcomes than a small group of experts, even if members of the crowd don't know all the facts or choose, individually, to act irrationally. . . . People's errors balance each other out; and including all opinions guarantees that the results are 'smarter' than if a single expert had been in charge." The market is smarter than any participant in it. Without the collective intelligence, an index fund could not work.

The markets are good at sorting out rational thoughts, and are equally good at responding to emotional factors, which leads to a sleepwalking herd instinct. At some point, markets need to punish overexuberance. Markets find the price that balances supplying sellers with demanding buyers. If either group is wildly overrepresented, markets cannot find clearing prices. The transaction mechanism staggers and fails. Like the unusual sight that overturns the ferryboat, the black swans stampede the crowd in the same direction at the same time.

Thus fear, or its extreme, panic, is a necessary factor in the operation of any market. Remove fear and the markets cannot restrain rampant greed and exuberance. The only way to right the imbalance was for the unsupportable guarantees to default, thus creating an unforgettable psychological experience for many supposedly sophisticated investors.

The stock market is among the most uncertain and anxiety-producing areas of human endeavor. Nothing is assured; nothing works at all times. Not even the best of intellect, research, ardor, and our most motivated and intensive efforts can guarantee the desired results. We need to apply the best of both our science and art, but a few strokes of serendipity always come in handy.[11]

Hubris

Hubris? In this industry? Among the Masters of the Universe?

Remember the scene in *History of the World Part I*, where Caesar enters the city in a triumphal procession, while a slave whispers in his ear "Remember, thou art mortal"? Caesar's response, unprintable here, echoes the sentiments of a portfolio manager who just turned in a top-decile performance, or the pension manager who reduced the unfunded liability by 25 percent.

Oh, yes, hubris grows very well in this industry. Indeed, a financial manager who doesn't display great confidence in his own ability is not likely to attract many customers. He must play guru to those who are unsure of their own competence. To them, he must appear to be able to foresee the future. The danger for the guru is that sooner or later he will start believing it himself. Guru-ing is a tough business.

Fortunately, going through the wringer is a good curative for hubris, as many seasoned veterans know. Until it's happened to you, well, it's hard to develop a true appreciation for how swift and devastating the experience can be. As Fred Schwed said in *Where Are the Customers' Yachts?*,[12] "There are certain things that cannot be adequately explained to a virgin, either by words or pictures. Like all of life's rich emotional experiences, the full flavor of losing important money cannot be conveyed by literature."

"More things can happen than will happen." This statement from Elroy Dimson about risk captures the essence of the problem: Rather than worry about the myriad possibilities, we desensitize to possible outcomes with low probabilities. Yet, as Rahl's chart shows, low-probability events occur with surprising regularity. I propose an inversion of Dimson's statement: *More things that can't happen do happen.* Surprise, it seems, is always around the corner.

Here's where Charles Prince went wrong. He—and many others like him—thought his group was smart enough to know when to run for the exits. So did everyone else.

Overexuberance

So you've thought and experimented and labored to come up with a new wrinkle in your investment strategy, and it's working well. Hey, when you're hot, you're hot! Once you've found an edge, the natural desire is to double down and maximize the benefit. If *Tickle Me Elmo* dolls are the hot

Christmas gift fad in 1996, we crank up production so we don't run short before December 25 of that year. Guess wrong, and we own a warehouse full of the stupid dolls.

In finance, the obvious double-down is to apply leverage to the strategy. If the mechanism produces small but consistent outperformance, perhaps with leverage we can significantly enhance the rewards—and the risks. Nothing exceeds like excess. They don't ring a bell when it's time to sell. Just ask Nick Leeson, the rogue trader whose unchecked risk-taking single-handedly caused the overnight collapse of the 223-year-old Barings Bank.

Self-Delusional Raptures

There are many investment strategies that trade off small but highly likely payoffs against a remote but catastrophic loss. Many option-writing strategies have that property, as do market making and insurance policy underwriting. My friend Chris Keith says, "The hard part of trading is not making money on most trades, it is keeping from being killed on the remainder."

When we experience one of these low-probability/highly adverse consequences, the losses mount quickly and inexorably. When a player of games of chance runs out of money, it's called *gambler's ruin*. When a financial institution runs out of capital, it's called *bankruptcy*. Again, just ask Nick Leeson.

Willful Blindness

Saul Hansell published an article in the *New York Times* describing how bankers worked their way around the regulators' requirement to monitor their risk positions. They lied to their computers, says Hansell:[13]

> *The people who ran the financial firms chose to program their risk-management systems with overly optimistic assumptions and to feed them oversimplified data.[14] This kept them from sounding the alarm early enough.*
>
> *Top bankers couldn't simply ignore the computer models, because after the last round of big financial losses, regulators now require them to monitor their risk positions. Indeed, if the models say a firm's risk has increased, the firm must either reduce its bets or set aside more capital as a cushion in case things go wrong.*
>
> *In other words, the computer is supposed to monitor the temperature of the party and drain the punch bowl as things get hot. And just as drunken revelers may want to put the thermostat in the freezer, Wall Street executives had lots of incentives to make sure their risk systems didn't see much risk.*

"There was a willful designing of the systems to measure the risks in a certain way that would not necessarily pick up all the right risks," said Gregg Berman, the co-head of the risk-management group at RiskMetrics. *"They wanted to keep their capital base as stable as possible so that the limits they imposed on their trading desks and portfolio managers would be stable."*

This is using statistics like a drunk uses a lamppost—more for support than illumination. It's junk science, pure and simple. How do you reconcile that behavior with "putting shareholder interests first" or "prudent ethical concerns"?

STAYING AHEAD OF THE GAME: A POTPOURRI OF IDEAS

Throughout this chapter, we have hinted at some of the ideas that might help to avoid destruction by discontinuous market events. There are no easy answers here—in many cases, there are no satisfactory answers at all. The following is a list of thoughts about possible methods to address the challenges that discontinuities bring.

Idea #1: The *Thrive and Survive* Strategy

Set in place a thrive/survive strategy: Thrive in Normal times and survive the discontinuities when they occur.

Think of Normal times as the typical sunny days in Southern California, and discontinuities as the earthquakes. We need to be systematic about how to thrive in normal times; we need to heed the overwhelming likelihood and prepare for it. But complement that skill by preparing for the inevitable discontinuities. Understand that:

- Such episodes *will* occur.
- They will come at unexpected times.
- They will throw our Normal thought processes off-kilter.
- They will affect our expectations and well-laid plans in unpredictable and unpleasant ways.

Learn from the current discontinuities and prepare to survive the next discontinuity. As Ralph Waldo Emerson said, "Bad times have a scientific value. They are occasions a good learner should not miss." We have an opportunity to prepare ourselves to behave in a different way than we might have in the past.

Idea #2: Rethink Risk

Develop a better understanding of risk. Risk is not a number, as Bill Sharpe has pointed out. Risk needs to be thought of as an emotional response—something felt in the gut because it throws us into a world of great uncertainty and potentially irreparable harm. Risk is probabilities multiplied by consequences, and consequences are what matter to pension executives and mutual fund shareholders. Pay attention to the old-fashioned standards of prudence and ethical concern. Isn't avoiding the consequences of the discontinuities what our clients value more than anything else?

That's easier said than done. No one believed Cassandra, and no one will pay more than bemused attention to the doomsayer who's been wrong year after year.

Idea #3: Widen the View

Rethink the knowledge base: Resist the rapid, preprogrammed automatic sifting and winnowing of information. Step back at times and try to see more like a camera, taking in the whole view before the bounded rationality kicks in and throws useful but abnormal information away. Isn't avoiding the consequences of the discontinuities what our clients value more than anything else?

Not that this is easy—no one believed the boy who cried wolf, and no one will pay attention to a gloom-and-doom manager when he's been wrong year after year.

Idea #4: Define the *Thrive* Strategy

Clarify your understanding of what works in Normal times; pay special attention to where the self-delusional blindspots might lie.

Do *not* throw away the past knowledge and science that worked in normal times. Jason Lanier notes that in normal times, the collective isn't stupid.[15]

In some special cases the collective can be brilliant. For instance, there's a demonstrative ritual often presented to incoming students at business schools. In one version of the ritual, a large jar of jellybeans is placed in the front of a classroom. Each student guesses how many beans there are. While the guesses vary widely, the average is usually accurate to an uncanny degree.

This is an example of the special kind of intelligence offered by a collective. It is that peculiar trait that has been celebrated as the "Wisdom of Crowds," though I think the word "wisdom" is misleading. It is part of what makes Adam Smith's Invisible Hand clever, and is connected to the reasons Google's page rank algorithms work. It was long ago adapted to futurism, where it was known as the Delphi technique. The phenomenon is real, and immensely useful.

Lanier points out that the collective is not infinitely useful. The collective can be stupid, too. Witness tulip crazes and stock bubbles and subprime mortgages. These are the times when intelligent thought really matters.

Stay in control. Be decisive, even when the best option appears to be to do nothing.

Idea #5: Do Not Underestimate Liquidity Risk

As the next discontinuity hits, most managers will miss the signals and find themselves locked into riding the discontinuity downward. Once the panic starts, the exit doors will be jammed. There may be no way out. Consider the thoughts of Howard Marks of Oaktree Capital:

> *We have no choice but to assume that this isn't the end, but just another cycle to take advantage of. I must admit it: I say that primarily because it is the only viable position.*
> *Here are my reasons:*
> - *It's impossible to assign a high enough probability to the meltdown scenario to justify acting on it.*
> - *Even if you did, there isn't much you could do about it.*
> - *The things you might do if convinced of a meltdown would turn out to be disastrous if the meltdown didn't occur.*
> - *Most of the time, the end of the world doesn't happen. The rumored collapses due to Black Monday in 1987 and Long-Term Capital Management in 1998 turned out to be just that.*
> - *Money has to be someplace; where would you put yours?*

Idea #6: Define a *Survive* Strategy

Know that you will be unlikely to avoid the damage when the discontinuity hits; but there are steps that can be taken to reduce the potential damage. Think "earthquake preparedness."

One of the easiest remedies is to set up some guardrails around your normal process. Establish some diversification targets, and enforce a calendared discipline to reduce the overexposures and rebalance the overexposures back to target.

Beware the overly complicated hedging devices. If you don't understand them, stay away. Watch out for the rare events, the whiplash of the tail of the distribution of events. Remember, the financial world is fundamentally different at the tails—new regimes, new modes of interactions, different codependencies come into play. The hedges may not protect you when you need it the most—when counterparties fail, liquidity disappears, and all the correlations go to 1.0.

Don't give up on trying new things and new ideas. Consequences stemming from the discontinuity will require new solutions. But don't try to compensate for a low-return environment by upping the risk. Do not confuse the absence of volatility with the absence of risk: When the market needs volatility to find the clearing price, the volatility will appear.

Idea #7: Refine Quantitative Thinking

Quants need to get in touch with how data inaccuracy, statistical misuse, and misspecified probability distributions lead to errors. Watch out for GIGO. Question whether standard deviations can be accepted as risk numbers. Think about skewed outcome possibilities and fat distribution tails—how might they affect results? None of this stuff is easy, and the best we can probably hope for is an awareness and sensitivity, not a mathematical solution.

Do not passively assume that the computer and the equations possess some mystical insight. Make sure you understand the mechanisms and apply common sense. Think beyond the numbers to the pitfalls and the consequences. Consider putting under retainer a mathematical statistician and an epistemologist as consultants to backstop your eager young financial engineers and economists.

Idea #8: Reassess Quantitative Education

We need to broaden the process that educates quantitative analysts. It's easy to fault the Master of Financial Engineering (MFE) curricula. These programs need to develop a required course entitled something like, "Do You Really Know What You Think You Know?" Taleb's books would be the reading assignment for such a course.[16] Furthermore, *The Black Swan* should be required reading for the CFA exams!

Idea #9: Beware the Consequences of Political Solutions

Don't assume that governmental leaders know how to fix the problem. They will tinker and they will regulate, but they must accommodate widely divergent demands, many of them political rather than economic in nature.

Remember that these solons have no more experience with this discontinuity than you do.

Once the discontinuity has run its course, expect to be subjected to remedies, particularly politically laudable but economically reckless remedies, purportedly designed to prevent a reoccurrence of the disaster. Markets are very good at wringing out the excesses, but, as Bloom said, political actions must have primacy over economic actions.

CONCLUSION

Chaos can be avoided in the same way it has always been, albeit imperfectly, through the slower processes of deliberation and lengthened horizons in investment management, and by elections and court proceedings in the political world. Take a deep breath.

We can *never* gather enough data. Therefore, we need to supplant our normal decision processes based on statistics with nonstatistical, intuitive, consequence-aware, carbon-based logic systems overseen by prudent experts.

In short, the way to survive is through heightened enlightenment, integrity-reasoned, rational, and skeptical expectations, and above all, *parsimony*, in the multiple senses of the word: (1) frugality, (2) economy, and, (3) Occam's Razor—the simplest explanation is most likely to be insightful.

"Once burned, twice shy" behavior will protect those who've been through the experience, but the corollary is "Never burned, not the least bit shy." How are we to help the virgins, the new kids on the block? Guardrails, fatherly advice, or what? At the end of this path lies Fred Schwed's admonition: ". . . the full flavor of losing important money cannot be conveyed by literature." Unfortunately, that includes this chapter.

There is an old Chinese curse that says, "May you live in interesting times." Stay prepared: An interesting time may be just around the corner—licking its chops.

NOTES

1. http://www.cmra.com/crises.php.
2. Allan Bloom, *The Closing of the American Mind* (New York: Simon & Schuster, 1987).
3. http://dealbook.blogs.nytimes.com/2007/07/10/citi-chief-on-buyout-loans-were-still-dancing/.
4. Nassim N. Taleb, *The Black Swan* (New York: Random House, 2007).
5. http://www.edge.org/3rd_culture/taleb08/taleb08_index.html.

6. Benoit Mandelbrot, *The (Mis)behavior of Markets* (New York: Basic Books, 2004).

7. http://mathworld.wolfram.com/NormalDistribution.html.

8. Taleb, op cit.

9. Herbert Simon, *Models of Man* (New York: John Wiley & Sons, 1957).

10. James Surowiecki, *The Wisdom of Crowds* (New York: Random House, 2004).

11. Wayne H. Wagner, "A Curious Dilemma," *CFA*, May/June 2007, pp. 6–7.

12. Fred Schwed and Peter Arno, *Where Are the Customers' Yachts? Or, A Good Hard Look at Wall Street*, (New York: John Wiley & Sons, 1991).

13. http://bits.blogs.nytimes.com/2008/09/18/how-wall-streets-quants-lied-to-their-computers/.

14. Did I just hear a pension fund administrator say, "actuarial assumption of expected rates of return on plan assets?"

15. http://www.edge.org/3rd_culture/lanier06/lanier06_index.html.

16. A personal footnote: As a graduate student in Statistics/Management Science, I was required to take a "real-world applications" course. A team of students was assigned to the United Airlines maintenance facility at San Francisco Airport, and our assignment was to try to improve maintenance scheduling. We had all the theories in hand but the data we were able to gather was spotty, clearly incorrect—and unclearly incorrect—and self-contradictory. The final study report was, as a result, a botch of evasions and mumbles. At the time, I thought the course was a waste of time; but I soon learned that this was likely the most important course of all: that the data rarely conforms to the statistical model. The learned (and caustic) Sir Josiah Stamp said it well: "The government are very keen on amassing statistics. They collect them, add them, raise them to the nth power, take the cube root and prepare wonderful diagrams. But you must never forget that every one of these figures comes in the first instance from the village watchman who puts down what he damn pleases."

CHAPTER 2

The Sub-Prime Crisis as a "Predictable Surprise"

Strategic Lessons to Be Learned

Keith Ambachtsheer
KPA Advisory Services, LTD

We have also seen the emergence of a whole range of intermediaries, whose size and appetite for risk may expand over the cycle . . . accentuating real fluctuations, and exposing themselves to tail risks . . .
—Raghuram Rajan, University of Chicago, September 2005

When the music stops, in terms of liquidity, things will get complicated. But as long as the music is playing, you've got to get up and dance. We're still dancing . . .
—Charles Prince, CEO, Citigroup, July 2007

The fallout from the events of 2007–2008 has engendered several million words of criticism, constructive and otherwise. Yet, very little relevant appraisal has come from the money management industry. An enduring champion of pension reform describes the collective actions than can be effectively marshaled to avoid another asset erosion. Why, in this case, Bazerman and Watkins are more relevant than Taleb.

Adapted from an article of the same title printed in "The Ambachtsheer Letter #256," published February 2008.

FROM BLACK SWANS TO PREDICTABLE SURPRISES

Veteran trading speaker and sagacious author Nassim Taleb defines his *black swan* events as unexpected outliers that have extreme impact, and that are rationalized as predictable and explainable after the fact. Black swans are the ultimate "unknown unknowns."[1] This view of the world has strategic implications for institutional investors, such as:

1. Make room for unanticipated contingencies in your strategic plans and decision-making processes.
2. Weight your expectations not by perceived plausibility, but by the harm they might cause if you are wrong.
3. Consider adopting *barbell* investment strategies (e.g., when adopting a risky strategy, consider buying downside insurance).
4. Replace "normal" distributions with *power law* distributions in simulations. The latter recognize asymmetrical outcomes such as Pareto's 80/20 rule.

In contrast to Taleb, strategic advisor Michael Watkins talks and writes about "predictable surprises," which sound a lot like Taleb's black swans, except for one important difference. Watkins' extreme-impact events really were predictable, and were actually predicted before the fact. The predictions were simply not acted on.[2]

What are some examples of predictable surprises that turned bad? There were serious airline security concerns well before 9/11. There were serious auditor-independence concerns well before Enron. There were serious hurricane preparedness concerns well before *Katrina*, and yes, there were serious financial intermediation industry concerns expressed well before the sub-prime mortgage crisis hit the headlines in August 2007. The Rajan and Prince quotes above are but two examples indicating that knowledgeable observers were aware of the buildup of a toxic combination of factors that would produce the sub-prime crisis well before it actually erupted into the open in August 2007.

So Watkins' predictable surprises have an additional strategic management implication beyond those that follow from Taleb's unknowable black swan events. It is to construct triggers that move organizations beyond just predicting bad outcomes to taking action to prevent them. In other words, Watkins' thesis takes us out of Taleb's fatalistic black swan world, into a more hopeful, proactive one. This chapter explores this powerful idea, focusing on the financial intermediation industry in general, and its pension investments sector in particular.

BARRIERS TO PREVENTING PREDICTABLE SURPRISES THAT TURN BAD

Why do public- and private-sector organizations have such difficulty preventing predictable surprises? Watkins offers four broad reasons:

1. *Decision making under uncertainty is intrinsically difficult.* Our brains are wired for optimism; low-probability–high-consequence events are often ignored; information is seldom symmetrically distributed; incentives are skewed to short-horizon outcomes.
2. *Agency costs are unavoidable.* Perfect alignment of interests between agents and principals is impossible. Continuous observation and control of agents is also impossible. Agents often have agents, further magnifying agency problems.
3. *Solutions create winners and losers.* There are usually many players in the game, with either gains concentrated tightly and losses spread broadly or vice versa. This leads to asymmetrical motivation and single-issue politics.
4. *There are barriers to collective action.* Incentive structures promote defensive behavior and freeriding. The lack of trust is pervasive and the authority to impose efficient outcomes or enforce agreements is often missing.

The toughest collective action problems we face today have all four of these elements in play. Global warming and serious pension reform are two obvious examples. Yet, by understanding the reasons why predictable bad surprises have happened, and continue to happen, we put ourselves in a better position to prevent them. We now examine the current sub-prime crisis in this context.

THE SUB-PRIME CRISIS AS A PREDICTABLE SURPRISE

As the basis of our examination, we use a 2005 paper by Raghuram Rajan, titled "Has Financial Development Made the World Riskier?"[3] The author believed the answer to his question was "yes," and offered the following logic sequence:

1. *Financial systems have undergone revolutionary change.* Technical changes include rapid communications and computation, and financial engineering; deregulation has removed barriers to entry; institutional changes have led to the rise of new entities such as hedge funds and private equity firms.

2. *Savings have been "reintermediated."* Banks are no longer the primary recipients of savings—these now flow mainly through mutual funds, insurance companies, and pension funds.

3. *Banks now repackage and sell what they originate.* Mortgages are an example; however, some *tail risk* (e.g., first losses) has to be retained. As a consequence, bank balance sheets have become more risky and less liquid.

4. *Financial incentives have been altered.* Bank managers used to be paid fixed salaries, and the key focus was not to "break the bank." Today, the focus is on earning performance-based compensation. Thus while banker compensation used to be concave in returns, today it is convex (i.e., there is less downside and more upside today from generating excess returns). As a result, the incentive to take risk has been cranked way up.

5. *How "excess return" is measured matters.* If compensation is going to be performance based, *performance* must be properly defined and measured. Failing to do so can induce perverse behavior. For example, there is now a strong incentive to conceal risk, thus making *outperformance* easier to achieve. This makes taking on hidden tail risks an attractive proposition.

6. *"Herding" now makes sense.* Losing when everyone else is losing is less risky than losing alone.

7. *Low interest rates increase financial markets risk.* Unhedged fixed rate commitments go "underwater" if interest rates fall, and can be saved only though risk taking. Meanwhile, credit spreads and volatility drops, creating the aura of a low-risk environment.

8. *Hiding tail risks + herding + low interest rates is a toxic combination.* All three behaviors reinforce themselves in asset booms. An important implication is that banks will not be able to provide liquidity when the asset boom comes to an end.

The key thing to keep in mind is that this highly accurate description of the causes and dynamics of the sub-prime crisis was written in 2005, a full two years before it became a visible predictable surprise. And, of course, Raghuram Rajan was not alone in making this prediction. The sub-prime crisis may well be the most predicted predictable surprise of all time.

HOW COULD THE SUB-PRIME CRISIS HAVE BEEN PREVENTED?

It is useful here to reflect on the Charles Prince quote, "When the music stops, in terms of liquidity, things will get complicated. But as long as the music is playing, you've got to get up and dance. We're still dancing. . . ."

It's tempting to call this dance "the dance of death." It's easy to string along while the money's flowing in, *but how do you know when to stop?* Those who leave the dance too early leave money on the table and initially look like dopes. However, a fully committed player can't get out when the building's on fire and everybody wants out at the same time—a whole ballroom filled with dopes. As we've seen, hardly anybody, not excepting Mr. Prince, knew how to call that timing very well.

"Haven't we been here before?" you might ask. In retrospect, all these crises look similar. But each time the players are different, the litany sounds new, and there's money to be made. We've seen junk bonds bring down the S&Ls, we've seen Russian bonds bring down LTCM, but we've never experimented with junk mortgages before. The downfall is always the liquidity: In this game of musical chairs, all the chairs disappear at once while the music is still playing. "Nobody rings a bell when it's time to sell," says the wise old Wall Street adage.

Thus, despite its predictability, the sub-prime crisis occurred anyway. What could have been done to prevent it? Let's use Watkins' four barriers to preventing predictable surprises as the basis for drawing up a prevention roadmap:

1. *Decision making under uncertainty is intrinsically difficult.* While we're not going to change human nature, strong measures could have been taken. At a micro level, informational playing fields could have been leveled inside financial intermediaries themselves. Risk assessments could have been de-biased and more rigorous (e.g., properly capturing tail risks). Limits on discretion could have been set and enforced by people of integrity. Incentive compensation could have been based on properly measured, longer-term results and better alignment of interests. At a macro level, monetary policymakers should at least have been aware of these pro-cyclical risk dynamics in their rate-setting decisions. Regulatory practices (especially regarding risk assessment and capital requirements) could also have been more effective.

2. *Agency costs are unavoidable.* Yes, but their impact could have been reduced. The same micromeasures relating to complete and timely information, risk assessment and management, and incentive compensation, mentioned in item 1, had they been rigorously applied, could have materially reduced the outsized agency costs spawned by the sub-prime crisis. Organizationally, this implies oversight functions (e.g., boards of directors) should have converted presumable expertise, experience, sense of public duty, and decisiveness into an insistence that these risk mitigation measures be taken by financial intermediaries.

3. *Solutions create winners and losers.* Was there, or is there now, some way to force the sub-prime crisis winners (i.e., the collectors of outsized compensation packages inside financial intermediaries) to share their loot with the losers (i.e., house evictees, financial intermediary shareholders)? Through the legal system? The tax system? Through collective action by institutional shareholders? (The 2007 bonuses to be paid out at the top five Wall Street investment banks alone are estimated to total $39B.)
4. *There are barriers to collective action.* Was there some way for the potential sub-prime crisis losers to band together in (say) 2005 to prevent the sub-prime dynamic already underway from becoming a full-fledged crisis in 2007? Clearly, the macro regulatory and micro governance processes in place were not up to the task. What about the globe's thought-leading pension funds and their investment managers? Where were they? Were there collective action vehicles they could/should have used to defuse the sub-prime dynamic before it exploded into a full-fledged crisis? For example, as their presumably knowledgeable owners, could/should these pension funds have collectively insisted back in 2005 that the financial intermediaries at the heart of the sub-prime dynamic deal with such internal issues as the distribution of information, risk assessment and management, incentive compensation, and responsible, even-handed oversight?

It is tempting at this point to shake one's head and say, "no way," and to argue that there are far too many *could/should haves* in the laundry list of sub-prime preventative measures set out above—in other words, that despite its ready predictability, the unfolding of the sub-prime crisis was still unstoppable. And worse, so are future financial crises based on the same set of dynamics. Yet, Watkins reminds us, not all hard problems have eluded eventual solutions. The Cold War was resolved without nuclear conflict. Northern Ireland is finally conflict-free (okay, it took 400 years). International trade has flourished since WWII ended. The European Union has succeeded (well, sort of). The Montreal Accord of 1989 ended the serious global threat of ozone depletion.

So what can institutional investors in general, and pension funds in particular, do to prevent future financial crises with sub-prime-type dynamics?

A THREE-STEP INSTITUTIONAL CALL TO ACTION

The prior analysis makes a clear distinction between macro actions and micro actions. *Macro actions* focus on steps multinational institutions, such as the IMF, and national institutions, such as central banks and regulatory agencies, can take to break the kind of negative financial dynamic exemplified by the sub-prime crisis.

William McChesney Martin, former chairman of the Federal Reserve Bank (serving from 1951 to 1970, under five presidents), is famous for saying that the job of a good central banker is to take away the punchbowl just as the party gets going. The problem, though, is that the government is usually reactive and reliant on rule-based procedures necessarily rooted in previous experience. However, there are exceptions where the Fed can mobilize quickly, such as with the LTCM and Bear Stearns debacles.

Micro actions focus on what steps individual financial institutions such as pension funds can take, either collectively through collaboration mechanisms they create for the purpose, or individually. However, despite this important macro/micro distinction, there is an important first step common to both.

Understand the Problem Correctly

Any action steps taken should be based on a clear understanding of the problem the action is supposed to address. The creative, integrative thinking of analysts such as Watkins and Rajan exemplify the importance of first understanding the problem before attempting to fix it. As Albert Einstein once observed, solving complex problems requires a higher level of thinking than was used to create them. The implication is that we must support ongoing research efforts (both basic and translational; both academic and professional) that lead to higher levels of thinking about both problems and possible solutions.

Developing a detailed macro action list falls outside the ambit of this chapter. We simply note the Einstein rule that multinational and national monetary/regulatory policies cannot be improved without higher levels of thinking about the problem being addressed. As the Watkins and Rajan analyses make clear, such higher levels of thinking are multidisciplinary/ multidimensional in their approaches. Watkins' insights come from integrating behavioral finance elements with organizational structure elements, with political motivation elements, and with game-theoretical elements. Rajan's insights come from integrating historical elements with economic elements, with behavioral elements, and with technical elements related to the measurement of risk and "performance."

Our micro action list for investment institutions in general, and pension funds in particular, devolves into the two branches of collective action and individual action. Watkins' and Rajan's insights remind us of the power, but also of the organizational challenges, of effective collective action.

Take Effective Collective Action

Effective collective action by investment institutions can play an important role in preventing future financial crises. The key sub-prime collective action *could/should have* we identified above was the potential for institutional investors, as major shareholders of financial intermediaries, to impact and modify the behavior of these intermediaries that turned out to be so destructive (i.e., asymmetrical distribution of information, incomplete risk assessment and management, inappropriate incentive compensation structures, dysfunctional oversight at the board level). We sense an increasing recognition (especially by large pension funds) of the power of this type of collective action. The Rotman International Centre for Pension Management recently commissioned a study on devising and implementing optimal collaboration strategies.[4]

Finally, what about individual investment institutions, especially pension funds, themselves? What can they do on their own? Quite a lot.

Improve Your Own Governance and Decision-Making Processes

Individual pension funds can lead the way by improving their own governance and decision-making processes. Stating the obvious, pension funds are financial intermediaries themselves. So they have their own issues related to distribution of information, risk assessment and management, incentive compensation structures, and board governance. The better they deal with these issues inside their own organizations, the more credible advocates they become on the outside. Especially when everyone else seems to have tipped the fear:greed ratio away from worries about risk, a pension plan needs some method for keeping the pension fund out of the deep end. One way, although not by any means an easy thing to do, is to preestablish long-term guardrails on risk that will pull back the risk exposure before major damage is done.

We explore the implications of this step further.

DECISION MAKING UNDER UNCERTAINTY IN A PENSION FUND CONTEXT

What can we do to make decision making under uncertainty in a pension fund context as effective as possible? That's a simple question with no simple answer. A reverse-engineered design perspective offers a useful starting point. What outcome do we want to create? What are the key success-drivers to creating that outcome? How can those success-drivers best be assembled? How do we measure results? And maybe most importantly: Where are the weak links in this design chain? Our short best answers to these questions today in a pension fund context are:

1. *Desired outcome:* Deliver target pension payments at expected cost.
2. *Key success-drivers:* Realistic investment beliefs, broad investment opportunity set, sustainable pension design/adequate contribution rate, relevant risk measurement and management, relevant information production and distribution, qualified/motivated people.
3. *Success-driver assembly:* Functional organization design and decision delegation, balanced compensation structure.
4. *Results measurement:* Measure what should be managed (i.e., account for risk and costs as well as returns), link outcomes to compensation.
5. *Weak links:* Conventional thinking/herding, poor integration across key functions, unfocused results measurement (especially regarding risk and cost-effectiveness), insufficient/inadequate human resources.

Each of these short answers deserves further elaboration. Exhibit 2.1 helps by graphically linking some of the individual design answers from this list together. A picture of the key strategic elements of an integrated pension fund decision-making process begins to emerge, as do a new set of critical questions.

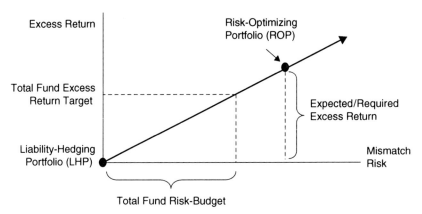

EXHIBIT 2.1 Integrated Pension Fund Decision Making: Key Strategic Elements

MORE HARD QUESTIONS

Exhibit 2.1 identifies four key elements and their linkages in any effective pension fund decision-making process:

1. *Liability-hedging portfolio (LHP):* Regardless of the specifics of any pension arrangement, the ultimate goal is to deliver a series of future pension payments. In theory, the LHP does so with zero mismatch risk. In practice, perfect matching is impossible. Further, taking on a modest amount of LHP mismatch risk (e.g., some credit risk) may generate worthwhile excess returns. Thus, practical questions are: Who is going to manage the LHP and its components? With what risk budget and excess return target? What part of the investment universe may be accessed? What will the size of the LHP be in relation to total fund assets? How will total LHP excess return be measured and, if earned net of expenses and a price-of-risk-based haircut, compensated?[5]

2. *Risk-optimizing portfolio (ROP):* In theory, the ROP is the cap-weighted investable universe of risky investments. In practice, it is some subset of that universe, opportunistically assembled by pension fund management to outperform the broader universe, ideally with less mismatch risk. Thus, practical questions are: Who is going to manage the ROP and its components? With what risk budget and excess return target? What part of the investment universe may be accessed? What will the size of the ROP be in relation to total fund assets? How will total ROP excess return be measured and, if earned net of expenses and a price-of-risk-based haircut, compensated? How is this measurement/ compensation process best repeated at the ROP component level (e.g., *public equity, private equity,* private real estate, absolute return strategies, etc.)?

3. *Risk measurement and management:* The ultimate financial risk in any pension system is that fund excess returns are zero to negative for an extended period of time. In this case, it is likely that the system will not be able to deliver the target post-work pension payments at an affordable cost. Avoiding this outcome requires two things. First, overall mismatch risk exposure (including those nasty, hard-to-measure tail risks) needs to be kept within the predefined total fund risk budget. This controls the extent of bad outcomes in the short and medium terms. Second, over the long term, risk taking (regardless of its source) must produce a materially positive excess return payoff. Thus, the practical questions are: How is the "total fund risk budget" best established? Given that risk measurement and management are mission-critical, is this function properly positioned within the organization? Has the function been allocated the

necessary resources? Does the function have the authority to say "no" when risk boundaries are overstepped?

4. *Expected/required excess return:* The *expected/required* duality in Figure 2.1 expresses the constant tension between difficult-to-foresee excess return expectations and a difficult-to-define excess return requirement. The *expectations* dimension should be grounded on an explicit set of defensible investment beliefs. What should the *requirement* dimension be grounded on? This is a yet-to-be resolved question in pension finance. At its essence is risk tolerance. But whose risk tolerance? Collective plans (e.g., Defined Benefit (DB)) feature collective risk bearing, with various stakeholder groups having different risk tolerances and facing different risk exposures. While individual plans (e.g., Defined Contribution (DC)) avoid the collective conundrum, the essential risk tolerance question remains. Specifically, how should a pension system put a price on risk, and in what units should that price be expressed? A seemingly objective pricing approach is to calculate the put option value that guarantees the LHP return as the minimum fund return with full utilization of the mismatch risk budget (e.g., a 4 percent put price at 10 percent excess return volatility, or a 0.4 reward/risk ratio, is a realistic estimate in this case). However, in the end, the resulting high price of risk is no more objective than any lower price of risk (e.g., 0.3 or even 0.2 in terms of an excess return/mismatch risk ratio).

WEAK LINKS IN THE CHAIN

Just as some pension fund organizations are addressing the hard questions just discussed, others are not. The four above-cited weak organization links in achieving high management effectiveness standards in the pensions arena are still with us:

1. *Conventional thinking/herding:* We have often characterized the management effectiveness struggle in pension funds as a governance quality struggle. Strong governance fosters creative thinking and actions that flow "from the inside out." Weak governance permits the continued acceptance of the status-quo views imposed by influential outsiders (e.g., pension lawyers, consultants, and others).

2. *Poor integration across key functions:* Eliminating *silos* is always a daunting management task, doubly so if many of the key management functions are externally delegated. Silo structures lead to decision-making processes that react to events rather than manage dynamically to anticipate them. Risk measurement and

management suffer especially in nonintegrated decision-making environments.

3. *Unfocused results measurement:* The lowest common results-measurement denominator is to simply compare gross returns among funds over the short term. Net returns offer a higher standard of comparison than gross returns. Risk-adjusted net returns over longer horizons offer an even higher standard, but as we noted, there is sill no consensus on how to risk-adjust.

4. *Insufficient/inadequate human resources:* This deficiency, too, ultimately represents a governance failure. It is the duty of pension fund governors to ensure that the organization has the financial resources to hire the right number of people with the right skill set.

So much for a collection of thoughts on how pension funds can make decision making under uncertainty less daunting and more focused. We close with some thoughts on the relevance of Michael Watkins' other three contributors to the predictable surprises phenomenon.

AGENCY, ASYMMETRY, AND COLLECTIVE ACTION ISSUES

A key *agency issue* of for-profit financial intermediaries is how managements deal with the respective economic interests of clients, shareholders, and themselves. Unless these interests are clearly separated and managed, there will be a natural tendency for managements to look after their own interests first. This tendency no doubt played an important role in the shifting composition of bank balance sheets on the way to the eventual sub-prime crisis. Life is simpler for pension fund managements in the sense that their organizations are not-for-profit, or at least not directly for-profit. However, this does not automatically make pension fund organizations conflict-of-interest-free.

For example, large own-company stock positions in some corporate DC plans continue to be a problem. As another example, the governance structures of some public-sector pension funds continue to be populated by special-interests members. In some cases, these members use their fiduciary positions on pension boards as political platforms. Others further labor union interests. Still others are only interested in the financial interests of the specific plan member group they represent. Thus, there are agency issues in the pensions sector that could spark unpleasant predictable surprises. Hence, agency issues must be vigorously identified and managed in the pension fund sector, too.

Regarding the *asymmetrical distribution of winners and losers,* the largest danger we see is in pension plans that collectivize individual financial interests. For example, it now becomes possible for one group (e.g., current pensioners) to simultaneously receive a guaranteed pension as well as have a call on additional financial benefits in scenarios where balance sheet surpluses arise. This was a common occurrence in public-sector plans in the 1990s. As another example, underfunded corporate DB plans present a radically different asymmetry of winners and losers, especially if there is a pension benefit guaranty fund. Now it makes sense for managements to roll the dice by loading up the pension balance sheet with risk. If the risk-taking pays off, the balance sheet recovers. If it does not, the employer can "put" the balance sheet to the guaranty fund. The United Airlines saga is a case in point. As a third asymmetry example, financial services providers in retirement savings plans can (and often do) charge fees in excess of the value of the services provided because plan participants don't understand the financial implications. In short, the asymmetry factor has salience in the pensions field, too, and must be carefully monitored (and ideally neutralized) over time.

Finally, there is the issue of mustering *collective action* initiatives against common predictable surprise threats. Leading pension funds are using the power of collaboration and collective action in a growing numbers of areas. Improving corporate governance practices is an obvious example, with an increasing number of pension fund–led national and international councils, coalitions, and other bodies banding together to press for a better alignment of interests between corporate managements and shareholders. The scope for collaboration has expanded beyond just corporate governance in recent years, with, for example, pension funds playing a leading role in the establishment of the UN Principles for Responsible Investment. The emerging trend of two or more pension funds establishing special-purpose coinvestment vehicles is yet another example. In yet a different sphere, organizations such as the Rotman International Centre for Pension Management at the University of Toronto offer opportunities for pension funds to pool their research dollars and conduct vigorous debates on important industry issues. Indeed, the sub-prime crisis has already spawned the Network for Sustainable Financial Markets, a group of investment professionals and academics studying ways in which financial markets can be made less crisis-prone.[6] Constructive collective action is one area where pension funds seem to be running well ahead of other classes of financial intermediaries.

LEADING THE WAY

This chapter offered four reasons why predictable surprises are often not nipped in the bud before they unleash their destructive forces. The sub-prime crisis offers a graphic case study of the *predictable surprise phenomenon*, with valuable lessons for the management of pension funds. We showed that decision making under uncertainty *can* be made less daunting and more focused. Agency-driven misalignments of interest *can* be neutralized. The pleasure and pain of reward and risk *can* be symmetrically distributed. Collective action *can* be effectively marshaled. All that remains is for the leadership of the pensions industry to turn these possibilities into realities.

NOTES

1. See Taleb (2007).
2. See Bazerman and Watkins (2004).
3. See Rajan (2005).
4. For more on the Rotman International Centre for Pension Management, see www.rotman.utoronto.ca/icpm. The commissioned study on collaboration can be accessed through this website. See Guyatt (2007).
5. For more on risk measurement and management in a pensions context, see Parts V and VI of Ambachtsheer (2007).
6. See www.sustainablefinancialmarkets.net for more information.

REFERENCES

Ambachtsheer, Keith. 2007. *Pension Revolution: A Solution to the Pensions Crisis.* Hoboken, NJ: John Wiley & Sons.

Bazerman, Max H., and Michael D. Watkins. 2004. *Predictable Surprises.* Cambridge MA: Harvard Business School Press.

Guyatt, Danyelle. 2007. *Identifying and Mobilizing Win–Win Opportunities for Collaboration among Pension Fund Institutions and Their Agents.* Rotman ICPM Working Paper. Rotman School of Management. University of Toronto.

Rajan, Raghuram G. 2005. *Has Financial Development Made the World Riskier?* NBER Working Paper 11728. National Bureau of Economic Research Inc.

Taleb, Nassim Nicholas. 2007. *The Black Swan: The Impact of the Highly Improbable.* New York: Random House.

CHAPTER 3

The Solidarity Challenge

David G. Tittsworth
Executive Director, Investment Advisers Association

United we stand, divided we fall.

—Aesop

Even if you're on the right track, you'll get run over if you just sit there.

—Will Rogers

In the wake of the 2008 financial crisis, the prospects for significant financial services regulatory "reform" are clear. The author examines the solidarity challenge facing the investment advisory profession in dealing with fundamental policy decisions—decisions that could dramatically affect how investment advisory firms are regulated and the standards to which they are held. He begins by examining key factors that contribute to the lack of solidarity among investment advisory firms, including: the diversity of firms, the absence of an accepted lexicon, the multiplicity of groups representing investment advisory interests, as well as historical and cultural factors. He then describes the characteristics that investment advisers have in common, and makes the case for a more cohesive and coordinated advocacy and education effort by the profession.

T he investment advisory profession is facing a number of serious policy issues that could dramatically alter the manner in which it is regulated and transform the high ethical standards that have been a hallmark of the profession for decades. As the 111th Congress commenced its work in 2009, "financial services reform" was high on the priority list in the wake of the seismic changes wrought by the subprime debacle. Other developments, notably the Bernard Madoff scandal involving an alleged $50 billion Ponzi scheme, have created a perfect storm environment for consideration of unprecedented changes to the manner in which investment advisers are regulated.

Possibilities that were nearly unthinkable a short time ago are now open for active discussion and potential action. In Congressional hearings examining the Madoff scandal, SEC officials have spoken openly about the need to "harmonize" investment adviser and broker-dealer laws and regulations and suggested the creation of a self-regulatory organization (SRO) for investment advisers. In January 2009, the Senate Banking Committee convened a hearing to confirm Mary Schapiro as SEC Chairman. Ms. Schapiro, the former CEO of FINRA, lamented that "far fewer resources are available for inspection and oversight" of investment advisers than for broker-dealers. Elisse Walter, another SEC Commissioner who previously served as a FINRA executive, has stated that "the biggest gap between brokers and advisors isn't how they're paid or the standards to which they are held, but the way they are regulated," noting that brokers—unlike advisers—are subject to self-regulation by FINRA. And FINRA (formerly NASD), the SRO for broker-dealers, has used the Madoff scandal to argue for extending its regulatory reach over investment advisers, stating that the "absence of FINRA-type oversight of the investment adviser industry leaves their customers without an important layer of protection inherent in a vigorous examination and enforcement program and the imposition of specific rules and requirements. It simply makes no sense to deprive investment adviser customers of the same level of oversight that broker-dealers customers receive."

The Securities and Exchange Commission, which among other roles serves as the regulator for the investment advisory profession, has been heavily criticized for its role in the Madoff scandal and for its alleged failure to regulate firms and practices that contributed to the financial crisis. As such, it is not inconceivable that the SEC could be abolished or significantly transformed as Congress debates regulatory changes (perhaps in favor of a single regulator system similar to the Financial Services Authority in the U.K.). How the regulation of investment advisory firms would be affected by such a sweeping proposal would obviously depend upon many devilish details. What is clear is that, in the context of the broad discussion taking place in the policy arena, the odds have increased that a fundamental restructuring of securities laws and regulations will occur.

Even before the 2008 meltdown, and the Madoff scandal, numerous studies, reports, and commissions were calling for changes to the current regulatory structure. For example, in March 2008, the U.S. Treasury Department issued a "blueprint" outlining changes that should be made in regulating financial institutions. The Treasury blueprint set forth two explicit recommendations that would dramatically affect how investment advisers are regulated: (1) to "harmonize" the Advisers Act with the law regulating broker-dealers, and (2) to subject investment advisers to over-sight by a self-regulatory organization.

These recommendations stem from the fact that traditional lines separating investment advisers from brokers have blurred during the past decade. An increasing number of brokers have moved away from conventional commission-based execution services, and now are offering fee-based advisory services. In 1999, the SEC initiated a rulemaking to address how such fee-based services should be treated under the Invest-ment Advisers Act. Ultimately, the rule spawned litigation and a 2007 court decision invalidated the rule adopted by the SEC. As it stands now, the legal issues concerning the distinctions between advisory and brokerage services largely remain unresolved. If and when Congress takes action in this important area, it could alter the fundamental fiduci-ary standard governing the advisory profession while subjecting advis-ory firms to costly oversight by FINRA, the self-regulatory organization for the brokerage industry.

In light of the Madoff scandal, the current composition of the SEC, and the worst economic crisis of our lifetime, it is abundantly clear that the environment is ripe for legislation and regulations that could dra-matically change the current framework governing the investment advis-ory profession. A rational person would conclude that these and other important policy debates would lead all investment advisers to take concerted action. The need for solidarity in addressing these develop-ments is compelling.

Yet, to a large degree, it remains elusive.

This chapter examines the solidarity challenge facing the investment advisory profession. It begins by examining key factors that contribute to the lack of solidarity among investment advisory firms, including: the diversity of firms, the absence of an accepted lexicon, the multiplicity of groups representing investment advisory interests, as well as historical and cultural factors. The chapter then examines the characteristics that investment advisers share, including fiduciary duty, and makes the case for a more cohesive and coordinated advocacy and education effort by the profession.

THE SLEEPING GIANT

In terms of sheer numbers, the U.S. investment advisory profession is a giant. The profession consists of more than 11,000 SEC-registered firms[1] that collectively manage more than $40 trillion[2] for nearly 20 million clients.[3] Clients run the full spectrum, from individuals and families who want a financial professional to handle their investments, to institutions such as pension funds, state and local governments, corporations, banks, insurance companies, mutual funds, endowments, foundations, and hedge funds. Simply looking at the vast amount of assets entrusted to investment advisers, it is clear that the performance of the profession is critical to the financial health and future wellbeing of millions of people.

Despite its size, the investment advisory profession has not done an adequate job of explaining who it is and what it does. Few investors understand the core characteristics of an investment adviser, or appreciate the key differences between investment advisers and other financial services providers. Even "specialists" in the financial media are not well-informed and many tend to characterize large mutual fund or brokerage complexes as "typical" investment adviser shops. Many policymakers, including members of Congress who have responsibility to craft laws governing investment advisers, have little understanding about the basics of the profession.

For these reasons, some might think of the investment advisory profession as a "sleeping giant" that has yet to reach its full potential by engaging in advocacy and educational efforts commensurate with its size.

Perhaps a more fitting description is that of a "dysfunctional" giant. Investment advisory firms come in all shapes and sizes. There is enormous diversity even among investment advisory firms that appear to be similar. By and large, advisory firms do not conduct business with each other. Thus, it should come as no surprise that the advisory profession often is described as "fragmented." Accordingly, many investment advisers do not feel any particular kinship with each other, despite the fact that the law treats them similarly. This leads to an insular mentality and a lack of solidarity in pursuing a common agenda.

CHALLENGE #1: THE DIVERSITY OF FIRMS

The investment advisory profession is characterized by its variety. On one level, the sheer size of advisory firms runs the gamut from very small to very large. Even among firms that are similar in size, there can be huge differences in investment philosophy, clientele, business structure, and services.

Here's a simple example that demonstrates the wide gulf that tends to separate investment advisers:

Everyman Wealth Management Company is an investment advisory firm located in Smalltown, USA. Ernest Everyman, 68, a CPA, founded the firm in 1976 when his accounting clients increasingly began asking for investment advice. His son, Ernest, Jr., is also a CPA and, among other duties, serves as the firm's chief operating officer. The firm employs two others, who primarily perform administrative functions. The firm has 190 accounts and manages $140 million in client assets, primarily for individuals. The firm provides financial planning, investment, tax, and accounting services.

Global Financial Company is an investment advisory firm with offices in New York, Los Angeles, London, and Hong Kong. The firm is majority-owned by a European bank. The firm concentrates on institutional clients, including public funds, central banks, insurance companies, endowments, foundations, and retirement plan sponsors. The firm offers a variety of investment products, including mutual funds, hedge funds, wrap fee programs, and separate accounts. The firm has an affiliated broker-dealer used primarily to distribute the firm's mutual funds. The firm has more than 1,500 employees and manages more than $300 billion in client assets.

Everyman and Global illustrate the solidarity challenge confronting the investment advisory profession. They are very different enterprises. Their clients are different. Their investment services are different. Their resources and focus are different. What, if anything, do Everyman and Global have in common? Are there any compelling reasons why they should work together to achieve shared goals? Do they even *have* any shared goals? Why should either firm be concerned about achieving solidarity with the other?

CHALLENGE #2: THE LEXICON CHALLENGE

At a very basic level, the lack of a broadly accepted and well-understood lexicon contributes to the solidarity challenge facing the investment advisory profession.

Terms used to describe those who provide investment advisory services include:

Investment adviser or advisor[4]
Asset manager
Investment manager
Portfolio manager
Financial adviser
Financial consultant

Financial counselor
Financial manager
Money manager
Wealth manager
Investment counsel or counselor
Financial planner

Complicating matters, some of these terms are used by other financial service providers, such as individuals who are employed by or associated with brokerage firms. The 2008 report of the RAND Corporation, commissioned by the SEC to examine the business activities of investment advisers and brokers, concludes that investors have "difficulty distinguishing among industry professionals and perceiving the web of relationships among service providers":

> We presented [investors] with a list of services and obligations and asked them to indicate which items applied to investment advisers, brokers, financial advisers or consultants, or financial planners. Their responses indicate that they view financial advisors and financial consultants as being more similar to investment advisers than to brokers in terms of services and duties. However, regardless of the type of service (advisory or brokerage) received from the individual professional, the most commonly cited titles are generic titles, such as advisor, financial advisor, or financial consultant. Focus-group participants shed further light on this confusion when they commented that the interchangeable titles and "we do it all" advertisements made it difficult to discern broker-dealers from investment advisers.[5]

The lexicon challenge (and related investor confusion) is further exacerbated by complexities related to various professional designations. While federal laws and regulations do not specify any minimal certification or educational requirements for investment advisers, there is an array of certifications, accreditations, and designations investment professionals can acquire to burnish their credentials. For example, the Chartered Financial Analyst and Certified Financial Planner designations are well-recognized, established designations that require significant time and effort to attain, including successful completion of certifying examinations. There are literally dozens of other professional titles that financial professionals may acquire, including accreditations for estate planners, financial counselors, tax advisers, employee benefit specialists, fund specialists, senior advisers, retirement counselors, and trust and financial advisers. Certainly, there is nothing wrong with professional certifications, and in fact many such programs assist in elevating educational standards and the technical proficiency of investment professionals. But considering the lack of an accepted "brand" for investment advisers, the plethora of certifications do little to help investors, the media, and policymakers understand the advisory profession.

Part of the solidarity challenge is for investment advisers to use the same terms to describe themselves and their peers, at least for purposes of advocating their common interests. It is inevitable that firms will use different words, phrases, tag lines, and brands to portray unique aspects of their services and products and to differentiate themselves from their competitors. But the profession could help itself simply by identifying and using certain key terms so that investors, the media, and policymakers will have a more profound appreciation of the fact that all investment advisers—in spite of their great diversity—fall under a big umbrella and are united by certain core characteristics.

One approach is to use the term *investment adviser* to describe all individuals and firms that are in the business of providing investment advisory services. The rationale for this approach is very simple—this is the defined term used in the Investment Advisers Act of 1940, the law that governs all investment advisers.[6] The Advisers Act defines *investment adviser* as "any person who, for compensation, engages in the business of advising others, as to the value of securities or as to the advisability of investing in, purchasing, or selling securities. . . . " Encouraging all investment advisers to acknowledge their legal status as investment advisers will lead to a better understanding of the profession.

I also prefer the term *profession* to describe the investment adviser community. Considering the impressive education and experience of most investment advisers—as well as the fact that all investment advisers are subject to a broad fiduciary duty—the word *profession* is more appropriate and descriptive than other terms.

CHALLENGE #3: ALPHABET SOUP

Washington, DC, is home to hundreds of trade groups and associations. Like investment advisers, they come in every size and shape. There are high-profile groups like AARP and the National Rifle Association, as well as scores of lesser-known organizations like the National Candle Association, the Popcorn Board, and the International Carwash Association. Virtually every industry and interest group has a membership organization that represents its collective interests.

At their core, associations work to advance and promote the interests of their members by serving as the liaison between industry and government. Membership organizations typically perform a wide variety of other services for their constituencies and may be involved in one or more of the following activities: providing information, research, and statistical data; education/professional development; developing standards, codes of ethics, and certification programs; and providing a forum to discuss common problems and solutions.

A number of groups compete to represent investment advisers, including the following:

- *Investment Adviser Association (IAA).* Represents more than 500 SEC-registered investment advisory firms that collectively manage more than $9 trillion in client assets. The IAA focuses on advocacy, compliance, and education activities. Its primary advocacy focus is the Investment Advisers Act of 1940 and related regulations.
- *Investment Company Institute (ICI).* Represents U.S. investment companies, including mutual funds, closed-end funds, exchange-traded funds, and unit investment trusts. ICI members manage total assets of more than $12 trillion and serve almost 90 million shareholders. Its primary advocacy focus is the Investment Company Act of 1940 and related regulations.
- *Financial Planning Association (FPA).* Represents financial planners, attorneys, accountants, bankers, insurance agents, stockbrokers, investment consultants, money managers, and others involved in the financial planning process. FPA's membership consists of about 28,000 individuals. The organization is focused on financial planning, best practices, and professional development.
- *Securities Industry and Financial Markets Association (SIFMA).* Represents 650 financial services firms, primarily broker-dealer firms. SIFMA was created in 2006 when the Securities Industry Association and the Bond Market Association merged. The organization is involved in a wide variety of advocacy, educational, and informational activities.
- *Managed Funds Association (MFA).* Represents the hedge fund industry. Members include professionals in hedge funds, funds of funds, and managed futures funds. MFA members represent the vast majority of the largest hedge fund groups in the world who manage a substantial portion of the approximately $2 trillion invested in absolute return strategies.
- *American Bankers Association (ABA).* ABA is the largest association that represents the banking industry. Its members include community, regional, and money center banks and holding companies, as well as

savings associations, trust companies, and savings banks. The organization represents over 95 percent of the industry's $12.7 trillion in assets.

Each of these organizations has some level of membership participation by investment advisory firms. In fact, some firms or their employees are members of more than one of these organizations. For example, a number of investment advisory firms that manage mutual funds belong both to IAA and ICI. Some of the larger diversified investment advisory businesses that are connected with brokerage firms belong both to IAA and to the asset management group within SIFMA. Some investment advisory firms belong to IAA, while some of their employees are members of FPA.

There are yet more groups representing subsets of these organizations. For example, while FPA is the largest organization representing financial planners, there are other groups—such as the National Association of Personal Financial Planners (the "fee-only" planners) and the Financial Services Institute (representing "independent brokers and financial advisors")—that also represent certain types of financial planners.

It is unrealistic to believe that the alphabet soup of investment adviser organizations will ever converge into one big happy family. The variety of organizations exists because investment advisory firms have a variety of issues, concerns, ownership structures, objectives, services, and products. Although there is some degree of overlap, it is probably inevitable that separate organizations will continue to exist to represent investment advisers, brokers, mutual funds, and financial planners. And as long as someone is willing to pay for access and exposure, enterprising individuals will continue to create advocacy organizations, even if no particular vacuum exists!

The confusing conglomeration of organizations representing investment advisers contributes to the general lack of understanding about the advisory profession. If you are a Member of Congress and two different groups (or more) purporting to represent the interests of investment advisers come to you with very different positions, what are you to conclude? What policies are you supposed to support? Whose side are you on? On the other hand, if you are a member of Congress and every SEC-registered investment adviser in your district comes to you with a unified message, it increases the odds that you will appreciate and understand their concerns and positions on key issues.

To the extent that investment advisers believe that their specific and collective interests as investment advisers deserve representation, they must devote the resources and energy to an investment adviser-centric association that can effectively make the case before policymakers in Washington, DC—and around the globe. They should not rely on associations that may have competing or conflicting membership interests to carry the ball. If investment advisers want to see particular changes or a different emphasis in policies, legislation, or regulations—or if they want the media, investors, and the public to understand the profession better—they must support a collective effort to make it happen.

CHALLENGE #4: THE GDI SYNDROME

As a general proposition, investment advisers are fiercely independent. They are highly intelligent and well-educated GDIs (gosh-darn independents). They tend to be self-reliant and self-supporting. They have worked hard to get where they are. They revel in intensive research and creative thought. Many would be flattered to be referred to as *contrarian*.

By nature, they are tough. The business of making investment decisions for clients is not easy. Investment advisers must deal with a host of complex and ever-changing issues. Unless an investment adviser has a solid understanding of the markets and specific securities and the acumen and discipline to focus on and follow a consistent investment strategy—not to mention the management skills to operate a business—things can unravel rather quickly.

Independent, tough—and autonomous. Investment advisers tend to abhor the herd mentality. Instead, they admire those who really "know their stuff" and who demonstrate originality based on thorough and objective analysis. Many have developed unique approaches to investment research and portfolio management based on rigorous analysis and steady application.

It logically follows that investment advisers are not exactly what one would call natural born "joiners." Even if an association is solely dedicated to representing their interests, the innate reaction of many advisers is one of healthy skepticism, if not outright suspicion.

For those who advocate solidarity within the ranks of the advisory profession, the GDI syndrome presents a significant challenge. One of the goals of an effective advocacy program is to get people—preferably as many different people as possible—rowing in the same direction. Trying to convince investment advisers to admit that they share interests with other investment advisers can be challenging. But it is not insurmountable. Investment professionals tend to be logical and can be convinced on the merits. Enlisting support from a broad cross-section of investment advisers will require a concerted and persistent effort of education, but the results will be worth it. The goal is to convince the vast majority of investment advisers to understand that they must work together to inform important debates and influence policies that affect their businesses.

CHALLENGE #5: AVERSION TO PUBLICITY

The traditional investment advisory business is based on a high level of discretion and confidentiality. Older generations of investment counselors would not even acknowledge their advisory clients when passing them on the street. Advertisements were eschewed as vulgar. Speaking with reporters was generally avoided if at all possible.

These historical tendencies of the investment advisory profession are somewhat at odds with well-run advocacy and educational initiatives that, by definition, need to highlight the profession, its attributes, and details of relevant issues. Advocacy results generally are tied to concerted, visible, and often widely publicized activities.

A trade organization can provide cover for individuals and firms that would prefer not to be on the frontline of particular advocacy debates. The investment advisory profession must come to grips with the reality that public discourse—from dealing with the financial media to meeting with policymakers—is a necessary element of effective advocacy.

CHALLENGE #6: WHO LIKES REGULATION?

Sometimes, the issues just aren't that "sexy." Most advocacy issues are directly tied to legislative and regulatory policies. The reality is that many advisers view legal, regulatory, and compliance issues as nothing more than a detraction and distraction from their primary job of serving clients. Moreover, legal and regulatory issues may be complex and difficult to grasp for senior management not immersed in the day-to-day nuances of compliance. As such, there is a natural tendency on the part of many investment advisory firms to avoid—or at least ignore—nascent legal and regulatory matters and conclude that it's "someone else's job" to try to deal with them.

Effective advocacy requires the active involvement of leaders in the advisory profession. Legal, regulatory, and compliance issues have become more visible during the past few years, and the level of awareness among leaders in the profession has been elevated. Transforming this awareness into active support for collective action will be a key to achieving a greater level of solidarity.

CORE CHARACTERISTICS AND SHARED VALUES

Let's return to our original questions. Do Everyman Wealth Management Company and Global Financial Company have anything in common? Are there any compelling reasons why Everyman and Global should work together to achieve any shared goals or objectives? Should either firm be concerned about achieving solidarity with each other?

The answers are yes, yes, and yes.

Everyman and Global are both "investment advisers" within the meaning of the Investment Advisers Act. Even though their firms appear to be completely dissimilar, both are in the business of providing investment advisory services to their clients. They are subject to the same SEC registration and disclosure requirements. Both owe a fiduciary duty to their clients. Both are subject to regulations under the Advisers Act, including the compliance program, code of ethics, proxy voting, privacy, custody, insider trading, books and records, and advertising rules. They are subject to examinations by the SEC. They both have serious risks related to noncompliance. They both face potentially negative consequences if the laws and regulations governing the profession become overly burdensome or are not appropriately tailored to the investment advisory business.

Everyman and Global also can benefit from positive perceptions of their profession—by investors, the media, and policymakers. They both have a critical stake in promoting high ethical standards for their profession. And they both can gain from organized and collective efforts to promote a better understanding of their profession.

Given these shared core characteristics, Everyman and Global have enormous incentives to work together. Both have a shared interest to preserve what's good about the statutory framework under which they operate and to oppose ill-advised and unsuitable laws. Both have a compelling interest in ensuring that regulations under the Advisers Act are reasonable and appropriate and to establish an ongoing working relationship with regulators to achieve an appreciation for the profession and their concerns. Both can benefit from positive and proactive government, public, and media relations. By working together, both Everyman and Global can strive to achieve a better understanding of their profession and in the process increase their own odds for success.

Fiduciary Duty: A Rallying Cry for Solidarity

Perhaps the most important shared characteristic of Everyman, Global, and every other SEC-registered investment adviser is fiduciary duty.

While the word never appears in the Investment Advisers Act, investment advisers are subject to an overarching *fiduciary* duty. This duty has been upheld by the U.S. Supreme Court[7] and reiterated by numerous regulatory pronouncements over the years. Fiduciary duty is one of the primary distinctions between investment advisers and others in the financial services industry. As a fiduciary, an investment adviser must at all times act in its clients' best interests. As such, an adviser's conduct will be measured against a higher standard of conduct than that used for mere commercial transactions. It is based on the premise that an advisory relationship is based on trust and confidence.

Fiduciary duty is not susceptible to strict definition or formulaic application but rather is dependent on facts and circumstances. However, certain core principles of an adviser's fiduciary duty have been well-established, as reflected in the following excerpt from the *Standards of Practice* of the Investment Adviser Association:

> I. *Fiduciary Duty and Professional Responsibility*
>
> *An investment adviser stands in a special relationship of trust and confidence with, and therefore is a fiduciary to, its clients. As a fiduciary, an investment adviser has an affirmative duty of care, loyalty, honesty, and good faith to act in the best interests of its clients. The parameters of an investment adviser's duty depend on the scope of the advisory relationship and generally include:*
> 1. *the duty at all times to place the interests of clients first;*
> 2. *the duty to have a reasonable basis for its investment advice;*
> 3. *the duty to seek best execution for client securities transactions where the adviser directs such transactions;*
> 4. *the duty to make investment decisions consistent with any mutually agreed upon client objectives, strategies, policies, guidelines, and restrictions;*
> 5. *the duty to treat clients fairly;*
> 6. *the duty to make full and fair disclosure to clients of all material facts about the advisory relationship, particularly regarding conflicts of interest; and*
> 7. *the duty to respect the confidentiality of client information.*

Fiduciary duty can and should be a rallying cry for investment advisers. It is a critical distinguishing feature of the advisory profession. It implicates a higher ethical standard and duty of care. It is designed to help avoid potential conflicts of interest and to cultivate a culture where the client's interests are paramount. It applies to all investment advisers, regardless of size or services. It is a key ingredient of solidarity.

THE CASE FOR SOLIDARITY: WHAT'S AT STAKE

What should investment advisers be fighting for (or against)?

The basic elements of the legal and regulatory structure governing investment advisers have much to offer. Compared to many other laws, the statutory framework of the Investment Advisers Act is relatively simple and straightforward. Since 1996, the law has designated a single regulator—the SEC—to oversee investment advisers that manage at least $25 million in assets. If appropriately implemented, the single-regulator model promotes efficiency, accountability, and subject-matter expertise. The Advisers Act is principles based. The law relies on broad anti-fraud authority rather than specific statutory requirements and prohibitions—it makes it unlawful for any adviser to "employ any device, scheme, or artifice to defraud any client or prospective client," to engage in "any transaction, practice, or course of business which operates as a fraud or deceit upon any client or prospective client."[8] The Advisers Act largely relies on full and fair disclosure to effectuate its purposes.

The following statement from former SEC Chairman Arthur Levitt summarizes the essential ingredients of the Advisers Act:

> *Unlike some of the other securities laws, the Advisers Act does not contain detailed rules governing the way advisers conduct their businesses. Rather, the Act broadly prohibits fraud and holds advisers to rigorous fiduciary standards when dealing with clients. Investment advisers have two choices under the Act. They must rid themselves of all conflicts of interest with their clients—conflicts that might influence them to act in their own best interest rather than in the best interest of their clients. Or, they must fully disclose any conflicts to clients and prospective clients.*[9]

One of the central purposes of the Advisers Act is investor protection. The fact that investment advisers have a legal responsibility—a fiduciary duty—to place the interests of their clients ahead of their own interests is central to the design of ensuring that investors will be protected.

That the Advisers Act has worked well for decades—particularly when considering the extreme diversity within the advisory profession and the dramatic changes that have taken place since its inception—is a testament to its relative simplicity and flexibility. The essential building blocks of the investment adviser law are sound—and worth fighting for.

This is not to say that investment advisers enjoy a perfect regulatory environment. During the past few years, a literal revolution in investment adviser regulation has occurred (much of it on the heels of the mutual fund "scandals" that arose in September 2003). A number of new and sweeping regulations have been adopted. As a result, the compliance burden for investment advisers has increased significantly. SEC oversight has become more aggressive. The complexity and costs of regulation have proliferated dramatically. In fact, one of the important reasons to support solidarity within the advisory profession is to advocate for appropriate and reasonable regulations. There is a compelling need for the profession to support a unified effort to engage in a dialogue with regulators and other policymakers, to develop relevant data and facts to support its positions, and to do the things that are required to be "on the record" (such as filing written comment letters on regulatory proposals).

Preserving what's good about how the advisory profession is governed—including a single regulator, anti-fraud and disclosure-based rules, and overarching fiduciary duty—will require concerted action by the advisory profession. It will not just take care of itself. Many of the basic building blocks that have served as the foundation for the advisory profession are in danger. Solidarity among investment advisers will be required to reestablish this foundation.

THE ASSAULT ON THE ADVISERS ACT

Coming full circle, let's return to the current discussions in Washington, DC, about changing the basic structure of how financial services firms are regulated.

In the fall of 2007, the Treasury Department requested public comment on a sweeping "regulatory review."[10] The proposal essentially asked for suggestions about how financial institutions—including banks, insurance companies, and securities firms—should be regulated. Following the formal comment period, the Department published a 218-page document in March 2008, entitled "Blueprint for a Modernized Financial Regulatory Structure," that sets forth a number of short-term, intermediate, and long-term options for improving the regulation of U.S. financial institutions.

The "intermediate-term" recommendations include a discussion pertaining to broker-dealer and investment adviser regulation. The document begins by noting that "convergence" is occurring in the securities industry and is "demonstrated by the ongoing debate regarding broker-dealer regulation and investment adviser regulation." It states that the regulations relating to broker-dealers and investment advisers originate in two distinct laws—the Securities Exchange Act of 1934 and the Investment Advisers Act of 1940—and summarizes various characteristics of each. In outlining differences between broker-dealer and investment adviser regulation, the report explicitly recognizes the fiduciary duty owed by investment advisers:

> *One critical factor that distinguishes investment advisers from broker-dealers is that investment advisers are fiduciaries, which means that they owe undivided loyalty to their customers and may not*

engage in any practices that conflict with their clients' interests (unless their clients have consented). Investment advisers, therefore, are generally required to take into account clients' financial resources, investment objectives, risk tolerance, and experience so as to provide their clients only with investment advice that is "suitable" for their particular needs and circumstances. Broker-dealers, which are subject to strong standards of conduct and "suitability" requirements, generally are not fiduciaries of their clients and thus are perceived by some as having weaker obligations to customers.

The blueprint describes the "convergence" of brokerage and advisory activities that has occurred in the decades that have passed since the laws were originally enacted:

Upon passage of the federal securities laws in the 1930s and 1940s, there was a clear difference between a broker-dealer and an investment adviser based primarily on how they were compensated. These differences have largely disappeared.

The report outlines the growth of fee-based brokerage accounts that prompted the SEC to commence a rulemaking in 1999 that "would have exempted a broker-dealer from registering as an investment adviser if the broker-dealer was not exercising investment discretion over the account, the investment advice was solely incidental to the brokerage services, and the broker-dealer disclosed to its clients the accounts were brokerage accounts." It goes on to outline the tortured history of the SEC rulemaking and the court decision, delivered March 30, 2007, that ultimately vacated the final rule adopted by the SEC in 2005. The narrative portion of the report ends with a description of the 2008 RAND report, which found that investors often are unable to distinguish between broker-dealers and investment advisers and "fail to understand the differences in the standards of care of broker-dealers and investment advisers. . . . "

The blueprint then sets forth the following recommendations:

Treasury notes the rapid and continued convergence of the services provided by broker-dealers and investment advisers and the resulting regulatory confusion due to a statutory regime reflecting the brokerage and investment advisory industries of decades ago. An objective of this report is to identify regulatory coverage gaps and inefficiencies. This is one such situation in which the U.S. regulatory system has failed to adjust to market developments, leading to investor confusion. Accordingly, Treasury recommends statutory changes to harmonize the regulation and oversight of broker-dealers and investment advisers offering similar services to retail investors. In that vein, Treasury also believes that self-regulation of the investment advisory industry should enhance investor protection and be more cost-effective than direct SEC regulation. Thus, in effectuating this statutory harmonization, Treasury recommends that investment advisers be subject to a self-regulatory regime similar to that of broker-dealers.[11]

Since the blueprint's publication, Treasury officials have confirmed that FINRA—the self-regulatory organization (SRO) formed by the merger of the NASD and the regulatory and enforcement arms of the New York Stock Exchange in 2007—would be the SRO for investment advisers.[12] FINRA currently serves as the SRO for broker-dealers. Ironically, FINRA was the only entity that filed comments with Treasury indicating that a SRO for investment advisers should be considered (the Investment Adviser Association argued against the SRO in its comment letter).

The Treasury recommendations are an example of how rational public policy can be turned upside down. The Treasury report actually does a credible job of stating the facts. It is true that broker and adviser services have converged as an increasing number of brokers have migrated toward the advice model (due in large measure to the fact that the traditional commission model for equity trades has been transformed with the advent of electronic trading). It is true that investors are confused and have difficulty understanding the differences between brokers, investment advisers, financial planners, and others who provide some form of investment advice.

But why should those facts translate to the *need* for an investment adviser SRO? If anything, it is more logical to conclude that those who provide investment advice (or market themselves as such) should be subject to the blanket fiduciary duty under the Investment Advisers Act. It is more logical to conclude that the principles-based structure of the Advisers Act should apply consistently to anyone who provides investment advisory services. It is more logical to conclude that the SEC should continue to be the regulator for investment advisers, rather than FINRA, the self-regulatory organization that oversees broker-dealers.

Similarly, FINRA has used the Bernard Madoff scandal to argue for an extension of its jurisdiction over investment advisers. At the January 27, 2009 hearing before the Senate Bank Committee, Columbia Law Professor John Coffee noted that he could "see no reason that FINRA (or at that time the NASD) should have abstained from examining and monitoring the advisory side of Madoff Securities." Other legal experts and practitioners have confirmed this view. Nonetheless, FINRA has used the scandal to argue that Congressional action is needed to fill the "regulatory gap" between brokerage and advisory activities by extending broker-dealer rules to investment advisers and subjecting investment advisers to "FINRA-type" oversight. FINRA's recommendation to "harmonize" broker and adviser regulation and oversight could eviscerate or water down fiduciary, disclosure, and other important requirements of the Advisers Act, such as eliminating provisions of the law that restrict investment advisers from self-dealing by trading to or from their own accounts with clients (referred to as principal trading).

These examples should serve as a wake-up call for the investment advisory profession. They represent the compelling need for investment advisers to come together to deal with potential issues that would affect the basics of how the profession is regulated and the standards that govern the profession.

If the advisory profession cares about the outcome, concerted and collective advocacy action is required to educate members of Congress and their staffs about relevant issues. Typical Congressional advocacy activities can involve a wide range of activities, including writing letters and meeting with elected officials, analyzing proposed legislation, providing testimony to Congressional committees, making political contributions, and communicating with executive branch officials and other appropriate agencies (such as the SEC).

Whether it is called advocacy or government relations or lobbying, exercising our First Amendment right to petition the government requires time, resources, and organization. Effective advocacy means supporting an organized effort designed specifically for the purpose of representing the interests of investment advisers. One hires an investment adviser when one needs advice about investments. Similarly, investment advisers need to hire professionals when legislative and regulatory issues are being debated and resolved. And, as with investments, a longer time horizon is much better than a short one. Running up to plead one's case on Capitol Hill or at the SEC only when "nuclear" issues are being considered is generally less effective than establishing long-term working relationships designed to promote a better understanding of the profession and its issues.

THE BOTTOM LINE—AND THE CHOICE

At first blush, it may seem that investment advisory firms have little in common. Everyman and Global epitomize the extreme diversity within the advisory profession. They are wholly separate enterprises that serve different clients, offer different advisory services, and deal with completely different business, operational, and financial issues.

Yet, despite the enormous gulf that separates them, Everyman and Global share a number of critical key characteristics. They are investment advisers within the meaning of the Investment Advisers Act. They are subject to SEC regulations and oversight. Both owe a fiduciary duty to their clients. Both are affected by significant changes to the laws and regulations governing all investment advisers.

The basic legal and regulatory structure that has governed investment advisers or decades is being debated. Key public officials have characterized the current statutory framework as "outdated" and "losing its relevance."[13] The 2008 financial crisis will certainly lead to action by the Congress to address "reforms" that may implicate how investment advisers are regulated and the standards to which they are held.

Investment advisers have a choice. They can sit on the sideline and watch as other well-organized and well-financed groups seek to change the laws that serve the advisory profession well. Or they can work together in solidarity to ensure that their common interests are understood and represented.

What can investment advisers do to address the solidarity challenge facing their profession? Here are three suggestions:

1. *Understand.* The first step is awareness. Investment advisers do not have to become experts on every facet of every law and regulation. But they should have an appreciation for major policy issues that directly affect their business and their profession. It is essential for investment advisers to understand the basic legal and regulatory framework governing their profession. While there have been many significant developments in the financial services industry since the Investment Advisers Act was enacted in 1940, it is clear that the overall structure has generally worked well and served the interests of both investors and investment advisers. The fiduciary culture fostered by the Advisers Act continues to be a unique element that distinguishes the advisory profession from other financial services providers. Investment advisers must first understand the essential legal, regulatory, and cultural aspects of the profession (including the fact that all advisers share certain core characteristics) in order to appreciate the need to work together for a common purpose.

2. *Reach out.* All investment advisers can benefit from a continuing dialogue with others in the profession. The insular mentality that tends to separate advisers from each other is counterproductive to organized and collective efforts that are necessary to influence public policy. On one level, interacting with other investment advisers can yield numerous benefits, from providing new ideas and views on investment,

operational, management, and business issues to gaining valuable benchmarks and insights into industry practices. Those who are willing to share their experiences and discuss their concerns and issues with others in the profession stand to gain much from their competitors. On another level, networking is an essential element of effective advocacy. The simple truth is that investment advisers will be unable to shape laws and regulations governing the way they do business unless they work together. Investment advisers must reach out to each other to ensure that their collective voice is effectively communicated to—and understood by—policymakers. Creating a collective and unified voice of the investment advisory community will increase the chances for a successful advocacy effort.

3. *Get involved.* The investment advisory profession faces a serious solidarity challenge. Unfortunately, many investment advisers appear to be disinterested in supporting organized efforts designed to address major policy issues that could affect the manner in which their businesses are conducted, perceived, and regulated. Many investment advisers have left it to others to carry the advocacy flag. Obviously, doing nothing means that other interests will be able to control the public policy agenda. Unless and until investment advisers are willing to get involved, they don't stand a chance of influencing current debates about how financial professionals should be governed. Getting involved means understanding the process by which public policies are made. It means taking affirmative steps to join with others in the profession to promote a coordinated and sustained effort to address issues of common concern. It means working with other investment advisers to do what it takes to ensure that policymakers understand and appreciate their interests.

The solidarity challenge is alive and well. Where do you stand?

NOTES

1. As of April 2008, there were a total of 11,030 entities registered with the SEC as "investment advisers" (including 1,071 entities that reported less than $25 million in assets under management). See Evolution/Revolution 2008: A Profile of the Investment Advisory Profession. Investment Adviser Association and National Regulatory Services.

2. As of April 2008, total AUM reported by all SEC-registered advisers was $42.3 trillion. The data, however, overstate actual AUM because more than one adviser may "claim" the same AUM. See Evolution/Revolution 2008, available at www.investmentadviser.org.

3. Amendments to Form ADV, Rel. Nos. IA-2711; 34-57419; File No. S7-10-00 (Mar. 3, 2008), at p. 4 (available at www.sec.gov under "Proposed Rules").

4. There's not even consensus on whether to spell adviser with an "e" or an "o"! Many in the profession seem to prefer the "o" spelling despite the fact that Congress spelled adviser with an "e" when it enacted the Investment Advisers Act in 1940 (there is no difference in meaning).

5. Investor and Industry Perspectives on Investment Advisers and Broker-Dealers, LRN-RAND Center for Corporate Ethics, Law, and Governance (2008), p. xix.

6. The Advisers Act defines investment adviser as "any person who, for compensation, engages in the business of advising others, as to the value of securities or as to the advisability of investing in, purchasing, or selling securities, or who, for compensation and as part of a regular business, issues or promulgates analyses or reports concerning securities." There are a number of exceptions to the definition, including, in certain cases, banks, broker-dealers, accountants, and attorneys. The broker-dealer exception is the subject of continuing debate among policymakers and interested parties.

7. SEC v. Capital Gains Bureau, 375 U.S. 180 (1963).

8. Section 206, Investment Advisers Act of 1940.

9. Speech by SEC Chairman: "Amendments to Form ADV: Opening Statement" (April 5, 2000), available on the SEC website (www.sec.gov).

10. Review by the Treasury Department of the Regulatory Structure Associated with Financial Institutions, TREAS-DO-2007-0018 (October 11, 2007).

11. The Department of the Treasury Blueprint for a Modernized Financial Regulatory Structure (March 2008), pp. 125–126.

12. "Blueprint for Change—or Not," Financial Times (May 5, 2008), p. 15.

13. Statements of Christopher Cox, SEC Chairman, and Kathleen Casey, SEC Commissioner (September 11, 2007).

Keeping the Challenges
in Perspective

The Failure of Invariance

Peter L. Bernstein

When published in 1996, Against the Gods: The Remarkable Story of Risk *(John Wiley & Sons) took its place as one of the seminal history books written in the twentieth century. Here is Chapter 16 from that remarkable work. Many readers encountered for the first time Kahneman's and Tversky's "Prospect Theory." Investment managers who have not yet read* Against the Gods *are at a competitive disadvantage—big time.*

All of us think of ourselves as rational beings even in times of crisis, applying the laws of probability in cool and calculated fashion to the choices that confront us. We like to believe we are above average in skills, intelligence, farsightedness, experience, refinement, and leadership. Who admits to being an incompetent driver, a feckless debater, a stupid investor, or a person with an inferior taste in clothes?

Yet how realistic are such images? Not everyone can be above average. Furthermore, the most important decisions we make usually occur under complex, confusing, indistinct, or frightening conditions. Not much time to consult the laws of probability. Life is not a game of *balla*. It often comes trailing Kenneth Arrow's clouds of vagueness.

And yet most humans are not utterly irrational beings who take risks without forethought or who hide in a closet when anxiety strikes. As we shall see, the evidence suggests that we reach decisions in accord with an underlying structure that enables us to function predictably and, in most instances, systematically. The issue, rather, is the degree to which the reality in which we make our decisions deviates from the rational decision models of the Bernoullis, Jevons, and von Neumann. Psychologists have spawned a cottage industry to explore the nature and causes of these deviations.

Peter L. Bernstein, *Against the Gods: The Remarkable Story of Risk* (Hoboken, NJ: John Wiley and Sons, 1996), pp. 269–283. Reprinted with permission of John Wiley & Sons, Inc.

The classical models of rationality—the model on which game theory and most of Markowitz's concepts are based—specifies how people *should* make decisions in the face of risk and what the world would be like if people did in fact behave as specified. Extensive research and experimentation, however, reveal that departures from that model occur more frequently than most of us admit. You will discover yourself in many of the examples that follow.

The most influential research into how people manage risk and uncertainty has been conducted by two Israeli psychologists, Daniel Kahneman and Amos Tversky. Although they now live in the United States—one at Princeton and the other at Stanford—both served in the Israeli armed forces during the 1950s. Kahneman developed a psychological screening system for evaluating Israeli army recruits that is still in use. Tversky served as a paratroop captain and earned a citation for bravery. The two have been collaborating for nearly thirty years and now command an enthusiastic following among both scholars and practitioners in the field of finance and investing, where uncertainty influences every decision.[1]

Kahneman and Tversky call their concept Prospect Theory. After reading about Prospect Theory and discussing it in person with both Kahneman and Tversky, I began to wonder why its name bore no resemblance to its subject matter. I asked Kahneman where the name had come from. "We just wanted a name that people would notice and remember," he said.

Their association began in the mid-1960s when both were junior professors at Hebrew University in Jerusalem. At one of their first meetings, Kahneman told Tversky about an experience he had had while instructing flight instructors on the psychology of training. Referring to studies of pigeon behavior, he was trying to make the point that reward is a more effective teaching tool than punishment. Suddenly one of his students shouted, "With respect, Sir, what you're saying is literally for the birds. . . . My experience contradicts it."[2] The student explained that the trainees he praised for excellent performance almost always did worse on their next flight, while the ones he criticized for poor performance almost always improved.

Kahneman realized that this pattern was exactly what Francis Galton would have predicted. Just as large sweet peas give birth to smaller sweet peas, and vice versa, performance in any area is unlikely to go on improving or growing worse indefinitely. We swing back and forth in everything we do, continuously regressing toward what will turn out to be our average performance. The chances are that the quality of a student's next landing will have nothing to do with whether or not someone has told him that his last landing was good or bad.

"Once you become sensitized to it, you see regression everywhere," Kahneman pointed out to Tversky.[3] Whether your children do what they are told to do, whether a basketball player has a hot hand in tonight's game, or whether an investment manager's performance slips during this calendar quarter, their future performance is most likely to reflect regression to the mean regardless of whether they will be punished or rewarded for past performance.

Soon the two men were speculating on the possibility that ignoring regression to the mean was not the only way that people err in forecasting future performance from the facts of the past. A fruitful collaboration developed between them as they proceeded to conduct a series of clever experiments designed to reveal how people make choices when faced with uncertain outcomes.

Prospect Theory discovered behavior patterns that had never been recognized by proponents of rational decision-making. Kahneman and Tversky ascribe these patterns to two human shortcomings. First, emotion often destroys the self-control that is essential to rational decision-making. Second, people are often unable to understand fully what they are dealing with. They experience what psychologists call cognitive difficulties.

The heart of our difficulty is in sampling. As Leibniz reminded Jacob Bernoulli, nature is so varied and so complex that we have a hard time drawing valid generalizations from what we observe. We use shortcuts that lead us to erroneous perceptions, or we interpret small samples as representative of what larger samples would show.

Consequently, we tend to resort to more subjective kinds of measurement: Keynes's "degrees of belief" figure more often in our decision-making than Pascal's Triangle, and gut rules even when we think we are using measurement. Seven million people and one elephant!

We display risk-aversion when we are offered a choice in one setting and then turn into risk-*seekers* when we are offered the same choice in a different setting. We tend to ignore the common components of a problem and concentrate on each part in isolation—one reason why Markowitz's prescription for portfolio-building was so slow to find acceptance. We have trouble recognizing how much information is enough and how much is too much. We pay excessive attention to low-probability events accompanied by high drama and overlook events that happen in routine fashion. We treat costs and uncompensated losses differently, even though their impact on wealth is identical. We start out with a purely rational decision about how to manage our risks and then extrapolate from what may be only a run of good luck. As a result, we forget about regression to the mean, overstay our positions, and end up in trouble.

Here is a question that Kahneman and Tversky use to show how intuitive perceptions mislead us. Ask yourself whether the letter K appears more often as the first or as the third letter of English words.

You will probably answer that it appears more often as the first letter.

Actually, K appears as the third letter twice as often. Why the error? We find it easier to recall words with a certain letter at the beginning than words with that same letter somewhere else.

The asymmetry between the way we make decisions involving gains and decisions involving losses is one of the most striking findings of Prospect Theory. It is also one of the most useful.

Where significant sums are involved, most people will reject a fair gamble in favor of a certain gain—$100,000 certain is preferable to a 50–50 possibility of $200,000 or nothing. We are risk-averse, in other words.

But what about losses? Kahneman and Tversky's first paper on Prospect Theory, which appeared in 1979, describes an experiment showing that our choices between negative outcomes are mirror images of our choices between positive outcomes.[4] In one of their experiments they first asked the subjects to choose between an 80 percent chance of winning $4,000 and a 20 percent chance of winning nothing versus a 100 percent chance of receiving $3,000. Even though the risky choice has a higher mathematical expectation—$3,200—80 percent of the subjects chose the $3,000 certain. These people were risk-averse, just as Bernoulli would have predicted.

Then Kahneman and Tversky offered a choice between taking the risk of an 80 percent chance of losing $4,000 and a 20 percent chance of breaking even versus a 100 percent chance of losing $3,000. Now 92 percent of the respondents chose the gamble, even though its mathematical expectation of a loss of $3,200 was once again larger than the certain loss of $3,000. When the choice involves losses, we are risk-seekers, not risk-averse.

Kahneman and Tversky and many of their colleagues have found that this asymmetrical pattern appears consistently in a wide variety of experiments. On a later occasion, for example, Kahneman and Tversky proposed the following problem.[5] Imagine that a rare disease is breaking out in some community and is expected to kill 600 people. Two different programs are available to deal with the threat. If Program A is adopted, 200 people will be saved; if Program B is adopted, there is a 33 percent probability that everyone will be saved and a 67 percent probability that no one will be saved.

Which program would you choose? If most of us are risk-averse, rational people will prefer Plan A's certainty of saving 200 lives over Plan B's gamble, which has the same mathematical expectancy but involves taking the risk of a 67 percent chance that everyone will die. In the experiment, 72 percent of the subjects chose the risk-averse response represented by Program A.

Now consider the identical problem posed differently. If Program C is adopted, 400 of the 600 people will die, while Program D entails a 33 percent probability that nobody will die and a 67 percent probability that 600 people will die. Note that the first of the two choices is now expressed in terms of 400 deaths rather than 200 survivors, while the second program offers a 33 percent chance that no one will die. Kahneman and Tversky report that 78 percent of their subjects were risk-seekers and opted for the gamble: they could not tolerate the prospect of the sure loss of 400 lives.

This behavior, although understandable, is inconsistent with the assumptions of rational behavior. The answer to a question should be the same regardless of the setting in which it is posed. Kahneman and Tversky interpret the evidence produced by these experiments as a demonstration that people are not risk-averse: they are perfectly willing to choose a gamble when they consider it appropriate. But if they are not risk-averse, what are they?

"The major driving force is *loss aversion*," writes Tversky. "It is not so much that people hate uncertainty—but rather, they hate losing."[6] Losses will always loom larger than gains. Indeed, losses that go unresolved—such as the loss of a child or a large insurance claim that never gets settled—are likely to provoke intense, irrational, and abiding risk-aversion.[7]

Tversky offers an interesting speculation on this curious behavior:

> *Probably the most significant and pervasive characteristic of the human pleasure machine is that people are much more sensitive to negative than to positive stimuli. . . . [T]hink about how well you feel today, and then try to imagine how much better you could feel. . . . [T]here are a few things that would make you feel better, but the number of things that would make you feel worse is unbounded.*[8]

One of the insights to emerge from this research is that Bernoulli had it wrong when he declared, "The utility resulting from any small increase in wealth will be inversely proportionate to the quantity of goods previously possessed." Bernoulli believed that it is the pre-existing level of wealth that determines the value of a risky opportunity to become richer. Kahneman and Tversky found that the valuation of a risky opportunity appears to depend far more on the reference point from which the possible gain or loss will occur than on the final value of the assets that would result. It is not how rich you are that motivates your decision, but whether that decision will make you richer or poorer. As a consequence, Tversky warns, "our preferences . . . can be manipulated by changes in the reference points."[9]

He cites a survey in which respondents were asked to choose between a policy of high employment and high inflation and a policy of lower employment and lower inflation. When the issue was framed in terms of an unemployment rate of 10 percent or 5 percent, the vote was heavily in favor of accepting more inflation to get the unemployment rate down. When the respondents were asked to choose between a labor force that was 90 percent employed and a labor force that was 95 percent employed, low inflation appeared to be more important than raising the percentage employed by five points.

Richard Thaler has described an experiment that uses starting wealth to illustrate Tversky's warning.[10]

Thaler proposed to a class of students that they had just won $30 and were now offered the following choice: a coin flip where the individual wins $9 on heads and loses $9 on tails versus no coin flip. Seventy percent of the subjects selected the coin flip. Thaler offered his next class the following options: starting wealth of zero and then a coin flip where the individual wins $39 on heads and wins $21 on tails versus $30 for certain. Only 43% selected the coin flip.

Thaler describes this result as the "house money" effect. Although the choice of payoffs offered to both classes is identical—regardless of the amount of the starting wealth, the individual will end up with either $39 or $21 versus $30 for sure—people who start out with money in their pockets will choose the gamble, while people who start out with empty pockets will reject the gamble. Bernoulli would have predicted that the decision would be determined by the amounts $39, $30, or $21 whereas the students based their decisions on the reference point, which was $30 in the first case and zero in the second.

Edward Miller, an economics professor with an interest in behavioral matters, reports a variation on these themes. Although Bernoulli uses the expression "any small increase in wealth," he implies that what he has to say is independent of the size of the increase.[11] Miller cites various psychological studies that show significant differences in response, depending on whether the gain is a big one or a small one. Occasional large gains seem to sustain the interest of investors and gamblers for longer periods of time than consistent small winnings. That response is typical of investors who look on investing as a game and who fail to diversify; diversification is boring. Well-informed investors diversify because they do not believe that investing is a form of entertainment.

Kahneman and Tversky use the expression "failure of invariance" to describe inconsistent (not necessarily incorrect) choices when the same problem appears in different frames. Invariance means that if A is preferred to B and B is preferred to C, then rational people will prefer A to C; this feature is the core of von Neumann and Morgenstern's approach to utility. Or, in the case above, if 200 lives saved for certain is the rational decision in the first set, saving 200 lives for certain should be the rational decision in the second set as well.

But research suggests otherwise:

> *The failure of invariance is both pervasive and robust. It is common among sophisticated respondents as among naïve ones. . . . Respondents confronted with their conflicting answers are typically*

puzzled. Even after rereading the problems, they still wish to be risk averse in the "lives saved" version; they will be risk seeking in the "lives lost" version; and they also wish to obey invariance and give consistent answers to the two versions. . . .

The moral of these results is disturbing. Invariance is normatively essential [what we should *do], intuitively compelling, and psychologically unfeasible.*[12]

The failure of invariance is far more prevalent than most of us realize. The manner in which questions are framed in advertising may persuade people to buy something despite negative consequences that, in a different frame, might persuade them to refrain from buying. Public opinion polls often produce contradictory results when the same question is given different twists.

Kahneman and Tversky describe a situation in which doctors were concerned that there might be influencing patients who had to choose between the life-or-death risks in different forms of treatment.[13] The choice was between radiation and surgery in the treatment of lung cancer. Medical data at this hospital showed that no patients die during radiation but have a shorter life expectancy than patients who survive the risk of surgery; the overall difference in life expectancy was not great enough to provide a clear choice between the two forms of treatment. When the question was put in terms of risk of death during treatment, more than 40 percent of the choices favored radiation. When the question was put in terms of life expectancy, only about 20 percent favored radiation.

One of the most familiar manifestations of the failure of invariance is in the old Wall Street saw, "You never get poor by taking a profit." It would follow that cutting your losses is also a good idea, but investors hate to take losses, because, tax considerations aside, a loss taken is an acknowledgment of error. Loss-aversion combined with ego leads investors to gamble by clinging to their mistakes in the fond hope that someday the market will vindicate their judgment and make them whole. Von Neumann would not approve.

The failure of invariance frequently takes the form of what is known as "mental accounting," a process in which we separate the components of the total picture. In so doing we fail to recognize that a decision affecting each component will have an effect on the shape of the whole. Mental accounting is like focusing on the hole instead of the doughnut. It leads to conflicting answers to the same question.

Kahneman and Tversky ask you to imagine that you are on your way to see a Broadway play for which you have bought a ticket that cost $40.[14] When you arrive at the theater, you discover you have lost your ticket. Would you lay out $40 for another one?

Now suppose instead that you plan to buy the ticket when you arrive at the theater. As you step up to the box office, you find that you have $40 less in your pocket than you thought you had when you left home. Would you still buy the ticket?

In both cases, whether you lost the ticket or lost the $40, you would be out a total of $80 if you decided to see the show. You would be out only $40 if you abandoned the show and went home. Kahneman and Tversky found that most people would be reluctant to spend $40 to replace the lost ticket, while about the same number would be perfectly willing to lay out a second $40 to buy the ticket even though they had lost the original $40.

This is a clear case of the failure of invariance. If $80 is more than you want to spend on the theater, you should neither replace the ticket in the first instance nor buy the ticket in the second. If, on the other hand, you are willing to spend $80 on going to the theater, you should be just as willing to replace the lost ticket as you are to spend $40 on the ticket despite the disappearance of the original $40. *There is no difference other than in accounting conventions between a cost and a loss.*

Prospect Theory suggests that the inconsistent responses to these choices result from two separate mental accounts, one for going to the theater, and one for putting the $40 to other uses—next month's lunch money, for example. The theater account was charged $40 when the ticket was purchased, depleting that account. The lost $40 was charged to next month's lunch money, which has nothing to do with the theater account and is off in the future anyway. Consequently, the theater account is still awaiting its $40 charge.

Thaler recounts an amusing real-life example of mental accounting.[15] A professor of finance he knows has a clever strategy to help him deal with minor misfortunes. At the beginning of the year, the professor plans for a generous donation to his favorite charity. Anything untoward that happens in the course of the year—a speeding ticket, replacing a lost possession, an unwanted touch by an impecunious relative—is then charged to the charity account. The system makes the losses painless, because the charity does the paying. The charity receives whatever is left over in the account. Thaler has nominated his friend as the world's first Certified Mental Accountant.

In an interview with a magazine reporter, Kahneman himself confessed that he had succumbed to mental accounting. In his research with Tversky he had found that a loss is less painful when it is just an addition to a larger loss than when it is a free-standing loss: losing a second $100 after having already lost $100 is less painful than losing $100 on totally separate occasions. Keeping this concept in mind when moving into a new home, Kahneman and his wife bought all their furniture within a week after buying the house. If they had looked at the furniture as a separate account, they might have balked at the cost and ended up buying fewer pieces than they needed.[16]

We tend to believe that information is a necessary ingredient to rational decision-making and that the more information we have, the better we can manage the risks we face. Yet psychologists report circumstances in which additional information gets in the way and distorts decisions, leading to failures of invariance and offering opportunities for people in authority to manipulate the kinds of risk that people are willing to take.

Two medical researchers, Donald Redelmeier and Eldar Shafir, reported in the *Journal of the American Medical Association* on a study designed to reveal how doctors respond as the number of possible options for treatment is increased.[17] Any medical decision is risky—no one can know for certain what the consequences will be. In each of Redelmeier and Shafir's experiments, the introduction of additional options raised the probability that the physicians would choose either the original option or decide to do nothing.

In one experiment, several hundred physicians were asked to prescribe treatment for a 67-year-old man with chronic pain in his right hip. The doctors were given two choices: to prescribe a named medication or to "refer to orthopedics and do not start any new medication;" just about half voted against any medication. When the number of choices was raised from two to three by adding a second medication option, along with "refer to orthopedics," three-quarters of the doctors voted against medication and for "refer to orthopedics."

Tversky believes that "probability judgments are attached not to events but to descriptions of events . . . the judged probability of an event depends upon the explicitness of its description."[18] As a case in point, he describes an experiment in which 120 Stanford graduates were asked to assess the likelihood of various possible causes of death. Each student evaluated one of two different lists of causes; the first listed specific causes of death and the second grouped the causes under a generic heading like "natural causes."

The following table shows some of the estimated probabilities of death developed in this experiment:

	Group I	Group 2	Actual
Heart Disease	22		34
Cancer	18		23
Other Natural Causes	33		35
Total Natural Causes	73	58	92
Accident	32		5
Homicide	10		1
Other Unnatural Causes	11		2
Total Unnatural Causes	53	32	8

These students vastly overestimated the probabilities of violent deaths and underestimated deaths from natural causes. But the striking revelation in the table is that the estimated probability of dying under either set of circumstances was higher when the circumstances were explicit as compared with the cases where the students were asked to estimate only the total from natural or unnatural causes.

In another medical study described by Redelmeier and Tversky, two groups of physicians at Stanford University were surveyed for their diagnosis of a woman experiencing severe abdominal pain.[19] After receiving a detailed description of the symptoms, the first group was asked to decide on the probability that this woman was suffering from ectopic pregnancy, a gastroenteritis problem, or "none of the above." The second group was offered three additional possible diagnoses along with the choices of pregnancy, gastroenteritis, and "none of the above" that had been offered to the first group.

The interesting feature of this experiment was the handling of the "none of the above" option by the second group of doctors. Assuming that the average competence of the doctors in each group was essentially equal, one would expect that that option as presented to the first group would have included the three additional diagnoses with which the second group was presented. In that case, the second group would be expected to assign a probability to the three additional diagnoses plus "none of the above" that was approximately equal to the 50 percent probability assigned to "none of the above" by the first group.

That is not what happened. The second group of doctors assigned a 69 percent probability to "none of the above" plus the three additional diagnoses and only 31 percent to the possibility of pregnancy or gastroenteritis—to which the first group had assigned a 50 percent probability. Apparently, the greater the number of possibilities, the higher the probabilities assigned to them.

Daniel Ellsberg (the same Ellsberg as the Ellsberg of the Pentagon Papers) published a paper back in 1961 in which he defined a phenomenon he called "ambiguity aversion."[20] Ambiguity aversion means that people prefer to take risks on the basis of known rather than unknown probabilities. Information matters, in other words. For example, Ellsberg offered several groups of people a chance to bet on drawing either a red ball or a black ball from two different urns, each holding 100 balls. Urn 1 held 50 balls of each color; the breakdown in Urn 2 was unknown. Probability theory would suggest that Urn 2 was also split 50–50, for there was no basis for any other distribution. Yet the overwhelming preponderance of the respondents chose to bet on the draw from Urn 1.

Tversky and another colleague, Craig Fox, explored ambiguity aversion more deeply and discovered that matters are more complicated than

Ellsberg suggested.[21] They designed a series of experiments to discover whether people's preference for clear over vague probabilities appears in all instances or only in games of chance.

The answer came back loud and clear: people will bet on vague beliefs in situations where they feel especially competent or knowledgeable, but they prefer to bet on chance when they do not. Tversky and Fox concluded that ambiguity aversion "is driven by the feeling of incompetence . . . [and] will be present when subjects evaluate clear and vague prospects jointly, but it will greatly diminish or disappear when they evaluate each prospect in isolation."[22]

People who play dart games, for example, would rather play darts than games of chance, although the probability of success at darts is vague while the probability of success at games of chance is mathematically predetermined. People knowledgeable about politics and ignorant about football prefer betting on political events to betting on games of chance set at the same odds, but they will choose games of chance over sports events under the same conditions.

In a 1992 paper that summarized advances in Prospect Theory, Kahneman and Tversky made the following observation: "Theories of choice are at best approximate and incomplete. . . . Choice is a constructive and contingent process. When faced with a complex problem, people . . . use computational shortcuts and editing operations."[23] The evidence in this chapter, which summarizes only a tiny sample of a huge body of literature, reveals repeated patterns of irrationality, inconsistency, and incompetence in the ways human beings arrive at decisions and choices when faced with uncertainty.

Must we then abandon the theories of Bernoulli, Bentham, Jevons, and von Neumann? No. There is no reason to conclude that the frequent absence of rationality, *as originally defined*, must yield the point to Macbeth that life is a story told by an idiot.

The judgment of humanity implicit in Prospect Theory is not necessarily a pessimistic one. Kahneman and Tversky take issue with the assumption that "only rational behavior can survive in a competitive environment, and the fear that any treatment that abandons rationality will be chaotic and intractable." Instead, they report that most people can survive in a competitive environment even while succumbing to the quirks that make their behavior less than rational by Bernoulli's standards. "Perhaps more important," Tversky and Kahneman suggest, "the evidence indicates that human choices are orderly, although not always rational in the traditional sense of the word."[24] Thaler adds: "Quasi-rationality is neither fatal nor immediately self-defeating."[25] Since orderly decisions are predictable, there is no basis for the argument that behavior is going to be random and erratic merely because it fails to provide a perfect match with rigid theoretical assumptions.

Thaler makes the same point in another context. If we were always rational in making decisions, we would not need the elaborate mechanisms we employ to bolster our self-control, ranging all the way from dieting resorts, to having our income taxes withheld, to betting a few bucks on the horses but not to the point where we need to take out a second mortgage. We accept the certain loss we incur when buying insurance, which is an explicit recognition of uncertainty. We employ those mechanisms, and they work. Few people end up in either the poorhouse or the nuthouse as a result of their own decision-making.

Still, the true believers in rational behavior raise another question. With so much of this damaging evidence generated in psychology laboratories, in experiments with young students, in hypothetical situations where the penalties for error are minimal, how can we have any confidence that the findings are realistic, reliable, or relevant to the way people behave when they have to make decisions?

The question is an important one. There is a sharp contrast between generalizations based on theory and generalizations based on experiments. De Moivre first conceived of the bell curve by writing equations on a piece of paper, not, like Quetelet, by measuring the dimensions of soldiers. But Galton conceived of regression to the mean—a powerful concept that makes the bell curve operational in many instances—by studying sweet peas and generational change in human beings; he came up with the theory after looking at the facts.

Alvin Roth, an expert on experimental economics, has observed that Nicholas Bernoulli conducted the first known psychological experiment more than 250 years ago: he proposed the coin-tossing game between Peter and Paul that guided his uncle Daniel to the discovery of utility.[26] Experiments conducted by von Neumann and Morgenstern led them to conclude that the results "are not so good as might be hoped, but their general direction is correct."[27] The progression from experiment to theory has a distinguished and respectable history.

It is not easy to design experiments that overcome the artificiality of the classroom and the tendency of respondents to lie or to harbor disruptive biases—especially when they have little at stake. But we must be impressed by the remarkable consistency evident in the wide variety of experiments that tested the hypothesis of rational choice. Experimental research has developed into a high art.[*]

---

[*]Kahneman has described his introduction to experimentation when one of his professors told the story of a child being offered the choice between a small lollipop today or a larger lollipop tomorrow. The child's response to this simple question correlated with critical aspects of the child's life, such as family income, one or two parents present, and degree of trust.

Studies of investor behavior in the capital markets reveal that most of what Kahneman and Tversky and their associates hypothesized in the laboratory is played out by the behavior of investors who produce the avalanche of numbers that fill the financial pages of the daily paper. Far away from the laboratory of the classroom, this empirical research confirms a great deal of what experimental methods have suggested about decision-making, not just among investors, but among human beings in general.

As we shall see, the analysis will raise another question, a tantalizing one. If people are so dumb, how come more of us smart people don't get rich?

NOTES

1. A large literature is available on the theories and backgrounds of Kahneman and Tversky, but McKean, 1985, is the most illuminating for lay readers.
2. McKean, 1985, p. 24.
3. Ibid., p. 25.
4. Kahneman and Tversky, 1979, p. 268.
5. McKean, 1985, p. 22; see also Kahneman and Tversky, 1984.
6. Tversky, 1990, p. 75.
7. I am grateful to Dr. Richard Geist of Harvard Medical School for bringing this point to my attention.
8. Tversky, 1990, p. 75.
9. *Ibid.*, p. 75.
10. *Ibid.*, pp. 58–60.
11. Miller, 1995.
12. Kahneman and Tversky, 1984.
13. McKean, 1985, p. 31.
14. *Ibid.*, p. 29.
15. This anecdote appears in an unpublished Thaler paper titled, "Mental Accounting Matters."
16. McKean, 1985, p. 31.
17. Redelmeier and Shafir, 1995, pp. 302–305
18. Tversky and Koehler, 1994, p. 548.
19. Redelmeier, Koehler, Liebermann, and Tversky, 1995.
20. Ellsberg, 1961.
21. Fox and Tversky, 1995.
22. Ibid., pp. 587–588.
23. Tversky and Kahneman, 1992.
24. Kahneman and Tversky, 1979.
25. Thaler, 1995.
26. Kagel and Roth, 1995, p. 4.
27. Von Neumann and Morgenstern, 1944.

REFERENCES

Ellsberg, Daniel. 1961. Risk, Ambiguity, and the Savage Axioms. *Quarterly Journal of Economics* 75: 643–669.

Fox, Craig R., and Amos Tversky. 1995. Ambiguity Aversion and Comparative ignorance. *Quarterly Journal of Economics* 110(3): 585–603.

Kagel, John H., and Alvin E. Roth, eds. 1995. *The Handbook of Experimental Economics*. Princeton, NJ: Princeton University Press.

Kahneman, Daniel, and Amos Tversky. 1979. Prospect Theory: An Analysis of Decision Under Risk. *Econometrica* 47(2): 263–291.

Kahneman, Daniel, and Amos Tversky. 1984, April. Choices, Values, and Frames. *American Psychologist* 39(4): 342–347.

McKean, Kevin, 1985, June. Decisions. *Discover* pp. 22–31.

Miller, Edward M. 1995. Do the Ignorant Accumulate the Money? Working Paper, University of New Orleans, April 5.

Redelmeier, Donald A., D. J. Koehler, V. Z. Liebermann, and Amos Tversky. 1995. Probability Judgment in Medicine: Discounting Unspecified Alternatives. *Medical Decision Making* 15(3): 227–231.

Redelmeier, Donald H., and Eldar Shafir. 1995. Medical decision-making in situations that offer multiple alternatives. *Journal of the American Medical Association* 273(4): 302–305.

Thaler, Richard H. 1995. *Advances in behavioral finance*. New York: Russell Sage Foundation.

Tversky, Amos. 1990. "The Psychology of Risk." In Sharpe, 1990, p. 75.

Tversky, Amos, and Derek J. Koehler. 1994. Support theory: A Nonextensional Representation of Subjective Probability. *Psychological Review* 101(4): 547–567.

Tversky, Amos, and David Kahneman. 1992. Advances in Prospect Theory: Cumulative Representation of Uncertainty. *Journal of Risk and Uncertainty* 5(4): 297–323.

Von Neumann, John, and Oskar Morgenstern. 1944. *Theory of Games and Economic Behavior*. Princeton, NJ: Princeton University Press.

CHAPTER 5

Inverted Reasoning and Its Consequences

G.C. Seldon

It is hard for the average man to oppose what appears to be the general drift of public opinion. In the stock market, this is perhaps harder than elsewhere; for we all realize that the prices of stocks must, in the long run, be controlled by public opinion. The point we fail to remember is that public opinion in a speculative market is measured in dollars, not in population. One man controlling one million dollars has double the weight of five hundred men with one thousand dollars each. Dollars are the horsepower of the markets—the mere number of men does not signify.

This is why the great body of opinion appears bullish at the top and bearish at the bottom. The multitude of small traders must be, as a plain necessity, long when prices are at the top, and short or out of the market at the bottom. The very fact that they *are* long at the top shows that they have been supplied with stocks from some source.

Again, the man with one million dollars is a silent individual. The time when it was necessary for him to talk is past—his money now does the talking. But the one thousand men who have thousand dollars each are conversational, fluent, and verbose to the last degree.

It will be observed that the above course of reasoning leads up to the conclusion that most of those who talk about the market are more likely to be wrong than right, at least so far as speculative fluctuations are concerned. This is not complimentary to the "moulders of public opinion," but most

---

Taken from *The Psychology of the Stock Market*, published by the Fraser Publishing Company, 1965 edition (first published in 1912). Reprinted with permission. All rights reserved.

seasoned newspaper readers will agree that is it true. The daily press reflects, in a general way, the thoughts of the multitude, and in the stock market the multitude is necessarily, as a logical deduction from the facts of the case, likely to be bullish at high prices and bearish at low.

It has often been remarked that the average man is an optimist regarding his own enterprises and a pessimist regarding those of others. Certainly this is true of the professional trader in stocks. As a result of the reasoning outlined above, he comes habitually to expect that nearly everyone else will be wrong, but is, as a rule, confident that his own analysis of the situation will prove correct. He values the opinion of a few persons whom he believes to be generally successful; but aside from these few, the greater the number of the bullish opinions he hears, the more doubtful he becomes about the wisdom of following the bull side.

This apparent contrariness of the market, although easily understood when analyzed, breeds in professional traders a peculiar sort of skepticism—leads them always to distrust the obvious and to apply a kind of inverted reasoning to almost all stock market problems. Often, in the minds of traders who are not naturally logical, this inverted reasoning assumes causes that are of most erratic and grotesque forms, and it accounts for many apparently absurd fluctuations in prices which are commonly charged to manipulation.

For example, a trader starts with this assumption: The market has had a good advance; all the small traders are bullish; somebody must have sold them stock which they are carrying; hence the big capitalists are probably sold out or short and ready for a reaction or perhaps for a bear market. Then if a strong item of bullish news comes out—one, let us say, that really makes an important change in the situation—he says, "Ah, so this is what they have been bulling the market on! It has been discounted by the previous rise." Or he may say, "They are putting out this bull news to sell stocks on." He proceeds to sell out any long stocks he may have or perhaps to sell short.

His reasoning may be correct or may not; but at any rate his selling and that of others who reason in a similar way, is likely to produce at least a temporary decline on the announcement of the good news. This decline looks absurd to the outsider and he falls back on the old explanation "All manipulation."

The same principle is often carried further. You will find professional traders reasoning that favorable figures on the steel industry, for example, have been concocted to enable insiders to sell their Steel; or that gloomy reports are put in circulation to facilitate accumulation. Hence they may act in direct opposition to these and carry the market with them, for the time at least.

The less the trader knows about the fundamentals of the financial situation the more likely he is to be led astray in conclusions of this character. If he has confidence in the general strength of conditions he may be ready to accept as genuine and natural, a piece of news which he would otherwise receive with cynical skepticism and use as a basis for short sales. If he knows that fundamental conditions are unsound, he will not be so likely to interpret bad news as issued to assist in accumulation of stocks.

The same reasoning is applied to large purchases through brokers known to be associated with capitalists. In fact, in this case we often hear a double inversion, as it were. Such buying may impress the observer in three ways:

1. The "rank outsider" takes it at face value, as bullish.
2. A more experienced trader may say, "If they really wished to get the stocks they would not buy through their own brokers, but would endeavor to conceal their buying by scattering it among other houses."
3. A still more suspicious professional may turn another mental somersault and say, "They are buying through their own brokers so as to throw us off the scent and make us think someone else is using their brokers as a blind." By this double somersault such a trader arrives at the same conclusion as the outsider.

The reasoning of traders becomes even more complicated when large buying or selling is done openly by a big professional who is known to trade in and out for small profits. If he buys 50,000 shares, other traders are quite willing to sell to him and their opinion of the market is little influenced, simply because they know he may sell 50,000 the next day or even the next hour. For this reason great capitalists sometimes buy or sell through such big professional traders in order to execute their orders easily and without arousing suspicion. Hence the play of subtle intellects around big trading of this kind often becomes very elaborate.

It is to be noticed that this inverted reasoning is useful chiefly at the top or bottom of a movement when distribution or accumulation is taking place on a large scale. A market which repeatedly refuses to respond the good news after a considerable advance is likely to be "full of stocks." Likewise a market which will not go down on bad news is usually "bare of stock."

Between the extremes will be found long stretches in which capitalists have found very little cause to conceal their positions. Having accumulated their lines as low as possible, they are then willing to be known as leaders of the upward movement and have every reason to be perfectly open in their buying. This condition continues until they are ready to sell. Likewise, having sold as much as they desire, they have no reason to conceal their position further, even though a subsequent decline may run for months or a year.

It is during a long upward movement that the "lamb" makes money, because he accepts facts as facts, while the professional trader is often found fighting the advance and losing heavily because of the overdevelopment of cynicism and suspicion.

The successful trader eventually learns when to invert his natural mental processes to leave them in their usual position. Often he develops a sort of instinct which could scarcely be reduced to cold print. But in the hands of the tyro this form of reasoning is exceedingly dangerous, because it permits of putting an alternate construction on any event. Bull news either (1) is significant of a rising trend of prices, or (2) indicates that "they" are trying to make a market to sell on. Bad news may indicate either a genuinely bearish situation or a desire to accumulate stocks at low prices.

The inexperienced operator is therefore left very much at sea. He is playing with the professional's edged tools and is likely to cut himself. Of what use is it for him to try to apply his reason to stock market conditions when every event may be doubly interpreted?

Indeed, it is doubtful if the professional's distrust of the obvious is of much benefit to him in the long run. Most of us have met those deplorable mental wrecks, often found among the "chairwarmers" in brokers' offices, whose thinking machinery seems to have become permanently demoralized as a result of continued acrobatics.

They are always seeking an "ulterior motive" in everything. They credit—or debit—Morgan and Rockefeller with the smallest and meanest trickery and ascribe to them the most awful duplicity in matters which those "high financiers" would not stoop to notice. The continual reversal of the mental engine sometimes deranges its mechanism.

Probably no better general rule can be laid down than the brief one, "Stick to common sense." Maintain a balanced, receptive mind and avoid abstruse deductions. A few further suggestions may, however, be offered.

If you already have a position in the market, do not attempt to bolster up your failing faith by resorting to intellectual subtleties in the interpretation of obvious facts. If you are long or short of the market, you are not an unprejudiced judge, and you will be greatly tempted to put such an interpretation upon current events as will coincide with your preconceived opinion. It is hardly too much to say that this is the greatest obstacle to success. The least you can do is to avoid inverted reasoning in support of your own position.

After a prolonged advance: do not call inverted reasoning to your aid in order to prove that prices are going still higher; likewise after a big break do not let your bearish deductions become too complicated. Be suspicious of bull news at high prices, and of bear news at low prices.

Bear in mind that an item of news usually causes but *one* considerable movement of prices. If the movement takes place before the news comes out, as a result of rumors and expectations, then it is not likely to be repeated after the announcement is made; but if the movement of prices has not preceded, then the news contributes to the general strength or weakness of the situation and a movement of prices may follow.

CHAPTER 6

Fatal Attractions for Money Managers

Arnold S. Wood
President, Martingale Asset Management

An experienced and innovative investment manager reflects on "the triumph of temptation over reason," and offers a "list of ten causes of irrational, and occasionally bizarre, behavior by professional investors."

As a laboratory for the study of human behavior—and, in particular, the triumph of temptation over reason—the field of money management has much to recommend it. We money managers, together with our entourage of economists, analysts and traders, offer a large, robust sample, with observations plentiful enough for all the cross-sectional (snapshot) or longitudinal (historical) analyses you could ask for.

Money managers are, ostensibly, reasonable. We are, by and large, highly educated; many of us hold certificates nearly as demanding to come by as MDs and JDs. One might expect that our investment judgments, given our training and experience, would prove sound and profitable for our clients. But this is, strikingly, not true. (See Exhibit 6.1.)

What makes us so consistently poor at our profession? It seems to me that we are too frequently undone by three very human tendencies.

- Our feelings overcome our reason.
- We take shortcuts that violate logic.
- We don't learn, or want to learn, from experience.

But *why* are we so motivated to behave illogically? In the following pages I offer 10—not necessarily mutually exclusive—causes of irrational, and occasionally bizarre, behavior.

This article first appeared in the May/June 1989 issue of the *Financial Analysts Journal* and is reprinted with permission of the author.

EXHIBIT 6.1   Performance of the Experts

Time Period	S&P 500	Annualized SEI Equity Funds	Differences
1962–1974	5.3	4.1	−1.2
1966–1974	2.1	.04	−1.7
1970–1974	2.2	−0.3	−2.5
1975–1982	14.7	13.4	−1.3
1983	22.3	20.3	−2.0
1984	6.3	−2.0	−8.3
1985	31.7	30.0	−1.7
1986	18.3	16.7	−1.6
1987	5.2	4	−1.2

Source: SEI Funds Evaluation.

MINDLESS ROUTINE

Put simply, we are steeped in ritual.

An Indian legend has it that the buffalo return each season in response to the ritual buffalo dance. This is, literally, true. Why? Because the Indians don't stop dancing until the buffalo come back.

As money managers, we place our bets, and when the world comes to us, we feel that it is our persistence that is being rewarded. We accept all evidence that confirms this notion and dismiss any that contradicts it. Psychologists call this "cognitive dissonance."

Die-hard growth-stock apostles of the early 1970s are still waiting for the buffalo. Conversely, money managers who never could stomach utilities missed a 12-year spurt in which the S&P 40 provided a 16.9 percent compound annual return, versus 12.8 percent for the S&P 500. If you had invested $10 million in utilities in 1976, before the 1979 Three Mile Island disaster, you would be 150 percent better off than the S&P 500 today—and even better off compared with the median money manager.

One by-product of ritual and routine is comfort, and there's nothing like feelin' good. At the Berkeley Program in Finance in 1987, the word "factors" was used 222 times; I counted. This silly indicator told me that everyone—manager, academic, consultant and client—is hung up on managing and measuring performance by factors. How do you define yourself? By the factors you focus on—defensive . . . , sector rotation, small cap, yield, whatever. Are there any *stock* pickers, people with portfolios that aren't swamped by factor bets, left?

THE LAWS OF PROBABILITY

Consider a pinch hitter with four hits in 10 at-bats during the year. Is he a better hitter than Wade Boggs?

He has, after all, a .400 batting average, and that beats Boggs' .359. But Boggs had 189 hits in 527 at-bats. Probability speaking, there is a 99.9 percent chance that Boggs is a .300, hitter; there is only an 85 percent chance that our pinch hitter is.

Now consider an example from money management. Suppose a market timer is correct 55 percent of the time, and that he makes one decision every two years. How long would you have to wait to determine (with 99 percent probability) whether he really has any skill? The answer: 167 years!

INFORMATION OVERLOAD

Humans simply cannot process a great deal of data, let alone convert it into action.

Herbert Simon, 1987 Nobel Prize winner, has concluded that humans can digest only five to seven different things at once.[1] A study of horse racing bettors has shown that more information increases bettors' confidence in their bets, but does nothing to increase their accuracy (Exhibit 6.2).

Occam's Razor suggests that most complex problems have simple solutions. Why, then, do we make money management so incredibly complex? An MBA with a facility for Lotus Spreadsheet analysis can produce

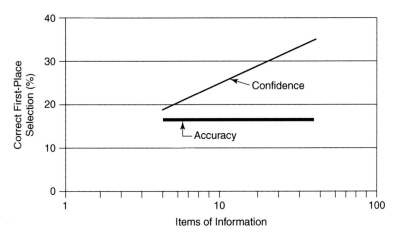

EXHIBIT 6.2 Changes in Confidence and Accuracy with Increasing Information

a limitless number of variables that complicate the process of making logical decisions.

PSYCHOLOGY OF CHOICE

Decision-framing is an intricate part of how we make choices, how we sort out alternatives. It stands behind one of the central tenets of investing, which is that people, given a 50/50 chance, would rather not lose a dollar than gain a dollar.

Most choices involving gains are risk-averse, most involving losses are risk-taking. The probabilities assigned to the possible outcomes of a life-and-death decision may be identical, but stating a problem in terms of lives lost versus lives saved evokes very different responses. Investing sometimes equates with loss of life, (job) and some irrational decisions result.

Measuring risk is tricky; measuring the perception of risk may be even trickier. Why, for example, do those pension plans with large surpluses tend to elect the more conservative investment policies? Why are people with more money than they ever plan to spend so reluctant to give it away? These choices may appear to be illogical, but we must take into account the entire framework within which the choice is made and that involves a complex balancing of gain and loss, age and wealth and myriad other factors.

FORECASTING

Given our failure to assign accurate statistical probabilities, it is obvious why we are lured into forecasting. But it goes beyond that.

Think of the lottery: Why do people pay to play? Simple: There is a huge payoff if you are right. You are willing to accept essentially a negative expected return for the possibility of a huge payoff, plus some fun in playing. Someone calculated that, on average, Massachusetts residents are spending at the rate of $106,000 per person to play the lottery over their collective lifetimes. (Do initial public offerings have a lower probability of payoff than roulette? Probably.)

A little monkey business may help to clarify our fascination with forecasting.[2] Imagine a room full of monkeys, a thousand of them. Each is trying to predict the direction of the market. Exhibit 6.3 shows that, at the end of 10 predictions, one monkey has a perfect record of 10 straight calls, while 10 have nine out of 10 and 44 eight out of 10. (By the way, all these outcomes are supported by probability theory.)

EXHIBIT 6.3 How Good Is that Monkey?

Out of 10 Possible Market Calls

Correct Calls	Number of Monkeys	Total (%)
10	1	0.1
9	10	1.0
8	44	4.4
7	117	11.7
6	205	20.5
5	246	24.6
4	205	20.5
3	117	11.7
2	44	4.4
1	10	1.0
0	1	0.1

What happens next? The 10-for-10 monkey starts its own firm. Large investment counselors hire the 9-for-10 monkeys. Bank trust departments, which can't afford to hire "top talent," lure the 44 who went 8 for 10. The unlucky monkeys stay home. This is a pure case of survivorship bias.

Rather than make market predictions, one of the unlucky monkeys figures out a system to predict the market, at least in hindsight. After many iterations, thanks to modern investment technology, the clever monkey figures out what combination of conditions would have led to a 10-for-10 record. With simulated results, this synthetic lucky monkey gets on the same plane with all the lucky monkeys to convince you that market timing is the only game in town.

OVERCONFIDENCE

Try answering the questions in Exhibit 6.4 giving "high" and "low" as well as "best" estimates for each one.[3]

The narrower the range between your high and low estimates, the more confidence you assign your best answer. Most of us think we know more than we do, or at least pretend a certainty we don't possess.

FOLLOW THE LEADER

In an uncertain world, we search for sign posts that will allay our fears and doubts.

EXHIBIT 6.4 Confidence Judgments

	Low Guess	Best Guess	High Guess
1. UPS delivers twice as many packages as the post office. How many packages did UPS deliver in 1980?			
2. How many credit cards were reported lost or stolen by U.S. consumers on a typical day in 1980?			
3. When you buy a dollar's worth of meat, how much does the rancher get?			
4. How much money was spent on tranquilizers in the U.S. in 1980?			

Suppose you are in a group in a completely dark room, or condition.[4] An intermittent dot of light is flashed on the wall, hitting the same spot each time. Each one in the room is asked how much the light is moving; guesses range from two to eight inches. The whole group is then asked the same question, and the range of answers narrows. Finally, a new person joins the group, declaring that he knows exactly the distance the light travels. The group will cling to this "authority's" estimate, achieving an even narrower consensus. (See Exhibit 6.5.)

Why do we all read the *Wall Street Journal*? Perhaps it is to look for leaders in an uncertain world.

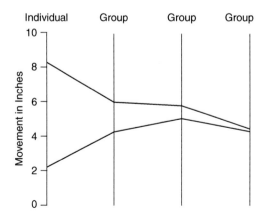

EXHIBIT 6.5 Convergence of Opinion
Source: M. Sherif and C. W. Sherif, *Social Psychology* (1969).

EXHIBIT 6.6   Illusion of Control

	Those Who Chose Their Own Card	Those Who Were Handed a Card
Initially Said They Would Not Sell	37%	19%
Average Price Offered for Sale	$8.96	$1.96

TOUCHY-FEELY SYNDROME

Exhibit 6.6 summarizes the results of an experiment in which individuals were either handed a card or selected a card, then asked to "sell" the card.[5]

Those who selected their cards were less likely to sell and received a much higher average price for their cards than those who were handed their cards. Visiting the management of a company can make you feel you know more than you really do. Furthermore, we tend to feel more favorably toward managers we have actually met. (Politicians don't go around shaking hands because they like to meet people.) We tend to overvalue persons and things we have actually "touched."

STATISTICAL BLACKOUT

October 19, 1987, when the Dow collapsed over 500 points, has statistically blocked out any logical, sensible response to such events.

Fear really damages an otherwise intelligent decision-maker. Our tendency to judge the future on the basis of the more immediate past is one of the most difficult behavioral flaws to overcome.

BAD DOG

Your dog chews on the carpet or jumps on a guest. You scold it, "Bad dog!" The dog looks sheepish.

Managers have their chances, some more than others, to be the Bad Dog. Poor performance, however your master wants to measure it, is ordinarily the reason for the scolding. (Well, that's one reason for paying someone—so you can blame him for not performing. . . .)

The differences between client and manager in environments, tasks, necessary skills and, more often than not, compensation levels make for a tenuous relationship to begin with, one prone to emotional outbursts and apprehensive behavior. (See Exhibit 6.7.) When the client sets a benchmark,

EXHIBIT 6.7 Friction between Client and Manager

	Corporate Mind	Investment Mind
Environment	Controllable	Capricious
Task	Complete	Incomplete
Skill	Measurable	Not Measurable
Pay Check	Medium	High

a performance bogey, and the money manager falls short, more friction is created and the relationship breaks down. Chief Financial Officer to corporate pension officer: "Those guys get too much to underperform. Tell them they're out if we see another quarter like that." The manager's response? Anxiety is an understatement. Is his judgment or skill impaired? I suspect so.

Money managers are human. Their behavioral responses are seldom as rational as might be expected from such an educated sample. Research in behavioral finance is only just getting more formal recognition for its value in identifying and measuring behavior. Clearly, there are managers who have learned from the past, recognize unreasoned behavior and are willing to seize upon the anxieties of others. Perhaps an awareness of the root causes for betraying sound analysis and logic will get us a Good Dog pat more often. Let's hope so.[6]

NOTES

1. H. A. Simon, "A Behavioral Model of Rational Choice," *Journal of Economics,* 1955, pp. 69, 91–118.
2. I am indebted to William Jacques of Martingale Asset Management for this example.
3. The answers are 1.4 billion packages, 30,000 credit cards, 55 cents and $2.3 billion. The example comes from Professor Fischhoff of Carnegie Mellon University.
4. This experiment is discussed in D. Dreman, *Contrarian Investment Strategy* (New York: Random House, 1979), p. 92.
5. The example comes from E. J. Langer, "The Illusion of Control," in D. Kahneman, P. Slovic, and A. Tversky, eds., *Judgment under Uncertainty: Heuristics and Biases* (Cambridge: Cambridge University Press, 1982).
6. Additional examples and insights for this article were provided by Robin Hogarth of the University of Chicago, John Carroll of MIT and Richard Thaler of Cornell.

CHAPTER 7

Renzo Gracie's Brazilian Jiu Jitsu Academy

Richard Bookstaber

An elegant analogy illustrating how innovation, endogenous risks, and regulation should be contemplated so as to assure a market "that is more robust and survivable." Excerpted from the best-selling book, A Demon of Our Own Design *(Bookstaber).*

In the basement of a rundown office building on West 30th Street in New York's Garment District resides Renzo Gracie's Brazilian Jiu Jitsu Academy. It is not only a place where I train several times a week, but one that also offers a great lesson in demonstrating a method for dealing with the endogenous risk of the market.

How "Jiu Jitsu" and "Brazilian" came to be joined in one breath is an interesting story. In 1912 a large group of Japanese immigrated to northern Brazil. They were assisted by Mitsuyo Maeda, a noted Japanese jujitsu expert who had traveled throughout the Americas and Europe teaching the art before emigrating to Brazil. Gastao Gracie, a diplomat and businessman, had befriended Maeda and arranged for the group's immigration. To show his appreciation, Maeda taught jujitsu to Gastao's oldest son, Carlos Gracie. He was just 14 when he began. A dedicated student, he adapted Maeda's techniques to be more effective for fighting in the Brazilian streets. He not only entered competitions, but also advertised in newspapers to find opponents against whom he could test and improve his style. Later he taught his younger brothers, the youngest of whom, Helio, became especially adept. Helio had a slight build, and to accommodate his small size and lack of strength he further modified the jujitsu style, focusing more on technique and less on power or athleticism. Helio fought more than 600

Richard Bookstaber, *A Demon of Our Own Design* (Hoboken, NJ: John Wiley and Sons, 2007), pp. 258–260. Reprinted with permission of John Wiley & Sons, Inc.

matches with only two defeats, both occurring when he was past the age of 45. The techniques refined by Carlos and Helio were passed on to their children and through them to the next generation as well. Carlos had 21 children and Helio had 9, so a dynasty of Brazilian Jiu Jitsu fighters was born. Today there are more than 40 Gracie family members who either teach or compete, Renzo being one of their number.

The confidence of the Gracies was manifest in an open challenge: Anyone could walk into their academy and demand a fight on the spot, with no time limit and no rules. Any challenger's notion of engaging in a bare-knuckle slugfest would be quickly disarmed by the nature of Brazilian Jiu Jitsu. Little if any damage would occur before the Gracies would take the fight to the ground. Once there, it would end with submission from either a choke hold or anoint lock. The opponent, sensing he would shortly lose consciousness in the first instance or would have his arm broken in the second, would "tap out" on the floor to signal his desire to end the contest. It makes the challenge workable both for the Gracies and for their foes. There was no harm done, but the superiority of the Gracie techniques was made clear. Over time these sorts of one-on-ones expanded to take place in open, no-holds-barred competitions called *vale tudo*, Portuguese for "anything goes," which became common throughout Brazil as a practical testing ground. These competitions came to the United States in 1994 when Rorion and Royce Gracie, two of Helio's sons, promoted mixed martial arts tournaments in the *vale tudo* tradition to demonstrate to the world at large the domination that Brazilian Jiu Jitsu had enjoyed in Brazil for the better part of a century.

The very existence of *vale tudo* competition points to the key aspect of Brazilian Jiu Jitsu that allowed it to gain superiority over other martial arts.

It was not just that it was actively improved through competition while other forms stayed rooted in tradition. It was that it had been developed in a way that allowed this competition and testing to occur in the first place. The techniques that formed the basis of Brazilian Jiu Jitsu could be practiced without causing harm. Many fighting techniques cannot be practiced live because they inevitably cause injury. The genius behind the development of Brazilian Jiu Jitsu was to select for inclusion only those techniques that are applied in a slow and measured way so that an opponent can stop before injury occurs.

What became apparent over time was that having a firm understanding of the actual application of a set of controlled techniques through live training and real fights was superior to having a quiver filled with techniques that were powerful in theory but could not be tried and refined until an actual fight occurred. You can see where this is leading when it comes to the markets. Does it make sense to do the same thing? Should we pull away from dangerous innovations, even if those innovations appear to be useful? And what constitutes those that are dangerous?

I believe the markets can better conquer their endogenous risks if we do not include every financial instrument that can be dreamed up, and take the time to gain experience with the standard instruments we already have. Just because you can turn some cash flow into a tradable asset doesn't mean you should; just because you can create a swap or forward contract to trade on some state variable doesn't mean it makes sense to do so. Well, in the efficient market paradigm it does, because there nirvana is attained when a position can be taken against every possible state of nature. But in the world of normal accidents and primal risk, limitless trading possibilities might cause more harm than good. Each innovation adds layers of increasing complexity and tight coupling. And these cannot be easily disarmed through oversight or regulation. If anything, attempts at regulating a complex system just make matters worse. Furthermore, if an innovation is predicated on behavior predicted by the efficient markets theory, then things may not operate as advertised: People just don't behave that way The point is that these innovations have externalities for the entire financial system that are hard to measure but dominate their apparent value. Rather than adding complexity and then tracing to manage its consequences with regulation, we should rein in the sources of complexity at the outset.

Linked to the need to reduce market complexity is the need to relax tight coupling. The easiest course for reducing tight coupling it to reduce the speed of market activity. This has been done in times of crisis through the imposition of bank holidays and so-called circuit breakers, but doing so on a day-to-day basis would turn back the clock on financial markets in an unacceptable way. A less disruptive course of action is to reduce the amount of leverage that comes as a result of the liquidity, since this is ultimately the culprit that high liquidity and speed of execution breeds. The externalities to high leverage are greater than they appear, because on most days everything runs smoothly But as we have seen time and again, in the instances where it really matters the liquidity that is supposed to justify the leverage will disappear with a resulting spiral into crisis.

Simpler financial instruments and less leverage make up a painfully obvious prescription for fixing the design of our markets. These modifications will lead to a financial marketplace that will be apparently less finely tuned and less responsive to investor needs. But, like the coarse response mechanism of the cockroach, when faced with the inevitable march of events that we cannot even contemplate, simpler financial instruments and less leverage will create a market that is more robust and survivable.

CHAPTER 8

Managing Outside the Box

Robert A. Jaeger, PhD
Senior Market Strategist, BNY Mellon Asset Management

This reflection on fads and fashion in the investment business provides an appropriate departure for studying Part Three of this book: The Challenges Under Transformation.

The investment business is dominated by a constantly changing mix of fads and fashions. For example, during the last several years there has been steadily growing interest in the general idea of "loosening the traditional investment constraints." This interest drives the current fascination with hedge funds and those long-only managers who are not totally obsessed with the standard benchmarks. The Australians call this "benchmark-unaware" management.

In theory, the investment management business should reward "thinking outside the box"—independent judgment, creativity, and courage. In practice, the investment management business often turns into a bureaucratic straightjacket in which clients and consultants obsess about the minutiae of performance measurement: benchmarks, tracking error, information ratios, style drift, and so forth. It is not surprising that many money managers have emigrated from the long-only world into the hedge-fund world, which offers the possibility of an intoxicating combination of greater freedom and higher fees. The irony, of course, is that the hedge fund world now has its own panoply of indices, style boxes, and consultants who worry about "style drift."

The desire to evade the tyranny of the benchmarks is very healthy—if implemented properly. The key to success is to have realistic expectations,

---

Previously published in *The Investment and Wealth Monitor*, January/February 2007 by The Investment Management Consultants Association. Reprinted with permission. All rights reserved.

thus avoiding the classic problem of throwing over one fad in order to be swept away by another. Maintaining a sense of historical perspective is critical. After all, the "traditional" constraints have not been with us forever—they are the result of specific market forces. To understand where we are, we need a clear picture of how we got here.

BENCHMARKS AND BULL MARKETS

Once upon a time, when dinosaurs roamed the earth, the main job of an equity manager was to deliver a real return over inflation when performance was measured over longer-term holding periods. There was a general realization that the ups and downs of "the market" had an important influence on results, but managers used a fairly broad range of tools in pursuit of their objective—and there was no single dominant measure of "the market." For example, managers sometimes raised cash, either as the result of a top-down market judgment or because their bottom-up investment process did not deliver enough stocks to buy. In addition, some managers were willing to adjust their sector exposures quite actively, either in response to top-down judgments, bottom-up processes, or some combination of the two. Those of us who were in the consulting business in the United States in the late 1970s and early 1980s remember a varied and colorful landscape of money managers.

What happened? Three things: (1) the institutionalization of the business; (2) an 18-year bull market; and (3) the growing hegemony of the index fund. "Institutionalization" covers a multitude of phenomena all related to the shift away from balanced managers who offered "one stop investment shopping," toward portfolios of multiple specialists. Building these portfolios became the job of the various investment consulting firms, who canvassed the universe for talented specialists to be blended together into a diversified portfolio. Consultants needed "style boxes," each with its appropriate benchmark. Thus there emerged the machinery of tracking error, style drift, information ratios, and all the other devices whose primary function was to make sure that managers stayed in their assigned boxes.

The second aggravating factor was a powerful bull market that dominated the U.S. investment scene from 1982 to 2000, with only minor pauses and interruptions. In this environment, money managers who held cash were likely to lag the market. Managers were therefore under strong pressure to remain fully invested at all times, which meant "equitizing" any available cash, an operation that became quite simple thanks to the development of the stock index futures market.

The third factor was the growing popularity of index funds and the growing difficulty of beating the indexes. This phenomenon became especially acute during the last stages of the bull market, when the market's gains were increasingly concentrated in a small number of mega-cap names that many active managers regarded as prohibitively overvalued.

Although passive management had various academic arguments in its favor, the ultimate argument was the performance argument: passive management *worked*. However, it worked not because of powerful theoretical reasons, but because of a unique kind of bull market. The defining feature of a bull market is that making money is easy: Indexing is the ideal bull market strategy. Consider the stark difference between the United States and Japan, where the 1990s and early 2000s presented to investors a lethal combination of low interest rates and weak equity markets. In that more hostile environment, passive management was not an option: Japanese investors were forced into multiple forms of active management, including hedge funds.

Herb Stein, Chairman of the Council of Economic Advisers under President Nixon, used to say that if something can't go on forever, it won't. The U.S. bull market lasted longer than most people expected, but it did eventually end. As the indices declined, interest in active management exploded. "Active management" here includes both "absolute return strategies" (hedge funds and so forth) and new tools for implementing "relative return strategies."

NEW WINE IN OLD BOTTLES

As institutional investors explore this brave new world, it is crucial to separate two ways of loosening the familiar investment constraints. On the one hand, there are investors mainly interested in finding new strategies for beating the traditional benchmarks. This is the "new wine in old bottles" approach. On the other hand, there are investors striving to build portfolios that are not so dependent on the traditional benchmarks. This is the "new bottle" approach.

The most prominent example of "new wine in old bottles" is portable alpha: yoking a multi-manager hedge fund portfolio to a derivatives hedge in order to create a synthetic equity portfolio or synthetic bond portfolio. More recently, we have seen the emergence of the "130/30" portfolio, in which an equity manager will be 130 percent long and 30 percent short, thus remaining 100 percent long at all times. This approach avoids the major predicament of the long-only index-oriented manager, who must cope with indices that are typically very "lumpy," combining a small number of large positions with a large number of small positions. In the S&P

500, for example, the ten largest stocks jointly account for 20 percent of the market capitalization of the index. However, there are 465 stocks that each account for less than 0.5 percent of the index. These stocks collectively account for 57 percent of the total index capitalization. Within this group of 465 stocks, the average position size is 0.12 percent. (Data as of December 31, 2007.) Even if a manager hates a stock with a 0.1 percent weight, the most that he/she can do is to be 0.1 percent underweight. In the 130/30 format, there is more room for expressing a negative opinion.

Both portable alpha and 130/30 have the potential to deliver meaningful alpha over a benchmark. Portable alpha has particular relevance for bond portfolios, which have drawn increased attention as investors have become more focused on liability-driven investing. The bond universe is a highly competitive universe in which benchmarks are hard to beat and the performance spread between the first and third quartiles is often measured in basis points, not percentage points. This makes it appealing to use equity-oriented strategies as the source of alpha, and then transport the alpha over into the fixed income universe.

In many situations the alpha source is a fund-of-funds portfolio, combining the talents of many hedge fund managers representing a well-diversified set of hedge fund strategies. This is a perfectly feasible strategy. However, the hedge fund universe offers its own unique set of challenges, especially in the current environment. There are more than 10,000 hedge funds, but genuine alpha is just as elusive in the hedge fund world as it is in the long-only world. Indeed, it is prudent to assume that the hedge fund business is a zero-sum game in which the better hedge funds (along with the better long-only managers) extract alpha from the less talented hedge funds (and the less talented long-only managers). Moreover, some (but not all) strategies occasionally show signs of overcrowding. In other words, strategy allocation and manager selection are critical. The key challenge in hedge fund investing is to maintain the right balance between excessive optimism ("Long-only management is dead; hedge funds are the only way to generate alpha") and excessive pessimism ("There's too much money in hedge funds; the game is over"). (For more on this theme, see the author's "Myths and Realities of Hedge Fund Investing," in *Hedge Funds: Crossing the Institutional Frontier*, Euromoney Books, 2006. See also "The Elusiveness of Investment Skill," Chapter 13 in this book.)

The essential point about portable alpha, 130/30, and the other new strategies is that they are subject to all the vicissitudes of active management. We are firm believers in active management, but we believe even more firmly in realistic expectations. Many institutions, disappointed by the performance of their long-only active managers, are competing to identify "the new, new thing" that will enable them to replace their long-only managers with something more "state of the art." This may be an unfortunate example of the "greener grass syndrome": the deep-seated conviction that the strategy that you haven't tried yet will work much better than the strategies that you have tried. The governing reality here is that genuine investment skill is rare throughout the investment world, even in the neighborhood of hedge funds and 130/30 strategies.

NEW BOTTLES

The preceding examples all fall under the general heading of "new wine in old bottles"—that is, new strategies for beating old benchmarks. How about the new bottles: portfolios that are not so benchmark driven? "Old-fashioned equity management," which ignores tracking error altogether, is a prime example. Hedge funds are another good example. Notice, however, that in these cases benchmarks are not completely absent. Rather, the benchmark is some positive number, related either to inflation or to some short-term interest rate. (Notice that liability-driven investing is not an "absolute return" approach. If the benchmark is the return on a client-specific stream of liabilities, then that benchmark will be negative in a rising interest rate environment.)

This point applies even, and perhaps especially, to those institutions that have been most innovative and opportunistic in thinking about their broad asset allocation posture. When institutions make substantial allocations to hedge funds, private equity, and other "alternatives," they do so because they want the total portfolio to generate an attractive absolute return. Similarly, when institutions hire "global asset allocators" to make tactical adjustments in the overall asset mix of the portfolio, their highly opportunistic approach is designed partly to avoid (or at least to mitigate) the pain that inevitably comes from static asset mixes. "The flight from 60/40" is driven by the conviction that positive returns are more important than beating a benchmark that may easily wind up in negative territory. (To be sure, even the more exotic "alternatives-heavy" portfolios are vulnerable to market forces that have the potential to produce negative returns. But these "alternative betas" are different from those that drive the standard 60/40 portfolio.)

This more opportunistic approach to investment management recalls some of Peter Bernstein's observations about "policy portfolios." (See especially "Are Policy Portfolios Obsolete?" in Bernstein's *Economics and Portfolio Strategy*, March 1, 2003.) Bernstein's basic argument is that flexibility and opportunism are the only appropriate responses to a world that is intrinsically uncertain and volatile. We agree, but, as always, it is important not to get carried away. There's often a fine line between getting carried away and getting carried out the door.

TWO KINDS OF STYLE DRIFT

For those who believe in "constrained" active management, "style drift" is the ultimate sin. But style drift can be either good or bad. Good style drift is a sensible response to changing circumstances. Bad style drift is aimless wandering, what the British call "losing the plot." Good style drift is healthy evolution, while bad style drift is unhealthy tampering, often driven by unrealistic expectations. Bernstein's plea for flexibility and opportunism can be seen as a plea for the right kind of style drift, both at the level of individual managers and at the level of the fiduciaries who employ those managers.

Markets are fickle and unpredictable. Indeed, some have joked that the stock market is a mechanism designed to inflict the maximum amount of humiliation on the maximum number of investors. When your enemy is unpredictable, it's foolish to limit yourself to a strict set of rules that are laid down in advance. The best investment managers are adaptable, flexible, and opportunistic. If "style consistency" becomes blind allegiance to what you've always done, then style consistency is a fatal error.

What is the final verdict on this new interest in loosening constraints? Is it good or bad? On the whole, we would say that it is good, since it is clear that "hyper-constrained money management" is a dead end. But flexibility and opportunism are double-edged swords: They can be used well or used badly. As Spiderman reminds us, with great power comes great responsibility. And responsibility means good judgment, not low tracking error.

PART

Three

The Challenges Under Transformation

CHAPTER 9

The Evolving Challenges of Quantitative Investing

Robert L. Hagin and
Kathleen T. DeRose
Hagin Investment Management

The authors suggest that fundamental analysis and quantitative analysis should not be considered as distinct from each other as some hold, or as an acrimonious "man-versus-machine" imbroglio. The increasing rate of technological change precludes holding firm opinions about the efficacy of one over the other. Don't discount the convergence of other disciplines. Advances in them could transform our understanding of investing.

> *The problem with computers . . . is that they only give you answers.*
> —Picasso

Investors face a continuous challenge: How do they best incorporate rapidly evolving technology into their thinking and behavior? Those present at the birth of modern computing never envisioned the raw muscle that technology would ultimately bring to investing. Alongside exponential increases in computing speed and storage capacity, this era also produced impressive advances in finance. For the first time, empirical tests of market hypotheses were possible. This historic revolution, with new theories and new technologies wedded hand-in-glove, enabled the creation and proliferation of new investment businesses, participants, products, and tools. It also spawned unimaginable increases in trading activity.

Yet investing remains a zero-sum game. Technology may actually have increased the efficiency of the market in some areas by enabling arbitrage. And it's certainly created an unforeseen problem: data proliferation. The quantitative investment arena, a product of the technology revolution, tackles this challenge every day.

Initially, quantitative investing appeared opposed to traditional, fundamental investing, a contrast between newfangled technology and old-fashioned stock-picking. Given that investors of both stripes require insight, even if they use different tools, this separation is a bit artificial. But when it comes to things clients care about, like having confidence that a manager will reproduce past successful performance in the future, more disciplined, (quantitative) investment processes better meet the test. Quantitative investors do have some shortcomings of their own, suggesting that the balancing act between judgmental and automated contributions to investing is still a very important one. This challenge is something both computer and investment pioneers foretold, and which remains tantalizingly unresolved today. As technology continues its bold progression, we should expect exciting new chapters in the ongoing story of "man and machine."

COMPUTERS AND FINANCE: THE BIRTH OF QUANTITATIVE INVESTING

The first computer, ENIAC (Electrical Numerical Integrator and Calculator), was developed in 1946 at the Moore School of Electrical Engineering at the University of Pennsylvania. Creators of early computers could not have imagined the technological improvements as computers moved from vacuum tubes, to transistors, to solid-state circuitry and beyond.

To put ENIAC in perspective, it had 17,840 vacuum tubes; the chips in our PCs each have 152 million transistors. The ENIAC could process 5,000 additions per second; the 2006 Intel Core Duo chips in the rather generic PCs that we are using to write this chapter can process 21.6 *billion* operations per second. Even so, Penn professor Irving Brainerd speculated that during the 80,223 hours that ENIAC operated (until it was destroyed by lightning in 1955) it performed more calculations than had been performed by all of humanity since the beginning of time.

Computers were not an instant success. Almost ten years elapsed between ENIAC and the time the first computer was installed in a business enterprise. But it was not until the introduction of "third-generation" computers using solid-state circuits and programming languages such as FORTRAN in the early 1960s that computers were used to study financial markets. Markets, with their dynamic, stochastic processes, were a logical application for computer-based research.

Rapid advances in processing technology followed these early strides. In 1965, Intel co-founder Gordon Moore made the bold prediction that the number of transistors on a silicon chip would double approximately every two years. In the more than 40 intervening years, what came to be known as "Moore's Law" has become a reality. Today, computer technology has advanced to the point where the lines on chips are smaller than a virus, and are 1,000 times thinner than a human hair. Miraculously, computer technologies have advanced so dramatically that the cost of a transistor on a silicon chip is now roughly the same as the price that we pay for *one* printed character on a newspaper. The stunning drop in costs has enabled many functions requiring rapid calculations over great spans of data— like those performed by investment management researchers—to migrate to computers.

Meanwhile, researchers in investing were also rethinking many previous notions about how markets behave. The evolution of modern investment management and risk control began in the mid-1960s. Even though Harry Markowitz wrote his book on a theory of portfolio construction in 1952, its importance was not widely appreciated until 1963, when Bill Sharpe articulated a theory of asset pricing in which risk plays a pivotal role. Sharpe introduced us to *alpha* and *beta* and set forth the insight that only a positive alpha is worth an active management fee. Even though questions had been raised about the value-added by early fundamental managers in places such as Fred Schwed Jr.'s best-selling 1940 book, *Where Are the Customers' Yachts?*, it was Sharpe's separation of alpha (which has an expected value of *zero*) and beta that launched the performance-measurement industry.

In 1965, Eugene Fama set forth the *efficient market hypothesis (EMH)*, providing a theory that explains why consistent records of above-average returns are so elusive. According to Fama's EMH, all that is known about stocks is instantaneously embedded into their prices so that there is no advantage to investors trading with information derived from investment analysis. In Fama's words, "I'd compare stock pickers to astrologers, but I don't want to bad-mouth astrologers." The widespread acceptance of the EMH argument in academic circles even swayed Benjamin Graham—the father of security analysis—to recant his belief in the usefulness of security analysis.

Obviously, assertions of the EMH were anathema to fundamental investment managers of the day. Picking up the gauntlet, legions of academics used computers to analyze historical financial data as they set about the quest to find "anomalies" that would refute the EMH. These researchers provided a new breed of *quantitative* investors with insights into factors-based subsets of the market (such as small stocks and stocks with low price/earnings ratios) that appeared to provide above-average risk-adjusted returns.

Until the turn of the 21st century, Fama and other EMH disciples countered the discoveries that certain factors lead to above-average returns by saying that these returns had to be compensation for unspecified risks. Moreover, something of renewed interest today, they emphasized that as skillful individuals identify and exploit the same investment opportunities, the opportunities will be arbitraged away—leaving an efficient market.

The next milestone in the development modern investing was the insightful work of Fischer Black, Myron Scholes, and Robert Merton on option-pricing theory. Their work laid the foundation for calculating the prices of options and a host of other derivative securities.

These advances in technology and in finance created many new investment businesses, attracted new entrants to the industry, inspired the creation of a host of complex derivative products, and produced sophisticated new tools for investors. Trading volume soared and the typical holding period for a stock fell from over a year to barely a week. Yet we have seen no net gain in outperformance for most market participants. The reason is that data does not equal insight. Users of ENIAC and today's computers share a common problem: how to harness computing power to provide decision makers with useful information. Imagine people sitting around in the post-WWII period with the H-bomb and other weaponry calculations finished, trying to decide what they might do with ENIAC. One project was to grind out books of logarithms to ten significant digits. Today's equivalent might be the weeks spent extracting illusory signals from the same in-sample market study period, or arcane volatility calculations for equity-derived securities that investors probably shouldn't buy.

From the perspective of decision theory, investors suffer from an over-abundance of irrelevant information. Smart investors train themselves to set aside massive amounts of "noise" and focus explicitly on the information that improves the accuracy of their investment decisions.

As we contrast *quantitative* and *fundamental* approaches to active investing, it is instructive to emphasize that (with a few lawbreaking scoundrels aside) there are thousands of hardworking investment professionals who toil diligently to provide value-added services to their clients. When comparing investment managers, it is important to remember that investing is a zero-sum game. We do not live in Garrison Keillor's fictional Lake Wobegon, where "all the children are above average." Outside of Lake Wobegon, half of the investors are above average and half are below average. Moreover, in this highly competitive industry, the returns of investors who earn above-average returns must be offset by investors who earn below-average returns.

The next step in the evolution of modern investment management was the mid-1980s introduction of desktop computers and the availability of extensive computer-readable databases with financial histories. This brought both technology and finance to the typical professional investor's desktop. Real client money could now be managed using exclusively quantitative techniques. The quantitative-versus-fundamental controversy moved out of the ivy tower and into the investment trenches, kindling the debate about investment processes that still burns today.

QUANTITATIVE INVESTING GROWS UP

The PC revolution turbocharged quantitative investing, allowing it to move out of the laboratory and into portfolios. Suddenly, investing was no longer about individuals and exceptions, but about computers and systematic effects. The quintessential stock analyst fished a future McDonalds from a sea of hamburger pretenders. Now, a prototypical quantitative investor, powered with speed and memory, nets a whole portfolio of champions from proven market-feeding grounds. A philosophical rift opened between traditionalists evaluating one stock at a time, and statisticians looking for common factors and ways to control risk. The need for human industry and intuition did not disappear. Despite the hardened factions, each with its heroes and villains (sometimes represented by the same people, like Nobel Prize winners who blow up large hedge funds), this divide is really procedural, not ideological. The PC has replaced the pencil, but not the intellect, for all investors. However, if one believes that process determines outcome, then style is substance; the rocket scientists with the computers clearly have the superior technique. The problem with quants can be lack of imagination, not lack of design. Meanwhile, below the surface tension created by pitting fundamental against quantitative lies an undercurrent of real controversy and future excitement: Who invests, people or machines? As computers have become increasingly powerful, even "intelligent," what is their proper role (if it is even ours to assign) in functions previously the exclusive province of mind?

By the early 1980s, low-cost processing power made primitive investment search-and-discovery missions possible for professional investors. From screening for high book-to-price it was a short step to correlating valuation with returns. It was a second small leap to identifying other winning attributes, from additional "risk" factors like market capitalization to unique company advantages, like rising return on equity. Combining them, quants created the first multifactor stock selection models. Risk models and portfolio optimizers followed, complementing alpha models. The models, becoming ever more sophisticated, produced above-average performance, and by the late 1980s, quantitative asset management was a credible and growing business. In 1987, portfolio insurance gave mechanistic techniques a black eye. In 1998, the unraveling of hedge fund Long Term

Capital challenged the hegemony of geniuses and their models. In the late 1990s, the tech bubble temporarily inverted normal statistical relationships. Then, in the summer of 2007, the beginnings of the credit crunch and forced liquidations dislocated factor-based portfolios. Despite these setbacks, quants mostly prospered in the 1990s and 2000s, feasting on unprecedented risk premia in the post-tech-bubble market, while producing their fastest growth to date. By 2008, quantitative firms managed significant assets and accounted for a meaningful proportion of all trading activity.

Meanwhile, technology also transformed traditional investing. Twenty-five years ago, an analyst scrutinizing a company telephoned the Investor Relations contact, requested an annual report, receiving it a week later by "snail mail," and used paper and pencil to construct her earnings forecast. Today, the click of a mouse button produces the financial history of the company, and multiple third-party research engines provide canned earnings and valuation analysis. Despite the cottage industry of advice about how to invest where you shop, most traditional investors use screens to sift for stocks to research, and borrow some risk management tools from quants. While still focused on the search for exceptional opportunities, rather than common-factor ones, fundamental investors have surely benefited from desktop technology. Silicon-based processing has reconfigured every aspect of investing, from data gathering to diversifying. The handmaiden of fundamental investors, technology is the animator of quantitative ones.

FUNDAMENTAL OR QUANTITATIVE: ART OR SCIENCE?

Yet a philosophical division developed between fundamental and quantitative tribes, who argue that the two approaches are ideological antipodes, one "art" and the other "science." Fundamental investors pride themselves on their roving armies of analysts, their close relationships with managements, and their carefully honed earnings forecasts, scoffing that no computer could possibly capture these intangibles. They describe the future, and they appeal to clients' affection for warm-and-fuzzy stories that illustrate their stock-picking prowess. Meanwhile, quantitative investors trumpet their discipline of empirical proofs and innovative algorithms, convinced that the analytical processes reveal all. They base their premises in the past, and they appeal to clients' desire, however elusive, to avoid uncertainty. Since both methods succeed and fail with similar frequency, the polarity is less about philosophy and more about mechanics. Technology is no guarantor of results, promising only faster, better procedures. Both types of investors need a framework to discriminate information from noise. Insight is still scarce, and alpha is hard to come by. The dividing line is not as hardened as perceived.

Both approaches rely on investment "laws of nature." Good investors generally use immanent economic and market principles to explain why they expect to outperform. (There is an expected relationship between growth and valuation.) The fundamental investor and the quantitative one count on such well-described phenomena, and in many cases, they also depend on the same information. To identify alpha, each seeks misalignments in the expected natural order. The fundamental investor quizzes the CFO about his cost of capital and his mounting inventories, while the quantitative one's models capture the deteriorating return on invested capital versus weighted average cost of capital spread, and increases in accruals. The fundamentalist seeks growth, while the quant creates a valuation algorithm. And they share biases. The fundamental investors' blithe confidence in their investment "themes" (such as "globalization") is equivalent to the quantitative investors' naïve conviction in their ratios—both fall into the logic trap that they are the "smart money" in a sea of irrational investment dunces. Both also expect reversion to a tidy Gaussian mean. Part "machine" and part "mind," both employ technology but still require judgment to extract information from the data fog. Each has equal probability of outperforming in their quest for the unique insight necessary to succeed.

QUANTITATIVE INVESTING: LONG LIVE THE KING

If successful outcomes (above-average performance) hinge on sound processes, then quantitative investors, who employ the king of all processes, the scientific method, have the edge over fundamental ones. Quantitative investors rightfully expect that a compelling process will increase the frequency of superior results. They parse each step and understand the potency of a 55 percent hit rate. Quantitative investors gather assets because they better meet widely accepted tests used by clients and consultants to evaluate investment processes. In the process-driven environment created by technology, the engineer wins.

Most quantitative investors readily articulate their underlying hypotheses and assumptions, demonstrating empirically why their particular recipe should prevail. They are in tune with advances in finance theory (or at least more willing to scrutinize the academic papers for ideas). Quantitative investors translate their theses into algorithms, outflanking fundamental ones who buy "stocks that they believe will go up." Admittedly, even the finest theories still fail to explain and predict market behavior.

Otherwise, there would be no opportunity—that is the mystery of markets. Quantitative investors are more inclined to acknowledge this paradox.

Quantitative investors' processes are generally transparent, more blue-print than sketch. They separate "beta" (which can be replicated cheaply) from "alpha" derived from proprietary sources. They routinely exploit "behavioral" biases in the market, capturing the value premium and avoiding high-expectation stocks. If they have a few quirks of their own, they more freely acknowledge these sins. Overall, quantitative investors willingly specify the details of security selection rather than offering anecdotes about buying "good" companies and selling "bad" ones.

The gulf between quantitative and fundamental investors widens when it comes to portfolio construction—here the engineering advantage really counts. Using an optimizer and a risk model, quants build portfolios to explicit objectives and constraints versus a benchmark. Meanwhile "star" fundamental managers pilot portfolios that are built of opinions and are opaque about risk. The trend toward concentrated portfolios of "best ideas" typifies this problem as active investors struggle to produce alpha while distancing themselves from index offerings. Quantitative investors rigorously measure and manage ex-post risk, while fundamental ones take an ad-hoc approach, trimming and adding to positions as sentiment warrants. A mental risk map cannot compete with a sophisticated co-variance matrix.

Quants can attribute performance, or assign blame, to each step in the investment process, from universe construction to risk management, while fundamentalists ascribe all alpha to portfolio manager alchemy and all mistakes to bad market weather. While fundamental investors rarely predict when their approach will falter, quantitative processes allow for stress testing in different market environments, providing better insight into when a strategy will—and won't—perform. Quants, more readily than fundamentalists, meet or exceed the requirements for the sustainable, repeatable investment process hoped for by prospective clients.

PITFALLS FOR QUANTS: THE SHINY ROCK

The problem with quants is that they sometimes act like denizens of "Flat-land," Edwin Abbot's satirical world of two-dimensional inhabitants, where residents stick to a limited, linear worldview because they cannot conceive of higher dimensions—even though reasoning by analogy suggests they exist. Dazzled by the elegance and utility of binary computing, we forget technology's inherent limits, particularly when applied by fallible human hands to complex, probabilistic problems. These blemishes range from the mundane to the unnerving. Quantitative investors are not inoculated against investment hazards, and can fall victim to pitfalls of their own design.

Quants love the past. They use the past to predict the future, although factor returns based on historical relationships are known to be volatile, or to disappear. Thanks to technology, there is too much data to mine and a temptation to overfit. The data "cloud" is now so dense that it obfuscates meaning, or worse, discourages the search for relevance. Who needs an explanation when the data looks so good? Quants routinely mistake correlation for causation. Moreover, data used in quantitative investing comes from just a few primary sources. If quantitative investors are all feasting at the same backtest buffet (using Point-in-Time data, for example), is it a surprise that they chase similar anomalies? Anomalies found in data-mining subsequently evaporate in real portfolios as investors crowd one another. Data is not insight, and insight—a scarce commodity—is still necessary to separate bankable investment bullion from deceptive "shiny rocks."

Even the most automatic processes still require judgment; humans must tend machines. At many junctures, there is not one right answer, but a continuum of choices, from how and where to truncate data to which risk model is employed. Linear processes can be slow to adapt to discontinuous change like industry deregulation, which renders previous statistical data incomparable and models useless. Static models have to be modified. More seriously, few quants incorporate "model failure" into their processes since by definition collapse comes from events outside of expected model boundaries. Even more disturbing are failures of imagination, where investors cling to questionable assumptions—like a flawed belief in normal distributions—which recent market realities have challenged. Sometimes quants forget to ask the right questions. The overwhelming success of the binary approach to the world can blind us to the possibilities of additional dimensions and, more broadly, to the ambiguities of mind versus machine.

THE BEST OF BOTH WORLDS: ART AND SCIENCE

For now, quantitative approaches that rest on a solid fundamental footing—a conceptual foundation built apart from the invading thicket of data—currently offer the most appealing compromise between discipline and intuition. Quants who rely only on a few, unheroic, simplifying assumptions, like the gears of capitalism continuing to grind, rather than those that depend on complex or esoteric statistical residuals, are most likely to survive and prosper. The high ground is a balance between empiricism and pragmatism. Quantitative investors lay better claim to this turf than fundamental ones do, because of their superior (if imperfect) clarity about what is automatic and what is assumed.

So, a demarcation line should not be drawn between the yin/yang of fundamental/quantitative, but delineated somewhere on the continuum of mind and machine. Rapid technological advances now make this line very difficult to discern. In the future, can we speculate about what investment functions will be best assumed by computers, and what will remain the property of intellect?

Quantitative problem-solving techniques, made possible by accelerating processing speeds and by increasing memory, have evolved in parallel with computing power and alongside advances in finance. They are engineered approaches. Quantitative investing is a technical improvement over prior designs, just as a washing machine is superior to a washboard. As advances in procedure, more than in philosophy, quantitative techniques may have already extracted most of the benefits of 20 years of enrichment in digital technology. Today, a slightly faster, slightly cheaper tool is not necessarily a better one. Progress under the existing paradigm seems incremental from here.

This may all be about to change, as computers, and now the Internet, move beyond reductive, arithmetical logic, taking on the subtleties of reason. Quantitative investors must now advance philosophy as well as practice, exploring the epistemological frontier between mind and machine. We need a new paradigm, not a new PC. Isn't investing, where emotion is a liability, the perfect application for a sci-fi solution—especially if artificial intelligence can finally adopt the very human shortcomings that convey evolutionary adaptability?

Computer science, economics, and biology are converging to redefine mental and physical models of markets. The new paradigm may be that an evolutionary model best fits market patterns of "creative destruction," with implications for humans and machines. In permanent states of disequilibria, repetitive, linear techniques may give way to self-organizing, recursive ones. Search and "learning" capabilities already possible on the Web have yet to be fully exploited by investors. Advances from these and from other philosophical and scientific developments we can barely envision will transform our understanding of investing. Yet, in the future as in the past, only one in three players will deliver above-average risk-adjusted returns after fees. As the unprecedented advances in computing have shown, the next technological revolution will not necessarily revolutionize the rules of the investment game.

EMH and the Matter at Hand

Wayne H. Wagner and
Ralph A. Rieves

Efficient adj. Acting or producing effectively with a minimum of waste, expense, or unnecessary effort.

Hypothesis n. Something to be taken to be true for the purpose of argument or investigation; an assumption.
— The American Heritage Dictionary, *3rd Edition*

Do nanosecond changes in "publicly available information" and the behavioral school's challenge require a reappraisal of a fundamental postulate of investment theory? Why is Taleb relevant?

In the preface to this book, we state that the theme is "how the stewards of the world's assets should think about their thinking." Harry Liem's interview with a reflective Steve Brown ("The Academic Challenge," Chapter 12 in this book) is an engaging point of departure in thinking about academic theory. The purpose of this chapter is to address only one core postulate of academic theory, and that is the *efficient market hypothesis (EMH): Market prices fully reflect **all** available information.*

A WELL-REASONED ASSUMPTION

We might refine the above definition of the hypothesis as a "well-reasoned" assumption. Let us agree that EMH earns the *well-reasoned* distinction by having been subjected to over 50 years of study, research, and discourse.

Peter L. Bernstein has reminded us many times, "You get it right all the time as a matter of luck." However, that reminder begs the question: Has a half-century of study, research, and discourse gotten EMH "right all the time"? No such luck. But not getting it right all the time doesn't necessarily mean getting it wrong. It can mean getting it not quite right.

An Outsider's Questions

Someone who is not currently engaged in financial economics, upon first encountering the EMH, might ask, "At the present speed of information transmission and decay, how can the EMH be true? It seems unlikely that everyone will encounter and process information at the same rate and at the same time." Most likely, that intuitive response is triggered by the word *all*. Further reflection by our skeptic might prompt another question: "What constitutes available information?" Then our perplexed outsider might conclude, "You mean there is no advantage to gathering information? How do people decide what assets to buy and sell? If the EMH is an accurate representation of the real world, then why are there even markets?" With all of this weight, all of these piles of information and interpretation sensitive to price changes, is it any wonder that markets are so volatile at the point of transaction that a 100-share trade can affect the value of millions of shares?

The Efficiency of Physical Systems

Rather than respond to our outsider with semantics, probability studies, and equilibrium models, let's stay with the "not quite right" characterization. Doing so, we can answer with an analogy to something familiar to our skeptic. The analogy suggested by Andrew W. Lo is that of a piston engine. Here it is as he presents it in *The New Palgrave Dictionary of Economics*:

> *Physical systems are often given an efficiency rating based on the relative proportion of energy or fuel converted to useful work. Therefore, a piston engine may be rated at 60 percent efficiency, meaning that on average 60 percent of the energy contained in the engine's fuel is used to turn the crankshaft, with the remaining 40 percent lost to other forms of work, such as heat, light, or noise.*
>
> *Few engineers would ever consider performing a statistical test to determine whether or not a given engine is perfectly efficient—such an engine exists only in the idealized frictionless world of the imagination. But measuring relative efficiency—relative to the frictionless ideal—is commonplace. . . . Therefore, from a practical point of view . . . the EMH is a useful benchmark for measuring relative efficiency.*[1]

Lo says that such a concept of relative efficiency is more advantageous to understanding markets than the all-or-nothing notion. However, there are participants and academics who have taken the critique of EMH even further, some of whom argue whether EMH has any relevance to modern global markets. Reviewing those observations and insights might help place EMH in a strategic perspective when actually managing investments.

THE BEHAVIORALIST TAKE—AND THAT OF OTHERS

The most widely accepted challenges to EMH have come from an amalgam of disciplines (psychology, economics, and statistics), the generally accepted description for which is *the behavioral school*. The behavioral school has concluded that people frequently don't act in ways that enhance the "efficiency" of their daily lives or their investment decisions.

The behavioralists contend that investors often do not make rational, information-based decisions. Therefore, the argument that prices reflect all available information is compromised by decisions that arise from irrational, noneconomic sources. They contend that the EMH needs considerable refinement.

What follows is a summary of some of the most representative work of the behavioral school.

Kahneman and Tversky

Daniel Kahneman and the late Amos Tversky were awarded a Nobel Prize in Economics for their studies about how people deal with financial risk. The two main concepts that evolved from their work were *prospect theory* and *narrow framing*.

Prospect theory states that investors don't make decisions within the context of an overall investment strategy, but think in terms of distinct gains and losses. And further, investors are more sensitive to a loss. Kahneman and Tversky (K & T) conducted several experimental studies to observe how people evaluate risk. The structures of those studies are available in a number of sources, so we won't discuss them in this chapter. The conclusions of these experiments were startling: Investors are risk-averse about low-probability losses, but risk-seeking when confronted with low-probability gains. EMH rests on an assumption of a smooth, sloping curve—K & T found bumps and twists in that road.

Narrow framing is another characteristic of investors K & T derived from their experimental studies. Again, risk aversion prevailed among the participants in these studies. In the context of an overall investment strategy, an investor should consider how choosing one investment will be offset by the choices that are made among several investments. However, the subjects in the experiments evaluated risk in isolation. K & T offered a bet on a coin flip (win $100 + 10\%$ on heads or lose $100 on tails), and most people turned down the bet. The pain of a $100 loss overrides the attractiveness of a 50–50 chance of winning $110. Here were even more bends and twists in the road. K&T concluded that most people think of the likelihood of a loss as an isolated, separate event.

Statman and Shefrin

Meir Statman and Hersh Shefrin are two other prominent researchers who contributed to the data about investor behavior. One of their most impacting focuses has been on why investors are predisposed to sell their winners (assets with prices that have exceeded their buy prices) too soon and hold onto their losing assets too long. They gave this behavior the elegant label of the *disposition effect*.

The early stages of developing the disposition effect emphasized the behavior of individual investors. Recently, Statman and Shefrin have directed their studies to the behavior of investment managers and the impact of that specific behavior on market prices. They concluded that professionals who discipline themselves to a more logical/rigorous trading strategy (inoculating themselves from the prevailing predisposition) outperform their counterparts.

Several Others

Other significant research about investor behavior is being conducted. Among those whose work is most frequently cited are Terrance Odean, Richard Thaler, William DeBondt, Josef Lakonishok, and Daniel T. Gilbert. (Since all of their respective papers and critiques of them can be easily retrieved on the commonly used search engines, we are not noting these citations at the end of this chapter.)

And Then There Is Darwin

Yet another avenue of study being explored is called the *adaptive market hypothesis*. This framework approaches economic behavior in the context of evolutionary biology. This school studies how to apply the principles of natural selection to human interactions, and by extension, to marketplace behavior. According to Andrew Lo, the degree of market efficiency is related to environmental factors characterizing market ecology, such as the number of competitors in the market, the magnitude of profit opportunities available, and the adaptability of the market participants.

HOW CAN IT WORK WHEN IT DOESN'T WORK?

The EMH theory says all information is free, everyone knows everything, and transaction costs don't exist. It implies that risk is measurable and mathematically tractable. None of these assertions are true, yet for a theory so apparently unrealistic, it stands at the base of almost everything we've learned and practiced about investing for the last half-century. Standing on the shoulders of Markowitz and Sharpe, Black, Scholes, and Merton conceived the option-pricing model, which has provided a structural framework for changing our perception of risk and managing our exposures to it.

Why has this unrealistic EMH become so useful? We believe it's because it has forced us to rethink how we apply our understanding of personal biases, risk, skill, mathematical tractability, and implementability.

Let's look at these one by one:

■ *Personal biases:* Yes, we are all experienced, wise, and accredited experts, but the market is too complicated and dynamic for anyone fully to understand. This describes Herbert Simon's *bounded rationality* phenomenon. We can hold only a few things in our mind at once, so we simplify. We dip into our well of knowledge and experience and dredge up a handful of things that seemed to have worked well in the past. We've satisfied, rather than optimized, our quest for the predictive— and we all know it. We pretend a confidence we don't feel, and hope for a little luck.

  Our clients try to seize success by hitching up to past successes. When things go wrong, the standard defense is, "Gee, he had such a great track record! How were we to know he had just had a couple of lucky years?"

■ *Skill:* EMH says that all available information is imbedded in the price. But not everyone falls into the category of the hapless *hoi polloi.* Consider what motivates a Buffett or an Icahn or Kerkorian to make a bid for a company, as well as the managers who focus on alpha hunting. One can argue for superior instincts or long-holding horizons, but the key factor for these talented investors is *control* of the resources of the company, particularly if that company is perceived to be poorly run. EMH in its purest form preaches passivity, while these canny investors appreciate the power of negotiation.

▪ *Risk:* It gets worse. In the previous paragraphs we talked about the things we could potentially know, things that *somebody* knows now. But the future is bound to surprise us all, individually and collectively. When and where will the next giant earthquake or volcanic eruption strike the world? Who will be devastated, and who will be untouched? Our point is that there is no *rational* portfolio response to a serious event of which the location, timing, and severity are completely unknowable. When an unexpected event hits, all portfolios are affected, some much worse than others. There are winners and losers—black swan effects, to be sure.

  Elroy Dimson (London Business School) puts it perfectly: "More things can happen than will happen." There it is: The most intuitive definition of risk ever presented, and not open to computational prowess.

▪ *Tractability:* Perhaps we brush these unknown unknowables aside, and work in whatever dimensional space works best for us. We clutch to our breasts the Gaussian stepwise-regression analyses, even though we know that the fat tails of the distribution are very real, and we vastly understate the likelihood of devastation. (Ask any banker who assessed his exposure to the mortgage meltdown through a VAR model.)

▪ *Implementability:* An explicit assumption of the EMH is that decisions can be implemented at no cost. Translated into the real world, markets will remain liquid, with roughly equal pressure from buyers and sellers. But, as many a highly levered portfolio manager has found out, liquidity can evaporate in times of severe strain. "Severe strain" translates into liquidity becoming more important than investment prospects. As local liquidity disappears, leveraged investors search everywhere for sources of portfolio liquidity. The result is contagion, where market strain spreads to unrelated sectors. As Myron Scholes poignantly said, "all correlations converge to one." (For further insight, read Khandani and Lo's paper, "What Happened to the Quants in August 2007?"[2])

Summary

Earlier, we presumed that someone outside of financial economics might question EMH, particularly the construct of "all available information." Moreover, a conscientious fiduciary or trustee could infer that EMH needs to be more thorough in its categorizations. As we have seen, critics of EMH haven't left the challenge to EMH to just that. They argue that asset selections by humans can often be irrational, so those selections do not enhance efficiency. Proponents defend EMH as central to understanding the consequence of many market participants attempting to profit from their actions. We expect the discourse among different schools to go on for a long time.

A familiarity with all sides of the EMH debate should heighten our consciousness about the uncertainty and the disequilibrium we are likely to confront within the capital markets.

So, that's enough. Next we should examine the most agitating element of uncertainty, that overriding part of the human experience—luck.

LUCK

All sides of the EMH debate state that introducing luck into their respective arguments is irrelevant, because it is a nonmeasurable variable. We agree, that is an appropriate reason for exclusion in academic discourse. However, talking about luck is relevant to this discussion of EMH and global investing.

Our challenge was to introduce luck in way that would be framed in the context of investing. We choose to do so by sharing the insights of Nassim N. Taleb. Taleb has been a professor and a derivatives trader. He was accomplished at both. For the past few years, he has devoted his time to speaking, research, and writing. From the start, his observations have been relevant, insightful, and engaging. Here is one of our favorites:

> *If you funded 1,000,000 unemployed people endowed with no more than the ability to say "buy" or "sell," odds are that you will break even in the aggregate, minus transaction costs, but a few will hit the jackpot, simply because the base cohort is very large. It will be almost impossible not to have small Warren Buffetts by luck alone. After the fact they will be very visible and will derive precise and well-sounding explanations about why they made it. It is difficult to argue with them; "nothing succeeds like success." All those retrospective explanations are pervasive, but there are scientific methods to correct for bias . . . but the public will remain convinced that "some" of these investors have skills.*[3]

Taleb is the author of three books, the most recent of which is called *The Black Swan: The Impact of the Highly Improbable* (Random House, 2006). The title of the book is taken from an article Taleb wrote in 2004 for the op-ed page of the *New York Times:* "Learning to Expect the Unexpected."

> *A black swan is an outlier, an event that lies beyond the real of normal expectations. Most people expect all swans to be white because that's what their experience tells them; a black swan is by definition a surprise. Nevertheless, people tend to concoct explanations for them after the fact, which makes them appear more predictable,*

and less random than they are. Our minds are designed to retain, for efficient storage, past information that fits into a compressed narrative. This distortion, called the hindsight bias, prevents us from adequately learning from the past.[4]

Again, addressing surprises and occurrences outside one's realm of expectations *is relevant to this discussion* of EMH and global investment management. And so we introduce Taleb's work and insights here.

Taleb has acknowledged that the works of Kahneman, Tversky, Gilbert, and the other behavioralists enhance our knowledge about the way we try to make decisions. He also vigorously expounds on the existence of random events. Thus, both sides of the EMH dialogue think he belongs to their side. However, they have approached his writing in a cursory manner, gleaning what suits their respective positions.

Taleb is not a member of either persuasion. He has his own unique perspective. His mission is to heighten awareness of randomness and the unexpected, so as to overcome what he labels *hindsight biases*. He strives to encourage a multidisciplinary approach to studying uncertainty and the impact of unpredictable events. One of his goals is to heighten our awareness of the role both kinds of luck play in life and work. We recommend that you read his work. A familiarity with Taleb's work will reinforce an appreciation of that most intriguing aspect of capital markets activity: *We don't know what we don't know.*

CONCLUSION

The EMH provides a point from which to think seriously about the business of funding peoples' businesses and lives.

Earlier, we proposed a modest acceptance of EMH as a well-reasoned assumption. Well-reasoned assumptions serve as mental models. As John Minahan observes in "Investment Belief Systems" (Chapter 23 in this book), "Mental models are tools for thinking through tangled problems in a structured manner." Minahan reinforces the value of theories with an insightful observation: ". . . theories are extremely valuable as 'inversions.' That is, if you provide a list of conditions under which something is irrelevant, the inverses of these conditions constitute the reasons the item matters."

Later in the chapter, he discusses the use of *inverted* EMH in evaluating investment managers:

I find the efficient market theory extremely helpful in guiding an interview so as to uncover answers. . . . More specifically, I find inverted *efficient market theory helpful* . . . *the basic idea is that the process of trading on information or a point of view causes that information or view to be reflected in asset prices. Once reflected in prices, the information can no longer be used to generate superior returns. The inverse of this statement is this: "If a manager is to generate superior returns, he must be able to trade on value-relevant information or perspectives before that information becomes reflected in price." This is the value of the efficient market theory as a logical construct. It simplifies all the possible reasons for superior performance into one focused question: How does the manager trade before his perspective or information is reflected in prices?* . . . Unless a manager can explain why his perspective is not reflected in the prices of what he buys or sells, there is no reason to expect he will outperform. *(Emphasis added.)*

The above quote is a significant argument for the relevance of the efficient market hypothesis.

NOTES

1. Steven N. Durlauf and Lawrence E. Blume, eds., *The New Palgrave Dictionary of Economics* (New York: Palgrave Macmillan, 2008).
2. Amir E. Khandani and Andrew W. Lo, "What Happened to the Quants in August 2007?" (http://web.mit.edu/alo/www/Papers/august07.pdf).
3. Nassim Nicholas Taleb in a 2004 interview with *EDGE/The Third Culture* (www.edge.org), April 19, 2004.
4. Nassim Nicholas Taleb, "Learning to Expect the Unexpected," *New York Times,* April 8, 2004.

CHAPTER 11

The Attribution Challenge

Ron Surz
PPCA, Inc.

Where misunderstanding serves others as an advantage, one is helpless to make oneself understood.
—Lionel Trilling, Author (1905–1975)

Performance standards focus on accurate measurements and reporting. But the most accurate measurements can be misinterpreted when compared to faulty benchmarks. Here is an extensive discussion about accurate benchmarking and rigorous attribution analysis. Tiger Woods' bowling scores are not relevant to his achievements.

Investment performance attribution determines why performance is good or bad, singling out what worked and what didn't. In the hierarchy of search criteria for manager talent, attribution ranks way above evaluation and is far more forward-looking. The skillful can stumble and the unskilled can get lucky. We want to know the difference, and more importantly, we want to know how mistakes are being corrected and what proficiencies are being groomed. Some of the "noble challenges" in performance attribution are as follows:

- *Differentiate not just between luck and skill, but between* style, *luck, and skill*: The relatively recent awareness of the importance of style goes a long way toward identifying true skill. It's easy to confuse style with skill, but extremely difficult to make good decisions in the face of this mistake. Buying skill, not style, is akin to buying alpha, not beta.

■ *Deal with the active–passive trade-off:* Use all the active managers you can find who have demonstrated this skill, and complete the portfolio with passive investments to fill in parts of the market where talent has not been found. It should matter only that the manager adds value, not that value is added in a particular style box.

■ *Put style boxes to good use:* Insisting that a manager fit into a style box is absurd. We miss too much talent that way, and mostly end up with index huggers. No offense to index huggers, but even the most skillful managers can't deliver under the constraint of living in a box. Rather, investment managers should be evaluated against custom style blends that reflect their people, process, and philosophy. The due diligence process involves two central questions: (1) Do we like what this manager does?, and (2) Does (s)he do it well? The answer to the first question shouldn't revolve around style boxes, and the presence of blended boxes should be used to answer the second question.

■ *Regain control of the assets:* Financial consultants and institutional investors have relinquished control of their assets to investment managers. They do this primarily through the type of sales and account management that manipulates the client in various ways, including "creative" performance reporting. Granted, investment managers are the smarter lot, but the assets are not theirs.

■ *Compensate investment professionals for delivering value added:* Attribution determines which analysts are succeeding and failing, as well as the effects of the portfolio managers on overall performance. Knowing which players own which pieces of the performance puzzle, as well as who is contributing and who is not, is important for professional retention and morale. *Compensation should be tied to contribution.* Unfortunately, bonuses are typically based on ad-hoc rules of thumb that ultimately make them discretionary. This creates a dynamic that rewards dominant personalities and pointy-haired bosses rather than talent.

To address these challenges, performance attribution must take away all of the hiding places that managers have used for the past 40 years (the relatively short history of this profession). Fair is fair, and it's time for investors to get the real story: All of the cards in this poker game need to be dealt face up. This chapter goes beyond the valiant efforts of the CFA Institute and its Global Investment Performance Standards (GIPs). The GIPs focus primarily on accurate measurements and reporting, but even the most accurate measurements can be misinterpreted when compared to faulty benchmarks, regardless of intent. And once the benchmark is wrong, all of the analytics, including attribution, are wrong. It's the old garbage-in-garage-out (GIGO) problem. So, this chapter starts with a discussion of accurate benchmarking and then shows how solid attribution analysis uses the best benchmarks to expose and remove the hiding places. The investor sees the real story, warts and all. What's good for the goose is good for the gander. Solid attribution analysis is also good for the investment management profession, especially when it comes to discretionary compensation—namely bonuses.

GETTING THE BENCHMARK RIGHT

The central challenge in identifying investment talent is knowing who is winning and who is losing. We've failed to meet this challenge because we usually get the benchmark wrong. It's like evaluating Tiger Woods as a bowler. Style analysis goes a long way toward correcting this problem, but we're currently stuck using flawed executions of an excellent idea. This total performance evaluation and attribution picture is shown in Exhibit 11.1.

The last couple of decades have taught us that Modern Portfolio Theory (MPT) does not work when it comes to evaluating investment performance. Specifically, the Capital Asset Pricing Model (CAPM) does not work when value investing is in favor, and markets are rising, because low-beta stocks outperform high-beta stocks in this environment. "Beta is dead" heralded the introduction of Arbitrage Pricing Theory (APT). APT has morphed into our current use of *style analysis*. Beta is dead because style effects are so strong. Of course, broad market effects remain paramount in determining portfolio returns, but not beta-adjusted market effects. In fact, the largest component of return is usually the market return, followed by the style

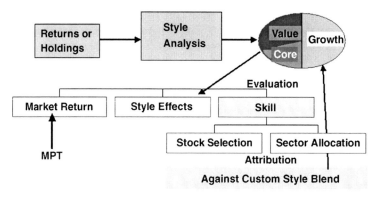

EXHIBIT 11.1   Sources of Return

effect, and then a far distant third component might be attributable to skill. Note that while alpha, or skill, can be estimated using either holdings or returns, holdings are required to complete the picture with the components of skill, or attribution analysis. Note also that it is important that style be taken into account in both performance evaluation and performance attribution. As a practical matter, the search for skill ought to begin at the macro level with managers whose performance is good. Then due diligence can proceed with an understanding of the people, process, and philosophy that produced the good performance. Then last, but not least, performance attribution confirms that the sources of this exceptional performance are consistent with the people, process, and philosophy. Throughout this process we keep in mind that the resultant decisions are all about the future, even though we use the past as a guide.

As shown in the exhibit, the benchmark used in this quest must be both market and style driven. Customization of the style component is important. A benchmark establishes a goal for the investment manager. A reasonable goal is to earn a return that exceeds a low-cost, passive implementation of the manager's investment approach, because the investor always has the choice of active or passive management. The relatively recent introduction of style indexes helps, but these need to be employed wisely, using blended rather than off-the-shelf style indexes. Before style indexes were developed, there was wide acceptance and support for the concept of a "normal portfolio," which is a customized list of stocks with their neutral weights. "Normals" were intended to capture the essence of the people, process, and philosophy behind an investment product. However, only a couple of consulting firms were any good at constructing these custom benchmarks. Today we can approximate these "designer benchmarks" with style analysis, sometimes called "the poor man's normals." While style analysis may not be as comprehensive as the original idea of normal portfolios, it at least makes it possible for many firms to now partake in this custom blending of style indexes. Style analysis can be conducted with returns or holdings. Both approaches are designed to identify a style blend that—like normals—captures the people, process, and philosophy of the investment product.

Whether the returns or holdings approach to style analysis is used, the starting point is well-defined investment styles. The classification of stocks into styles leads to style indexes, which are akin to sector indexes such as technology or energy. It's important to recognize the distinction between indexes and benchmarks. Indexes are barometers of price changes in segments of the market. Benchmarks are passive alternatives to active management. Historically, common practice has been to use indexes as benchmarks, which works fine for index huggers, but there are many skillful managers who work best without the comfort of hugs. Style analyses have shown that most managers are best characterized as using a blend of styles. As a practical matter, we are no worse off with style blends, as the old practice is considered in the solution. So there's always the possibility that the best "blend" is a single index. Some managers feel compelled to complete the sentence, "I manage the _____ index." This is counterproductive and a convenience that helps no one, unless, again, the manager is an index hugger. Also, the sentence is frequently completed with the index *du jour* for the Request For Proposal (RFP).

One form of style analysis is *returns-based style analysis (RBSA)*. RBSA regresses a manager's returns against a family of style indexes to determine the combination of indexes that best tracks the manager's performance. The interpretation of the *fit* is that the manager is employing this "effective" style mix because performance could be approximately replicated with this passive blend. Another approach, called *holdings-based style analysis (HBSA)*, examines the stocks actually held in the investment portfolio and maps these into styles at points in time. Once a sufficient history of these holdings-based snapshots is developed, an estimate of the manager's average style profile can be developed and used as the custom benchmark. Note that HBSA, like normal portfolios, starts at the individual security level. Both normal portfolios and holdings-based style analysis examine the history of holdings. The departure occurs at the blending. Normal portfolios blend stocks to create a portfolio profile that is consistent with investment philosophy, whereas HBSA makes an inference from the pattern of point-in-time style profiles and translates the investment philosophy into style.

The choice between RBSA and HBSA is complicated and involves several considerations. Although RBSA has gained popularity, this doesn't necessarily mean that it's the best choice. The major trade-off between the two approaches is ease of use (RBSA) versus accuracy and ease of understanding (HBSA). RBSA has become a commodity that is quickly available and operated with a few point-and-clicks. Some websites offer free RBSA for a wide range of investment firms and products. Find the product, click on it, and out comes a style profile. Offsetting this ease of use is the potential for error. RBSA uses sophisticated regression analysis to do its job. As in any statistical process, data problems can go undetected and unrecognized, leading to faulty inferences. One such problem is multicollinearity, which exists when the style indexes used in the regression overlap in membership. Multicollinearity invalidates the regression and usually produces spurious results. The user of RBSA must trust the "black box," because the regression can't explain why that particular blend is the best solution. In his article that introduced RBSA, Nobel laureate Dr. William Sharpe (1988) set forth recommendations for the style indexes used in RBSA, known as the *style palette*:

It is desirable that the selected asset classes be:

- *Mutually exclusive (no class should overlap with another)*
- *Exhaustive (all securities should fit in the set of asset classes)*
- *Investable (it should be possible to replicate the return of each class at relatively low cost)*
- *Macro-consistent (the performance of the entire set should be replicable with some combination of asset classes)*

The mutually exclusive criterion addresses the multicollinearity problem, and the other criteria provide solid regressors for the style match. The only indexes that currently meet all of these criteria are provided by Morningstar and Surz. Both index series are readily available on a wide variety of platforms, such as Zephyr and MPI. Morningstar is available for U.S. stocks, while Surz indexes are provided for U.S., international, and global stock markets. Using indexes that do not meet Dr. Sharpe's criteria is like using low-octane fuel in your high-performance car. See Picerno (2003, 2006) for an extensive discussion of a proper style palette.

Holdings-based style analysis (HBSA) provides an alternative to RBSA. The major benefits of HBSA are that the analyst can both observe the classification of every stock in the portfolio, as well as question these classifications. This results in total transparency and understanding, but at a cost of additional operational complexity. HBSA requires more information than RBSA; that is, it needs individual security holdings at various points in time rather than returns. Since these holdings are generally not available on the Internet, as returns are, the holdings must be fed into the analysis system through some means other than point-and-click. This additional work, sometimes called *throughput*, is not that difficult and is well worth the effort. Like RBSA, HBSA also requires that stocks be classified into style groups, or indexes. Dr. Sharpe's criteria work for both RBSA and HBSA. For consistency purposes, the same palette should be used for both types of style analysis. Note that the "mutually exclusive" and "exhaustive" criteria are particularly important in HBSA, as it is highly desirable to have stocks in only one style group and to classify all stocks.

In certain circumstances, deciding between RBSA and HBSA is really a matter of Hobson's choice. When holdings data is difficult to obtain (as can be the case with some mutual funds and unregistered investment products such as hedge funds, or when derivatives are used in the portfolio), RBSA is simply the only choice. RBSA can also be used to calculate information ratios, which are style-adjusted return-to-risk measures. Some researchers are finding persistence in information ratios, so they should be used as a first cut for identifying skill. Similarly, when it is necessary to detect style drift or to fully understand the portfolio's actual holdings, HBSA is the only choice. Holdings are also required for performance attribution analysis that is focused on differentiating skill from luck and style—an important distinction. This level of analysis must use holdings because performance must be decomposed into stock selection and sector allocation. Returns cannot make this distinction.

Custom benchmarks developed through either RBSA or HBSA solve the GIGO problem, but statisticians estimate that it takes decades to develop confidence in a manager's success at beating the benchmark—even one that is customized. This is because when custom benchmarks are used, the hypothesis test "Performance is good" is conducted across time. An alternative is to perform this test in the cross-section of other active managers, which is the role of peer-group comparisons. We'll examine this alternative as it is integrated into performance attribution, discussed in the next section.

PERFORMANCE ATTRIBUTION

There has been an evolution in performance attribution. Much of the attribution analyses that had been used until recently were developed back in the 1980s, when we were only beginning to understand that there was more to life than MPT and had moved on to APT. We knew back then that characteristics like capitalization, price/earnings ratio, and dividend yield mattered, but we hadn't figured out how to best integrate these factors into attribution analysis. Consequently, we wrote "slicers and dicers" that segmented the portfolio and the benchmark by whatever characteristic we liked. Want to see how the segment of your portfolio with high P/Es fared against the comparable segment of stocks in the S&P500? No problem— just draw the P/E line wherever you want, and *voilà*. The problems with these old approaches are standardization and benchmark inflexibility. If you draw the P/E line at 15 and I draw it at 20, we'll each get different insights. Also, as described above, we'd like to use a custom style blend as the benchmark, but we can't do so with the 1980s technology because it doesn't provide the ability to customize the benchmark as a blend of indexes. So, with the old technology we can peel the apple like an orange or slice the orange like an apple, but all we've got to show for it is fruit salad.

By contrast, contemporary technologies encourage the use of custom style-blended benchmarks, and standardize style definitions so there is comparability across managers. In this way, a manager's stock selection and sector allocation skills are not confused with his style. Exhibit 11.2 summarizes this evolution.

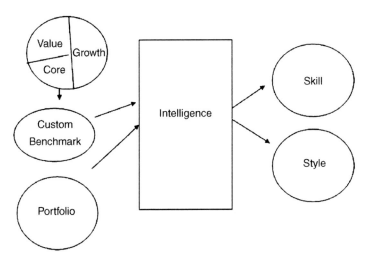

EXHIBIT 11.2 Today's Craft

In the search for skill, we look for persistence in the reason(s) for good performance, and for confirmation of the people, process, and philosophy. Exhibit 11.3 shows a real-life manager who has consistently added value through stock selection, although the amount of value added has slowed somewhat in the recent past. This particular manager is a bottom-up stock picker, and the attribution analysis confirms his skill in this endeavor. Sector Allocation has also added some value, which is consistent with bottom-up stock picking. Only Trading Activity has had a modest negative effect on

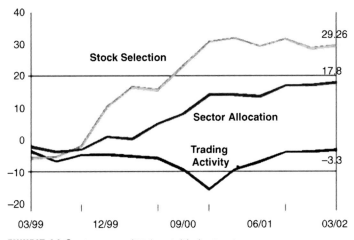

EXHIBIT 11.3 Sources of Value Added—Persistence

performance. Trading Activity measures the intraperiod effects on performance of transactions executed during the period. If this manager were looking for ways to improve performance, a place to start would be the trading desk.

These relatively new tools give the professional evaluator insights needed to determine whether good performance is likely to continue into the future. To rely on this analysis we need to be confident that the benchmark is correct. This is achieved by careful examination of the style profile of the manager, as well as the period-by-period attributions against a custom style profile. Let's take a closer look at these style attribution details.

Exhibit 11.4 shows a portfolio's composition and performance broken out by style. There are two scales on this graph. The scale on the left is for return and applies to the dots and floating bars, and the scale on the right is for allocation and applies to the shaded area and line on the bottom of the exhibit.

Let's start with allocations. The shaded area shows the portfolio's allocations to styles, and the line shows the custom benchmark's allocations. In this case, we see that a style bet has been made in overweighting large-value companies while underweighting mid- and small-size companies. The floating bars in the exhibit tell us that this bet paid off because large value was in favor. The opportunities in this style, while narrow, tended to exceed the opportunities in other styles for this period. Then, looking at the dots in the exhibit, we see how well or poorly this portfolio performed relative to the opportunities in each style. Note that performance in large companies was near or below median, while performance in mid- and small-size companies tends to be above median, although the small company results should be ignored because the allocations are negligible. This manager did a better job of selecting smaller companies. We can run this analysis for any

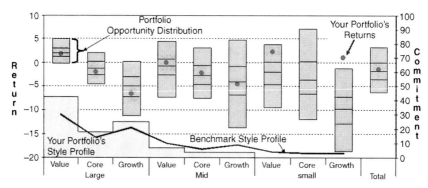

EXHIBIT 11.4 Style Attribution

time period we choose, and examine the details by style and by individual stock. The longer the time period of the analyses, the more meaningful the results.

The opportunity sets shown in the exhibit are special peer groups. Traditional peer groups come with a boatload of biases that render them totally useless. These include classification, composition, and survivorship biases as described in the following:

- *Classification* bias results from the practice of forcing every manager into a prespecified pigeonhole, such as growth or value. It is now commonly understood that most managers employ a blend of styles, so that pigeonhole classifications misrepresent the manager's actual style as well as those employed by peers. Classification bias is the reason that a style index ranks well, outperforming the majority of managers in an associated style peer group, *when that style is in favor.* Conversely, the majority of managers in an out-of-favor style tend to outperform an associated index. Until recently it was believed that skillful managers excelled when their style was out of favor. However, research has shown that this phenomenon is a direct result of the fact that many managers in a given style peer group are not "style pure," and it is this impurity, or classification bias, that leads to success or failure versus the index. See Hanachi (2000) and Surz (2006) for more details. Exhibit 11.5 demonstrates the effect of

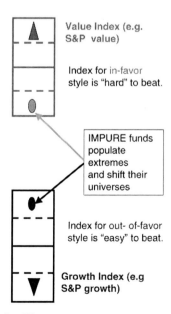

EXHIBIT 11.5 Classification Bias

classification bias. The scatter charts in this exhibit use RBSA to locate members of the Morningstar peer group in style space. As you can see, the tendency is for the funds to be somewhat similar, but significant compromises have been made.

Classification bias is a boon to client relations personnel because there is always an easy target to beat. When your style is out of favor, you beat the index; when it's in favor, you beat the median.

- *Composition* bias results from the fact that each peer group provider has its own collection of fund data. This bias is particularly pronounced when a provider's database contains concentrations of certain fund types, such as bank commingled funds, and when it contains only a few funds, creating a small sample size. For example, international managers and socially responsible managers cannot be properly evaluated using peer groups because there are no databases of adequate size. Composition bias is the reason why managers frequently rank well in one peer group, but simultaneously rank poorly against a similar group of another provider, as documented by Eley (2004). Don't like your ranking? Pick another peer group provider. It is frequently the case that a manager's performance result is judged to be both a success and a failure because the performance ranks differently in different peer groups for the same mandate, such as large-cap value.

- *Survivorship* bias is the best understood and most documented problem with peer groups. Survivor bias causes performance results to be overstated because defunct accounts, some of which may have underperformed, are no longer in the database. For example, an unsuccessful management product that was terminated in the past is excluded from current peer groups. This removal of losers results in an overstatement of past performance. A related bias is called *backfill bias*, which results from managers withholding their performance data for new funds from peer group databases until an incubator period produces good performance. Both survivor and backfill biases raise the bar. A simple illustration of the way survivor bias skews results is provided by the "marathon analogy," which asks: If only 100 runners in a 1,000-contestant marathon actually finish, is the 100th runner last? Or in the top 10 percent?

But we can use the notion of a peer group to solve the waiting-time problem mentioned above with custom benchmarks. Namely, we need to wait decades for regression analyses against custom benchmarks to produce statistically significant results. This is because we are testing the hypothesis "Performance is good" across time. (The statistician would say that we are rejecting the hypothesis that performance is mediocre, or near average.)

To solve this waiting problem, we structure the test in the cross-section of all possible portfolios, or at least a reasonably good sample of all possible portfolios, that could have been held when selecting stocks in the benchmark. It's classical statistics using Monte Carlo simulations. The hypothesis is tested by comparing the actual performance outcome to all of the possible outcomes, so if the observed return exceeds 90 percent of the possible returns, we say the result is a statistically significant success at the 90 percent confidence level. The provider of such simulation technologies has some choices to make. The simulations can be parametric, that is, tied to a specific form of probability distribution, or nonparametric. I advocate nonparametric approaches, especially when it comes to hedge funds. Another consideration is trading. Academics have performed portfolio simulations in the past, and always use buy-and-hold returns over cumulative time periods. This is not real-world. A solid simulation approach should incorporate portfolio trading through time.

When the evaluator is confident that style attribution is using an accurate style benchmark, this attribution can be extended to sector and country attribution, which can be used for analyst and manager compensation, in addition to taking away all of the old hiding places. Let's focus on the positive application of manager compensation.

ATTRIBUTION FOR ANALYST AND MANAGER INCENTIVE COMPENSATION

A fair incentive formula should incorporate the following elements:

1. *Responsibility:* What part of the overall investment process does this employee influence?
2. *Expectation:* Some measure of the employee's performance must be agreed on, and a barometer of what is expected must be established.
3. *Impact:* The significance of the employee's contribution, beyond expectations, should be specified as an independent variable in the bonus formula. "If you add x, you can expect a bonus of y."

Current compensation schemes use indexes and/or peer groups to address these three requirements, but there is now science that combines the better characteristics of benchmarks with those of peer groups to create a superior new compensation formula. Monte Carlo simulations serve as reference points for determining not only the success or failure of the professional, but also the significance of this success or failure. Here are the details.

Responsibility for a research analyst is the list of companies from which recommendations can be made—the eligible list. Ideally, neutral weights are assigned to the list to create a normal portfolio for the analyst. Responsibility for a portfolio manager is the rollup of analyst responsibilities, weighted by neutral allocations to each analyst's economic sector. In other words, custom benchmarks are created for each analyst and aggregated to create a custom manager benchmark. An alternative approach is to begin with a custom benchmark for the manager and to disaggregate it into economic sectors, like utilities and technology. The returns on these custom benchmarks represent expectations that need to be exceeded to earn a bonus. It's extremely important that these benchmarks are customized, or at least that the benefits of customization have been considered. Processes for establishing custom benchmarks are presented above.

The measure of actual performance for a portfolio manager is straightforward: It's the return on the total portfolio. Analyst results can be tracked in two ways: as the actual return on the analyst's economic sector, and as a paper portfolio return representing the analyst's recommendations. The difference between these two portfolios is, of course, a reflection of the analyst's ability to sell recommendations to the manager.

At this point, we have sufficient data to calculate attribution measures for both managers and analysts, conducted at the security level (i.e., holdings-based attribution analysis). As a result, we know how much each professional has succeeded and why. We're now ready to determine impact, or the significance of success. Current common practice is to set the same threshold for everyone, like 2 percent above the benchmark. This is neither fair nor realistic. Two percent in some environments may be extremely easy or hard, plus some economic sectors are more volatile than others, so 2 percent is easier for some analysts than others. What we really need is some sense of the opportunities for each professional, a custom peer group for each. This is a great concept, but one that cannot be implemented in practice. Peer groups cannot work despite frequent attempts to make them work.

Enter Monte Carlo simulations. Virtual peer groups are created from each custom benchmark by creating a reasonable representation of all possible portfolios that the professional might have held. This requires the specification of portfolio construction rules, like industry and security constraints, and the number of stocks. Impact is then determined as the ranking within this virtual peer group. This is fair because the professional's actual decisions are compared to all of the decisions that might have been made instead: the cost or benefit of untaken paths. Value added is placed into perspective as its statistical significance within this framework. The ranking in a Monte Carlo opportunity set is the statistical distance of actual performance away from expectation.

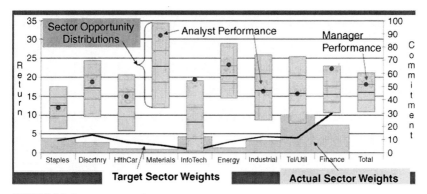

EXHIBIT 11.6 Example of a New Compensation Approach

An example will help to clarify this new approach. Exhibit 11.6 shows a one-year attribution for an investment product with nine sector analysts. In the far-right bar, the portfolio manager is ranked against a total custom opportunity set. The line running along the bottom of the exhibit is the benchmark, or neutral, allocation to each sector, and the shaded area is the actual average allocation. We can see sector-by-sector where this manager has over- and underweighted sectors, as well as the ranking of each sector's performance. These sector rankings belong primarily to the responsible analysts, and, as suggested above, the analysts' paper portfolios could also be located in this framework. In this example, we have started with a total custom benchmark and disaggregated it into sectors. But you could just as easily take the opposite approach of aggregating custom sector benchmarks.

Here's how to read the exhibit. The Materials analyst has delivered a 31 percent return, dwarfing the InfoTech return of 19 percent and Finance return of 22 percent. But the virtual peer group rankings of the InfoTech and Finance analysts are better than that of the Materials analyst, and the allocations to InfoTech and Finance are higher than that to Materials. The Energy analyst performed in the top quartile, even though performance was only 2 percent above benchmark. The performance of the remaining five analysts is in line with expectations.

Let's develop a sample bonus formula to see how each professional would be compensated. Using the convention that the top of the distribution is a rank of 100, a bonus could be specified as 1 percent of additional pay for each 1 percent that the ranking is above 55 percent. Exhibit 11.7 shows how everyone would be compensated on this basis, or at least where the bonus discussions would start.

EXHIBIT 11.7 Sample Bonus Formula Using the New Approach

Consumer Discretionary Analyst	2%
Healthcare Analyst	15
Materials Analyst	35
Information Technology Analyst	45
Energy Analyst	20
Financial Analyst	40
All Other Analysts	None
Portfolio Manager(s)	20

This new virtual peer group approach is fair, accurate, timely, objective, and easy. It's fair because compensation is tied to the significance of achievement, instead of relying on some arbitrary thresholds. It's accurate if good custom benchmarks are employed, which I recommend. It's timely because simulations can be run any time during the year on demand. It's objective because the rules are straightforward—a 1 percent improvement in ranking earns an x percent bonus. And it's easy to understand and monitor.

CONCLUSION

The search for investment manager talent puts a lot of emphasis on recent past performance. Unfortunately, in evaluating past performance, style is routinely confused with skill. The retirement industry is particularly notable for making this mistake as a group. Perhaps it's because the test of fiduciary prudence rests partially with what other fiduciaries have done.

Solid performance attribution is very careful about getting the benchmark right, so we avoid the GIGO problem. It also drills down into style, sector, and country details so there is no place for the manager to hide. Some investment management marketing and relationship personnel benefit from the current obfuscation. They are among the "others" in the quote at the beginning of this article who are served by misunderstanding. These folks are some of the best *spinmeisters* in the world, and are well-compensated for their talents. Like the affably charismatic lawyers on the TV show, *Boston Legal*, good spinmeisters always win, even when they should not. But we can stop the confusion and manipulation, and replace it with accuracy and fairness. "Live and let live" is a nice mantra, but not if it betrays client trust or breaches fiduciary duty. Fiduciaries have the duties of both prudence and care. Prudence argues for common practice, but care trumps prudence and requires best practice.

REFERENCES

Eley, Randall R. 2004. Database dysfunction. *Pensions & Investments*, September 6, p. 12.

Hanachi, Shervin. 2000. Can the average U.S. equity fund beat the benchmarks? *Journal of Investing*, Summer.

Picerno, James. 2003. In the quest to identify investment skill, Ron Surz claims he has the better mousetrap. *Bloomberg Wealth Manager*, June, pp. 80–82.

Picerno, James. 2006. A style all his own. *Wealth Manager*, September, pp. 64–66.

Sharpe, William F. 1988. Determining a fund's effective asset mix. *Investment Management Review*, December, pp. 59–69.

Surz, Ronald J. 2006. A fresh look at investment performance evaluation: Unifying best practices to improve timeliness and accuracy. *Journal of Portfolio Management*, Summer, pp. 54–65.

CHAPTER 12

The Academic Challenge

An Interview with Professor Stephen Brown on Developments in Modern Finance

Harry Liem
MERCER in Sydney

Some great questions of financial theory remain with us. A respected academic candidly answers some well-posed questions about "book-smart" and "street-smart." The answers are relevant and pertinent, regardless of an occasional systemic disorder.

> *Prediction is very difficult, especially if it's about the future.*
> —Niels Bohr (1885–1962)

Stephen J. Brown is David S. Loeb Professor of Finance at the Leonard N. Stern School of Business, New York University, and Professor of Melbourne Business School of the University of Melbourne. He was one of the founding editors of the *Review of Financial Studies*.

Stephen, many thanks for this interview. First, can you introduce our readers to what you consider to be the most interesting and fertile topics of discussion in modern finance today?

Most of the more interesting and fertile topics of discussion today have to do with the role of institutions within markets.

Risk research attracts attention. The simple-minded covariance-based definitions of risk have been effectively challenged by the development in

---

Originally published as "What's New in Modern Finance?" a chapter in *2020 Vision: Investment Wisdom for Tomorrow*, by Harry Liem of Mercer, Australia. Published with permission of the author. All rights reserved.

the recent past of the hedge fund industry. This has spotlighted the importance of more nuanced measures of downside risk, tail risk and operational risk, which is my current area of interest and research. The same set of concerns has raised issues both in terms of the importance of systemic risk, and also in terms of corporate governance. This has reinvigorated interest and research on these topics.

Behavioral finance. Some of the original great promise of the behavioral view of the markets has been tempered somewhat by what I would term *the failure to generate a unified paradigm of asset pricing* through this analysis. Some of the emphasis in this literature has shifted away from the macro level question of how asset prices are determined to a more micro level understanding of the behavior of corporate managers in setting corporate financial policy and in terms of the behavior of traders in real-time markets.

Some of the great questions of financial theory remain with us, in particular the way in which expected returns relates to the measures of risk. A celebrated paper by Lettau and Ludvigson[1] shows that the apparent disconnect between asset prices and the real economy, one of the principal arguments posited for the behavioral view of the markets, can be ascribed to the failure to control for the dynamic changes that have occurred between the markets over the last 50 years. Controlling for these factors does indeed explain the cross-sectional dispersion of expected returns relative to risk.

Which discussions are most likely to affect the way that institutional investors behave in the near future?

At least in the United States, *the first concern of most investment fiduciaries is risk management.* Paradoxically it is this concern that is leading many fiduciaries to hedge funds, not in the naive belief that hedge funds are in fact hedged, but rather as a tool for effective diversification.

However, the failure of Amaranth Advisors last year was a wake-up call for many investors. The lack of transparency of most hedge funds is a source of considerable operational risk, and there is a considerable interest in devising more sophisticated measures of risk. Hedge funds are also an expensive way to obtain effective diversification, and this has led recently to the growth of beta funds, passively managed vehicles that mimic the risk characteristics of hedge funds but without the high cost structures and operational risk features of typical hedge funds.

Do you want to comment on any interesting trends you see in the quantitative research field?[2]

This is very much a matter of taste. I am intrigued by what I am reading about the behavior of individual investors from some of the large-scale databases in the United States and in Sweden, particularly in the work of Zoran Ivkovic and others.[3] Contrary to the assumptions and predictions of modern portfolio theory, individual investors do not hold well-diversified portfolios and tend to invest in only the familiar. While of course consistent with the behavioral hypothesis, this does tend to challenge the perceived wisdom on return for risk trade-offs, and has significant implications that might explain why there appears to be such a pronounced home bias in international investing.

Meanwhile the increased attention to institutions and markets in United States–based research is challenging some of the cherished examples cited in the Behavioral literature. The discount at which closed-end funds trade relative to the value of assets under management is often presented as an unexplained anomaly or rather as evidence for a behavioral view of the markets. Stephen Ross at MIT argues that this and many other so-called anomalies arise out of an incomplete understanding of the institutional features and tax regimes much overlooked by U.S.-based researchers. His recent book is a must-read.[4]

Many former academics have left the ivory tower to pursue active careers in fund management; for example, Josef Lakonishok (LSV), Richard Roh (Roll and Ross Asset Management), Jim Simons (Renaissance) and even Eugene Fama himself. You yourself are at present associated with MIR. What's your view on this:

(a) In terms of what it implies for the EMH?
(b) Does book-smart win over street-smart?
(c) Does exposure to day-to-day funds management issues assist an academic in developing insights and ideas for further research?

(a) What it implies for EMH:

Many in funds management see the role of academics as seekers after regularities in the market, regularities that are profitable. Given the faith that many academics seem to have in the efficient markets hypothesis, there is perceived to be some tension here between what they seem to believe in and what they aspire to do. Hence there is some skepticism of their role, a skepticism that is reflected in Roger Lowenstein's aptly titled book on the collapse of Long Term Capital Management, *When Genius Failed*. What can possibly be the role of these pointy-headed folks in the real work of funds management?

I am convinced that this characterization of the role of academics is as much a straw man as is the representation of the efficient markets hypothesis they are said to believe in.

The academic perspective gives a useful reality check on exuberance, a hard-edged understanding of the trade-off of return for risk, and most of all, an important measure of humility both in terms of the history of the markets and the powerlessness of any individual to correct or stop general market movements. For me, this is what the EMH means. It is not a straw man view that it is impossible to make money trading. Rather, it is a dose of healthy skepticism. When you see a security that is trading considerably less than its intrinsic value, do you *buy* or ask *why?*

(b) Does book-smart win over street-smart?

I am not of the view that there is a contest between "book-smart" and "street-smart." There is room for both. A qualitative seat-of-the-pants approach may lead to quick decisions but may lack discipline. Quantitative approaches, to use a phrase of my friend Michael Triguboff, are often blunt tools that attribute value to factors otherwise left out of the analysis. My funds management experience shows very clearly the value of a carefully mediated compromise between these approaches. And it is not a one-way street. Most of the important advances in academic research, in asset allocation, performance measurement and derivative pricing have arisen from observations of the markets and the curiosity and the need to explain regularities that are otherwise hard to understand. The very term "anomaly" refers to the fact that there are things that as academics we cannot explain and need to explain, and has been a large part of the motivation for the growth and development of the behavioral finance area.

However, there is a temptation to label everything we cannot understand as "behavioral." Burton Malkiel and Richard Quandt in 1969 wrote a book[5] in which the odd behavior of option traders was discussed and the fact that they used a simple rule of thumb $d*S - b*PV(\text{exercise})$ to value options which gave valuations for out-of-the-money calls and puts that were too high and valuations for in-the-money options that were too low relative to the actuarial models of valuation, then popular among academics. This formula was described in a doctoral dissertation at the University of Chicago in 1962 by James Boness, but it reflected current practice. This was therefore an anomaly. It was not until the work of Black and Scholes published in 1971 that we came to understand the rational basis of this formula.

Indeed, I believe that the major contribution of academics has been the growth and development of financial technology, exemplified by the option pricing model, a cornerstone of all new financial claims markets. Coincidentally, these developments have been matched by computational innovations that have made these markets feasible. One unintended consequence of this technology has been to make redundant the old seat-of-the-pants trader. I discourage students from going into sales and trading as I foresee that many of the jobs in the field are being taken by cyber-traders, of the kind pioneered by Jim Signons at Renaissance Technologies, traders who don't sleep, who don't have temper tantrums and who never confuse buy and sell orders.

Beyond these very specific examples, academics can play a very important role in funds management by providing a fresh and sometimes

completely different perspective. Academics are not driven by the imperative of devising ever new trading rules and searching out market opportunities. They are thus in a position to provide a reality check to fund managers
who have data mined and backtested just one time too many.

(c) Does exposure to day-to-day funds management issues assist academic research?

In a real sense, I have been associated with fund management since I left
graduate school in 1976, first at AT&T's Pension Fund, then at Yamaichi
Securities in Tokyo, and now at MIR.

Fund management can provide the academic with significant benefits by
assessing the practical limitations that confront the implementation of
research ideas. We had a term for this at Bell Labs. It was referred to as
"reduction to practice," a term from patent law that reflected the fashioning
of pure research and indeed the research agenda to the practical limitations
of implementation.

Every one of the Nobel Prize winners at Bell Labs had done first-rate
pure research with path-breaking practical implications. Even Arno Penzias
who discovered the echo of the Big Bang (for which he won the Nobel) was
chiefly interested in the application of this research to the particular problems of reducing interference in long-distance radiotelephony.

Dr. Penzias as President of Bell Labs came into my office once and challenged me to explain the possible benefits of my web-cited research on event
studies, the empirical analysis of information events on stock prices. How
could this research have any possible benefit to the telephone company?
I asked him whether he participated in AT&T's $35 billion superannuation
fund. Did he know that there was very little understood about the statistical
properties of measures used to assess the performance of the 108 manager
mandates? I then laid out for him the close, indeed intimate, relationship
between my academic research and matters of the greatest practical concern
for the company, questions that had motivated my research in the first
place. This was exactly what he wanted to hear.

I notice that you co-authored an article on the Dow theory back in 1998,
which concluded that the taming strategy actually yielded a positive alpha.[6]
Can you outline for our readers your view on the EMH in its various forms?

Twenty years ago or so, the tobacco industry in the United States went
on a publicity offensive arguing that because science could not attribute all
lung cancer to smoking, it was okay to light up.

In the same way many fund management companies argue today that
because the EMH does not explain all regularities in asset pricing, it is okay
to engage in simple-minded market-timing strategies. It is all a question of
degree and context. Yes, the data is indeed in conflict with the EMH in its
various flavors and degrees.

This does not mean that it is easy to make money in the markets. Sophisticated hedge funds in the city can make money from the regularities that academic research has found in the markets. People out in the country with full-time jobs outside the financial sector and lacking timely information may as well assume that the EMH is literally true.

This point is illustrated by my research on the Dow theory. Many people believe they know what the Dow theory is, but in fact it was never written down by Charles Dow. All we know about this theory is what was written by his most earnest acolyte, William Peter Hamilton. And his writings were not altogether transparent. Many people believe that the Dow theory was simply a matter of observing head and shoulders formations in simple charts. But it was never that simple. My co-authors and I used advanced neural net procedures to capture the essence of the Dow theory from the writings of Hamilton given the market conditions of the time. We were able therefore to create a Hamilton automaton that survived his death. This automaton made money from the early thirties through the fifties, but then struggled as the markets became more sophisticated and the easy money filtered away. In context it was possible to yield positive alpha through this rather mechanical timing strategy but not now, not in today's market conditions. Now of course, Hamilton and his mentor Charles Dow were very sophisticated analysts. In conducting this experiment, my co-authors were very tempted to allow the Hamilton automaton to live and to learn.

I am sure that Hamilton, were he to be living today would find a way of profiting from the time series regularities in the market. But it would not be Dow's theory. Simple-minded mechanical black-boxes that worked in the 1920s and 1930s cannot be expected to work in the much more sophisticated market conditions of today.

What's your view on behavioral finance? Does it work, and if so, is there any prospect that enough of us will be able to reprogram ourselves so that it will stop working?

In the academic literature, there is much excitement about the potential of behavioral finance to explain many apparent and otherwise inexplicable regularities in the financial markets. The great challenge of this theory is to develop a united or single theory which will coherently explain asset prices. At the moment, this body of work represents a series of ill-connected examples which severally explain certain market regularities. But as G. K. Chesterton wrote many years ago, "ten false philosophies will fit the universe."

Many of these behavioral stories, while plausible by themselves, need to be shown to work together to explain asset prices. Many of the brightest people in the U.S. are working to meet this challenge.

My good friend and mentor Stephen Ross of MIT presents a strong challenge to the behavioral literature in his recent book.[7] Just because we as academics are not able to explain a particular regularity in the markets does not make it irrational or behavioral. Perhaps we need to work just a little harder?

In the funds management area behavioral finance is a Siren call that can bring many on to the rocks. The academic literature is very convincing. It does work. But it is dangerous to try to make money from it for we must necessarily assume that the fund manager is immune from the behavioral biases that infect everyone else. It is therefore self-defeating in practice.

In Homer's epic, Odysseus understands that to listen to the Sirens is to drive his boat on to the rocks on which they sit. He therefore commanded his crew to tie him to the mast and to put wax in their ears. He was entranced by the call of the Sirens and called on his crew to steer the boat toward them. But they did not hear him and he sailed to safety. The only effective way to profit from behavioral biases is to buy on valuation differences and pre-commit not to sell on the short term, no matter how compelling the desire is to do so. Few fund managers have the courage to do this, and few fund managers can really profit from these strategies.

Have you any comments about the work by Andrew Lo on evolutionary dynamics as applied to the market place? Apart from the adaptive markets hypothesis, are there any other new frameworks being developed?

Professor Lo is a good friend and colleague, and I have great respect for his work. His adaptive markets hypothesis is undoubtedly true. I was the editor who handled his first major assault on the EMH.[8]

His view then that the EMH was captured by a rigid and somewhat simplistic random walk hypothesis he now views to be somewhat extreme, and he now espouses an evolutionary view that posits that markets evolve in a behaviorally adaptive way. However, at every step along the way behavioral biases will imply profit opportunities.

To this extent, his views are unexceptionable. It is true that there has been tremendous innovation in the capital markets. Indeed, I tend to believe that this innovation has had and will have as profound an impact on the world economy as the growth of railroads and the resulting expansion of the steel industry had in the nineteenth century. New Carnegies and Rockefellers have come to the fore, and the hedge fund industry will generate new dynasties that will last to the fifth generation. But is this innovation a cause or effect of these new profit opportunities opening up? Silicon is the new steel, and the development and spread of information technology has at least as important a role to play in this financial innovation as has the profit opportunities that this innovation has given rise to.

In terms of fundamental strategic research, which areas do you think institutional investors should focus on? For example, strategic asset allocation (beta), security selection (alpha), new beta markets (for example, alternatives), TAR, portfolio construction (the MPT, PMPT),[9] risk management, etc.

While many in the funds management business are intrigued by academic studies of anomalies, this literature troubles academics because anomalies by very definition constitute what we cannot explain. This is really at the heart of the current interest in behavioral finance, a hope that this structure will give us understanding of what is otherwise inexplicable.

There is much that we don't understand, and the job of academics is to try to give form and function to this understanding. *While much of the attention among practitioners has been on the application of these new theories to the possibility of generating excess return, a neglected area is that of risk management.* Here, the newest literature on behavioral finance tells us something very disturbing. Loss-averse trading patterns (also known as doubling down) are a characteristic of behavioral trading that can magnify potential downside risk, and may in fact be a complete explanation of recent rogue trading episodes.[10]

We do not blame the tiger for stalking its prey. But we do blame the zookeeper for leaving the cage door open. Recent academic findings suggest that there may be a rational explanation for the failures of supervision evident in the Australian Prudential Regulation Authority report and PriceWaterhouseCoopers' reports on the National Australia Bank currency desk problems of 2004, and of the findings of the 1995 Bank of England report on the Barings disaster.

One of the most profoundly important new papers circulating today is the work by Goetzmann and others on the development of manipulation-proof performance measures.[11] This is a very scary paper, a must-read by all serious institutional investors. While written in a technical language, the implications are very clear. By constructing a portfolio whose returns are concave to benchmark (for example, an LTCM-style short volatility strategy implemented by buying units of the benchmark and scribing out-of-the-money uncovered calls and puts), any money manager can generate a Sharpe ratio superior to that of the benchmark without employing any skill whatsoever. If we then allow the manager to leverage this portfolio, the alpha will be positive, limited only to the amount of margin he or she is allowed. They show that all performance measures are subject to the same problem, including more recent proposals, such as the Sortino ratio. The problem of course is that there is potentially unbounded downside risk, particularly when the strategy is leveraged sufficiently.

What is frightening is that this research suggests that modern performance metrics set up a necessary conflict between a manager's supervision and the risk management team. The supervisor rewards the trader and is in turn rewarded on the basis of these performance measures. The risk management team is concerned about both downside risk due to these strategies, and operational risk that arises when the negative consequences of these strategies are obscured. A classic and extreme case of concave portfolio strategies is the doubling-down strategies implicated in recent rogue trading episodes. I remember discussing this issue at a meeting in Melbourne in October 2003 where I met with the senior risk management teams from leading Australian financial institutions. I remember being taken to task by the representative from the National Australia Bank, who argued that they were immune from this problem because they employed sophisticated value-at-risk technology. My response, that value at risk without reference to trading behavior was part of the problem, not part of the solution (because it gave supervision a false sense of security), was widely quoted in the Australian press subsequent to the rogue trading episode at that bank that was revealed in January 2004.

U.S. foundations have attracted a lot of press coverage for their superior investment performance, much of which can be traced back to their early asset allocation decision to move into alternatives (private equity, hedge funds, etc.) and out of especially U.S. fixed income and stocks. Many of the highest profile foundations are attached to leading universities. Do you think their superior performance is due to a more innovative culture or access to thought leadership emanating from the academic world? Or does it have more to do with the fact that they are less constrained than other institutional investors such as pension funds, or something else?

The foundation we hear most of is the Yale endowment. This foundation has an appetite for risk unusual among foundations in the United States. Kingman Brewster, the President of Yale back in the late 1960s, was a visionary who saw looming what he termed an educational deficit at that institution. The income from the endowment, conservatively managed, was insufficient to propel the University into first place in the sciences. He took heed of a Ford Foundation report that in the late 1960s argued that university endowments were being managed too conservatively and proposed instead a "total return" approach to investing. As a consequence, the endorsement was invested aggressively into a growth equity portfolio that had high returns for several years and at least one negative return. At that point, the University launched a Campaign for Yale, and from the success of this endeavor, due in large part to the great wealth of its alumni population, learned that the downside risk of its high-risk strategy was of minimal consequence. Subsequently the fund—led by David Swensen, a doctoral graduate from its own Economics Department—has maintained an unusually aggressive investment strategy which in the event has paid handsome dividends for the University. *Many foundations seek to emulate Yale's investment success, but few have the foundation resources sufficient to support its considerable appetite for risk.*

Of some concern is the move by many pension funds to emulate this model and seek high returns that would offset future pension fund costs. As with the case of the Yale endowment, they have a deep pocket to support them in the case of a significant downturn. But it is not clear that this deep pocket, the U.S. Pension Benefit Guarantee Corporation, can in fact support U.S. Treasury Bill risk, let alone the risk emanating from alternative investments and exotic investment strategies.

What do you see as the hallmark of a successful long-term institutional investor?

What I have learned in my experience is that one hallmark of a successful long-term investor is the strength, and indeed courage, to temper the seat-of-the-pants approach characteristic of fundamental research with the hard edge of quantitative analysis, to learn not merely from experience but also from first principles. Such an approach involves a commitment to allocate resources to ongoing research to continually upgrade their investment process. This is a characteristic of the very best institutional managers. Such managers are able to understand in a realistic way the reason why they have succeeded in the past, and to articulate a comprehensive and realistic statement of their investment process going forward into the future. Part of this process necessarily involves a periodic review to accommodate to changing markets and circumstances. Black box analyses or "trust me" key persons are a common feature of fund management failure.

Let's talk a bit about the topic of hedge funds and the state of the industry. You recently gave a testimony before the U.S. House of Representatives Committee. Can you for our readers give a brief overview of what you presented and its implications for the wider industry?[12]

I was originally invited to testify before the U.S. Congress House Financial Services Committee hearing on Hedge Funds and Systemic Risk in the Financial markets on the basis of my recent research on hedge fund operational risk and optimal disclosure.[13] However, the terms of reference expanded and I was asked to give my views on the status of the industry and my views on systemic and operational risk. *My main points were that contrary to popular perception, there is remarkable diversity among hedge funds.* The industry is loath to disclose any information at all about their activities and as a result many believe that hedge funds are a monolithic whole. The danger is of course that the sins of the few will be visited on the many. I observed that contrary to popular perception hedge funds actually reduce systemic risk by taking on risk that would otherwise fall on the banking system. They provide valuable diversification opportunities for institutional investors, and reduce liquidity risk in the markets by buying when no-one is willing to buy and selling when no-one is willing to sell. More information would certainly help. But does this detract from the due diligence of sophisticated investors? With colleagues I studied the recent controversial and ultimately unsuccessful SEC attempt to increase hedge fund disclosure. We examined disclosures filed by many hedge funds in February 2006. I explained that leverage and ownership structures as of December 2005 suggest that lenders and hedge fund equity investors were already aware of hedge fund operational risk revealed in these forms. However, operational risk does not mediate the naive tendency of investors to chase past returns. Investors either lack this information, or regard it as immaterial. I concluded by emphasizing the importance of selective disclosure. There is no need to know proprietary trading information, and the industry (or at least their representatives, the Managed Fund Association in the U.S.) has now come to the view that by being more forthcoming they can allay public concern about systemic risk and operational risk.

What do you see as the main areas of academic research into the hedge fund industry at the moment? Is it all about the cloning and alternative beta (for example, Lo, Jaeger, Ibbotson) or is something else emerging?

I can really only talk about my own research. I think we have put a stake in the heart of the myth of market neutrality. *Zero beta is not a strategy but is rather the outcomes of an investment strategy. Playing the slot machines is a zero beta investment strategy but is not by that fact desirable or particularly low risk.* I am fascinated by the idea that we might be able for the first time to develop a quantitative measure of operational risk, a measure which seems to explain the pattern of lending to hedge funds. I am also involved in new research on the measurement and management of tail risk.

Hedge funds are often blamed for volatility such as that which occurred during the Asia currency crisis of 1997–98. You wrote a paper in 1998 in which you argued that there was no empirical evidence that hedge fund managers were responsible. We all know that many famous hedge fund managers (such as Niederhoffer, Merriwether) lost tons of money during that crisis. Have you any insight as to who was on the other side of their trades? Who was responsible for that volatility? Are there any lessons from that experience which remain valid today, or has the market already evolved too much?

My evidence seems to show that while Soros and other currency traders lost significant sums during that period it is not clear in the data which trades lost the most money. My data seems to show that many hedge funds had unwound their currency positions before the crisis. There was currency flight during that period, but at least in the Malaysian case it seems to be domestic in origin. A reading of the Australian financial press during the period of the crisis reveals that many Malaysian property trusts were heavily investing in Australian urban real estate at the very height of the crisis.[14] The most interesting aspect of this whole story was the credence given the views of Mahathir bin Mohamad, who argued in the pages of the *Wall Street Journal* (23 September 1997) that Soros was responsible for the crisis. He provided no evidence for this position, and there was in fact no evidence at all to support it. Soros was in fact famous as a currency trader for having bet and won $3.2 billion that the European Rate Mechanism would not hold in 1992. According to press accounts at the time, the counterpart to that trade was in fact a major Malaysian financial institution!

I notice that you're also on the board of the *Pacific Basin Finance Journal*. What are some of the topics, academic and other, that attract your interest in the Asian region?

I am fascinated by the institutional differences in the markets and what we may learn from them. My most important published research on this topic relates to the reported underperformance of Japanese unit trust companies.[15] We found that this underperformance could be almost entirely attributed to the onerous and idiosyncratic tax environment under which Japanese unit trust companies were forced to operate. This paper was cited in the Japanese parliamentary discussions that led to a major revision in the unit trust tax code.

As you grew up in Australia, but have since moved to the U.S., I'd like to ask you a question on how the two compare. In general, I find the extent of financial innovation and even the quality of intellectual capital available in the Australian investment community to be high, especially given the small size of our economy.[16]A lot of foreign visitors comment on how far ahead we are in terms of industry developments such as sophistication of pension scheme investment management, retail platform distributions, and preparedness to embrace new products. And yet much of the innovation occurring in the northern hemisphere as a result of the liability-driven investment trend is passing Australia by because of the different liability structure here. How would you compare Australia to the U.S. since you've worked in both?

I would definitely second the view that the quality of Australian intellectual capital is very high, and is much valued both in industry and in academic circles, particularly in the areas of finance and accounting. Australians are in high demand both on Wall Street and, as Ph.D. students, in top tier U.S. academic institutions.

There are differences in focus that have a substantial basis in the historical development of the two markets. Institutions in the United States are very focused on their fiduciary responsibilities. In the first instance, this was a result of ERISA legislation that governs private pension plans. Of recent interest is the Prudent Investor Law of New York passed in 1995 and which has spread across the United States, which reinforces the primary duties of fiduciaries, their responsibilities and potential liability. This focus has led to a major emphasis on risk management and technology to support this area.

The weight of the tax burden in Australia has focused attention here much more on tax-efficient investing, a focus many in the United States find interesting and indeed a little curious, as tax issues are a little more straightforward in the U.S. Finally the influence of accounting is far greater in Australia than in the U.S. and this has influenced academic research to a much greater extent. Finance as an academic discipline here has branched out as a sub-discipline of accounting, where in the United States it is more often perceived as a branch of economics. This also leads to a different focus in terms of research interests.

What new academic research projects are you working on at the moment?

I am working on a number of projects both in the U.S. and with Australian researchers. However, the most important research is the work I have done on optimal disclosure and hedge fund operational risk.[17] Required disclosure is a regulatory tool intended to allow market participants to assess manager risks without constraining manager actions. We use the recent controversial and ultimately unsuccessful SEC attempt to increase hedge fund disclosure to examine the value of disclosure to investors. By examining SEC mandated disclosures filed by a large number of hedge funds in February 2006, we were able to construct a measure of operational risk distinct from market risk. Leverage and ownership structures as of December 2005 suggest that lenders and hedge fund equity investors were already aware of hedge fund operational risk characteristics. However, operational risk does not seem to mediate the naive tendency of investors to chase past returns, suggesting that investors either lack this information, or they do not regard it as material. These findings suggest that any consideration of disclosure requirements should take into account the endogenous production of information within the industry and the marginal benefit of required disclosure on different investment clienteles.

How do you see the investment industry in 10 years' time?

Investment technology is changing with great speed, led by cutting-edge hedge funds like Renaissance Technologies. Cyber trading is replacing the trading desk, and humans are being taken out of the investment process at the high end. There will always be small traders, but the easy money is gone. I am convinced that without appropriate checks and balances these machines can go awry, and that there will always be an important role for human judgment. The most successful funds will be those which learn to integrate these machine-based systems with seat-of-the-pants checks and balances that can most effectively introduce common sense into the process.

Finally—investment: art, science, or skill?

As my previous response indicates, I am convinced investment is both art and science. The proper balance is what I might term *skill*.

SUMMARY

Stephen is among the most cited academics in the world. A few things sprang out of the interview:

The academic literature on behavioral finance is very convincing. Yet, the problems with implementing behavioral finance are often underestimated. As Stephen mentions, it is about believing that "everybody but me is mad."

Many of the behavioral stories, while plausible by themselves, need to be shown to work together to explain asset prices. Many of the brightest people in the U.S. are working to meet this challenge.

Stephen took great care to explain the increased research focus on risk management, and especially the work by Goetzmann et al. (2004) on Portfolio performance manipulation. He made clear why oft-used measures such as Sharpe or Sortino may be deemed insufficient to model the derivatives nowadays used in (hedge) funds. Exhibit 12.1 is one of the diagrams he drew for us during the interview.

A traditional portfolio will fluctuate with a 1:1 relationship with the market (as represented by the dotted line, with a 45-degree angle). However, by passively adding derivatives (in this case, selling uncovered calls

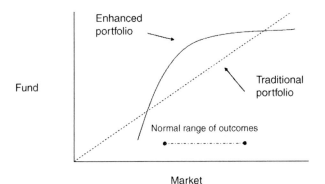

EXHIBIT 12.1 Impact of Selling Options on Sharpe Ratios

and puts) we can see that for a range of market outcomes (the "normal" range) the portfolio returns are enhanced, at the expense of tail risk. Hence we have a concave outcome. It is clear that the enhanced portfolio has a Sharpe ratio superior to the normal fund under the range of normal outcomes. The alpha can in fact be leveraged up, so in that sense, there is unlimited alpha. Stephen emphasizes that this is exactly the way many hedge funds operate; by using leverage and assuming tail risk which is not captured in the traditional ratios, they deliver superior Sharpe ratios.[18]

■ Similar *portfolio insurance* can be deemed to have lower Sharpe ratios under normal circumstances, as we're now taking on the convex diagram, or the opposite side of the trade, whereby we cover off tail risk. This is in contrast to popular thinking whereby portfolio insurance is deemed useful to help improve short-term performance (Exhibit 12.2).

■ Academics play a very important role in the investment management industry, as they provide fresh and sometimes completely different perspectives. As Stephen mentions, beware of the people who can successfully combine book-smart and street-smart, as the new breed of cyber traders who don't sleep, don't have tantrums, and never confuse buy and sell orders. Investment technology is changing with great speed, and cyber trading is replacing the trading desk. Humans are being taken out of the investment process at the high end. There will always be small traders, but the easy money is gone.

■ There will always be an important role for human judgment. The most successful funds will be those which learn to integrate these machine-based systems with seat-of-the-pants checks and balances that can most effectively introduce common sense into the process.

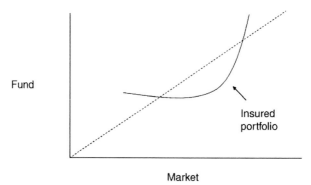

EXHIBIT 12.2 Impact of Buying Portfolio Insurance on Sharpe Ratios

NOTES

1. Martin Lettau and Sydney Ludvigson, "Resurrecting the [C]CAPM: A Cross-Sectional Test When Risk Premia Are Time-Varying," *Journal of Political Economy* 109(2001):1238–1287.
2. As noted above, Stephen also serves as Managing Editor of the *Journal of Financial and Quantitative Analysis*.
3. While this emerging literature is very large, the paper of S. Ivkovich, C. Sialm, and S. J. Weisbenner, "Portfolio Concentration and the Performance of Individual Investors," AFA 2006 Boston Meetings (available at SSRN: http://ssrn.com/abstract=568156), forthcoming in the *JFQA*, is a very good example.
4. S. Ross, *Neoclassical Finance* (Princeton: Princeton University Press, 2004).
5. *Strategies and Rational Decisions in the Securities Options Market* (Cambridge, MIT Press, 1969).
6. Alfred Cowles' (1933) test of the Dow theory apparently provided strong evidence against the ability of Wall Street's most famous chartist to forecast the stock market. In Stephen's paper, he reviewed Cowles' evidence and found that it supports the contrary conclusion—that the Dow theory, as applied by its major practitioner, William Peter Hamilton, over the period of 1902 to 1929, yielded positive risk-adjusted returns. A reanalysis of the Hamilton editorials suggests that his timing strategies yield high Sharpe ratios and positive alphas.
7. S. Ross, *Neoclassical Finance* (Princeton: Princeton University Press, 2004).
8. A. Lo, and A. C. Mackinlay, "Stock Market Prices Do Not Follow Random Walks: Evidence from a Simple Specification Test." *Review of Financial Studies* 1(1988):41–66.
9. Interestingly enough, Markowitz himself at some stage suggested that a model based on the semi-variance might be preferable. Recent advances in portfolio and financial theory, coupled with today's computing power, have led to a number of expanded risk/return paradigms also known as postmodern portfolio theory (PMPT), focusing on the downside risk using semivariance and Sortino. Thus, MPT becomes a (symmetrical) special case of PMPT; see Rom and Ferguson (1993). Note that this proposed framework does not have any relationship with the PMPT alternative introduced by Ray Dalio earlier in our book, which diversifies among risk-adjusted betas (although, coincidentally, the two theories bear the same name).
10. Doubling down refers to the behavior of doubling the bet size when on a losing streak, rather than taking the more prudent approach of cutting losses.
11. W. N. Goetzmann, J. E. Ingersoll Jr., M. I. Spiegel, and I. Welch, "Portfolio Performance Manipulation and Manipulation-Proof Performance Measures," November 2004, Yale ICF Working Paper No. 02-08. (Available at SSRN: http://ssrn.com/abstract=302815 or DOI: 10.2139/ssrn.302815.)
12. "Hedge Funds and Systemic Risk in the Financial Markets," hearing held on March 13, 2007.
13. S. J. Brown, W. N. Goetzmann, B. Liang, and C. Schwarz, "Optimal Disclosure and Operational Risk: Evidence from Hedge Fund Registration," January 7,

2007, Yale ICF Working Paper No. 06-15. (Available at SSRN: http//ssrn.com/abstract=918461.)

14. S. Brown, "Hedge Funds: Omniscient or Just Plain Wrong," *Pacific-Basin Finance Journal* 9(2001):301–311.

15. S. Brown, with W. Goetzmann, T. Hiraki, T. Otsuki, and N. Shiraihi, "The Japanese Open End Fund Puzzle," *Journal of Business* 74(2001):59–77.

16. This could potentially reflect the number of immigrants, as there's lots of technology transfer and entrepreneurs. For example, Australia is by some considered the hedge fund capital of Asia, in terms of assets managed, beating even centers such as Hong Kong, London, and New York. Australia has also won a large number of AsiaHedge awards.

17. S. J. Brown, W. N. Goetzmann, B. Liang, and C. Schwarz, "Optimal Disclosure and Operational Risk: Evidence from Hedge Fund Registration," January 7, 2007, Yale ICF Working Paper No. 06-15.

18. The fact that they are deemed "market neutral" does not impress him. He mentions one case he remembers where the client invested in a market-neutral fund, the market didn't move anything, and yet the client lost everything. In the strict sense of the word, the fund was indeed "market neutral." As Stephen mentions, it could have made a one-way bet on the winner of the Superbowl as a legitimate neutral action.

REFERENCES

Brown, SJ, Goetzmann, WN, and B. Liang, 2004, "Fees on Fees in Funds of Funds," Yale ICF Working Paper No. 02–33

Lo, AW, 2004, "The Adaptive Markets Hypothesis: Market Efficiency from an Evolutionary Perspective." *Journal of Portfolio Management*, 30, 15–29.

Rom, BM, and K. Ferguson, 1993, "Post-modern Portfolio Theory Comes of Age," *Journal of Investing* (Winter 1993).

CHAPTER 13

The Elusiveness of Investment Skill

Robert A. Jaeger, PhD
Senior Market Strategist, BNY Mellon Asset Management

The author of this chapter turns from commenting on fads and fashions to reflecting on investment skill. It is elusive, but not illusionary. He argues that skill is real precisely because it is elusive. "The barriers to entry in the hedge fund business are seductively low; the barriers to success are formidably high."

The investment management business is all about skill, but skill is elusive. Indeed, some have suggested that skill is not just elusive but illusory: there is no such thing as skill, or no reliable way of identifying it. This suggestion is a key component of the efficient market view of the world (EMV), which has posed a major challenge to active investment management.

The EMV no longer dominates academic finance. We now have a host of alternative theories, such as behavioral finance, the adaptive market hypothesis, complex adaptive systems, chaos theory, catastrophe theory, and fractal geometry. Thus it may seem that the EMV no longer poses a threat to active investment management.

Not so. The EMV is a combination of insights and myths. The insights do present a challenge to active management, but that challenge can be met. However, meeting that challenge forces us to think more clearly about what skill really is. If you have the wrong ideas about skill, the insights of the EMV will force you to conclude that it doesn't exist.

Previously published in the *Journal of Wealth Management*, Fall 2008, by Institutional Investor Inc. Reprinted with permission. All rights reserved.

This chapter is organized into eight sections. Section 1 makes some preliminary points about skill: it is rare, hard to quantify, and takes many forms. Section 2 addresses the main insights of the EMV: There Are No Free Lunches (no market inefficiencies) and Nobody Knows Anything (markets are unpredictable). These insights do not rule out skill: they tell us what skill is *not*. Section 3 separates the "no free lunch" insight from the myth that investors are totally rational. Similarly, Sections 4 and 5 separate the "nobody knows anything" insight from the myth that markets follow a random walk. Section 6 separates skill from "investment systems," while Sections 7 and 8 explore the loose linkage between skill and performance. The EMV does not rule out skill: it rules out the myth that skill can be detected from historical performance alone and is a reliable predictor of future success.

SCARCITY AND VARIETY

Before confronting the EMV head on, let's note three preliminary points about skill. The first and most obvious point is that skill is rare. There are lots of competent money managers, but competence is not the same as the kind of talent that gives you a competitive edge. Furthermore, skill is rare throughout the investment world. Hedge fund enthusiasts talk about a brain drain in which the most talented managers have left the long-only world to seek the greater freedom (and higher fees) available in the hedge fund world. However, genuine skill is as rare in the hedge fund world as it is elsewhere in the investment business. Hedge fund managers operate with fewer investment constraints than long-only managers. This is a great advantage for the skilled manager, but gives the less skilled manager more ways of getting into trouble. The transition from long-only investing to hedge fund investing is not easy. Many hedge fund managers are not as talented as they claim to be, and there are many talented long-only managers who have their own reasons for not joining the rush into hedge funds. The barriers to entry in the hedge fund business are seductively low; the barriers to success are formidably high.

The second point is that we don't know exactly how rare skill is, since there are no generally agreed-upon criteria for determining whether a manager is skilled. There are no "reliable techniques" for separating the skilled from the unskilled. It's easy to count the number of managers who meet specified performance criteria, but, as we shall see in more detail later on, the linkage between skill and performance is loose. This means, by the way, that skill is not the same thing as alpha, since alpha can be measured but skill cannot. Once you've calculated the alpha from a series of historical returns, the question is: Does this alpha reflect real skill, or did the manager just happen to be in the right place at the right time? Calculating the t-statistic of the alpha does not conclusively settle the question: smart and well-informed people may disagree about the level of skill that lies behind a good record. Pronouncing a manager to be skilled is a value judgment, like pronouncing a stock to be attractively priced. So the ability to identify skill is itself a form of investment skill. When you're hunting for skilled investors, it takes one to know one.

The third point is that skill is multi-faceted: it is not some monolithic quality that takes the same form in every case. For example, skill involves a combination of "book smarts," "street smarts," and "emotional intelligence," but the proportions vary considerably from manager to manager. And there are wide variations in risk attitudes: some skilled managers are very risk averse, quick to exit losing positions, while others are more loss-tolerant, and may even double down on losing positions. The variations of skill are endless. Buffett's skill is utterly different from George Soros', just as Picasso's genius is utterly different from Rembrandt's.

THE TWO MAIN INSIGHTS

The EMV's critique of active management is based on two insights: *There Are No Free Lunches* and *Nobody Knows Anything*. The first point reminds us that return requires risk: there are no opportunities for risk-free arbitrage, no $100 bills sitting on the sidewalk waiting to be picked up. In the language of the EMV, there are no "market inefficiencies," precisely because so many people are looking for them. The EMV is based on a giant negative feedback loop, or a Zen riddle: we all try so hard that we are bound to fail. (Here the Zen master would insert various inscrutable remarks about the futility of all human striving.)

It is unrealistic to insist dogmatically that there are no market inefficiencies. There may be a few "pricing anomalies" lying around. However, if there are any market inefficiencies, then they are few and far between, not abundant enough to support the multi-trillion-dollar business of active investment management. In particular, the hedge fund business is not designed to exploit market inefficiencies. There are many hedge fund strategies that call themselves "arbitrage"—merger arbitrage, convertible arbitrage, fixed income arbitrage, capital structure arbitrage, and so forth—but all these strategies involve risk. This is true even in the current environment. Investor fear is creating some exceptional opportunities, but they are not risk-free. It takes skill to catch a falling knife.

The second insight, *Nobody Knows Anything*, reminds us that Wall Street is just like Hollywood. In each place, people in the business know a lot, but they don't know what they really want to know. In Hollywood, nobody can predict whether a movie will be a smash or a bomb. On Wall Street, nobody can predict stock prices or manager performance.

The academic literature tells us that the future is not a simple extrapolation of the past. But even people who make fun of the academic literature accept the fact of unpredictability. We make jokes about generals who fight the last war and people who drive by looking in the rear-view mirror. Money managers who pay little attention to the EMV will cheerfully confess, "Hey, if I could predict the future do you think I'd be working for a living?"

The two insights of the EMV tell us something about manager skill. If skill required exploiting market inefficiencies and/or predicting the future, then there would be no such thing as skill. But skill does not require inefficiencies: it requires the ability to make intelligent judgments about risk and reward. Similarly, skill does not require predicting the future: it requires the ability to form reasonable expectations and to respond intelligently when those expectations are confounded. As George Soros observed, the question is not whether you're right or wrong—it's how much you make when you're right and how much you lose when you're wrong.

INEFFICIENT MARKETS VS. MARKET INEFFICIENCIES

Although there are no market inefficiencies, the stock market is not efficient. An efficient market is a community of totally rational investors who jointly constitute a highly efficient information processing mechanism. These investors are either immune to fear and greed, or those mundane emotions are held in check by a powerful economic calculating machine. This myth is now dead, or near death. In the real world, there are bubbles and panics. A bubble is an epidemic of greed, while a panic is an epidemic of fear. Bubbles and panics aren't rare, but they don't happen every day. Greed and fear are with us every day. Greed drives the search for return, while fear drives the sensitivity to risk. Investing is all about the tradeoff between return and risk, which can sometimes get pretty abstract. The daily conflict between fear and greed is not abstract.

In addition to fear and greed, there is a long list of "investor biases" catalogued by students of behavioral finance. Indeed, the main purpose of behavioral finance is to understand the many forms of investment behavior that defy the simple EMV models of rationality and efficiency. Behavioral finance folks talk about "heuristics and biases"; David Letterman would call them "stupid investor tricks."

Flesh-and-blood investors do not behave like economic calculating machines. In that sense, the market is not efficient. Then why are there no market inefficiencies, i.e., free lunches? The answer comes from Keynes: markets can remain irrational longer than you can remain solvent. It's tempting to divide the world into "smart money" and "dumb money," with the smart money earning "alpha" from the irrational behavior of the dumb money. The problem is that the dumb money can set prices longer than the smart money can remain solvent. This is especially true if the so-called smart money is using big leverage.

The recent housing bubble offers a perfect example of this phenomenon. Lots of smart people knew that the U.S. housing market was a ticking time bomb, but bubbles almost always last longer than smart people expect. Many investors made money from the unwinding of the credit bubble, but a lot of smart people went short too early. Timing is everything.

UNPREDICTABILITY VS. RANDOM WALKS

The EMV is right to emphasize the unpredictability of markets, but wrong to confuse unpredictability with randomness. A random walk is like a sequence of coin tosses, where each toss is independent of every other toss and you can't predict the next toss from the prior 100 tosses. Random sequences are unpredictable, but not all unpredictable sequences are random: randomness is a very specific kind of unpredictability. In particular, the things that investors really care about—economic cycles and market trends—are unpredictable but not random.

The outcome of a coin toss is neither predictable in advance nor explainable in retrospect. Economic and market phenomena are different: we can explain them after the fact even though they are not predictable in advance. They are explainable because they have a structure: they are not sequences of totally independent events. The housing bubble and the recent panic are perfect examples of explanation without prediction. We can identify multiple forces that shaped the bubble and triggered the panic, but nobody could have predicted the turning point in advance.

Market trends and economic cycles reinforce themselves until they destroy themselves. In a bubble, rising prices attract more buyers, who drive prices higher. The opposite holds in a panic. A run on the bank (remember Bear Stearns?) is a classic case of a self-reinforcing trend: nobody wants to be the last to sell. Similarly, in a bubble nobody wants to be the last to buy.

Self-reinforcement takes place mainly in the early and middle stages of a trend. In the later stages the trend begins to plant the seeds of its own destruction: there aren't enough new converts available. That's why trends ultimately destroy themselves.

Trends are real, but there is no "science of trends" that enables us to predict the turning points. Naïve investors believe that, if there are trends, then there must be some way to make predictions. The EMV counters that prediction is not possible, so there are no trends: only random walks. Both sides make the same mistake: they link trends with prediction.

The unpredictability of markets has two very different sources. Consider the current anxiety about the possibility of a severe recession in the U.S. This anxiety presents two problems: we don't know how bad the economic news will get, and we don't know how much bad news is built into current prices. There are no recession futures, and even if there were recession futures the expectations reflected in that market might be different from the expectations reflected in the market at large. So we have to read market entrails in order to decipher what the market expects. Smart people will disagree about what the entrails say. We all talk confidently about what the market expects, but in many cases we don't really know what the market expects.

Ironically, the EMV underestimates the unpredictability of markets. According to the EMV, current prices reflect everything that we know about the future, so prices will move only in response to what we don't know. The market is thus a price-setting mechanism whose output, a price, is unpredictable because we don't know what the relevant inputs will be. But there is a bigger problem: even if we knew the inputs, we might not be able to predict the output. If the Fed delivers another bigger-than-expected rate cut, will that be received as good news (because the Fed is taking more bold action) or bad news (because the Fed knows how bad the situation really is)?

The non-mechanistic character of markets is most obvious on the days when markets experience wild intra-day swings. What we see then is not a homogeneous group responding instantaneously to new information, buying on the good news and selling on the bad news. What we see instead is a highly non-homogeneous group trying to figure out what the news really means. We have been spoiled by several years of unusually low market volatility, during which disagreements among investors tended to be polite and orderly. What we have now is a shouting match among investors with very different perceptions of what's going on.

UNPREDICTABILITY AND PHYSICS ENVY

The unpredictability of markets flows ultimately not from any specific financial theory but from the chronic unpredictability of human behavior. Prices reflect the combined impact of millions of investment decisions, many of which are *hard* decisions. Investors spend a good deal of their working lives poised on a knife's edge, torn between Buy and Sell. The hallmark of a tough decision is that even the person making the decision doesn't know what he'll decide. Tough decisions are thus another example of explanation without prediction: the person making the decision doesn't know what he'll decide, but after the fact he can explain why he made the decision that he did.

The literature of behavioral finance focuses on highly simplified and idealized decision-making conditions in which it's possible to predict how the experimental subject will behave. This is totally legitimate: the whole point of experimentation is to simplify. The experiments help isolate important "forces" that influence investment decisions, but that's very different from understanding the full complexity of a tough call. The same issue arises in physics: we perform experiments under tightly controlled conditions that are radically different from the messy complexities of real life.

The physical sciences look like paradigms of predictability. For example, the website of the National Aeronautics and Space Administration tells us that there will be a total eclipse of the sun on September 4, 2100. The eclipse will last 3 minutes 33 seconds; it will be visible from Africa and Antarctica but not from the U.S. Our knowledge is so detailed that this eclipse, which will happen 92 years in the future, may seem inevitable, or predetermined: given the current state of the universe, the eclipse must happen.

Not so: even when the world seems most predictable, there is unpredictability lurking beneath the surface. [G. K. Chesterton makes the point somewhat melodramatically: "Life is not an illogicality; yet it is a trap for logicians. . . . Its exactitude is obvious, but its inexactitude is hidden; its wildness lies in wait."] There is a wide range of events that might prevent the eclipse, of which some are "random" and some involve human decision making. A sample random event would be a distant supernova that might slightly alter the relative positions of the earth, moon, and sun. As an example of human decision making, imagine a bizarre science-fiction scenario in which we must delay the eclipse of 2100 in order to avoid some major cataclysm. This scenario is a souped-up version of the crisis in the movie *Armageddon*, in which an asteroid is predicted to strike the earth. When the equations of celestial mechanics predict a disaster, people do not sit back and wait for the inevitable: they do everything in their power to prevent the "inevitable" from happening.

People often joke that investing isn't rocket science. Though usually intended as a comment about the average I.Q. of the investment community, the joke also marks an apparent chasm between the hard sciences and the world of investing. The hard sciences offer order, precision, and predictability. The world of investing bristles with chaos, imprecision, and unpredictability. But real-life rocket science is surprisingly like investing, since the real-world applications of the physical sciences are filled with unpredictability. The gritty business of managing a space mission is saturated with uncertainty and risk, unlike the elegant universe presented in physics and chemistry texts.

Investing isn't rocket science, but real-world rocket science isn't the rocket science of idealized laboratory conditions.

Social scientists often suffer from physics envy: the grass looks more orderly and predictable on the other side of the fence. But this envy is based on two misconceptions. First, even in the physical sciences the predictability is not total. Second, even when there is no prediction there can still be plenty of room for interesting and powerful explanations.

NEGATIVE FEEDBACK LOOPS

To dig deeper into investment skill, let's take a closer look at two specific applications of the main EMV insights. *No Free Lunches* includes the claim that there are no "systems" for extracting incremental return from the markets. The argument here is based on a negative feedback loop: if there were such a system, then the widespread acceptance of the system would destroy the opportunities that the system is designed to exploit. *Nobody Knows Anything* includes the claim that the past performance of a money manager does not predict the future performance, which takes us back to the earlier idea of a "loose linkage" between skill and results.

Negative feedback loops are familiar in markets. If too many people try to exploit the January effect, then the January effect becomes the December effect and eventually disappears. When an undiscovered opportunity becomes an over-crowded trade, the opportunity is gone. However, this fact about markets does not rule out manager skill. First, having skill is not the same as having a "trade" or a "system." A system is a set of trading rules that can be mechanized. Skill involves talent, judgment, and the kind of flexibility and adaptability that cannot be mechanized. Second, negative feedback loops do not operate instantaneously: it takes time for a strategy to destroy itself. Early adopters can make money even if the late entrants are left holding the bag. This leaves room for manager skill as the ability to make informed judgments about where we are in the life cycle of a trade. But, since we're talking about skill, there are no rules for making these judgments.

A CLOSER LOOK AT THE COIN-TOSSING ANALOGY

As for the loose linkage between skill and results, the unpredictability of manager performance rules out the following line of thought: this manager has had superb historical performance, therefore the manager has skill, and hence the manager will do well in the future. This line of thought uses skill as the magical missing link that converts past success into future success. But there is no such missing link. Past success does not always indicate skill, and skill does not always indicate future success.

The EMV literature is filled with coin-tossing contests in which some lucky contestant throws Heads 20 times in a row. When we're looking at an unusually good investment record, how do we distinguish luck from skill? A closer look at coin tossing will help answer the question.

Coin-tossing contests always feature *fair* coins, i.e., coins whose physical constitution makes Heads and Tails equally likely. But a fair coin may produce a long run of Heads, since the outcome of a particular toss depends on a long list of factors other than the physical constitution of the coin. (For a fascinating discussion of the physics of coin tossing, see E. T. Jaynes, *Probability Theory*, especially Chapter 10, "Physics of Random Experiments.")[1] Now let's think about *unfair* coins. Let's say that a coin is *Heads-biased* if it is imbalanced in such a way that Heads is more likely than Tails. For example, imagine a sandwich construction, half metal and half Styrofoam, so the coin tends to land on the heavier side. A Heads-biased coin has an edge in producing runs of Heads, but an edge is not an ironclad link. Just as a fair coin may produce a long run of Heads, so a Heads-biased coin may produce a long run of Tails.

To determine whether a coin is Heads-biased, the best approach is not to flip the coin but to perform other tests that are focused more directly on the physical constitution of the coin. For example, we might examine the coin for signs of a suspicious sandwich construction, or stand it on edge to see if it tends to fall toward one side, or drop it in a vertical orientation to see if it tends to land on one side.

Similarly, to determine whether a manager is skilled the best approach is not to examine the performance record but to examine the manager. The performance record reflects the interaction of "manager factors" (his/her intellectual and business acumen, the strength of the team, etc.) and "market factors," just as the outcome of a particular coin toss reflects the interaction between the physical constitution of the coin and the myriad specific circumstances of the toss. The performance record helps shed light on the "manager factors," but the record is just part of the story.

HOT HANDS, SKILL, AND PERFORMANCE

In thinking about coin tosses and manager performance, it is essential to distinguish between *bias* and *independence*. A Heads-biased coin has an edge in producing Heads, but still the result of each toss is independent of the result of every other toss. Similarly, a skilled manager has an edge in producing good performance, but it may still turn out that performance in one time period is statistically independent of performance in other time periods.

This point is closely related to the phenomenon of "the hot hand." In a classic paper Gilovich, Vallone, and Tversky (the same Tversky who would have shared the 2002 Nobel Prize in Economic Science with Kahneman if he had lived) studied the hot hand phenomenon in basketball. They demonstrated that when players shoot for the basket, the result of each shot is statistically independent of the results of the preceding shots. However, as the authors emphasize, statistical independence is consistent with the fact that some players are more skilled than others, and thus have a higher probability of making the basket. Similarly, some managers are more skilled than others, and thus have a higher probability of doing well, even though sequences of returns may show various types of statistical independence. [The hot hand paper is Gilovich, T., Vallone, R., & Tversky, A. (1985): The Hot Hand in Basketball: On the Misperception of Random Sequences, *Cognitive Psychology* 17:295–314.]

Past success does not always indicate skill (maybe it was good luck), and skill does not always predict future success (since there's always room for bad luck). However, this is just the beginning of the story, not the end. The contrast between skill and luck is a hopelessly crude tool in thinking about manager performance. In analyzing historical performance, the key is to get beyond that crude tool in order to develop a more subtle understanding of how the "manager factors" interacted with the changing market environment.

A similar point applies to future performance. When you worry that a skilled manager may fail to perform in the future, it's useless to worry about "bad luck." The only useful worries are specific worries linked to the specific reasons why skilled managers often fail. Sometimes the problem is over-confidence: success breeds hubris, which breeds a higher risk profile, which breeds failure. The epitaph reads, "He was a victim of his own success." Sometimes the problem is under-confidence: the manager becomes overly concerned about defending the historical record and "chokes up," thus becoming merely average. Sometimes the problem is failure to adapt to changing market conditions. The list of potential problems is endless. A skilled manager is not a bond with "alpha coupons" attached. Having identified a skilled manager, you have to be vigilant for the various syndromes that sometimes prevent skill from generating return.

Skill is elusive, but it's not illusory. Indeed, it is real precisely because it is elusive. If your conception of investment skill is unrealistically simple, then the insights of the EMV will force you to conclude that skill does not exist. What makes skill real is the fact that it's more complicated than you might think.

NOTE

1. E.T. Jaynes, *Probability Theory*, (New York: Cambridge University Press, 2003)

The Clients' Challenges

The Client Challenge—Trustees as Leaders

Fiduciary 360

Recent events have generated a new challenge for trustees. How boards are led has emerged as an even more critical issue than it has been. The author reminds stewards of the four characteristics of a prudent procedure for discharging fiduciary duties: organize, formalize, implement, and monitor.

The principal audience for this book is the investment management professional whose current and prospective client bases are large institutions. This chapter and its associated chapters are included to provide a better understanding about the concerns and organizational dynamics of those client bases. This chapter is also intended for those clients' investment committees—the members of which must stay abreast of those intrinsic and extrinsic factors that affect how they conduct their fiduciary activities.

A QUICK REVIEW

Trustees oversee much of the global liquid wealth. Trustees manage the assets of other parties, and stand in a special relationship of confidence and legal responsibility. The majority of these trustees are investment board members who supervise pension plans—both defined benefit (DB) and defined contribution (DC) plans. Other trustees oversee the investment of endowments and foundations, many of which have assets in the billions of dollars (U.S.).

This chapter is adapted from *Prudent Practices for Investment Advisors*. Copyright 2008 by Fiduciary 360. All right reserved by Fiduciary 360.

Trustees undergo a high degree of scrutiny—complaints and/or lawsuits alleging financial committee misconduct or negligence are not uncommon.

PROCEDURAL PRUDENCE

Participants in the global capital markets must remember that investment performance is not necessarily a factor in determining whether a trustee has been malfeasant or negligent (untrustworthy). *Procedural prudence* is the legal term that has evolved to describe whether trustees conducted their oversight in an appropriate manner—that is, whether a prudent process was followed in deciding how and where the entrusted assets were to be invested. Much of the fiduciary litigation is about the omission of some prudent investment procedures, rather than the commission of some chicanery. Commonly used investment products and risk management tactics are not inherently imprudent. The manner in which decisions are made about their use determines whether the standard of procedural prudence has been met. The most aggressive and unconventional investment tactic can meet the procedural prudence standard, if conducted through a fundamentally sound process. A conservative and traditional investment tactic may be judged negligent if there is no evidence of fundamentally sound process.

SOME HISTORY

The Employee Retirement Security Income Act of 1974 (ERISA) established the legal standards for overseeing pension assets. Trustee investment decisions became subject to the regulatory oversight of the Department of Labor (DOL). The Pension Protection Act of 2006 (PPA) prescribed further standards, notably for overseeing DC plans.

After ERISA, pension trustees served under an embedded legal liability that was subject to review by a federal agency. The need for informed advice and sage counsel about procedural prudence accentuated the growth of investment consulting practices. What evolved were two areas of business activity to serve institutional investors: investment consultants and investment managers.

Investment Consultants

Fiduciary liability committed institutional investors to developing thoughtful, long-term investment strategies. Trustees needed informed advice from an objective, independent third party to guide them through the increasingly complex global capital markets and investment strategies. The practice of advising institutional investors grew from a collegial, and somewhat passive, "hand-holding" service to a deliberately focused role. The consultant actively advised on the management of the institution's investment management decisions. Specifically, the consultant was expected to:

- Assist in the development of an asset allocation strategy.
- Assist in the preparation of a written investment policy statement (IPS).
- Assist in the documentation of all investment decisions.
- Assist in the selection of investment managers who would make investment decisions consistent with the IPS.
- Assist in the control of investment expenses.
- Monitor the activities of the contracted investment managers and service vendors.
- Educate the trustees on their fiduciary responsibilities, and the fundamentals of investment management.
- Assure that there are never any conflicts of interest.

Investment Managers

The role of the investment consultant is *not to make investment decisions.* Investment managers (IMs) comprise that set of professionals who have the discretion to select specific securities and employ specific tactics within a designated strategy. Investment decisions should be ceded by the trustees to IMs under some very specific ERISA requirements:

- Investment decisions are to be made by prudent experts.
- A due diligence process must be followed in selecting an IM.
- IMs must be provided with general investment direction.
- IMs must acknowledge their co-fiduciary status in writing.
- The activities of the IMs must be monitored.

The means by which trustees monitored an IM's compliance with these requirements were generally acquired from the consultants. The investment consultant would offer training to trustees as it related to the trustees' responsibilities. The assiduous consultant would encourage and inspire the trustee to learn how to distinguish "great" investment process from "adequate" investment process.

An Emerging Condition

The changes occurring in the capital markets (along with the 2001–2002 and 2007–2008 systemic shocks) directed attention away from an emerging condition that was changing the protocol that had evolved after the enactment of ERISA.

Some institutional consultants were opting for becoming IMs. The fee-based revenues were highly attractive. Obvious concerns about conflicts of interest thus precluded them from continuing as consultants. The next generation of aspiring players in the capital markets are mostly fee-based broker-dealers or fledgling investment/hedge fund managers. Very few aspire to be consultants.

So, the number of institutional consultants has decreased. At the same time the assets entrusted to institutions increased in unprecedented amounts. The issues with respect to this situation are discussed more fully in Chapter 17 of this book, "The Marketing Challenge."

THE CHALLENGE

It is uncertain how endemic staffing problems will affect the practice of investment consulting. Some revisions to compensation practices may solve them. However, some pessimistic observers speculate that the shrinking supply of qualified people will erode the practice into insignificance. Another scenario might be the emergence of a small oligopoly of firms with an elitist, high-achiever ethos—the impact of which would be a prevailing inelasticity of fees. That might be a short-term phenomenon, but its impact on the fiduciary concerns about expenses cannot be ignored. Trustee boards might forgo the retention of consultants as part of their cost-control practices. There now is a situation where there are too few competent consultants upon whom trustees can rely.

A Culture of Initiative

If in the near future there are no consultants (or only a few high-cost consultants), trustees will have to take initiative in addressing the oversight of procedural prudence. The following is about how trustees are approaching a situation where there are scant consulting services.

Building an effective leadership team will be the overriding challenge of a board of trustees. Any analysis of fiduciary organizations that have underperformed or abrogated their oversight will reveal that key positions were held by people who were ineffective leaders.

The remainder of this chapter will describe a leadership and fiduciary development process that the Foundation for Fiduciary Studies (FFS) and the Centre for Fiduciary Excellence (CEFEX) have formed over several years of engagement with institutional investors.

This is not a generic, off-the-shelf curriculum. In the spirit of this book, what follows is not prescriptive. Rather, this is an ordering of concerns that need to be addressed by fiduciary committees/boards.

INVESTMENT MANAGERS AND THE FFS LEADERSHIP PROGRAM

The FFS leadership and fiduciary development program was devised to provide a standard of excellence in overseeing the prudent management of investable wealth. The program is structured around the four actions: Organize, Formalize, Implement, and Monitor.

1. **Organize**

    Trustees must put together an orderly, functional, and structured process to assess whether their investment managers are in conformance with recognized fiduciary and industry best practices. What follows is a checklist to aid the trustee in conducting such an assessment.

    1.1 Does the IM demonstrate an awareness of fiduciary duties and responsibilities?

    > Does the IM have a well-defined mission statement for the organization?

    > Does the IM have a business-development plan, and a defined approach to plan for and control assets under management?

    > Does the IM have suitable support structure for each type of client?

    1.2 Does the IM manage in accord with applicable laws, trust documents, and the written investment policy statement (IPS)?

    > Is there a committee to set strategy and boundary constraints on the IM's investment strategies?

    > Is there a formal portfolio review process to ensure adherence to investment policies and mandates?

    > Do the portfolio managers have adequate technical support to plan investment actions, and monitor portfolio constraints?

    > Is there a system in place to capture required mandates and any changes to mandates that may come from clients, regulators, or internal sources?

    1.3 Has the IM defined, documented, and acknowledged the roles and responsibilities of all parties?

    > Does the IM's governance board exercise authority within the context of a prescribed system of checks and balances?

    > Within the IM firm, is there effective communication between the administration and the portfolio management functions to ensure compliance?

    > Does the IM firm have backup procedures and a disaster recovery plan in place?

1.4 Is the IM firm organized in a manner that assures that no conflicts of interest exist?

> Are policies and procedures for overseeing and managing potential conflicts of interest documented?
>
> Are there senior staff members especially assigned to oversee and enforce conflict-of-interest safeguards?
>
> Do all employees annually acknowledge, in writing, the firm's ethics policies and agree to disclose any potential conflicts of interest?
>
> Is there is a policy outlining how employee and manager compensation aligns with clients' interest?
>
> Are there documented guidelines for sales and marketing practices?

1.5 Are all service agreements and contracts with the IM in writing?

> Are all agreements and contracts periodically reviewed to ensure consistency with the needs of the managed portfolios?
>
> Are all the agreements and contracts periodically reviewed by legal counsel?
>
> Are all third-party service providers competitively selected and periodically evaluated?

1.6 Are all assets managed within the jurisdiction of appropriate courts to assure protection from theft and embezzlement?

> Are all assets adequately secured through a suitable custodian, and within the purview of the relevant judicial body?
>
> Are there, if needed, underwritten surety bonds?
>
> Is there adequate insurance protection?
>
> Are the assets priced in a timely, accurate, and independent manner?

2. Formalize

Trustees must establish proper procedures in accord with accepted conduct, conventions, and regulations.

2.1 Has an investment horizon been identified?

> Is there a system in place to monitor and manage short-term client cash?
>
> Has the IM discussed with the trustees how the time horizon was determined?
>
> With respect to a DB plan, has a vetted asset/liability study been factored into the time horizon?
>
> With respect to a foundation or endowment, has receipt and disbursement of gifts been factored into the time horizon?

2.2 Has a risk level been determined?

> Has the degree of risk of each investment strategy been described, understood, and documented?
>
> Has a worst-case scenario been considered for each strategy?
>
> Does the firm's senior management regularly review the defined risk management parameters?
>
> Is there a designated risk management oversight committee that regularly reviews the efficiency of the systems for monitoring and managing investment risks?
>
> Are backup procedures and a disaster recovery plan in place?
>
> Is there an effective process for evaluating the firm's business risk so as to assure business continuity?
>
> Are validated and generally accepted tools and methodologies employed to assess portfolio risks?
>
> Are broker/dealer/vendor relationships structured in a manner that minimizes counterparty risks?

2.3 Given the stipulated investment objectives, has a minimum expected return been modeled?

> Does each of the IM's proposed strategies have a modeled return expectation?
>
> Are the modeled return assumptions for each asset class based on reasonable risk-premium assumptions?

2.4 Are the asset classes that are selected consistent with the identified risk-return parameters and the time horizon?

> Are the securities diversified to conform to the specified time horizon and risk?
>
> Is the methodology used to establish appropriate diversification effective, and is it consistently applied?

2.5 Are selected asset classes consistently implemented and monitored?

> Does the IM have the time, inclination, and knowledge to effectively implement and monitor the assets selected for the investment strategy?
>
> Are the processes and tools used effective for implementing and monitoring the assets?
>
> Does the IM demonstrate some innovation in employing products and techniques?

2.6 Does the IM have a written investment policy statement (IPS) that defines, implements, and monitors each investment strategy that it offers?

> Are each IPS's diversification and rebalancing guidelines consistent with risk/return parameters and the time horizon?

> Does each IPS define the due diligence criteria for selecting securities?
>
> Does each IPS define the monitoring criteria for the securities?
>
> Does each IPS define the procedure for controlling and accounting for investment expenses?

2.7 Where applicable, does the IPS define the appropriately structured *sustainable investment strategies*? [This is often called *socially responsible investing* (SI), or *environmental, social, and governance investing* (ESGI).]

3. Implement

Trustees must put into practical effect those established activities necessary for procedural prudence.

3.1 Is the selected investment strategy being implemented according to the required level of prudence?

> Is each investment strategy clearly designed, focused, and documented?
>
> Is each investment strategy applied consistently over time and through market cycles?
>
> Is credit (fixed income) and investment research (equities) documented and subject to review?
>
> Are trading allocation policies well-defined, fair, and reviewed on a regular basis?

3.2 Are applicable "safe harbor" provisions being followed?

3.3 Are the investment vehicles being employed appropriate?

> Are decisions about the use of separately managed and commingled accounts documented and appropriately implemented?
>
> Are decisions regarding passive and active investment strategies documented and appropriately implemented?

3.4 Is due diligence practiced in selecting service providers, including custodians?

> Does each custodian have adequate insurance?
>
> Are there appropriate procedures for selecting and monitoring money market accounts used for sweeping?
>
> Is each custodian capable of providing performance reports and tax statements?
>
> Are broker-dealer relationships closely monitored for "value-added" services?
>
> Are investment products accurately and timely accounted for?
>
> Do the trade execution systems provide timely and accurate trading?

4. Monitor

Trustees must supervise and control the implementation of those formalized activities necessary for procedural prudence.

4.1 Will the IM provide periodic reports comparing its performance against appropriate indices, peer groups, and IPS objectives?

> Is investment performance calculated and verified in compliance with Global Investment Performance Standards (GIPS)?
>
> Are clients provided with timely and appropriate communications?

4.2 Are clients informed about changes and qualifications of the IM's investment decision makers?

> Does the IM conduct periodic evaluations of the qualitative factors that affect the performance of each investment decision maker?
>
> Will the IM document and act appropriately on learning that a investment decision maker is alleged to have acted outside the IM's prescribed operating policies?
>
> Will the IM report significant organizational changes within the firm to clients in a timely manner?

4.3 Does the IM keep clients aware of every compensated party and vendor involved in its investment activities, including the amount of compensation and an assessment of the value of the services rendered?

> Will the IM permit periodic audits of all fees paid to various third parties?
>
> Will the IM provide evidence that fee-paid services were consistent with contract stipulations, and that the fees compared favorably with industry benchmarks?

4.4 Does the IM have controls in place to account for and report about service fees for activities such as best execution, soft dollars, and proxy voting?

> Are there defined and documented securities lending procedures?
>
> Are directed brokerage and commission recapture mandates transparent, monitored, and enforced?
>
> Is the IM willing to send trade confirmations and periodic brokerage activity statements to clients if so requested?

4.5 Does the IM have in place a process wherein it and the client periodically can review how effectively the IM is meeting its fiduciary responsibilities?

Are appropriate policies and procedures in place and maintained to address all fiduciary obligations?

Is each IPS up to date?

Are the assessments conducted in a way to assure an objective and reasonable appraisal of the IM's commitment to sound fiduciary practice?

CONCLUSION

This chapter was included to heighten investment managers' awareness of how trustees should devise their oversight and auditing practices. There should be common agreement between trustees, consultants, investment managers, and *beneficiaries* so that all will honor these practices.

CHAPTER 15

The Kool-Aid® Quandary and the Enduring Lure of Outperformance

Edward Siedle, Esq.
President, Benchmark Financial Services, Inc.

A seasoned observer of the money management industry reminds readers about the myth and the reality of sustained outperformance. Clients who can't distinguish between myth and reality are more likely to be subject to chicanery. The burden is on clients to make this distinction, not on regulators or SROs—a theme that is reiterated in our other chapters.

THE DREAM

Some make the Kool-Aid®; some sell the Kool-Aid; some drink the Kool-Aid. Everyone wants the Kool-Aid. But what's in the Kool-Aid? It is the myth or dream that there are money managers out there who can outperform the market year after year, never giving back their superior results or reverting to the mean. In Chapter 4 of this book, "The Failure of Invariance," Peter L. Bernstein describes, with his customary elegance, why in truth no such manager can exist.

Bernstein discusses the myth or dream of invariance in the context of behavioral economics. One can read that chapter with clients and prospective clients in mind (Kool-Aid drinkers). But investment managers (Kool-Aid makers) and their marketing staffs (Kool-Aid sellers) are advised to read that chapter with themselves in mind. Doing so is an effective exercise in enhancing self-awareness.

Investment managers are by nature competitive and seek performance that's better than the other players on the field or court. Some need to reinforce their self-image by earning entrance into an exclusive investment club, such as a hedge fund. Whatever the reason, the allure of outperformance is strong. Again, as Bernstein says, "We like to believe we are above-average in skills, intelligence, farsightedness, experience, refinement, and leadership."

Trustees, beneficiaries, and regulators can live with the egos of overachievers in the Kool-Aid business, as long as they are mindful of their own prejudices and limitations. And they should look at their responsibilities with an awareness of real-world probability, and be vigilant when the Kool-Aid makers represent their various flavors as having been made with prudence, safety, and a healthy regard for uncertainty and probability.

Unfortunately, such fiduciary awareness is not yet pervasive. As long as lots of people want to believe someone out there can sustain a long career batting average of 1.000, the Kool-Aid will continue to sell briskly.

The money management profession is one of the few in the world where virtually everyone involved fails to deliver the service that is being sold. Almost all money managers do not perform up to the benchmark standards they have established for themselves. Only Las Vegas gambling casinos enjoy the same customer loyalty. In Vegas, too, there are few winners but the players keep coming back hoping to beat the odds. How exaggerated is the harsh charge that some investors have mindsets that are no different from gamblers'?

THE HIGH COST OF DREAMING

Here's a paradox: Investors willingly pay dearly to chase the improbable dream of getting rich riding on the coattails of a super-talented money manager who can beat the market. On the other hand, investors are reluctant to pay very little for the certainty that they can receive a market rate of return—nothing more, nothing less.

The existence of this paradox is acknowledged and acted upon by far too many in the money management industry. They know the easy big money is to be made selling the dream. Why earn a smaller return marketing a reality-based product that stewards are reluctant to consider? For the same marketing outlays, a firm can more easily sell a dubiously appealing product for significantly higher fees.

It takes a far more mature, disciplined mind to accept that dreams of consistently beating the market or getting rich quick will end in disappointment. And it takes a far more ethical mindset on the part of money management firms not to offer products or services that result in vast assets under management and high fees (but poorer performance).

You get what you pay for is an axiom of conventional wisdom. But there are many notable exceptions to this bit of conventional wisdom. It may be counterintuitive, but sometimes paying less nets the same result and sometimes paying less gets you more. A Seiko watch tells the same time as a Rolex.

For most institutions, the single most important decision they face is whom to trust to manage the assets entrusted to them. Therefore, investors need to know whether paying more will increase the likelihood of superior performance. The answer to this question is well-documented and empirically substantiated. The highest-cost investment products, such as hedge funds, are far less likely to consistently produce net returns at or above the market. Yet the "hot hands" still retain star appeal. However, human stars burn out quickly. Again, low-cost portfolios, such as indexed ones, are the most likely to guarantee a market rate of return over most funding horizons.

SELLING THE DREAM

More often than not, the money management business is about convincing clients that they will beat the odds consistently—despite the fact that decades of data show they cannot do so. This means that a lot of people in the profession have learned to live in a spurious state. All managers know in their heart of hearts that clients will not receive the performance they are led to believe is possible. Of course, a few money managers *promise* superior results. That will get them sued. Indeed, every discussion of past performance is likely to be accompanied with the warning, consistent with SEC requirements, that "past performance is not indicative of future results." But the profession knows that in investors' minds past performance *suggests* future results.

Even regulators, such as the Securities and Exchange Commission, know investors are routinely misled by past-performance figures. It is well known to them that investors chase past returns. Regulators allow the game of advertising past performance as long as there are cautionary footnotes. Despite the countless assets that are eroded annually, regulators perceive their mandate to involve a *balancing* of the interests of the financial institutions against those of investors. Regulators are not solely focused upon investor protection. They have equal or even greater concern for what is benignly referred to as "financial innovation." Critics contend that the degree of this concern creates a situation wherein the industry has too much influence upon regulatory agencies.

The money management industry wants to retain the power to market to the public any financial product, however improbable. The industry will agree to limitations that appear to reduce the likelihood that investors will be cheated, such as disclosure in footnotes, as long as marketing effort is unimpeded. Investor confidence in the system is required to sustain it.

Expediently crafted products and unsavory sales practices persist. The regulators are aware of them because they have allowed them to persist.

Successful money managers learn to sell the dream *within the limits of the law*. That is, while the investor does not receive what he was led to expect (which, by the way, the manager knew the investor would not), the manager can defend himself by showing he didn't really promise the superior results. The fault generally lies with the investor's expectations, not the manager. However, to come full circle, the industry creates and markets products designed to appeal to investors' unrealistic desires.

Regulatory compliance notwithstanding, honest investment management professionals must admit that trustees and fiduciaries get hoodwinked. Stewards with less financial sophistication will buy a faulted product from buy-side or sell-side operatives who have greater financial sophistication.

WHEN DREAMS FAIL TO MATERIALIZE

Since most financial products do not provide the investor with the sought-after return within the time allotted, successful money management firms must be extremely adept at providing satisfactory explanations for unsatisfactory results. The investor must be convinced either that the performance already received is adequate or that by staying invested the dream of better performance will materialize sometime in the future. Managers are skilled at employing whatever devices circumstances require to retain assets under management, regardless of performance.

While in law school in Boston, I worked as a summer intern in the Boston Regional Office of the Securities and Exchange Commission. This regional office, due to the large number of money managers in the Boston area, had great expertise in inspections and investigations of money managers. My first week of the internship I was allowed to sit in on a deposition of a prominent money manager who had invested (and lost) a substantial portion of a local college's endowment in a speculative oil-and-gas deal. He and his legal counsel argued that in an era of high inflation, an oil-and-gas investment that had a projected return of 20 percent was, in fact, conservative because the return would merely keep pace with inflation. The deposition was such a polite, fascinating exchange of investment philosophy that I had to keep reminding myself that the college had been screwed. I found myself wanting to believe the investment advisor. The rarified air of the money management profession was intoxicating to a newcomer.

When a money manager fails to perform up to the benchmark he has established for himself, the manager might simply acknowledge his poor performance or change the benchmark to one that will make his performance appear better. If performance falters in the short term, managers will likely acknowledge the problem and offer a plausible explanation. For example, "Value investing is out-of favor."

If performance continues to be poor, the manager will begin the desperate search for a benchmark against which his performance looks good. Investors may endure short-term underperformance. However, if the manager can't improve his performance within an acceptable period of time, he looks for a scheme for making bad look as if it were good. Changing the benchmark is only one of the many devices available to managers to improve the appearance of performance. Not surprisingly, violations of money manager performance reporting are the most commonplace of all violations.

Today, with the proliferation of hedge funds, another alternative exists when performance falters: Close up shop and start another firm. The structure of hedge fund performance fees makes it all but impossible for managers to dig their way out of years of bad performance precluding an outsized performance-based fee. The *modus operandi* of this industry is to walk away from the disasters created.

Sometimes managers choose not to go it alone. Managers may enlist others in their battle against bad performance.

A LITTLE HELP FROM FRIENDS

Managers may enlist others in obscuring or ignoring performance reporting chicanery.

A fee-based or commissioned-based agent with a personal relationship with a client is most capable of assuaging the inevitable disappointment of underperformance. Moreover, these agents are well compensated from the addition of substantial fees for the delivery (and retention) of the products, thus significantly reducing the likelihood of any superior net performance. Dispassionate observers of the money management industry contend that adopters of this business model do not focus on returns at all. These firms' objectives are to continue growing AUM by encouraging expectations that they know they can never meet.

The logical inference is that the needs of clients and beneficiaries are much less important than the needs of the firm.

CONCLUSION

Competitive pressures, hubris, and the trillions of dollars needing harbor have created business models that are long on expedience and short on ethics. James Ware and James Dethmer forthrightly address this sad state of affairs in Chapter 24, "Ethical Leadership in the Investment Firm." Marketing professionals within the industry can depart from misrepresentation and exaggeration by practicing the communication methods and organizational structures discussed by Ron Gold in Chapter 17, "The Marketing Challenge."

The candid counsel and forthright recommendations in the aforementioned chapters are deliberate steps to furthering the message that *there are zero nutrients in the Kool-Aid*.

Readers of this chapter can correctly infer that the burden of procedural prudence by trustees and plan sponsors has increased. The circumstances described above require that the concept of *prudent process* be expanded from careful diligence to extreme vigilance—toward a heightened consciousness of probabilities and actualities. In Chapter 14, "The Client Challenge: Trustees as Leaders," FI 360 staff encourages trustees and sponsors to undertake a systematic program to lead their staff (and beneficiaries) to an understanding of the myths and realities of institutional investing.

Once upon a time, the thoughtful money manager understood and honored the fiduciary tradition, the standard to which he was held under the law: *to put the clients' interest before your own*. That fiduciary tradition many times required extremely successful managers to turn assets away rather than disappoint. As the number of registered and unregistered money managers has exploded in the last 30 years, the business of money management has lost touch with these ethical principles. There is substantial overcapacity in the industry. Yet finding reliable managers is harder than ever. I contend that it is time to prune the investment management tree.

The pruning tools are *education*, *self-awareness*, and *vigilance*.

CHAPTER 16

The ESGI (née SRI) Challenge

'Dove Green'

The term socially responsible investing *(SRI) has morphed into* environmental, social, and governance investing *(ESGI), and is sometime referred to as* sustainable investing. *Each of these terms has been used by cadres of activists to describe their persuasive campaigns—the targets for which are now trustees, investment managers, and corporations. Here is a discussion about the concerns of shareholder activists and social activists. Are ESG policies and procedures the new intangibles? Whatever the cause, fiduciary duty still trumps all.*

This chapter is intended as a survey of issues for public companies and fund trustees, as well as for investment managers. What follows are discussions about the most common issues prevalent in a dialogue that is increasing in frequency and in fervor. In some instances, these issues are not only described, but their descriptions are appended with some comments on why some parties think they are issues that merit concern.

TWO-AND-A-HALF TRILLION, AND COUNTING

[I]t is extraordinarily difficult, in a world where our major corporations have a variety of associations and interests, to make any clear moral judgments. . . .
—Burton G. Malkiel in an address
at a 1971 Endowment Conference

Malkiel's address was given almost 40 years ago. He was recounting his experience as chairman of a faculty committee advising Princeton University about investment policy, when students demanded that the

Princeton Endowment sell holdings that had subsidiaries or affiliates operating in apartheid South Africa.

The Princeton incident, while not a precedent encounter, was an uncommon event. Today, greater degrees of institutional and global investing have generated a tsunami of demands that fund pools incorporate "moral criteria" into their investment practices. Informed sources (both private consultants and the Department of Labor) estimate that broad-based "moral" funds account for about $2.5 trillion in just the United States. There are an estimated 200 such funds. They are becoming a major factor in allocation decisions.

THE OVERRIDING CONSIDERATION

The fervor of activists pales in importance compared with concerns about fiduciary or director responsibility. Oversight accountability, or more accurately, procedure prudence, overrides any activist agenda. Such prudence is not merely a concept—it is a duty grounded in statutes. Persons of ascribed responsibility whose imprudent actions diminish the value of a pool of assets entrusted to them are liable to severe penalties, not to mention lawsuits. Readers of this chapter should keep this in mind. There will be reminders about this throughout.

Moreover, readers should keep in mind that there are informed people who characterize activists as persons who want to exercise power without any responsibility for consequences. Some of those same people think that activism has no effect other than to cause massive portfolio distortions—and that more harm than good results from their actions.

In the spirit of this book, we have tried not to express any opinions about particular agendas or views. We address the issues and concerns in a manner that prompts readers to "think about their thinking" with respect to activist investing.

A NEW LABEL

Besides the advocacy issues of employment practices, environmental impacts, and offshore operations, intramural oversight of corporate activities is always on a list of "rightful concerns." Hence the concept of *socially responsible investing (SRI)* has been expanded to include governance. Rather than rally around the old SRI label, activists and advocates for the redress of perceived wrongs now employ the acronym *ESGI (environmental, social, and governance investing).*

But those acronyms, and the words for which they stand, are not precise enough to use in discussing agency issues; therefore, we will employ more commonly used terms. In this chapter, we will distinguish between the two primary groups of activists. We will refer to those who champion transparency and fiscal accountability as *shareholder activists*. Shareholder activists' concerns will be discussed in the context of corporate governance. Those who weigh shareholder value as less of a concern than how a company adheres to values held by their particular advocacy will be referred to as *social activists*. Those values-based concerns will be discussed separately from the transparency and fiscal accountability issues.

The concerns of shareholder activists are the least complex. Governance issues have more specificity. We will discuss corporate governance first.

CORPORATE GOVERNANCE

The concerns about corporate governance are easily identified and defined. Recently, the chief concern has been egregious financial reporting practices. Many investment professionals and fiduciaries think the Sarbanes-Oxley (SOX) Act of 2002 has assured that accounting and disclosure chicanery are no longer barriers to analysis and valuation. All concede that SOX should keep honest people honest.

SOX prescribes procedures and practices that are to be followed when overseeing financial reports, whether under Financial Accounting Standards Board (FASB) or under International Financial Reporting Standards (IFRS). The consequences of not complying "in all good faith" with the provisions of SOX are as severe as the consequences of not doing so with regulations prescribed by the EEOC, EPA, and IRS. Complying with the spirit and letter of regulations regarding hiring practices, environmental safeguards, and tax obligations is an ordinary business practice.

Investors, directors, and activists must keep this in mind: Compliance is just a component of a well-reasoned and structured corporate governance policy. Compliance is not governance.

What Is Governance?

Governance is overseeing practices that assure a systematic increase in shareholder equity, as well as assuring shareholder rights to information about corporate activities, exposures, and funding. The main characteristics of effective governance are perspective and judgment.

The consensus of experienced investors is that there are four areas of activity from which one can grade governance: qualifications of board members, executive compensation practices, merger and acquisition (M&A) strategies, and capital structure.

Qualifications of Board Members   Governance should be conducted within the context of the corporation's industry best practices. It follows then that a board member should know what those best practices are. The board member with the least experience in the given industry should still have an understanding of the comparative measures by which companies in that industry are valued. One comparative measure is how well a company complies with regulations relevant to its business activities. For example, EPA dictates will impact the manner in which a manufacturing company or an extractive company goes about business. It follows, then, that at least one director of such companies should be very knowledgeable about environmental regulations and strictures.

> *The audit committee:* All public companies are subject to Securities and Exchange Commission (SEC) financial reporting requirements. The SEC does mandate that a board have an audit committee. The SEC does not stipulate that each member of the audit committee should have a background in accounting or corporate finance. The SEC does encourage publicly held companies to have "at least one financial expert" on the audit committee. The SEC defines a financial expert as someone with an understanding of financial statement auditing, of financial reporting, and of generally accepted accounting principles (GAAP). If there is no financial expert on the auditing committee, the company is required to report to the SEC why there isn't one. The major value of having one is that such a person can assume the role of coach and guide for the other members of the committee.
>
> *Derivatives strategies:* Many companies employ derivatives strategies to manage risks incurred in foreign exchange, debt management, and raw materials purchasing. In those companies, one board member should have a working knowledge of derivatives. That person should be able to explain concepts such as counterparty risks, as well as pose the questions: "How much do our earnings depend on hedging transactions, how much do these contracts really add to shareholder value, and what is our exposure on the downside of these contracts?"
>
> *Leadership experience:* Experienced investors agree that the most important attribute of independent board members is leadership experience. The most effective members will be those who have successfully managed organizations that consistently exceeded performance benchmarks in their respective areas: whether business,

education, or government. They know how to ask the tough, probing questions. They have developed a feel for the deep-down dynamics that have the most impact on an organization. They can direct their fellow board members' focus to the critical activities that enhance shareholder value.

Executive Compensation Practices   The responsible view is that compensation plans should be structured to hire and retain the kind of people who will grow the company's market capitalization at a rate appropriate to the risks and costs the investor is assuming. This policy is not as easily implemented as inexperienced shareholder activists think. Experienced investors want evidence that a lot of thought has been given to establishing a compensation plan that links short-term performance with sustained increases in shareholder value. Excluding benefits, executive compensation generally consists of base salary, short-term incentives like bonuses, and purchase options on listed stock.

> *Base salary:* Compensation consultants hold that salary should reflect experience and sustained performance. Moreover, they counsel that base salaries should be set on the basis of "going market rate" for similar positions in the company's industry sector. Personnel turnover is a key concern of experienced investors, particularly the turnover rate of key executives. Annual raises must be weighted as much on retention as on short-term performances. Salaries are sources of contention for shareholders and for employees; therefore the salary portion of any executive's compensation, over time, should be the smallest portion of the total compensation.
>
> *Bonuses:* Conventional wisdom holds that the danger of awarding performance bonuses on an annual basis is that executives will focus on short-term goals. Like salary, bonus plans may be necessary for retention as well as for motivation. Bonus programs should be tied to functional performance—that is, how a specific activity contributes to enhancing share value. If a company is a manufacturing company, how well the purchasing department manages the cost and delivery of materials is a logical performance measure on which to base bonuses. All experienced investors agree that if a company institutes a performance bonus program, the amount of bonuses paid should not be capped.
>
> *Stock options:* Experienced investors should be concerned about how contingent expenses will impact earnings when stock options are exercised. The Financial Accounting Standards Board requires companies to specifically expense stock options. Companies are

also required to detail in their financial statements the valuation method used. The bedeviling aspect of this new requirement is how to choose among the alternative methods. None of the methods will yield anything but an approximation of expense impact. Investors should look for a demonstrated "best efforts" approach to complying with the FASB dictate. Despite the accounting burden, many companies still offer options. The experienced investor looks for whether the history of a corporation's stock option program correlates with an increased earnings pattern.

All investors, regardless of their degrees of experience, concur that resetting "under the water" strike prices is an unacceptable practice. Such practice is a legitimate grievance for shareholder activists.

Merger and Acquisition Strategies　Mergers and acquisitions are the most demanding, exacting, and perilous of all corporate activities. Investors and shareholders are advised to scrutinize every aspect of the activities associated with M&A. They should think about the fees a company will pay out to investment bankers, accountants, tax experts, and attorneys. There is the matter of additional compliance and disclosure headaches. There can be antitrust issues.

And overriding all other concerns, investors must not overlook the subjective ones: What do the current market values of either company's stock really represent? Over what time period should incremental cash flows be projected? Is one party's discount rate more appropriate than another party's? What criteria will be used to discharge or retain members of the combined workforce? What about the argument of "enhancing a competitive position"? Will that position prevail tomorrow in the face of unforeseen changes that most assuredly are coming?

There is another consideration with respect to a target company. Recently, there have been instances when shareholder activists (like hedge funds) abet the acquisition of the company whose shares they hold. Since expectations of an impending acquisition often substantially increase the share price of the target company, the short-term strategy of those activists is "take the money and run." In such cases, those subjective concerns described above are of no concern to the target company shareholders. And, of course, the target company's employees have a whole different set of concerns.

Capital Structure　Experienced inventors and governance proctors point out that how management deploys a hoard of cash is a reliable measure of its judgment and potential for sustaining shareholder value.

Depending on the industry, a company's mix of debt, equity, and cash should be governed by how and where assets need to be directed. In technology companies, particularly biomedical and pharmaceutical companies, research and development (R&D) expenses comprise the greatest part of their operating budgets and equity funding is not likely to provide for these heavy outlays. A successful product can generate considerable amounts of cash, much of which could fund the research and development of a product with the potential for the same degree of success.

Using the greater part of large cash positions to raise dividends, re-purchase company stock, or achieve "that great strategic fit" rather than fund further R&D programs might be a reason for a greater degree of oversight.

Benchmarks, with respect to equity and debt capitalizations, vary among industry groups. Rather than focus on the balance between a company's stock value and the sum of its long-term debt, experienced investors and shareholder activists look at how the company's debt is rated. They reason that present and future debt service costs are more relevant to sustained growth than some arbitrary ratio of debt-to-equity.

There can be instances when well-managed companies may need to raise cash through some special issuance such as preferred stock, convertible securities, or warrants. Informed shareholders might agree that such fund sourcing is prudent—and moreover, likely to enhance shareholder value. There is, however, one chief concern of conscientious investors and activists when apprising a special issue: The company should not undergo the aggra-vation and cost of special issues unless the money to be raised is sufficient to fund the designated activity/mission for a considerable length of time.

Going back to the market for more special-issue capital could indicate that the company is not as deliberate in its capital budgeting as it could be. A review of how capital budgeting decisions are approved, and the manner in which capital is acquired, are considered to be legitimate governance queries.

Conclusions about Governance

Experienced, responsible, and sincere shareholder activists understand that governance is not compliance. Governance is overseeing practices that assure a systematic increase in shareholder value, as well as supporting shareholder rights. There are four areas of activity that experienced share-holder advocates can monitor: the composition of the board, executive compensation practices, M&A activities, and the financial structure of the corporation. Assuring that these activities are managed judiciously and transparently is the best way by which to grade governance.

SOCIAL ACTIVISM

There is a long history of social activism, whether directed at government institutions or businesses. Many social activists will disagree with Malkiel's comment at the beginning of this chapter. Social activists, religious groups in particular, don't think that "it is extraordinarily difficult to make any clear moral judgments. . . ." They sincerely think it is easy (but not extraordinarily easy) to make some clear moral judgments, and align their investment decisions with their core values. Those core values evolve from concerns about the environment, human rights, justice, labor practices, product quality/safety, workforce diversity, abortion, and community involvement.

The Fiduciary Concern

Again, regardless of the relative ease of making moral judgments, fiduciary standards of procedural prudence must not be disregarded. The implied and explicit provisions of a pension plan's (or endowment's) investment policy may not permit moral judgments to be weighed with other factors in deciding how funds are invested. Trustees must proceed with care when crafting an investment policy that permits social activist criteria to be part of the oversight process. A fund should retain an outside counsel experienced in fiduciary law to review social activism within the context of the investment policy statement and associated trust documents.

Son of Boycott

For a long time, the most common ploy of a person or a group was to not invest in a public corporation whose policies were perceived as divergent from the values of that particular person or group. This passive protest was an extension of the *purchasing boycott* strategy. Some activists will argue that this passive tactic prevents using the moral suasion of a shareowner to change a corporation's business practices. The strength of that argument is proportionate to the number of shares held by said activists.

ESG-Constructed Portfolios

Our discussion of governance and shareholder activists required it to be framed within the context of a specific company. The discussion of social activists is best framed within the context of portfolio management.

"Voting with our feet" is still the most frequently used tactic for protesting against corporate policies and procedures; however, forgoing investing in values-divergent companies does not preclude social activists from earning market rates of returns from holdings in businesses that are values compatible. The means to earning market rates of return is constructing portfolios with screens that exclude holdings in values-divergent companies. Such exclusion screens needn't diminish a portfolio's relative rate of return.

Recent research reinforces the notion that the degree of tracking errors in ESG portfolios and in conventional portfolios is negligible. ESG portfolios will perform as well as their conventional counterparts. Nevertheless, the performance of well-constructed and well-managed ESG portfolios, like well-constructed and well-managed conventional portfolios, will sometimes vary from the generally accepted benchmarks.

The Challenge of Research Costs

As with conventional, actively managed funds, ESG actively managed portfolios' sustained returns trail ESG passively managed funds over long horizons. Social activists may now choose among many low-cost index funds invested in companies that are values compatible with a given social activist group: green funds, peace funds, health funds, and so forth. However, the cost ratios of such funds may not compare favorably with the cost ratios of "nonrestrictive" index funds and exchange-traded funds (ETFs).

Passive programs confront the same economic hurdle as the active programs, namely research costs. Social activists sometimes ignore this fact: The research-cost hurdle often makes ESGI more expensive than conventional investing practices, whether active or passive.

The most responsible arguments about the viability of ESGI focus on the quality of research. Managers of actively or passively managed ESG portfolios can be expected to confront higher research costs. More time must be invested in selecting "appropriate" issues to be included (or excluded) in an ESG index fund, just as more time is required to select representative issues in an actively managed ESG portfolio.

Most ESG investment professionals agree that going outside for independent research is not a viable cost-reduction option. Integrity Research Associates has over 25 firms in its database whose primary research methodology is ESG analysis. However, there are responsible concerns about the quality of those methodologies. Reviews of many of these firms' reports find that these reports can be vague and imprecise about a corporation's ESG commitment. Upon reflection, such a state of affairs should not be surprising. In an activity where emotions might override dispassion, subjectivity is most likely to override objectivity.

Conscientious ESG stewards and investment managers will be increasing their own research resources needed to develop screening criteria intended to reconcile ESG objectives with measures of shareholder value. Such research methodology is expensive to develop. The degree of commitment to ESGI is likely to be proportionate to the degree by which such screening expenses are controlled. And again, those expenses need to be addressed in the context of fiduciary concerns.

Sustainable Investing

The phrase *sustainable investing* is frequently used in more recent ESGI dialogue.

The term was introduced by environmental activists and is now used as the concise label for "balancing a growth economy, protecting the environment, and acting in a socially responsible way so as to assure an improving quality of life for ourselves and future generations." This is considered a most noble challenge by some, but an ignoble abrogation of fiduciary duty by others.

Like *holistic medicine*, the term is now used to denote a type of service that transcends the scope of traditional practices. Some of the more established ESGI managers are now marketing themselves as *sustainable investment advisors*. Can such a "style" lend itself to sophisticated attribution analysis? Stay tuned.

PROXY ACCESS

Any discussions about governance or shareholder activism will soon turn to the issue of proxy access. At the core of any proxy issue is the obvious question: "Where does stockholder power begin, and board power end?" The conventional answer is this: "Board power ends when more shares of stock vote against a board proposal than the number of shares of stock that voted with the board." It is a simple statement about a complex challenge.

Most large and medium capitalized public companies have a large shareholder base. Other than wanting a sustained increase on their investment, those shareholders often do not have any other common interests. Any attempt to unify them so as to challenge a board's business policies or its slate of directors is expensive in time and money. Only those dissident groups with very deep pockets can support sustained proxy fights. Those well-funded dissidents are becoming more successful in gaining board representation. In the first quarter of 2008, 32 companies had to seat dissidents as a result of election contests. And throughout that year, a lot of public companies conceded board seats rather than engage in an expensive proxy fight.

Some dissidents who weren't successful in acquiring board representation tried petitioning the SEC. When petitioned by dissidents to address the difficulty in leveraging proxy power, the SEC has chosen to pass proxy issues on to the judiciary. Delaware amended its state constitution to allow the SEC to request help from the Delaware courts in ruling on proxy imbroglios. In hearing cases brought before it, so far the Delaware Supreme Court has ruled in favor of boards. In 2008, however, a ruling favoring a sitting board was narrow enough to create a higher degree of concern about how the court might rule in subsequent cases brought before it.

A decision in 2008 (*CA Inc. v. AFSCME Employees Pension Plan*) narrowly ruled against the union's request to have the company reimburse the expenses the union incurred in conducting an election to seat a dissident. The decision overruled the union based on the court's interpretation of whether reimbursement would violate the board's fiduciary duties. Some observers think the narrowness of that ruling could energize dissidents to more carefully construct proxy petitions, in a way that would create rulings by the court in favor of dissident petitions. Investors and trustees need to stay abreast of the Delaware courts' activities, so as to ascertain any impact of future decisions on the companies in which they invest.

CONCLUSION

Investors, trustees, fiduciaries, and beneficiaries who are activists for environment, social, and governance matters can be classified into two groups: shareholder activists and social activists.

Shareholder activists' concerns are about sustaining an increase in a company's capital shares' values, as well as assuring shareholder rights. Those concerns are best addressed by corporate governance policies that dictate transparency, foresight, and judgment. These policies can be easily detected by monitoring four functions: the appointment of directors, the compensation of executives, prudent valuations of merger and acquisition opportunities, and the allocation of capital.

Social activists' concerns are about aligning their investment decisions with their core values. Social activists who are fiduciaries, trustees, or beneficiaries must assure that their funds' efforts to align investments with values do not conflict with explicit or implicit rules of the respective fund's charter or investment policy statement. The returns performances of ESG portfolios might not differ from conventional portfolios. However, the higher research costs particular to ESG portfolios may require higher fees, thus reducing net returns relative to conventional active and passive portfolios.

Some members from both sets of activists seek to extend their suasion by mounting campaigns for director seats on corporate boards. Not only are such campaigns expensive for the dissidents, they are just as expensive for the corporations—perhaps more so, because of the immeasurable costs of distracting sitting directors from overseeing the businesses they have been elected to govern.

Intangibles and Security Analysis—Some New Metrics?

Experienced investment analysts often consider the value of a corporation's *intangibles*, such as trademarks, R&D policies, and employee training programs. Valuing intangibles is becoming standard practice. Research professionals recognize that such intangibles cannot be valued like fixed assets. However, they can defend the inclusion of intangibles in a research report by recounting instances of cause-and-effect with respect to them. Some of the effects could be caused by the regard in which consumers, regulators, and the general public hold the intangibles.

Such circumstances thus beg this question: When will the demonstrated ESG practices of a corporation be considered valued intangibles in analysts' reports? Probably sooner than later—nevertheless, fiduciary concerns will still be the overriding factors.

CHAPTER 17

The Marketing Challenge

Ron Gold
Gold Consulting Inc.

Investment managers do not have to differentiate themselves from the competi-
tion in huge ways. The real marketing challenge is to articulate in a convincing
fashion how the differentiation "accrues to the benefit of the client." Here are
some insights and proposals for getting more than "just a ticket on the bus."

The stock market boom of the 1990s fueled the asset growth of many investment management firms. When looking back on that era, John Boneparth,
then Chief of Institutional Sales for Putnam Institutional Management, recalls
how even Zippy the Monkey could bring in new business.[1] All Zippy had to
do was sit by the phone and take calls from prospective clients seeking to
arrange a finalist interview for Putnam. Zippy was busy, and his job was easy.
Putnam made lots of finals presentations. Hundreds of new clients awarded
Putnam billions of dollars. The marketing challenge was simple.

Not any more—the days of Zippy the Monkey are long gone.

Today's marketplace is crowded with thousands of investment managers
offering investment products and strategies of all types to meet evolving
client needs around the globe. Competing for "shelf space" has never been
more difficult. It is not enough to offer a product of interest. Having good
historical performance is typically a necessary condition, but not a sufficient
one. Developing the right distribution channels is critical for the owners of
investment firms to "get it right," but it only gets them a ticket on a bus
filled with their strongest and best competitors.

We address five building-the-business issues in this chapter. Our thesis
is that the winning investment managers are more likely to be those who:

1. Acknowledge the importance of relationship building.
2. Recognize that the retail sales process has become institutionalized.

3. Focus on distinguishing themselves from others.
4. Get their story right and communicate it effectively and persuasively.
5. Leverage their resources by considering consultants as their best target market.

THE IMPORTANCE OF RELATIONSHIPS

Obie McKenzie addressed a room filled with sales executives at the AIMSE 16th Annual Fall Conference on October 10, 2007 in New York City. Obie is one of the industry's top sales veterans. He helped firms such as UBS, Merrill Lynch and now BlackRock develop successful sales efforts and gain substantial assets from new clients. A younger sales professional in the audience, new to the industry, asked Obie to define his secret to success. Obie didn't hesitate. He identified *relationship building* among a broad list of contacts as the single-most-important contributor to his success.

Technological improvements enable investment managers to implement cost-effective techniques for improving marketing efficiency, such as e-mail blasts, teleconferencing, Webinar presentations, and customer relationship management (CRM) systems. Nothing, however, is likely to replace good, old-fashioned, face-to-face communication geared toward creating and strengthening personal relationships that endure through time. Going forward, the economic benefits associated with building and maintaining strong relationships are likely to be significant. Why? Because of the huge amount of capital that will be up for grabs as investors rebalance their investment portfolios to comply with their ever-evolving asset-allocation policies.

Protecting Marketshare

A recent survey suggested that investors worldwide would allocate an additional \$2.5 trillion to alternative investments by 2011.[2] Much of this cash flow will be reallocated away from long-only portfolios. Protecting current market share will become a priority. The investment managers who have developed strong relationships with their long-only clients have a better chance of keeping their client and asset bases. They also have better chances of cross-selling their new or to-be-developed alternative investment strategies, which might have no track records (which is a selling situation involving the two words *trust us*). Trust is earned. Investment managers who treat the marketing function as a relationship-building function build credibility and earn the trust of their clients and prospects.

Having a broad contact list and building relationships is especially important to emerging and boutique managers. Every day, owners of these firms have the marketing challenge of competing against the mega managers, which continue to get bigger. Recent statistics showed that there were 12 investment organizations with global assets under management of at least $1 trillion.[3] Collectively, they managed approximately $18 trillion. BNY Mellon has since joined this group. There were a total of 63 organizations with assets in excess of $250 billion. The marketing muscle of these firms—their marketing spend—creates a challenge for the rest of the firms seeking to grow their businesses.

The Need to Be "Brilliant"

Emerging and boutique firms have scarce resources. Getting meetings, filling out RFPs, and making presentations require lots of time and effort. The use of third-party marketers has been a marketing solution for many of these firms. The third-party marketing industry is likely to expand as more and more "alpha" providers attempt to build their businesses. An appeal of third-party marketers is that they possess broad lists of contacts with whom they have been building relationships during the years.

Building and nurturing relationships is not a revolutionary idea—any good salesperson treasures his or her Rolodex®. What is changing is the way in which relationship building takes place. Entertainment is becoming a strategy of the past. Marketers need to be professional and technically savvy. They need to be perceived as part of their firms' investment teams. They need to know their products and strategies inside and out. In short, they need to be brilliant at every point of contact with the outside world, for they have only one opportunity to make a first impression.

INSTITUTIONALIZATION OF THE RETAIL SALES PROCESS

A consequence of the current regulatory environment is that there is an increased and well-placed focus on fiduciary responsibility. The decision-making processes that institutional boards of trustees and investment committees develop and implement are becoming commonplace in the retail markets, including family offices, the IRA rollover market, 401(k) plans, and mutual funds. This trend is likely to continue.

Exhibit 17.1 illustrates the disciplines that institutional investors follow when developing, implementing, and evaluating their investment programs.

Many investment managers have become accustomed to the special characteristics of the institutional market. Their marketing efforts reflect an understanding of the "buying" practices of institutional investors. This is a world where institutional investors typically retain consultants as

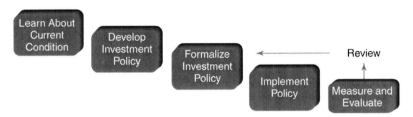

EXHIBIT 17.1 Five-Step Institutional Investment Management Process

gatekeepers to conduct investment manager due-diligence during a period of time, sometimes for two or more years, as they watch new managers.

The Broker-Dealers

Selling into the retail market will take on new challenges. For example, financial advisors at large broker-dealers will have newfound appreciation for their fiduciary responsibilities. They will better serve their clients by involving their regional and national offices in the financial-planning process and delivery of services. This means that investment managers are now selling into the broker-dealers at multiple levels. The level of due diligence conducted by broker-dealers is likely to continue to increase.[4] The marketing challenge for investment managers is to allocate new sales resources to these channels that used to require a lesser marketing spend.

The 401(k) Market

The 401(k) market deserves special attention because of its size and importance to the retirement of so many Americans. Since the passage of ERISA in 1974, pension staffs and investment committees of private corporations have learned the value of conducting rigorous due-diligence when hiring and evaluating managers for their defined-benefit (DB) pension plans. As fiduciaries, they acknowledged the importance of developing and implementing sound processes when hiring or firing investment managers.

It was uncommon, however, for plan sponsors to apply the same processes to the 401(k) savings plan. This has begun to change during the recent past. It now is becoming more common for plan sponsors to apply their DB practices to their defined-contribution (DC) plans. Investment managers offering investment-only services to DC plan sponsors need to make the switch to an institutional sale from a retail sale. As more plan sponsors introduce separately managed accounts into their platforms and reduce reliance on retail mutual funds, their need for information will increase. Investment managers serving the 401(k) market will need to allocate additional resources to their selling efforts.

Simple Match

Another marketing challenge unique to the 401(k) market is that surveys tend to show that plan sponsors are simplifying their investment platforms and offering fewer investment options than they once did. (A recent Hewitt Associates survey did show a slight increase in the average number of investment options to 17 from 14, but largely as a result of the introduction of premixed, lifecycle funds.[5]) The math is simple. If the typical number of investment options decreases, then the total number of manager searches conducted by plan sponsors each year also decreases. And a lesser number of manager searches equals a greater marketing challenge.

A Multiyear Campaign

Whether marketing within the institutional or retail marketplace, the challenge is to think about the sales process as a multiyear campaign. Exhibit 17.2 is a recommended list of the primary elements of an effective

EXHIBIT 17.2   Twenty-Four Elements of an Effective Marketing and Sales Campaign

1. Identify resources to allocate to the marketing and sales campaign.
2. Set realistic goals and objectives.
3. Identify and maintain a target universe of prospective clients.
4. Identify and maintain a target universe of consulting firms.
5. Develop compelling and persuasive "messaging."
6. Create and maintain effective sales material.
7. Develop effective presentation skills.
8. Create and maintain an effective website.
9. Get into and update consultant databases.
10. Create a written marketing and sales plan.
11. Meet with prospective clients.
12. Meet with consultants.
13. Send follow-up letters after each meeting.
14. Send sales material by mail to prospective clients and consultants.
15. Call prospective clients and consultants periodically by phone.
16. Send relevant e-mail communications to prospective clients and consultants.
17. Respond to requests for proposals (RFPs).
18. Advertise in the print media.
19. Conduct relevant and timely research and publish well-written papers.
20. Become members of the "right" trade groups and participate on committees.
21. Speak at conferences.
22. Work with the press.
23. Host an annual client event.
24. Meet monthly to review progress and priorities.

marketing and sales campaign. Large global investment firms have significant marketing resources, enabling them to allocate time and effort to all 24 elements. Small investment boutiques have scarcer resources, and thus have the added challenge of deciding where they should focus their marketing attention.

IDENTIFYING YOUR EDGE AND DISTINGUISHING CHARACTERISTICS

In a competitive marketplace with thousands of investment firms, managers owe it to themselves to find out where their strengths lie in finding market inefficiencies they can exploit to generate incremental returns. The starting place is to succinctly describe one's investment philosophy. What follows is an example of a statement of investment philosophy:

> *We believe that excess investment returns are achieved by taking a long-term, value-oriented approach to investments based upon detailed, fundamental research. When considering investments, our primary concern is to select quality companies that are priced conservatively.*

Although it is interesting to learn of an investment manager's investment philosophy, it is far more interesting to learn *why* the manager has adopted its investment philosophy. Yet, relatively few managers have taken the time to communicate to the marketplace the answer to the *why* question. The marketing challenge is to do just that—clearly describe why they have adopted their approach to adding value on behalf of clients. We suggest that an effective way to do this is for managers to trace their investment roots to the academic literature, and to describe the key academic findings that support their approach to investment management.

The Adding-Value Challenge

Why will this be important going forward? Because the trend of separating alpha and beta is likely to continue. Institutional investors are willing to pay relatively high active management fees to hedge fund managers and alpha boutiques that can demonstrate they have genuine skill that enables them to add value during all types of capital market conditions. Demonstrating one's skills starts with the careful articulation of one's core investment beliefs.

A marketing challenge for all active managers is to demonstrate they have perceived skill. A leading consulting firm, Ennis Knupp + Associates, thinks of this qualitative characteristic in four ways—cogent investment thesis, information advantage, unusual insight, and sound investment process.[6] Managers must be able to describe their investment thesis so that institutional investors and their consultants can understand it and repeat it. Claiming an information advantage is one thing. The challenge for managers is to demonstrate with solid empirical evidence that they do indeed have an information advantage. The marketing challenge of demonstrating that one has unusual insights about markets, securities, or prices gets to the heart of a manager's ability to generate alpha. Having a sound investment process that stands up to the scrutiny of the public domain is a necessary condition for marketing success. What investment managers need to think about is *how* they can effectively and persuasively demonstrate that they have perceived skill and *why* their perceived skill will persist in the future.

Identifying Your Edge

Investment managers can have edges by which they distinguish themselves from the competition in additional ways. The marketing challenge is to identify them, which often is a difficult exercise. One suggestion is for a firm's senior management to conduct an offsite retreat and to think about the factors contained in Exhibit 17.3.

EXHIBIT 17.3 Seventeen Factors to Consider When Determining a Manager's Edge and Distinguishing Characteristics

1. History and background
2. Mission and vision
3. Cultural values
4. Ownership and organizational structure
5. Professional and support resources
6. Investment products and strategies
7. Strengths and key competitive advantages
8. Weaknesses
9. Investment philosophy
10. Investment process
11. Risk management
12. Use of technology
13. Compliance and trading
14. Historical performance
15. Client-servicing and consultant-relations programs
16. Fees
17. Current marketplace perception

Investment managers need not be able to differentiate themselves from others in huge ways. Seemingly little differences can have enormous influences on the hiring decisions made by institutional investors. For example, having a clearly defined succession plan that is understood by the marketplace can be an edge for hedge fund managers and investment boutiques with lean investment staffs.

Describing an edge, distinguishing characteristic, or competitive advantage is only the beginning. The real marketing challenge is to articulate in a convincing fashion that the edge, distinguishing characteristic, or competitive advantage *accrues to the benefit of clients.* This is the linkage that must be made and that managers need to think about if they want to be successful gaining new clients in the challenging marketing environment that has emerged.

COMMUNICATING THE RIGHT STORY

Successful investment managers have learned the importance of telling their story in a way that makes it come to life. They have learned that institutional investors and their consultants need to be sold. This means spending more time on less—there is no need to get bogged down in detail or complicated charts. Consultants need to be able to wrap their arms around an investment manager's story and develop trust in what the manager does before recommending the manager to their clients. Consultants need to be able to easily repeat the manager's key messages.

The marketing challenge is for investment managers to develop the right messages and the right flow of their messages. The right flow is critical to audience understanding of the overall story. Some investment managers develop good messages, but then lose the audience by linking the messages together in a confusing fashion. Many managers use a variant of the four *P*s—people, philosophy, process, and performance. Although this flow is a reasonable structure for telling one's story, it results in many presentations sounding (and looking) alike.

It is reasonable for an investment manager to assume that the typical audience (consultant or fund sponsor) is uninformed, dubious, and resistant before they meet with an investment manager for the first time.[7] Many audiences probably are thinking something along these lines:

"Who are these guys?"
"What do they do and how do they do it?"
"How are they different—how do they distinguish themselves from their competitors?"

"Have their strategies worked in the past and are they likely to work in the future?"

"Do they have institutionally oriented client-servicing and consultant-relations programs?"

FIVE MEASURES OF SUCCESS

Investment managers need to think about how they can tell their story by essentially answering the five questions listed above and by focusing on benefits, not just features. The shift to benefits from features often is difficult, but is essential to a manager's long-term marketing success.

Although the successful investment managers offer different products and investment strategies, they share common traits, which can be categorized into these five common measures of success:

1. Good long-term performance
2. Controlled and steady asset growth
3. Organizational stability
4. Low turnover among key employees
5. Client satisfaction

Investment managers who communicate their story to consultants or prospective clients by demonstrating they have achieved good long-term performance, controlled and steady asset growth, organizational stability, low turnover, and client satisfaction are likely to be highly rated by consultants. We suggest it would be effective for investment managers to frame their story within the context of these five measures of success.

Good Long-Term Performance

The marketing challenge is for each investment manager to think about what *good*, *long term*, and *performance* mean. Good in relation to benchmark? Good in relation to peers? Good in relation to benchmark and peers? *Long term* for a large-cap growth manager and for a 130/30 manager are likely to be two different things. When a manager says it has generated good performance, what does it mean? Good gross-of-fee returns? Net-of-fee returns? Up- and down-market returns? Risk-adjusted returns? What types of risk-adjusted returns make the most sense for different types of long-only and hedge-fund strategies? Sharpe ratios? Information ratios? Other ratios? Investment managers need to consider these seemingly simple questions if they want to communicate their story in a fashion that resonates with the audience.

Controlled and Steady Asset Growth

Being able to demonstrate better-than-industry growth rates is a plus—success helps breed success. But there are other dimensions to this measure of success. Did the manager close a product (like they said they would) when assets reached a predetermined level in a capacity-constrained strategy such as small cap? Is the manager growing too fast and is the back office strained or is client servicing suffering? Communicating the right story includes addressing these matters

Organizational Stability

Merger and acquisition activity in the investment management industry ebbs and flows. Lift-outs of investment teams are fairly commonplace. It is common for consultants to place investment organizations experiencing an organizational change "on watch" until a period of stability returns. Firms that have achieved organizational stability have the marketing challenge of explaining what has led to their stability—for example, their strong culture or their reputation as being a terrific place to build a career. Managers going through a period of organizational change have the challenge of demonstrating that they can continue to stay focused on adding value for their clients.

Low Turnover Among Key Employees

Attracting and keeping talented investment professionals is critical to the long-term success of investment firms. Firms that have experienced turnover have the marketing challenge of convincing the marketplace that not all turnover is bad. In fact, strategic, or planned, turnover can be a good thing. The marketplace can be forgiving when an investment firm experiences turnover, but only if the firm's knowledge base remains intact. Firms experiencing "brain drains," particularly those with lean staffs and portfolio management "star" systems, lose clients and find it difficult to attract new clients.

Client Satisfaction

SEC rules and regulations prohibit the use of third-party testimonials. Investment firms have the challenge of demonstrating client satisfaction in other ways. One way is to communicate new cash flows from existing clients. Another way is to communicate the average length of client relationships. When communicating why an investment firm offers the best solution for a prospective client, we encourage managers to think about how they would complete the following sentence: "Our clients tell us that. . . ."

THE ROLE OF CONSULTANTS

The U.S. consulting industry started in the late 1960s when three firms— A. G. Becker, Callan Associates, and Frank Russell—began providing performance-measurement services to institutional investors with defined-benefit pension plans. There now are hundreds of consulting firms offering services that go well beyond performance measurement to investors around the globe. Today, approximately 70 percent of the reported manager searches involve a consultant in one capacity or another. Nevertheless, some question whether consultants will continue to be relevant in the future. Others question their viability as a result of revenue structures that have led to significant margin pressures. Chapter 14 in this book, "The Client Challenge: Trustees as Leaders," addresses the relevance and viability of consultants. What follows is our evaluation.

The Question of Relevance

Will consultants be relevant in the future? With respect to their role in the manager-search process, we propose that the answer to this question is "yes." Consultants know managers, maintain rate-of-return databases, and help trustees discharge their fiduciary responsibilities under Department of Labor regulations and guidelines. Beyond manager searches, the demand for consulting services is likely to increase for two particular reasons.

First, the 401(k) marketplace represents an enormous growth opportunity for those consultants who have the resources and expertise to assist plan sponsors in this area. Plan sponsors used to rely exclusively on retail mutual funds. They conducted their own manager searches without the assistance of consultants. This has changed and will continue to change as plan sponsors institutionalize their 401(k) plans by introducing separately managed accounts, preparing written statements of investment policy, conducting rigorous performance measurement, and replacing underperforming managers. Plan sponsors are beginning to increase their use of qualified consultants to help them develop, implement, and evaluate their 401(k) investment programs.

Second, the proliferation of new products and strategies, particularly in the alternatives area, is likely to continue. This represents opportunities for consultants who have the resources and expertise. Many institutional investors that include private equity, real estate, absolute return strategies, commodities, global tactical asset allocation (GTAA), portable alpha, short extension strategies (such as 130/30) and/or infrastructure in their portfolios are turning to qualified consultants for education and assistance. For example, Ennis, Knupp + Associates recently announced its intention to add substantial resources to its private equity consulting area. Four consultants left Wilshire Associates to form Cliffwater, a consulting firm that specializes in alternatives. The Townsend Company continues to be a force in the area of real estate consulting. These examples support the argument that consultants with the requisite skill set are likely to remain relevant.

The Question of Viability

Are consultants viable? For some, the answer might be "no." For those who acknowledge that their business models need to change, the answer is "yes." Consultants used to provide data and information to their clients. Now that data and information are commoditized, consultants need to change their business models so that they become at-the-table partners with their clients. To survive in the future, consultants need to recognize that they should be in the business of offering knowledge, wisdom, and solutions. Some have diversified their businesses. Some manage money. Some offer "outsourcing" services whereby they go beyond traditional consulting (making recommendations) and make decisions as an ERISA fiduciary (at a much greater fee).

Challenges remain for the consulting industry. Consultants must change their low-margin revenue model (fixed project or retainer fees) to a higher-margin, success-based model involving incentives. They need to develop better ways to attract and keep consulting talent. They need to be continuously inspired to look for new ways to better serve their clients. They also need to reenergize themselves as thought leaders and innovators.

Four Suggestions

To the extent consultants continue to be relevant and viable, they represent a target market into which investment managers should continue to sell. For those investment managers who choose to leverage their marketing efforts by calling on consultants, we offer four suggestions. They should:

1. Target a realistic number of consulting firms that they can thoroughly cover; focus their selling time and effort on those consultants who understand the segments of the capital markets in which they operate; seek out consultants who are likely to be supporters of their products and strategies; and do their homework.

2. Communicate their firm's investment strategies within the context of each consulting firm's philosophical premises and general beliefs about the capital markets; learn each consultant's opinions about manager structure (number and types of investment managers); and become knowledgeable about each consultant's performance measurement framework and ongoing manager-retention guidelines.
3. Focus their communications on their strengths, key competitive advantages, and distinguishing characteristics. Consultants and their clients have problems. Managers' marketing challenge is to convince them that they are the solution.
4. Read and reread Chapter 23 in this book, "Investment Belief Systems: A Cultural Perspective."

SUMMARY

The competitive landscape creates marketing challenges for investment managers. The winners will remember the importance of relationship building as our industry continues its march into the Internet age. The institutionalization of the retail sales process has increased the degree of difficulty selling into retail market segments. Distinguishing oneself from hundreds of strong and established competitors is not getting any easier. Getting the story right and communicating in an effective and persuasive fashion requires time and effort. The winners will continue to leverage their resources by working with consultants in the ways suggested above. Unlike prior eras, investment products will be sold, not bought, in the future.

Zippy the Monkey is unlikely to return to our industry any time soon.

NOTES

1. John Boneparth, speech given at Patriot Management's Investment Management Training Academy on June 20, 2007.
2. Merrill Lynch and Casey Quirk, "The Brave New World: Winning Investment Strategies for a Changing Global Market," September 2007.
3. P&I/Watson Wyatt, "World's 300 Largest Managers (as of December 31, 2006)," December 24, 2007.
4. McKinsey & Company, "The Asset Management Industry in 2010," p. 12.
5. Hewitt Associates, "2007 Trends and Experience in 401(k) Plans," November 2007.
6. Jim Ware, *Investment Leadership* (Hoboken, NJ: John Wiley & Sons, 2004), p. 267.
7. Jerry Weissman, *Presenting to Win* (Upper Saddle River: Prentice Hall, 2006), p. 7.

CHAPTER 18

The Selection and Termination of Investment Management Firms by Plan Sponsors

Amit Goyal
and Sunil Wahal, et al.

We examine the selection and termination of investment management firms by 3,400 plan sponsors between 1994 and 2003. Plan sponsors hire investment managers after large positive excess returns but this return-chasing behavior does not deliver positive excess returns thereafter. Investment managers are terminated for a variety of reasons, including but not limited to underperformance. Excess returns after terminations are typically in-

This was originally published in the *Journal of Finance* (Wiley-Blackwell, Volume 63, Issue 4, August 2008, pp. 1805–1847). Goyal is at the Goizueta Business School, Emory University, and Wahal is at the W. P. Carey School of Business, Arizona State University. We are indebted to Allison Howard and Nick Mencher at Invesco; David Baeckelandt, Maggie Griffin, and Robert Stein at Mercer Investment Consulting; Keith Arends at iisearches for assistance with data issues; and to the Goizueta Business School and the Q-Group for financial support. Jesse Ferlianto, Peter Left, Margaret Petri, Marko Svetina, and Fridge Vanzyp provided research assistance. We thank an anonymous referee, Roberto Barontini, George Benston, Mark Carhart, Chris Geczy, Charles Hadlock, Larry Harris, Narasimhan Jegadeesh, Kevin Johnson, Ananth Madhavan, and Ed Rice and the seminar participants at Hong Kong University of Science and Technology, the University of Washington, Goldman Sachs Asset Management, Arizona State University, University of California at Irvine, Barclays Global Investors, Boston College, Brown University, the European Finance Association Meetings in Moscow, the American Finance Association meetings in Boston, and the Mitsui Life Symposium at the University of Michigan for helpful comments and suggestions.

distinguishable from zero but are in some cases positive. In a sample of round-trip firing and hiring decisions, we find that if plan sponsors had stayed with fired investment managers, their excess returns would be no different from those delivered by newly hired managers. We uncover significant variation in pre- and post-hiring and firing returns that is related to plan sponsor characteristics.

A llen (2001) argues that financial institutions matter for asset pricing and laments the lack of attention to their behavior. Despite this clarion call, academic research has focused on two types of institutions, banks and mutual funds. There are good reasons for this. Banks have been a historically important component of the economy, and mutual funds are a relatively new but sizeable channel for retail investors to participate in capital markets. In addition, good data for both these types of institutions are widely available, permitting researchers to tackle issues with precision. However, another category of institutions, namely plan sponsors and institutional asset managers, is equally if not more important. At the end of 2003, there were 47,391 plan sponsors in the United States (corporate and public retirement plans, unions, endowments, and foundations), which were responsible for delegating investment of $6.3 trillion to institutional investment managers (Money Market Directory (2004)). At that time, there were 7,153 equity, bond, and hybrid mutual funds with total assets of $5.4 trillion (Investment Company Institute (2004)). The enormity of the assets under the jurisdiction of plan sponsors and their potential impact on asset prices are compelling reasons to examine their behavior.[1] Moreover, the fact that the assets managed by many plan sponsors fund the retirement incomes of their beneficiaries makes studying their behavior important from a personal and public policy perspective.

A comparison of institutional investment to the more widely studied retail marketplace provides some perspective. There are three basic streams to the retail investment/mutual fund literature: (1) investigations of performance, including persistence, (2) studies of the relationship between fund flows and returns, and (3) analyses of investment choices made by individual investors. The general conclusion that emerges from these streams is that the level of excess performance and the degree of persistence is weak and elusive, the relationship between flows and returns is convex, and retail investors make investment choices that can be construed as suboptimal by some and simply noisy by others.[2]

In the institutional realm, the streams are rivulets. Lakonishok, Shleifer, and Vishny (1992) provide the first investigation of performance and persistence. They persuasively argue that there are significant conflicts of interest in the money management industry and use proprietary data to examine the performance of 769 all-equity funds run by 341 investment managers. They paint a bleak picture of performance and argue, "[that] when all is said and done, we doubt that an industry that has added little if any value can continue to exist in its present form" (p. 341). Coggin, Fabozzi, and Rahman (1993) also use proprietary data to study a sample of pension fund managers and find that they have limited skill in selecting stocks. Christopherson, Ferson, and Glassman (1998) find evidence of persistence among institutional equity managers using conditional methods and Busse, Goyal, and Wahal (2007) find that persistence exists in domestic equity and fixed income portfolios. Del Guercio and Tkac (2002) examine the relation between asset flows and returns and find that excess (as opposed to raw) returns are the relevant metric for the flow–performance relationship in the institutional arena. With one exception, the third stream, the actual investment choices by plan sponsors is dry. The exception is Heisler et al. (2007), who indirectly study why plan sponsors hire and fire investment managers by examining asset flows and accounts. Ex ante, one might expect that the level of expertise of plan sponsors in delegating assets to institutional investment management firms is higher than that of individual investors picking retail mutual funds. Whether this expertise generates excess returns or not is ultimately an empirical question. Our paper is the first to tackle this issue directly in the institutional marketplace.

Plan sponsors have certain investment goals and, working under self or externally imposed restrictions, allocate funds across asset classes in an attempt to achieve their goals. Within each asset class, mandates of specific dollar amounts are then delegated to investment management firms to be invested in a particular investment style. The raison d'être of a plan sponsor is then twofold: (1) to conduct asset allocation and (2) to hire managers to deliver benchmarked returns, monitor, and if necessary, fire investment managers.[3] It is this second task, that is, the hiring and firing of investment managers by plan sponsors, that we focus on in this paper.

We compile a unique database of 8,755 hiring decisions by 3,417 plan sponsors that delegate $627 billion in mandates between 1994 and 2003. We examine benchmark-adjusted cumulative excess returns, information ratios, and calendar-time alphas from factor models up to 3 years before and after hiring. All measurement methods show that for domestic equity and fixed income mandates, pre-hiring returns are positive, large, and statistically significant, but that post-hiring returns are statistically indistinguishable from zero. For international equity mandates, however, both pre- and post-hiring excess returns are positive and large.

Plan sponsors hire investment managers either because new inflows need to be invested or to replace terminated investment managers. Our sample of terminations consists of 869 firing decisions by 482 plan sponsors that withdraw almost $105 billion in mandates between 1996 and 2003. The number of terminations is substantially smaller than hiring decisions because data sources are geared toward assisting investment managers in obtaining new business and because there is a natural disinclination to report terminations. One obvious reason for terminating investment managers is underperformance. But we find that plan sponsors also terminate investment managers for a host of reasons unrelated to performance. Nonperformance terminations are related to the plan sponsor (such as reallocations from one investment style to another or the merger of two plans) or events at the investment management firm (such as personnel turnover, the merger of two investment management firms, or regulatory actions). Excess returns prior to firing are negative for performance-based terminations but not for others. Post-firing excess returns for the entire sample are statistically indistinguishable from zero in the first 2 years after termination, but positive in the third year. Three-year post-firing returns are also positive for performance-based terminations.

To gauge the opportunity costs associated with both hiring and firing decisions, one has to compare post-hiring returns with the post-firing returns that would have been delivered by fired investment management firms. Since there are a multitude of complicated mechanisms by which firing and hiring decisions are coordinated, we build a sample of "round-trip" firing and hiring decisions manually. We identify 412 round-trip decisions between 1996 and 2003. For these decisions, the return difference between hired and fired managers prior to the round-trip is positive. After the round-trip the return differential is negative but with large standard errors.[4]

The aggregate results described above mask considerable variation in selection and termination. There are a number of different types of plan sponsors that run the gamut from defined benefit corporate plans to unions, foundations, public and private universities, and local-and state-level public plans. They vary in size from tiny multiemployer union plans like the Detroit Ironworkers Local 25 to behemoths such as the California Public Employees Retirement System. Size brings with it scale economies and perhaps expertise in selection and monitoring of investment managers. Consistent with this we find that larger plans are less likely to retain consultants to assist them in the selection process and have higher post-hiring excess returns than their smaller counterparts. Also important is the notion of "headline risk" in which some sponsors are sensitive to public scrutiny in the event of underperformance. We find that headline risk-sensitive sponsors are likely to chase investment styles with high returns in the past 3 years, to retain consultants to assist them in their hiring decisions, and to terminate managers for poor performance. But they have lower post-hiring returns than those that are headline risk-resistant or risk-neutral. Moreover, although consultants add value to hiring decisions on average (i.e., consultant-advised decisions have higher post-hiring returns), they destroy value in advising large plan sponsors. Lakonishok, Shleifer, and Vishny (1992) and Hart (1992) argue that overfunded corporate plans have little incentive to generate superior performance. Underfunding of plans, on the other hand, could generate large risk-taking incentives. For a limited sample of corporate and public plans for which we obtain funding ratios, we find that overfunded plans are less likely to engage in style-chasing and have lower post-hiring returns than underfunded plans. Underfunded plans are more likely to fire underperforming investment managers than overfunded plans. Finally, we also construct an asset allocation index that proxies for the lack of restrictions from investment policy statements and find that this index is positively correlated with post-hiring excess returns. The general picture that emerges from this cross-sectional analysis is that economic fundamentals such as size, the potential for adverse publicity, restrictions, and funding demands "matter," in the sense that they influence various aspects of hiring and firing.

Notwithstanding this variation, the conclusion to be drawn from our broad results depends largely on one's view of performance persistence, and of the role of frictional costs. Since all of our hiring decisions are for active investment managers, they represent an unsuccessful attempt by plan sponsors to seek excess post-hiring returns. This lack of success could be because there is no persistence in investment manager returns. But Christopherson et al. (1998) and Busse et al. (2007) show that there is persistence in institutional portfolios over one to two years. The fact that there is some persistence justifies the plan sponsor's conditioning of hiring on returns, at least on an ex ante basis. Zero post-hiring excess returns indicate that, on average, plan sponsors have no timing ability.

For hiring decisions necessitated by the termination of incumbent investment managers, one has to judge the hired manager's returns against the returns that the fired manager would have delivered (i.e., the opportunity costs described above), as well as frictional costs in moving portfolios. Since the difference between pre-hiring and pre-firing returns is large, hiring and firing decisions can be justified ex ante by plan sponsors. Ex post, there are some opportunity losses. Addressing the issue of how much transaction costs add to these losses is more difficult because there are no publicly available data on the costs of moving portfolios. The process of moving assets from the legacy portfolio of the fired investment manager to the target portfolio of the hired manager is frequently outsourced to "transition management firms" that attempt to minimize the costs associated with the transition. Estimates of transition costs by practitioners in the public press suggest that average costs range between 2 percent and 5 percent of the portfolio, with a standard deviation of 1 percent (see, for example, Proszek (2002), Bollen (2004), and Werner (2001)). Private estimates of all-in transition costs provided to us by an anonymous large transition management firm vary between 1.0 percent and 2.0 percent. This firm also indicates that transition costs are much higher for international, fixed income, and small-cap transitions, and when the legacy and target portfolios are in different asset classes. Regardless of the actual magnitude, the size of this transition business, estimated by some observers to be almost $2 trillion annually, suggests that transaction costs are substantial.[5]

Given our results, a reader could reasonably ask why plan sponsors make decisions that, ex post, appear to be costly. There are three plausible explanations. One is the hubristic belief among plan sponsors than they can time the hiring and firing decisions successfully. We stress that this behavior is not necessarily irrational, especially since there is persistence in performance. A second explanation is job preservation; to quote Lakonishok et al. (1992, p. 342), "those in charge of the plan must show that they are doing some work to preserve their position." Simply put, if plan sponsors did not hire and fire, their raison d'être would be nonexistent. We find that elements of hiring and firing tendencies, pre-event return thresholds, and post-event performance are related to plan sponsor attributes that reflect these agency relationships; broadly, the cross-sectional evidence is closely tied to this possibility. A third possible explanation is that these decisions are not as costly as our evidence would indicate because we are unable to fully measure the benefits. For example, it may be that termination disciplines fired investment managers and cause them to improve returns in the future. Indeed, investment managers who lose a larger fraction of their assets have higher post-termination returns. It may also be that termination disciplines incumbent (not fired) as well as potential investment managers. Unfortunately, we have no way of measuring this potentially offsetting benefit. Thus, while our results shed light on the efficacy of hiring and firing, we cannot necessarily conclude that these decisions are inefficient. The above explanations are not mutually exclusive. It is quite likely that all three play some role in the process.[6]

Our paper proceeds as follows. In Section I, we provide a brief description of the institutional marketplace and investment process. In Section II, we describe data sources and sample construction procedures. We present results on the selection of investment managers in Section III, and the termination of investment managers in Section IV, and round-trips in Section V. Section VI concludes.

I. INSTITUTIONAL DETAILS

In this section, we describe the institutional marketplace and the investment process followed by most plan sponsors. A more detailed description of the pension fund industry can be found in Fabozzi (1997), Lakonishok et al. (1992), Logue and Rader (1998), and Travers (2004).

A. The Institutional Marketplace

There are basically two types of plan sponsors, those that manage retirement assets and those that manage nonprofit assets. The former include corporate plans; public plans for employees at the city, county, or state level; single-employer plans; and Taft–Hartley multiemployer plans for organized labor.[7] The latter include foundations and endowments, including those for universities. Retirement plans can be set up as defined benefit plans, defined contribution plans, or both. In a defined benefit plan, beneficiaries receive a fixed set of payments upon retirement. The trustees of the plan are responsible for investing the beneficiaries' contributions to ensure that future benefits can be paid. In defined contribution plans, beneficiaries receive variable payments upon retirement. The plan sponsor typically selects providers of various investment options (such as Vanguard or Fidelity) who then allow beneficiaries to directly invest their assets in various funds. Some firms offer both defined benefit and defined contribution plans.

All plan sponsors share one common feature: The trustees of the plan are charged with the task of managing assets in the best interests of their beneficiaries. However, organizational structure and incentives can generate tremendous variation in behavior across plan sponsors. In corporate defined benefit plans, if the plan is overfunded, the excess funds belong to the corporation. This creates incentives for the treasurer's office (the trustee) to generate superior performance. But, Lakonishok et al. (1992) argue that firms' implicit contracts with employees may be such that excess funds are effectively handed over to employees. Hart (1992) argues that even if the excess funds belong to the corporation, considering agency issues, there is little incentive for management to generate superior performance. If the plan is underfunded this might provide an incentive to invest in risky assets, in part because, in the event of bankruptcy, the Pension Benefit Guarantee Corporation (PBGC) insures the benefits (up to a statutory limit) if the corporation has insufficient assets to cover its obligations. Lakonishok et al. (1992) note that this structure produces a bias against passive investment management (since it reduces the potential power of the treasurer's office), and against internal investment management (since it is easier to blame another organization for poor performance). In federal, state, or local government pension plans, the residual claimant is the government authority (and ultimately the taxpayer), and the trustees of the plan are political appointees and/or bureaucrats. Similarly, the residual claimants at single-employer union plans are union members and the PBGC provides downside protection. Trustees are drawn from members. However, in multiemployer Taft–Hartley plans, if one employer files for bankruptcy, the shortfall is assumed by solvent companies remaining in the plan. Non-retirement plans such as endowments and foundations do not receive any protection from the PBGC and do not have a residual claimant per se. Cash outflows for endowments and foundations have more of a discretionary element to them than retirement plans. If a foundation's performance is weak, it can lower distributions and curtail charitable activity whereas a retirement system has to fulfill its cash outflow obligations. Incentives are also provided by the market for human capital. Superior performance in managing the investment process can increase salaries and generate improved external employment opportunities. This appears to be the case, especially for endowments, where even though the residual claimant is not well-defined, executives that manage the investment process effectively generate significant human capital.[8]

B. The Investment Process

The above discussion suggests that the goals of a plan sponsor are influenced by the structure of claims and the nature of payouts. The investment process followed by plan sponsors is designed to achieve those goals. Typically this process begins with an investment policy statement drafted by the investment committee, often spearheaded by a chief investment officer. The investment policy statement describes the goals of the plan sponsor, the road map for reaching those goals, and any restrictions on the investment process. The restrictions originate from a desire to control risk and return profiles and can take a variety of forms, varying from broad strategic asset allocation decisions to tactical adjustments around strategic targets. They can influence the quantity and quality of asset classes available. For instance, certain asset classes (such as hedge funds or real estate) may be excluded or capped at a particular percentage of total assets. There may also be restrictions on specific securities to be held within qualified asset classes. Quality restrictions, for example, might involve excluding "sin" stocks or including only dividend-paying securities. Effectively, asset allocations can be thought of as one realization of the goals and restrictions in the investment policy statement.

Plan sponsor size also generates variation in the investment process across plan sponsors. Larger plan sponsors likely benefit from economies of scale in generating information and managing the investment process. In addition, large plan sponsors have an advantage in that they may be allowed preferential access to certain funds because they can provide large amounts of capital; most investment management firms have minimum investment requirements that small plan sponsors may not be able to meet.

C. The Hiring and Firing Process

Once broad asset allocations have been established, the search for managers begins. The plan sponsor puts out a request for proposals (RFP) and may retain a consultant to assist in the search. The process involves screening investment managers who provide investment products in the mandate stated by the plan sponsor. The mandate can be either broad (e.g., domestic equity) or narrow (e.g., small-cap equity value). The list of candidate managers is then culled based on relative performance. The list is further trimmed with written questionnaires and interviews, and the investment committee or trustees make a final choice.

For an investment manager, being part of the initial list of managers is a critical hurdle. As a result, most organizations voluntarily provide information to various databases that record performance and other characteristics. Such databases are produced by independent organizations, such as iisearches (affiliated with Institutional Investor publications) or Nelson's Directories (affiliated with Thomson Financial), as well as by pension consultants such as Mercer Investment Consulting. A list of common databases is contained in Travers (2004).

Since different plan sponsors conduct manager searches that are correlated in time and investment mandate, pension consultants can reap economies in gathering information. To the extent that larger plan sponsors make more hiring/firing decisions, they may be less likely to employ consultants. Plan sponsors may also employ a consultant to shield themselves from adverse publicity associated with negative outcomes from hiring decisions.

Once an investment management firm has been hired, its performance is generally monitored on a quarterly basis. If performance relative to a benchmark deteriorates over consecutive evaluation horizons, the firm may be put on a "watch list." If performance improves, the firm is removed from the watch list. Continued deterioration in performance may result in the firm's contract being terminated. If the firm is terminated, the assets are transferred to the newly hired investment manager's portfolio by a transition organization. Large investment houses, such as State Street Global Advisors and Barclays Global Investors, provide such transition management services, the aim of which is to minimize the frictional loss in transitioning between the legacy and target portfolios.

Aside from performance, there are other reasons why an investment management firm may be terminated. The plan sponsor may view the superior performance of the investment manager's portfolio as being directly attributable to a particular individual. If such an individual(s) leaves the firm, the plan sponsor may decide to terminate its relationship with the investment management firm. For example, in 1996 the two principal partners of Apodaca–Johnston

Capital Management separated to start their own investment management firms. As a result, the Los Angeles County Employees Retirement Association terminated its contract with the firm. In addition to personnel turnover, mergers between investment management firms can also prompt terminations. Finally, reasons that are specific to the plan sponsor, rather than the investment management firm, can cause terminations. For instance, a reorganization of the sponsor (perhaps because two corporations merged) may cause the reorganized plan to fire some investment managers. Alternatively, if the plan sponsor decides to change asset classes or investment styles, it may terminate investment managers in mandates that are downsized.

Hiring of investment managers also takes place for several reasons. The replacement of a fired manager or an increase in asset allocation to a particular mandate can trigger hiring. Additionally, if the size of the plan sponsor's asset base increases, it may hire new investment managers rather than increase allocations to existing managers.

II. DATA SOURCES AND SAMPLE CONSTRUCTION

A. Selection and Termination Data

We obtain data on the selection and termination of investment managers from three different sources: the "Tracker" database developed by Mercer Investment Consulting, the "iisearches" database created by *Institutional Investor Publications*, and electronic searches of articles published in *Pensions and Investments (P&I)*. The Tracker and iisearches databases are used by investment management firms to market their services to plan sponsors. These sources provide the name of the plan sponsor, the type of the plan sponsor, the name of the investment manager hired, the name of the consultant(s), the type and amount of the investment mandate, and a hiring date. Although similar in spirit, the two databases differ in three key ways. First, the Tracker database does not record the termination of investment managers. The iisearches database does record parallel information on investment managers that are fired, but the firing data are sparse and record only single-matching firing and hiring decisions. Therefore, round-trips cannot be extracted in a straightforward way from the database. Second, iisearches provides a column containing textual information about the hiring/firing that can help in identifying the reason for the termination. Here again, the data are sparse—only some records contain textual information. As a result, we use manual searches in trade journals to fill in the gaps. Third, the Tracker database contains data from 1994 through 2003, whereas the iisearches database starts in 1995.

We also perform electronic searches for articles in *P&I*, a widely used and respected source of weekly information for this industry. It reports on searches and terminations by major plan sponsors, often providing contextual information that is not recorded in the Tracker or iisearches databases. We perform keyword searches of all issues of *P&I* between 1996 and 2003 using the following phrases: "hiring," "firing," and "termination." We then read these articles and manually record the same data elements as Tracker and iisearches.

We remove all non-U.S. plan sponsors from each of these databases and discard observations where the hiring (or firing) concerns custodians or record keepers. We also remove observations for employee-directed (defined contribution) retirement plans. This results in 15,940 hiring observations from Tracker, 11,537 hiring observations from iisearches, and 1,184 observations from *P&I*.

We use these data sources to create as comprehensive a sample as possible and to cross-check information. To eliminate duplicates, we first create master files that uniquely identify different permutations and spellings of plan sponsor, investment manager, and consultant names. We then splice the data sets together, from which we identify duplicate observations as those in which the same plan sponsor hires/fires the same investment manager within 90 days of each other. When data sources disagree on other aspects of the hiring/firing, we use a reasonable algorithm to determine the final value for the field (for instance, taking the minimum value of the mandate amount). Where the data sources disagree on the investment mandate, we treat the mandate as unknown.

B. Plan Sponsor Information and Asset Allocation Data

We use Nelson's Directory of Plan Sponsors, the Money Market Directory of Investment Managers and Plan Sponsors, and internet searches to classify each plan sponsor into nine categories: corporate; endowments and foundations; local public plans that represent general retirement interests for cities and counties; state public plans that refer to statewide plans such as the California Public Employees Retirement System; miscellaneous public plans that include police, fire, and municipal employee retirement plans for cities and counties; unions (including Taft–Hartley plans); public universities; private universities; and a miscellaneous category that includes insurance plans, health and hospital plans, trusts, and anonymous plans.

For corporate plans, we calculate funding ratios for the year prior to hiring/firing based on the procedure outlined in Franzoni and Marín (2006), except that rather than scaling by market capitalization, we use the ratio of fair value of plan assets to the projected benefit obligation. For public plans, we manually collect funding ratios from plan sponsor websites, relying especially on the public retirement systems website (www.prism-assoc.org). Not surprisingly, there is a reporting bias: Only large plans report this information. Since the obligations of nonretirement plans are largely discretionary, the notion of a funding ratio is not well-defined. Therefore, our funding ratio tests are only for corporate and public plans.

We obtain information on asset allocations for plan sponsors from two sources. *P&I* surveys the largest 1,000 corporate and public retirement plans in each year and records information on broad asset allocations in the following general categories: domestic equity, domestic fixed income, international equity, international fixed income, cash, private equity, real estate, mortgages, and "others" (including distressed debt, oil and gas, timber, etc.). These data also contain the percentage of assets that are indexed and that are managed internally. There are several important qualifications to these data. First, they include only retirement plans and specifically exclude endowments, foundations, unions, and insurance plans. Second, prior to 1996, only the largest 200 plan sponsors are surveyed. Third, the asset class categories and gradations change over time. For example, in some years, only allocations to equity, rather than domestic and international equity, are recorded. Similarly, allocations to private equity are not recorded until later in the time series. We supplement these data with hand-collected information from Nelson's Directory of Plan Sponsors (2005). Nelson's coverage of plan sponsors is better in that it includes endowments, foundations, and union plans. However, its gradation of asset classes is not as fine as *P&I* and we only observe allocations at the end of our sample period.

C. Returns and Asset Size Data

We obtain return information from Mercer's Manager Performance Analytics database. This database contains quarterly returns (gross of fees) on approximately 9,000 products offered by 1,200 investment managers for the period from 1981 to 2005. These are "composite" returns for unrestricted portfolios. The actual returns earned by a plan sponsor may differ slightly from these composite returns if the plan imposes significant restrictions on the portfolio. The returns data are self-reported by investment management firms. Given that a successful track record of returns is critical for hiring, it is possible that some investment management firms "amend" prior years' returns in updating return information. We ensure that this is not the case—Mercer informs us that investment managers provide each quarter's return soon after the end of the quarter and are not permitted to update prior returns. In addition, the investment management firms in our sample comply with the performance reporting standards established by the CFA Institute (see http://www.cfainstitute.org/centre/ips).

Another potential concern is one of survivorship bias. We perform three checks to determine if survivorship bias influences our results. First, we compute attrition rates of investment managers and ensure that return histories disappear over time. Tabulations of return histories show an attrition rate of approximately 4 percent per year in our sample (by comparison, Carhart et al. (2002) report an average annual attrition rate of 3.6 percent for mutual funds). Second, we calculate the number of instances where pre-firing returns are available but post-firing returns are not. We find that the loss in data is trivial (10 observations for a one-year horizon), suggesting that post-firing returns do not disappear from the sample because the pre-firing returns are negative. Third, we reexamine the portion of our firing database for which we have no returns (either pre- or post-firing). A vast majority of firing decisions for which we have no returns are where the mandate is unknown or in an asset class not covered by our returns database (private equity, venture capital, real estate, and so on).

Mercer provides multiple benchmark return indices appropriate for each product category. For example, for the small-cap product category, Mercer provides 13 different benchmark indices. The correlation coefficients between these different indices are generally very high. Therefore, we select one index for each product category that we believe best describes the investment objective of that category. A list of each product category and the chosen index, along with a brief description, is provided in Exhibit 18.1. We obtain asset information from the Money Market Directory of Investment Managers. This database contains the investment management firms' name and the total assets under management in each year from 1996 to 2003.

D. Sample Construction

We match the hiring/firing database with the return data in two steps. We first match the names of investment management firms across the two databases. We use *Nelson's Directory of Investment Managers* (2004), the *Money Market Directory of Investment Managers and Plan Sponsors* (2004), and Internet searches to ensure that acquisitions of investment management firms are correctly accounted for in both databases. Second, we match information on the investment mandate from the hiring/firing database to one of the products in the returns database. This process results in a loss of some data for three reasons. First, Mercer's return database may not have returns for a particular investment management firm. Second, Mercer's return database may not have returns for the mandate for which the investment manager was hired or fired. This is often the case for "alternative asset" mandates that include venture capital and private equity. Third, we remove passive mandates from our sample since investment managers for these mandates are selected for their ability to provide low-cost passive exposure rather than beating a particular benchmark.

Sometimes, mandate information in the hiring/firing database is available only at a broad level while the returns are available at a refined level. For instance, a hiring record may indicate that XYZ Investment Partners was hired for a large-cap equity mandate. Our returns database may record return information for XYZ Investment Partners for large-cap growth, large-cap value, and large-cap core products. In such situations, we use an equally weighted average return across all the relevant products and match it to the investment mandate. We perform all our tests without this averaging and note that it does not affect our conclusions.

The intersection of the two databases produces a sample of 8,755 hiring decisions by 3,417 plan sponsors. These hiring decisions involve 602 investment managers hired to manage a total of $627 billion between 1994 and 2003. The firing database consists of 869 decisions by 482 plan sponsors between 1996 and 2003. These decisions involve the withdrawal of $105 billion from 247 investment managers.

E. Performance Measurement

We identify quarter zero as the quarter in which the hiring/firing takes place and then measure performance in several different ways. We calculate cumulative excess returns for the mandate (portfolio) of the investment manager as

$$CER_i(t, H) = \sum_{s=t}^{t+H-1} (R_{i,s} - R_{b,s}) \tag{1}$$

where $R_{i,s}$ is the return on the mandate type by the investment manager i in quarter s, and $R_{b,s}$ is the return on the benchmark in quarter s. We calculate CERs for 1, 2, and 3 years before and after an event, but we focus our discussion on the 3-year horizon because shorter period returns are noisy. In addition to CERs, we also report information ratios since they are widely used in the practitioner community, and calculate them as

$$IR_i(t, H) = \frac{\overline{CER}}{\sigma_{ER}} \tag{2}$$

where $\overline{CER}$ is the mean excess return over the appropriate horizon and σ_{ER} is the standard deviation of the excess return.

The assessment of the statistical significance for *CERs* is a nontrivial matter. In our data, plan sponsors and investment managers can appear multiple times for different decisions. This repetition, in combination with overlapping periods in long-horizon returns, introduces cross-sectional and time-series dependencies that render typical standard errors unreliable. We follow Jegadeesh and Karceski (2004) and calculate conservative standard errors based on a calendar-time procedure that accounts for cross-correlations, heteroskedasticity, and serial correlation. Details of the calculations of standard errors are contained in the Appendix.

Benchmark adjustments are not risk adjustments. One alternative is to estimate factor models in the spirit of the mutual fund literature (e.g., Elton, Gruber, and Blake (1996) or Carhart (1997)). Ideally, we would want to estimate alphas from a factor model before and after each event. However, the short time series, in addition to the fact that our returns are quarterly, limits our ability to do so. To get around this problem, we follow a calendar-time portfolio approach to estimating factor models. This allows us to estimate alphas for each year before and after the event. The disadvantage is that since we do not obtain alphas for each decision, we cannot examine cross-sectional variation in performance measured by alphas.

We calculate separate calendar-time portfolio returns for three years to one year before and after hiring/firing decisions (in other words, we calculate six separate calendar-time portfolios for each asset class). For instance, a hiring decision in December 1998 is included in the three-year pre-hiring calendar-time portfolio from December 1996 to November 1998. We then estimate alphas from factor models with the following specification for each of the calendar-time portfolios:

$$R_{p,t} = \alpha_p + \sum_{k=1}^{K} \beta_{p,k} f_{k,t} + \varepsilon_{p,t} \tag{3}$$

where R_p is the excess return on portfolio p, and f_k is the kth factor return. The models are estimated separately for domestic equity, fixed income, and international equity mandates. For domestic equity mandates, we follow Fama and French (1993) and use the market, size, and book-to-market factors obtained from Ken French's web site. For fixed income portfolios, we use the Lehman Brothers Aggregate Bond Index return, a term spread (computed as the difference between the long-term government bond return and the T-bill return), and a default spread return (computed as the difference between the corporate bond return and the long-term government bond). The default and term spread are obtained from Ibbotson Associates. For international equity mandates, we employ an international version of the three-factor model. We obtain the international market return and book-to-market factor from Ken French. The international size factor is computed as the difference between the S&P/Citigroup PMI World index return and the S&P/Citigroup EMI World index return, both of which exclude the United States (see http://www. globalindices. standardandpoors.com).

III. THE SELECTION OF INVESTMENT MANAGERS

A. Sample Distribution

Panel A of Exhibit 18.1 describes the distribution of hiring decisions. Of the 8,755 hiring decisions, 22 percent (1,927) originate from corporate plan sponsors. The average size of such sponsors is $3.7 billion and the average mandate is for $55 million. State-level public plans are extremely large, averaging $22.9 billion in size and present mandates that are over $200 million. Local and miscellaneous public plans are considerably smaller. Endowments and foundations are smaller than corporate and state or local public plans with an average size of only $1 billion. Their average mandate size is also smaller ($25 million). Single and multiemployer union plans represent over 10 percent of the sample and their average mandate is for $34 million. The miscellaneous category includes 890 hiring decisions by insurance plans, trusts, and anonymous defined benefit plans.

In Panel B, we collapse these types of plans into three categories that reflect their sensitivity to adverse publicity in the event of poor performance. This categorization is based on the premise that sponsors whose boards of directors or investment committee members are political appointments are more likely to be subject to headline risk. In the spirit of Brickley, Lease, and Smith (1988), we categorize plans into headline risk-sensitive, risk-resistant, and risk-neutral groups. Headline risk-sensitive sponsors include local, state, and miscellaneous public plans, unions, and public universities. In such public institutions, appointments to boards are either direct placements by elected officials (e.g., in the case of gubernatorial appointments at state plans) or take place via a process that involves behind-the-scenes political maneuvering. Headline risk-neutral sponsors include non-university endowments and foundations, and headline risk-resistant sponsors are corporate plans, private universities, and miscellaneous plans. The objectives of the latter group are well-defined and the political influence in the board appointment process is not as large as for headline risk-sensitive sponsors. Headline risk-sensitive sponsors are larger, in part because they include the extremely large state public plans.

In Panel C, we report size and mandate statistics for plans that are over- or underfunded in the year prior to the hiring decision. Since the residual

EXHIBIT 18.1 Distribution of Hiring Decisions by Plan Sponsors

Local public plans are those for cities and counties. State public plans are state-level retirement plans (such as Calpers). Misc. public plans include police, fire, municipal employee, and other such retirement plans at the city or county level. Unions include single and multiemployer unions and Taft–Hartley plans. The "miscellaneous" category includes anonymous corporate plans, insurance plans, health and hospital plans, and trusts. Headline risk-resistant plans are corporate plans, private universities, and miscellaneous plans. Headline risk-sensitive plans are local, state and miscellaneous public plans, unions, and public universities. Headline risk-neutral plans include nonuniversity endowments and foundations. Funding status for corporate pension plans is calculated as in Franzoni and Marín (2006). Funding ratios for public plans for the year prior to the hiring decision are obtained from the plan web sites.

	Number of Hirings	Plan Sponsor Size ($M)			Mandate Size ($M)		
		Mean	Median	N	Mean	Median	N
Panel A: Distribution by Type of Plan Sponsor							
Corporate	1,927	3,690	370	1,617	55	22	1,557
Endowments & foundations	729	1,080	190	532	25	12	625
Local public plans	1,655	7,952	500	1,601	98	25	1,545
State public plans	1,032	22,954	12,000	1,006	203	120	961
Misc. public plans	951	4,728	830	891	87	30	858
Unions	892	1,165	250	761	34	19	815
Public universities	351	1,297	200	324	36	12	317
Private universities	348	369	174	321	16	10	303
Miscellaneous	890	2,659	244	597	91	20	671
All	8,755	6,482	474	7,650	82	25	7,652
Panel B: Headline Risk							
Headline risk-sensitive	4,884	9,021	800	4,583	103	30	4,496
Headline risk-neutral	729	1,080	190	532	25	12	625
Headline risk-resistant	3,145	3,026	300	2,535	59	20	2,531
Panel C: Funding Status							
Corporate plans							
Underfunded	330	1,952	375	307	49	21	242
Overfunded	355	1,959	447	338	54	25	297
Public plans							
Underfunded	736	13,288	6,100	731	170	100	700
Overfunded	381	24,468	13,650	370	278	130	356

claimant and the nature of the guarantees (PBGC vs. taxpayers) are quite different for corporate versus public plans, we report separate statistics. Over- and underfunded corporate plans are quite similar in terms of size and mandate, but in the case of public plans, overfunded plans are significantly larger with bigger mandates.

Before RFPs can be issued and an investment management firm hired, a plan sponsor must create an asset allocation plan that incorporates its investment goals and restrictions. Unfortunately, to our knowledge, there is no database of restrictions and/or investment policy statements. Even though we cannot measure the restrictions imposed on a plan sponsor directly, we create a proxy by examining asset allocations. The idea is that plan sponsors that are relatively unrestricted are more likely to invest larger amounts in riskier asset classes; in effect, asset allocations represent a realization of constraints and investment policy statements. For instance, an endowment that allocates a large percentage of its assets to hedge funds is likely to be less restricted than one that is prohibited from such investments. To capture this idea, we create a simple allocation index that is the average of the allocation to equity (both domestic and international), alternative assets, nonindexed assets, and externally managed assets.[9] For plan sponsors without data on indexation or externally managed assets, the average is computed only from available data elements.[10]

Panel A of Exhibit 18.2 shows average asset allocations for the different types of plan sponsors. Since our data sources provide different and not always consistent classifications of assets, we collapse all allocation information into five asset classes: domestic equity, fixed income, international equity, alternative assets (buyout funds, venture capital, and hedge funds), and other assets (balanced, GICs, cash, real estate, timber, oil and gas, etc.).

Allocations to fixed income generate a more predictable stream of cash flows than those to equity. Therefore, plan sponsors that need to pay retirees might make higher allocations to fixed income than those whose outflows are more flexible. Consistent with this, public and union plans allocate between 33.6 percent and 37.6 percent of their assets to fixed income portfolios compared with endowments that only allocate 29.7 percent, and to public and private universities that allocate 26.3 percent and 21.5 percent, respectively. By this metric, allocations by corporate plans are relatively aggressive, allocating 48.5 percent of their assets toward domestic equity and only 26.8 percent to fixed income. Allocations to international equity portfolios are quite high from corporate and public plans (over 10 percent), particularly compared to unions that invest only 2 percent of their assets in international equity. Corporate plan and endowment allocations to alternative assets are also high, but surprisingly, allocations from union plans are also large.

EXHIBIT 18.2 Asset Allocations and Consultant Use

Alternative assets include buyout funds, venture capital, and hedge funds. Other assets include balanced, GICs, cash, real estate, timber, oil, and gas. The number of observations across asset classes and allocation attributes are not equal because of data collection procedures and, as a result, the sum of allocations is not equal to 100 percent. The allocation index is the average of the allocation to equity (both domestic and international), alternative assets, nonindexed assets, and externally managed assets. For plan sponsors without data on indexation and externally managed assets, the average is computed from the equity and alternative asset allocation. For probit regressions predicting the use of consultants, standard errors (in parentheses) account for clustering in observations where the investment manager is hired for a mandate in the same style and period by different plan sponsors.

Asset Allocation Information

	Asset Classes Allocations					Allocation Attributes			Number of Hirings			
	Domestic Equities	Fixed Income	International Equities	Alternative Assets	Other Assets	Indexed	Internal Management	Allocation Index	Domestic Equities	Fixed Equities	International Equities	International Consultant Use (%)
Panel A: Plan Sponsor Type												
Corporate	48.5	26.8	10.6	11.9	9.5	8.5	3.3	0.65	53	20	20	50
Endowments and foundations	48.6	29.7	7.5	6.9	6.3	—	—	0.34	60	19	13	58
Local public plans	46.8	35.4	9.9	1.9	6.3	17.3	10.3	0.45	45	23	21	82
State public plans	42.4	33.6	13.3	4.4	8.5	25.0	19.2	0.54	41	23	25	68
Miscellaneous public plans	45.9	34.8	10.6	2.8	7.3	20.1	6.6	0.50	49	24	19	73
Unions	41.5	37.6	2.4	10.9	12.6	8.1	0.2	0.45	61	24	4	67
Public universities	47.5	26.3	11.3	8.4	4.6	—	—	0.35	52	25	16	64
Private universities	55.3	21.5	6.7	7.1	6.2	—	—	0.35	60	18	17	61
Miscellaneous	49.7	24.7	4.9	14.7	5.9	—	—	0.39	50	30	14	41

Panel B: Headline Risk

	Plan Size	Portfolio Age	Headline Resistant	Headline Sensitive	Domestic Equity	Fixed Income	Intnl. Equity	Funding Indicator	Sample Size			
Sensitive	45.2	34.6	10.1	3.9	7.5	20.7	12.6	0.48	48	23	18	73
Neutral	48.6	29.7	7.5	6.9	6.3	—	—	0.34	60	20	13	58
Resistant	49.4	26.1	9.1	12.1	8.7	8.7	4.3	0.59	53	23	18	49

Panel C: Funding Status

	Plan Size	Portfolio Age	Headline Resistant	Headline Sensitive	Domestic Equity	Fixed Income	Intnl. Equity	Funding Indicator	Sample Size			
Public: underfunded	42.5	33.0	13.7	4.5	7.5	24.4	12.7	0.59	323	171	168	75
Public: overfunded	45.7	31.7	14.6	3.8	6.2	28.4	20.6	0.56	142	97	105	74
Corp.: underfunded	45.8	26.2	13.4	9.3	10.8	7.6	4.9	0.66	183	65	63	50
Corp.: overfunded	49.4	26.3	10.9	9.7	8.0	10.5	5.5	0.66	193	63	86	60

Panel D: Probit Regressions Predicting Consultant Use

	Intercept	Plan Size	Portfolio Age	Headline Resistant	Headline Sensitive	Domestic Equity	Fixed Income	Intnl. Equity	Funding Indicator	Sample Size
Full sample	0.40	-0.05	0.02	-0.26	0.42	0.29	0.13	0.26	—	7,328
	(0.14)	(0.01)	(0.03)	(0.06)	(0.06)	(0.07)	(0.08)	(0.08)		
Public plans	0.76	-0.09	0.12	—	—	0.49	0.42	0.38	0.07	1,060
	(0.36)	(0.03)	(0.06)			(0.14)	(0.15)	(0.15)	(0.09)	
Corporate plans	0.83	-0.19	0.01	—	—	0.36	0.30	0.48	0.26	615
	(0.42)	(0.03)	(0.06)			(0.27)	(0.29)	(0.29)	(0.10)	

Panel A also reports the percentage of assets that are indexed and managed internally. Since these data elements are only available from *P&I*, the sample does not match that for asset classes. In the available subsample, the data show that state public plans manage a significant proportion of their assets internally (19 percent) and also pursue indexation policies (25 percent), consistent with the increase in indexation reported by Lakonishok et al. (1992). In contrast, union plans rarely index and never manage their own assets.

The allocation index is highest for corporate plan sponsors (0.65). This is again consistent with the idea that corporate plan sponsors can be more aggressive in asset allocation because they are the residual claimant and because they are less constrained than other sponsors. Panel B shows asset allocations and the allocation index for plan sponsors classified by headline risk and Panel C shows the same data for public and corporate plans that are either over- or underfunded. Headline risk-resistant plan sponsors have higher allocations to domestic equity and alternative assets, and a significantly higher allocation index than for headline risk-sensitive plan sponsors. Interestingly, headline risk-neutral plan sponsors have the lowest allocation index. The correlation between funding status and asset allocation could reflect two opposing forces. It could be that plans with more restrictions become underfunded because these restrictions prevent them from constructing optimal portfolios. Or, it could be that plans with lower restrictions become underfunded because they unsuccessfully invested in riskier securities. Empirically, we find that funding status does not vary with asset allocations.

The last columns in Panels A, B, and C show variation in the use of consultants. For example, headline risk-sensitive sponsors are more likely to employ a consultant (73 percent) than headline risk-resistant sponsors (4 percent). But, such effects are likely correlated with other attributes such as the size of the plan sponsor or the asset class of the mandate. To provide a more complete description of this, we estimate multivariate probit models that predict the use of consultants in Panel D. The independent variables in these probit models proxy for the ideas discussed above. Plan sponsor size captures the notion that larger sponsors may have economies in hiring. We include the age of the portfolio managed by the investment management firm because consultants typically require a return history before recommending a portfolio to a sponsor. We also include indicator variables for headline risk-resistant and risk-sensitive plan sponsors, and allow the headline risk-neutral category to be picked up by the intercept. Since selection of investment managers in certain asset classes might require more expertise, we include indicator variables for domestic equity, international equity, and fixed income mandates.

Three versions of the probit model are reported in Panel D. Standard errors are reported in parentheses below the coefficients. The first model is estimated on the full sample and shows that headline risk-resistant (sensitive) plan sponsors are significantly less (more) likely to use a consultant. The implied probability changes from the coefficients are 10 percent for headline risk-resistant sponsors and 15 percent for headline risk-sensitive sponsors. The logarithm of plan sponsor size is negatively correlated with the use of consultants, consistent with our priors. Similar models augmented with an indicator variable for whether the plan is overfunded in the prior year for public (corporate) plans are also reported. The funding indicator is insignificant for public plans but positive for corporate plans.

B. Pre-hiring Performance

Plan sponsors hire investment managers to invest new asset inflows and to replace terminated investment managers. We examine pre-hiring performance in two ways. First, we modify the investment manager *CERs* described above to calculate style *CERs*. Our purpose is to determine the degree to which plan sponsors engage in style-chasing. Lakonishok et al. (1992) argue that the structure of this industry and the agency relationships within cause sponsors to allocate funds to different styles, rather than following a specific style or indexing. Barberis and Shleifer (2003) argue that style investing is particularly attractive to plan sponsors because style categorizations make it very easy to evaluate investment managers. Ideally, to detect style-chasing, we would like to directly examine shifts in asset classes and styles for each plan sponsor and correlate them with lagged market movements. Absent this information, we can provide some indirect evidence to bear on this issue by computing style excess returns and correlating them with hiring decisions. Specifically, we compute style *CERs* by cumulating the return of the investment style ($R_{b,s}$) minus the return of a broad index that reflects the return for that asset class. For example, to compute the style *CER* for small-cap growth, we cumulate the return difference between the small-cap growth benchmark (Russell 2500 Growth) and the Russell 3000 index. Second, we calculate investment manager *CERs* as described in Section II.E. Panel A of Exhibit 18.3 shows style and investment manager excess returns 1, 2, and 3 years before hiring with standard errors in parentheses.

There is some evidence of style-chasing in domestic equity: The three-year pre-hiring return is 1.20 percent, albeit with a standard error of 3.59 percent. In contrast, there is no style-chasing in either fixed income or international equity. In terms of pre-hiring performance, the cumulative excess returns for investment managers are consistently positive across all horizons and for all asset classes. They are the largest for international equity with a

EXHIBIT 18.3 Style and Investment Manager Excess Returns Prior to Hiring

Style excess returns are calculated by subtracting the average return for all styles in an asset class from the style return of the hiring decision. These excess returns are then cumulated over appropriate horizons. Style CERs are only shown for domestic equity mandates. Excess returns for investment managers are calculated by differencing the raw return for the manager in the hiring mandate from benchmark returns for the same mandate. Information on benchmarks is provided in Exhibit A.1 on page 272. Heteroskedasticity, serial, and cross-correlation consistent standard errors are calculated using the procedure described in Jegadeesh and Karceski (2004). Panel B shows the results of regressions with style or investment manager excess returns. The return regression is $y_j = \beta x_j + \delta z_j + \varepsilon_j$, where y_j is the 3-year pre-hiring cumulative excess return, x_j is a vector of explanatory variables, and z_j is a dummy variable for whether a consultant was employed. The selection equation is $z_j^* = \gamma w_j + u_j$, $z_j = \begin{cases} 1, & \text{if } z_j^* > 0 \\ 0, & \text{otherwise} \end{cases}$ and w_j is a vector of explanatory variables. The $z_j = \begin{cases} 1, & \text{if } z_j^* > 0 \\ 0, & \text{otherwise} \end{cases}$ selectivity correction is identical to the first model in Panel D of Exhibit 18.2.

	Style CERs			Investment Manager CERs		
	−3 to 0	−2 to 0	−1 to 0	−3 to 0	−2 to 0	−1 to 0
Panel A: Univariate Returns						
Domestic equity	1.20	0.95	0.49	12.21	8.54	4.21
	(3.59)	(2.62)	(1.17)	(2.50)	(2.27)	(1.52)
Fixed income	−0.43	−0.55	−0.26	3.55	2.28	1.15
	(1.01)	(0.70)	(0.33)	(0.27)	(0.29)	(0.22)
International equity	−0.30	−0.50	−0.58	17.05	11.80	5.70
	(1.47)	(0.85)	(0.67)	(3.61)	(2.66)	(1.37)

	Style CER (−3 to 0)			Investment Manager CER (−3 to 0)		
Panel B: Selectivity-Corrected Regressions Using 3-Year Pre-hiring Returns						
Constant	−5.93	−1.45	−3.52	−7.49	7.79	6.23
	(2.75)	(1.56)	(4.08)	(0.78)	(2.21)	(1.32)
Headline-sensitive indicator	3.17	5.59	1.95	−1.35	−0.27	0.29
	(1.20)	(3.10)	(1.66)	(0.74)	(1.80)	(1.11)
Log (plan sponsor size)	0.17	0.63	0.11	0.37	0.24	0.23
	(0.11)	(0.43)	(0.16)	(0.10)	(0.29)	(0.14)
Consultant indicator	9.75	11.39	4.81	1.63	0.99	1.83
	(3.97)	(7.67)	(0.54)	(0.66)	(1.53)	(1.09)
Consultant headline-sensitive	1.69	1.98	2.17	0.25	1.48	−0.28
	(0.74)	(1.55)	(1.12)	(0.91)	(2.01)	(1.33)

	Style CER (-3 to 0)			Investment Manager CER (-3 to 0)		
Overfunded indicator	—	-2.29	—	—	1.90	—
		(0.71)			(1.93)	
Allocation index	—	—	0.09	—	—	2.70
			(1.04)			(1.32)
Number of observations	7,594	1,746	4,444	6,648	1,544	3,898

three-year pre-hiring return of 17.05 percent and smallest for fixed income with a three-year pre-hiring excess return of 3.55 percent.

Clearly, and not surprisingly, plan sponsors condition their hiring decisions on the performance of investment managers.

In Panel B, we investigate how different attributes of plan sponsors are correlated with the return threshold at which investment managers are hired. The endogeneity of consultant use (see results in Panel D, Exhibit 18.2) necessitates a procedure that corrects for selectivity. We follow Madalla (1983) and estimate the following model:

$$y_j = \beta x_j + \delta z_j + \varepsilon_j \tag{4}$$

where y_j represents three-year pre-hiring cumulative style or investment manager excess return, x_j is a vector of explanatory variable, and z_j is a dummy variable for whether a consultant was employed. The selection equation is modeled as

$$z_j^* = \gamma wj + uj \tag{5}$$

where $z_j = \begin{cases} 1, \text{ if } z_j^* > 0 \\ 0, \text{ otherwise} \end{cases}$ and w_j is a vector of explanatory variables. The regressions otherwise are estimated via a two-stage procedure and standard errors account for clustering, where an investment management firm is hired for a mandate in the same style and period by different plan sponsors.

The selection equation that we use is identical to the first model in Panel D of Exhibit 18.2 and not shown in Exhibit 18.3. The independent variables (x_j) in the return regression measure plan sponsor attributes that, based on the discussion in Section I, we expect to be correlated with pre-hiring return thresholds. We present three regression models. The first model includes an indicator variable for headline-sensitive plan sponsors, the logarithm of plan sponsor size, a consultant indicator (from the first-stage regression), and an interaction effect between the consultant indicator and the headline-sensitive sponsor indicator. This base specification shows that sponsor size plays no role in style-chasing but that headline risk-sensitive plan sponsors engage in style-chasing. Sponsors that employ consultants also engage in more style-chasing than those that do not. An interaction effect between the two indicates that the presence of a consultant accentuates the style-chasing behavior in headline risk-sensitive plan sponsors rather than reducing it. In the second model, we add an indicator variable for whether the plan is over-funded. This drops the sample size since funding information is only available for a small sample of public and corporate plans. The overfunded indicator variable is significantly negative, indicating that overfunded plans do not engage in style-chasing, most likely because they have little incentive to do so. In the third model, we add the allocation index to the base model to see if our proxy for restrictions influences style returns. It does not.

We also study variation in investment manager pre-hiring returns using the same sets of models. The base model suggests that larger sponsors condition their hiring on larger investment manager returns. Similarly, the presence of consultants is positively correlated with pre-hiring investment manager returns. But neither funding levels nor the allocation index are related to pre-hiring investment manager returns. Overall, the data suggest that there is some style-chasing and that plan sponsors condition their hiring decisions on investment manager performance. The magnitudes of these effects are different for headline risk-sensitive plan sponsors and those that are advised by consultants. We turn now to an investigation of post-hiring performance.

C. Post-Hiring Performance

Exhibit 18.4 shows cumulative excess returns (Panel A), information ratios (Panel B), and alphas from factor models (Panel C) one, two, and three years after hiring. For comparison purposes, we also show pre-hiring returns over the same horizons. To ensure that changing sample sizes between the pre- and post-period do not drive our results, we report excess returns for a balanced sample in which returns can be computed for matched horizons before and after hiring. In addition to the full sample, we also show separate results for domestic equity, fixed income, and international equity.

As before, pre-hiring performance is significantly positive using all three measures of excess returns. For the full sample, post-hiring performance is statistically flat. Cumulative excess returns one, two, and three years after hiring are 0.4 percent, 1.1 percent, and 1.8 percent with standard errors of 0.6 percent, 0.8 percent, and 1.1 percent, respectively. The only case in which post-hiring excess returns are positive and statistically significant is for international equity mandates. This effect for international equity appears to be quite robust for all performance measures.

EXHIBIT 18.4 Investment Manager Excess Returns before and after Hiring

Panel A presents average cumulative excess returns computed by summing quarterly excess returns (raw minus benchmark return). Information on benchmarks is provided in Exhibit A.1. Heteroskedasticity, serial, and cross-correlation consistent standard errors are calculated using the procedure described in Jegadeesh and Karceski (2004). Panel B shows information ratios calculated by scaling the average excess return by its standard deviation. Panel C shows estimates of alphas from calendar-time regressions factor regressions with standard errors in parentheses. For domestic equity mandates, we use the Fama and French (1993) three-factor model with market, size, and book-to-market factors. For fixed income mandates, we employ a three-factor model with the Lehman Brothers Aggregate Bond Index return, a term spread (the difference between the long-term government bond return and the T-bill return), and a default spread (the difference between the corporate bond return and the long-term government bond return). For international equity mandates, we use international versions of the domestic equity three-factor models. In all pre- and post-return comparisons, we require a balanced sample (i.e., returns be available in matched pre- and post-hiring horizons).

	Pre-Hiring Period (Years)			Post-Hiring Period (Years)		
	−3 to 0	−2 to 0	−1 to 0	0 to 1	0 to 2	0 to 3
Panel A: Cumulative Excess Returns						
Full sample	10.39	7.04	3.42	0.42	1.12	1.88
	(1.87)	(1.45)	(0.97)	(0.61)	(0.85)	(1.11)
Domestic equity	12.54	8.72	4.25	−0.22	−0.07	0.77
	(2.85)	(2.31)	(1.52)	(0.85)	(1.31)	(1.86)
International equity	17.11	11.83	5.71	3.32	7.09	9.00
	(3.67)	(2.69)	(1.37)	(1.27)	(1.71)	(2.62)
Fixed income	3.72	2.32	1.16	0.30	0.65	0.80
	(0.24)	(0.29)	(0.23)	(0.23)	(0.42)	(0.55)
Panel B: Information Ratios						
Full sample	3.69	2.61	1.59	0.45	0.78	1.05
Domestic equity	3.14	2.31	1.34	−0.04	0.11	0.30
International equity	4.52	3.45	2.15	1.42	2.42	2.89
Fixed income	5.13	3.43	2.25	1.31	1.74	1.98
Panel C: Calendar-Time Alphas from Factor Regressions						
Domestic equity	1.10	1.09	1.06	−0.17	−0.13	−0.08
	(0.26)	(0.29)	(0.35)	(0.15)	(0.14)	(0.16)
International equity	1.47	1.54	1.31	0.77	0.68	0.61
	(0.45)	(0.53)	(0.55)	(0.33)	(0.32)	(0.27)
Fixed income	0.36	0.35	0.39	0.19	0.21	0.21
	(0.09)	(0.08)	(0.09)	(0.11)	(0.08)	(0.08)

Recall that the sample of hiring decisions is for active mandates in which, presumably, plan sponsors hope to earn future excess returns. Our results suggest that, on average, plan sponsors are unsuccessful in this endeavor. It could be that some plan sponsors are more successful than others because of differences in the nature of agency relationships and incentive structures. For example, the degree of headline risk faced by a plan sponsor could influence its ability to successfully pick managers that beat their benchmark. We study the degree to which such plan sponsor attributes result in superior post-hiring excess returns through selectivity-corrected return regressions analogous to those in Exhibit 18.4. The dependent variable is the three-year post-hiring cumulative excess return. The base regression model contains three-year pre-hiring cumulative excess returns, plan sponsor size, consultant indicator, and headline risk-resistant, risk-sensitive, and risk-neutral indicators as explanatory variables. Since all the headline risk indicators are included, the model is estimated without an intercept. Fixed effects for detailed investment styles (not shown) allow for intercept shifts in post-hiring returns that are not picked up by the benchmark used to compute excess returns.[11]

The base regressions in Exhibit 18.5 show strong evidence of return reversal. The negative coefficients on the pre-hiring return variable do not imply negative post-hiring returns, just that post-hiring returns are smaller than pre-hiring returns. Larger plan sponsors appear to generate superior post-hiring performance, consistent with scale economies at the plan sponsor level. The sensitivity to headline risk could influence hiring decisions in two opposing ways. It could be that increased public scrutiny improves incentives and results in higher post-hiring performance. Alternatively, headline risk sensitivity could be a response to the lack of incentives for plan sponsors to generate superior performance. Consistent with the latter explanation, we find that the performance of headline risk-sensitive plan sponsors is generally negative, particularly when compared to sponsors that are neutral to such risk. Finally, post-hiring returns are higher for decisions in which a consultant was used in selecting the investment manager.

The above results indicate that smaller plan sponsors have lower post-hiring performance and that consultants add value. Since larger plan sponsors are less likely to employ consultants, it is also interesting to examine whether consultants add more or less value for them. In the second model, we find that the interaction effect between sponsor size and consultant use is negative. This suggests that consultants add value for smaller plan sponsors but are detrimental to the post-hiring performance of larger plan sponsors. This could be because consultants do not bring scale economies or expertise to larger plans and are instead used as a shield in the case of poor hiring decisions.

EXHIBIT 18.5 Post-hiring Selectivity-Corrected Excess Return Regressions

The return regression $y_j = \beta x_j + \delta z_j + \varepsilon_j$, where y_j is the three-year post-hiring cumulative excess return, x_j is a vector of explanatory variables, and z_j is a dummy variable for whether a consultant was employed. The explanatory variables are computed as in earlier exhibits. The selection equation is $z_j^* = \gamma w_j + u_j$, where $z_j = \begin{cases} 1, & \text{if } z_j^* > 0 \\ 0, & \text{otherwise} \end{cases}$ and w_j is a vector of explanatory variables. The selectivity correction is done via a two-stage estimation procedure. The selection equations for the full sample, public plans, and corporate plans are as reported in Panel D of Exhibit 18.2 and are not reported in this exhibit. Standard errors (in parentheses) account for clustering in observations where the investment manager is hired for a mandate in the same style and period by different plan sponsors.

	All Plan Sponsors				Public Plans	Corporate Plans
Pre-hiring return	−0.17 (0.01)	−0.17 (0.01)	−0.24 (0.01)	−0.18 (0.02)	−0.17 (0.02)	−0.01 (0.05)
Log (plan sponsor size)	0.61 (0.09)	0.99 (0.14)	0.37 (0.14)	0.25 (0.13)	0.32 (0.31)	1.04 (0.44)
Headline risk-resistant indicator	−1.13 (0.80)	−2.87 (2.01)	1.01 (1.72)	−0.38 (1.18)	—	—
Headline risk-sensitive indicator	−1.70 (0.07)	−4.12 (1.06)	−0.22 (0.12)	−0.63 (1.18)	—	—
Headline risk-neutral indicator	0.26 (0.95)	2.28 (1.22)	1.17 (1.19)	1.06 (1.05)	—	—
Expected value of consultant	2.02 (0.43)	6.19 (1.37)	1.95 (0.62)	1.70 (0.59)	0.82 (1.10)	1.74 (1.44)
Consultant plan sponsor size	—	−0.64 (0.18)	—	—	—	—
Log (mandate/assets$_{t-1}$)	—	—	−0.22 (0.11)	—	—	—
Allocation index	—	—	—	4.11 (1.29)	—	—
Underfunded indicator$_{t-1}$	—	—	—	—	1.51 (3.01)	−4.48 (3.07)
Overfunded indicator$_{t-1}$	—	—			−1.62 (0.80)	−0.30 (0.14)
Number of observations	6,170	6,170	3,184	3,633	921	513

Scale diseconomies could be present for investment managers. Consider, for example, a small-cap growth manager that is at capacity with $1 billion under management. If this manager then receives a $200 million mandate from a state-level plan sponsor, its future returns could deteriorate because of higher trading costs. In the third model, we add the size of the mandate obtained by the investment manager, scaled by (lagged) assets under management. Mandate size scaled by assets is negatively related to post-hiring returns. In the fourth model, we augment the base regression with the asset allocation index. The regression shows a strong positive relation between post-hiring returns and the allocation index, suggesting that the imposition of restrictions is detrimental to performance. Finally, we would like to add the funding status of the plan in the year prior to the hiring decision to these regressions. But since these data are available only for a subset of public and corporate plans, we estimate such regressions separately for these sponsors (and accordingly drop the headline risk indicator variables). For both corporate and public plans, the overfunded plan indicator is negative and significant, consistent with Hart's (1992) argument that overfunded plans have little incentive to generate superior performance.

The economic magnitude of some of these effects is quite large. From the base specification, the average impact of a one-standard deviation increase in three-year pre-hiring returns (with other variables evaluated at their mean) implies a decrease in three-year post-hiring cumulative excess returns of 4.7 percent. Headline risk-sensitive sponsors have excess returns that are lower by 1.7 percent than their counterparts and the use of a consultant leads to an increase in three-year post-hiring returns by over 2.0 percent depending on the specification. Lower performance for overfunded plans (compared to underfunded plans) varies from 1.6 percent for public plans to 0.3 percent for corporate plans.

D. Discussion

Our aggregate results show that plan sponsors condition their hiring decisions on superior performance. However, post-hiring performance is essentially flat. One way to think about these results is to consider the role of persistence in investment manager returns. If there is little or no persistence in the performance of investment managers in general, then on average, hiring decisions should produce zero excess returns. This does not necessarily mean that plan sponsors achieve their objectives, since they hire investment managers in our sample to deliver excess returns. However, it does imply no ex-post losses. A full-scale analysis of persistence is beyond the scope of our paper. However, Christopherson et al. (1998) and Busse et al. (2007) undertake such an analysis for institutional investment managers and find evidence of persistence among winners for up to one year, and in some cases, longer. Their persistence results indicate that plan sponsors *could* generate excess returns by appropriately timing hiring decisions but, apparently, they do not.

However, the aggregate results mask considerable cross-sectional variation, not only in elements of pre-hiring decisions (return thresholds, style-chasing, consultant use), but also in post-hiring performance. This variation is tied to plan sponsor attributes that reflect agency problems and incentive structures across plans.

IV. THE TERMINATION OF INVESTMENT MANAGERS

A. Reasons for Termination

Our firing sample consists of 869 termination decisions. The number of termination decisions captured by the data collection process is substantially smaller than hiring decisions for three reasons. First, the data sources that we use (which to our knowledge are the only publicly available sources) serve a marketing function, that is, they are designed to inform subscribers that a plan sponsor is searching for an investment manager in a particular asset class/mandate. These sources are not designed to track performance or to assign blame. As such, the emphasis is on new accounts and revenue. Second, termination decisions are generally viewed with some distaste and there is a natural disinclination to report terminations. Certainly, investment managers have no incentive to report their own terminations. Plan sponsors may choose not to publicize terminations because they may employ the same manager for another mandate, either currently, or in the future. Third, there has been an increase in the assets under the administration of plan sponsors over the sample period. Ergo, the number of hiring decisions in the population is likely to be larger than of firing decisions.

Panel A of Exhibit 18.6 shows the distribution of termination decisions by type of plan sponsor and within headline risk category. Also shown are statistics on plan sponsor and mandate size. All major categories of sponsors except private universities are represented in our data. The number of terminations by endowments and foundations (in the headline risk-neutral category) are quite small. The size and mandate statistics are similar to those reported for hiring decisions. Although we do not show the time-series distribution, the number of firing observations increases over time because our data sources do a better job of capturing such decisions in the later years.

We use the textual information in our data sources to manually categorize the reasons for the termination of the investment manager into six categories.

EXHIBIT 18.6 Distribution of Firing Decisions by Plan Sponsors

Definitions for variables in Panels A and C are the same as those reported in Exhibit 18.1. Panel B shows the distribution of firing decisions by reasons identified by the data sources. Investment manager mergers may be either before the termination or impending. Regulatory action against the investment manager is both announced and ongoing. Personnel turnover at the investment management firm may be forced or voluntary. Plan reorganizations occur when two plans have to be merged. Plan reallocation category refers to firings because the plan sponsor has decided to move away from the asset allocation/investment style offered by the investment manager. The "not reported" category includes terminations in which the plan sponsors were asked the reason for the termination but deliberately did not offer a reason. When no public document contains information about the termination, the reason for the determination is determined to be missing.

	Number of Firings	Plan Sponsor Size ($M)			Mandate Size ($M)		
		Mean	Median	N	Mean	Median	N
Panel A: Headline Risk and Plan Sponsor Type							
Headline risk-resistant							
Corporate	112	2,209	700	777	95	37	80
Private universities	29	176	150	27	16	13	19
Miscellaneous	47	4225	350	33	197	62	35
Headline risk-neutral							
Endowments and foundations	29	6,899	722	24	31	35	13
Headline risk-sensitive							
Local public plans	238	5,716	650	197	104	50	213
State public plans	181	24,319	13,200	143	304	200	157
Miscellaneous public plans	128	3,494	618	101	107	50	111
Unions	75	383	190	57	103	20	70
Public universities	30	273	200	26	21	10	23

Panel B: Distribution of Firing Decisions by Stated Reason

Manager merger	22	5,951	1,100	19	142	55	15
Manager regulatory action	53	13,375	2,214	48	258	112	38
Manager personnel turnover	49	9,425	487	42	76	35	44
Manager performance	297	7,062	767	238	130	50	257
Plan reorganization	36	9,555	422	28	131	70	31
Plan reallocation	111	4,458	675	80	218	75	89
Not reported	104	8,181	433	88	108	38	94
Missing	197	9,081	870	142	144	55	153

Panel C: Distribution of Firing Decisions by Funding Status

Corporate Plans							
Underfunded	22	4,198	1,200	19	198	83	16
Overfunded	20	1,494	950	13	36	30	11
Public Plans							
Underfunded	182	19,966	8,350	164	237	200	161
Overfunded	76	21,593	12,000	52	286	200	60

Four of those categories are related to activities/events specific to the investment management firm: the merger of two investment management firms, regulatory action against the investment management firm, personnel turnover, and performance. Two of the categories are related to the plan sponsor itself: either a reorganization of the plan sponsor or a reallocation across asset classes.[12] If the text of the termination decision indicates that the plan sponsor executive willfully refused to provide the reason for the termination, we identify it as "not reported." This is different from "missing" because that category contains terminations for which we cannot find any information.

Only 34 percent (297 observations) of the total terminations (including those with unidentified reasons) are due to the performance of the investment manager. Activities and events at the investment manager firm that are unrelated to performance (mergers, regulatory action, and personnel turnover) account for another 14 percent. Plan sponsor changes (reorganizations and asset reallocations) are responsible for almost 17 percent of terminations.

There are two caveats associated with the termination reasons described above. First, the reasons are self-identified by the plan sponsor. Second, elements of current or future underperformance could creep into nonperformance categories. An acquisition of one investment management by another might take place after underperformance. Alternatively, a plan sponsor may terminate an investment manager after the departure of key personnel because it believes that the departure will cause underperformance in the future.

Panel C shows the distribution of firing decisions, sponsor size, and mandates by the funding status of corporate and public sponsors. Out of the 112 terminations from corporate plan sponsors, we only have funding information for 42, which are roughly evenly split between under- and overfunded plans. The underfunded corporate plans are considerably larger than the overfunded plans. Of the 546 public plans in the termination sample, we have funding information for 258, and a significant majority of those are underfunded (70 percent).

In Exhibit 18.7, we present a two-way frequency tabulation of the reasons for termination and plan sponsor attributes. As with hiring decisions, our purpose is to determine if headline risk, funding status, size, and consultant use influence the degree to which plan sponsors terminate investment managers for various reasons. Before presenting the results, we alert the reader to two important facts. First, some of the sample sizes for termination reasons are quite small. Although we report all cuts of the data, we only make inferences when sample sizes are reasonable. Second, our priors are well formed primarily for two termination reasons, performance and regulatory action. For example, we expect that headline risk-sensitive plan sponsors may be more likely to terminate managers for poor performance

EXHIBIT 18.7 Two-Way Frequency Distribution of Firing Decisions

The exhibit shows the number of firing decisions for each identified reason and subgroup (panel), as well as the percentage of observations in that column and category. For example, of the 297 terminations identified as due to poor performance, 79.1 percent originated from sponsors that are sensitive to headline risk. Frequency distributions are not shown for the "not reported" and missing categories. Frequencies are also not reported from intermediate groups (i.e., headline risk-neutral plan sponsors, medium-size plan sponsors, and sponsors with allocations indices in the middle group). Low and high cutoffs for the allocation index are based on the bottom and top quartiles. Similarly, small and large cutoffs for sponsor size are based on the bottom and top quartiles.

	Investment Manager Reasons				Plan Sponsor Reasons		
	Merger	Regulatory Action	Turnover	Performance	Reorganization	Reallocation	Total
Panel A: Headline Risk							
Headline risk-resistant	9.1	24.5	14.3	18.8	25.0	19.8	21.6
Headline risk-sensitive	90.9	67.6	81.6	79.1	75.0	73.9	75.0
Number of observations	22	53	49	297	36	111	869
Panel B: Public Plan Funding Status							
Underfunded plans	66.7	90.5	77.8	75.6	84.6	53.3	70.5
Overfunded plans	33.3	9.5	22.2	24.4	15.4	46.7	29.5
Number of observations	6	21	18	90	13	30	258
Panel C: Corporate Plan Funding Status							
Underfunded plans	0.0	100	33.3	64.7	0.0	20	52.4
Overfunded plans	0.0	0.0	66.7	35.3	100	80	47.6
Numbe rof observations	0	4	3	9	3	1	42

(*Continued*)

EXHIBIT 18.7 (*Continued*)

| | Investment Manager Reasons | | | | Plan Sponsor Reasons | | |
	Merger	Regulatory Action	Turnover	Performance	Reorganization	Reallocation	Total
Panel D: Allocation Index							
Low allocation index	35.0	25.0	35.7	30.8	30.0	37.8	32.1
High allocation index	20.0	12.5	16.7	22.3	6.7	16.3	20.9
Number of observations	20	48	42	247	30	98	708
Panel E: Consultant Use							
Noconsultant	22.7	15.1	20.4	22.7	30.6	21.6	22.9
Consultant	77.3	84.9	79.6	77.3	69.4	78.4	77.1
Number of observations	22	53	49	297	36	111	869
Panel F: Plan Sponsor Size							
Small plan sponsors	20	11.1	21.1	31.2	37.9	39.2	31.7
Large plan sponsors	25	37.8	26.3	21.7	27.6	20.6	21.8
Number of observations	20	45	38	263	29	97	757

or regulatory action than headline risk-resistant sponsors. We cannot a priori make the same claim for plan sponsor reorganizations/reallocations or even for investment manager personnel turnover. Again, we make inferences only where we have sensible priors.

With those qualifications in mind, Exhibit 18.7 presents the frequency of termination decisions across subcategories of sponsors in Panels A through F for each termination reason. Correct interpretation of these frequencies requires one to compare the frequency distribution across a subcategory and reason with the unconditional distribution across that subcategory (reported in the last column). For example, to determine if headline risk-sensitive plan sponsors are more likely to terminate for underperformance than headline risk-resistant sponsors, we compare their frequency distribution (79 percent vs. 18.8 percent) to that for all terminations (75 percent vs. 21 percent). Consistent with our expectations, headline risk-sensitive sponsors are more likely to terminate investment managers for poor performance (79 percent) than headline risk-resistant sponsors (18 percent); the p-value for this difference is 0.00. Overfunded plans may be less likely to terminate underperforming managers because they have some slack. Alternatively, they may be more likely to terminate for poor performance if they achieved overfunding via good firing decisions. We find that overfunded plans are less likely to terminate for poor performance than their counterparts, suggesting that the first effect dominates. Consultant-advised plans may be more likely to terminate underperforming managers because consultants want to distance themselves from the poor performance of investment managers. But we find that consultant-advised plans are no more likely to terminate investment managers for poor performance (and regulatory action) than those without consultants.

B. Pre- and Post-Firing Performance

In Exhibit 18.8, we show average cumulative excess returns for investment managers prior to the termination. Panel A shows the excess returns and standard errors for all terminations as well as by the reason for termination. The average excess return for all terminations is not different from zero: The three-year (one-year) excess return is 0.33 percent (-0.72 percent) with a standard error of 1.27 percent (0.68 percent). This reflects the heterogeneity in the reasons for termination. The excess returns prior to performance-based firing are significantly negative (-4.1 percent over three years with a standard error of 1.2 percent). In fact, poor performance and regulatory action are the only termination reasons that have negative pre-firing returns, although returns for the latter are not statistically significant. Excess returns prior to terminations due to mergers are positive but returns

EXHIBIT 18.8 Pre-Firing Investment Manager Excess Returns

The exhibit shows pre-Firing cumulative excess returns for investment management firms. Panel A shows returns for terminations due to each of the stated reasons. Panel B shows the results of regressions with investment manager excess returns. The return regression is $y_j = \beta x_j + \delta z_j + \varepsilon_j$, where y_j is the three-year pre-hiring cumulative excess return, x_j is a vector of explanatory variables, and z_j is a dummy variable for whether a consultant was employed. The selection equation is $z_j^* = \gamma w_j + u_j$, where $z_j = \begin{cases} 1, & \text{if } z_j^* > 0 \\ 0, & \text{otherwise} \end{cases}$ and w_j is a vector of explanatory variables. The selectivity correction is identical to the first model in Panel D of Exhibit 18.2. Heteroskedasticity, serial, and cross-correlation consistent standard errors are in parentheses and are calculated using the procedure described in Jegadeesh and Karceski (2004).

	Pre-Firing Period (Years)		
	−3 to 0	−2 to 0	−1 to 0
Panel A: Firing Reasons			
All	0.33 (1.27)	−2.11 (1.27)	−0.72 (0.68)
Merger	6.86 (2.74)	5.50 (1.38)	4.17 (1.51)
Regulatory action	−2.98 (5.31)	−1.87 (3.83)	−1.45 (3.19)
Turnover	4.49 (3.11)	−0.62 (4.74)	1.24 (3.52)
Performance	−4.14 (1.26)	−7.01 (1.80)	−3.71 (0.88)
Reorganization	3.22 (1.14)	0.33 (1.29)	−1.37 (0.93)
Reallocation	1.42 (1.75)	0.30 (1.13)	0.79 (1.27)
Not reported	4.00 (2.36)	−0.38 (0.98)	−0.62 (0.70)
Missing	3.27 (2.53)	1.29 (2.45)	2.25 (1.35)

Panel B: Selectivity-Corrected Regressions Using 3-Year Pre-Firing Returns for Performance-Based Firings

Constant	−10.76	−6.15	−13.10
	(11.91)	(17.48)	(19.93)
Headline-sensitive indicator	−5.71	−8.16	−0.52
	(9.18)	(12.61)	(8.50)
Headline-resistant indicator	−4.15	−3.05	—
	(9.22)	(13.25)	
Log (plan sponsor size)	0.68	1.39	2.35
	(0.62)	(0.83)	(1.70)
Consultant indicator	8.41	6.42	−14.73
	(10.25)	(14.80)	(15.73)
Allocation index	—	12.36	—
		(7.96)	
Overfunded indicator	—	—	5.65
			(6.12)
Number of observations	212	159	80

for the other termination reasons are statistically indistinguishable from zero. In Panel B we investigate whether headline risk, funding status, sponsor size, the allocation index, and consultant use are related to pre-firing returns using selectivity-corrected regressions similar to those employed earlier. These regressions are estimated for performance-based terminations only because that is where we expect such effects to be important. None of the variables that were important for pre- and post-hiring returns are important here, although it is entirely possible that the small size limits the ability of the regression to detect meaningful differences.

In Exhibit 18.9, we show cumulative excess returns (Panel A), information ratios (Panel B), and calendar-time alphas from factor regressions (Panel C) after termination. To allow for easy comparisons, we also show pre-firing results in the same table and break up the results for domestic equity, fixed income, and international equity. As before, pre-firing returns are generally statistically indistinguishable from zero. After firing, in the first two years, the cumulative excess returns are positive but with large standard errors. In some cases, in the third year, the excess returns are large and statistically significant; for the full sample, the three-year cumulative excess return is 3.3 percent with a standard error of 1.4 percent.

Investment manager termination could be correlated with changes in portfolio risk before and after termination and affect our inferences. For example, Brown, Harlow, and Starks (1996), Chevalier and Ellison (1999), and Busse (2001) show that underperforming mutual fund managers increase portfolio risk in an attempt to generate superior returns. Gallo and Lockwood (1997) show correlated changes in investment style. Such behavior may be prevalent in institutional investment management firms as well. Our calendar-time factor models allow us to test if these pre- and post-event betas are different from each other. Although we do not display the results, we mostly fail to reject the null hypothesis of constant beta. We suspect two reasons for this. First, most investment management firms have a large stable of clients. Losing one or two clients is unlikely to dramatically influence risk-taking incentives. Second, plan sponsor monitoring of tracking error (Del Guercio and Tkac (2002)) is likely to reduce incentives to change risk profiles dramatically.

C. Discussion

As a whole, our data appear to indicate that plan sponsors show limited timing ability in terminating investment managers. In the case of nonperformance terminations, a priori, one should not expect over- or underperformance subsequent to termination. In untabulated results, that is exactly what we find; post-firing excess returns for nonperformance-based firings are essentially zero. In the case of performance-based termination, expectations of post-firing

EXHIBIT 18.9 Investment Manager Excess Returns before and after Firing

Panel A presents average cumulative excess returns computed by summing quarterly excess returns. Information on benchmarks is provided in Exhibit A.1. Heteroskedasticity, serial, and cross-correlation consistent standard errors are calculated using the procedure described in Jegadeesh and Karceski (2004). Panel B shows information ratios calculated as the average excess return scaled by the standard deviation of the excess return. Panel C shows estimates of alphas from calendar-time factor regressions with standard errors in parentheses. For domestic equity mandates, we use the Fama and French (1993) three-factor model with market, size, and book-to-market factors. For fixed income mandates, we employ a three-factor model with the Lehman Brothers Aggregate Bond Index return, a term spread computed as the difference between the long-term government bond return and the T-bill return, and a default spread computed as the difference between the corporate bond return and the long-term government bond return. For international equity mandates, we use an international version of the domestic equity three-factor model. In all pre- and post-return comparisons, we require a balanced sample (i.e., that returns be available in matched pre- and post-firing horizons).

	Pre-Firing Period (Years)			Post-Firing Period (Years)		
	−3 to 0	−2 to 0	−1 to 0	0 to 1	0 to 2	0 to 3
Panel A: Cumulative Excess Returns						
Full sample	2.27	−2.06	−0.74	0.98	1.47	3.30
	(2.10)	(1.20)	(0.61)	(0.77)	(1.27)	(1.46)
Domestic equity	2.63	−3.28	−1.26	0.83	1.15	3.44
	(3.41)	(1.38)	(0.71)	(1.08)	(1.76)	(2.57)
International equity	9.15	3.72	2.42	1.52	2.66	4.10
	(0.82)	(1.87)	(1.61)	(1.35)	(3.11)	(3.59)
Fixed income	−1.54	−1.47	−0.86	0.91	1.51	2.19
	(0.86)	(1.39)	(0.62)	(0.55)	(1.04)	(1.58)
Panel B: Information Ratios						
Full sample	0.36	−0.37	−0.09	0.76	1.49	2.12
Domestic equity	0.63	−0.31	−0.15	0.30	0.97	1.39
International equity	2.18	0.74	0.67	0.12	0.66	0.62
Fixed income	−1.09	−1.09	−0.28	2.21	3.23	4.35
Panel C: Calendar-Time Alphas from Factor Regressions						
Domestic equity	−0.06	−0.42	−0.57	0.45	0.14	0.10
	(0.22)	(0.19)	(0.21)	(0.55)	(0.36)	(0.32)
International equity	0.42	0.01	−0.63	1.00	0.64	0.57
	(0.25)	(0.26)	(0.68)	(0.52)	(0.30)	(0.27)
Fixed income	0.03	0.15	0.19	0.33	0.30	0.30
	(0.14)	(0.11)	(0.13)	(0.09)	(0.09)	(0.08)

excess returns depend on the perspective of the evaluator. The plan sponsor terminating the investment manager presumably expects post-firing returns to be negative. Counterfactually, we find that the three-year post-firing excess return for performance-based terminations is 4.20 percent with a standard error of 1.87 percent. An independent observer could argue that post-firing excess returns should be zero (under mean reversion) or even positive, either under diseconomies of scale in investment management or if termination disciplines the investment manager. The diseconomies channel is simply that if the manager is capacity constrained, then removal of a mandate might allow the investment manager to improve returns, perhaps through lower trading costs. The disciplinary channel implies that termination improves performance by inducing greater effort. Both channels imply that post-firing returns should be correlated with the size of the lost mandate scaled by assets under management. In unreported regressions with post-firing excess returns as the dependent variable, we find that the coefficient on this scaled mandate is positive and significant (the coefficient is 0.008 with a t-statistic of 1.96), even in the presence of other control variables.

The extent to which such (mis)timing damages the performance of the plan sponsor depends on the performance of the investment managers hired to replace terminated managers. In other words, the appropriate comparison is the returns that the plan sponsor earned (post-hiring) relative to what it would have earned (post-firing). Although it is tempting to simply compare post-hiring returns in Exhibit 18.4 with post-firing returns in Exhibit 18.9 and conduct a cross-sectional analysis, we refrain from doing so because firing and hiring decisions are coordinated using complicated mechanisms. We proceed to an analysis of such "round-trips" below.

V. ROUND-TRIP TERMINATION AND SELECTION OF INVESTMENT MANAGERS

The best way to illustrate the complexity of a round-trip termination and selection decision is by way of examples.

> **Example 1.** In the first quarter of 2000, the St. Louis Employees Retirement System terminated 1,838 investment advisors for its core long-term fixed income portfolio, reportedly because of poor performance. It then hired Reams Asset Management to handle this $45 million portfolio. Watson Wyatt Investment Consulting assisted in the search.
>
> **Example 2.** In the first quarter of 2002, the Arapahoe County Employees Retirement System hired Barclays Global Investors to manage $15 million in passive global large-cap equity, Artisan Partners for a

$10-million active international all-cap equity mandate, Brazos for $9 million in active domestic micro-cap equity, and Royce for $5 million in active domestic small-cap equity. The Barclays hiring was funded by reallocating $15 million from a $44-million active domestic large-cap growth equities portfolio managed by Fayez Sarofim. Artisan's allocation came from terminating a $10-million active international all-cap equities portfolio managed by Brinson Partners. Brazos and Royce were funded by terminating a $14-million active domestic mid-cap growth equities portfolio managed by Denver Investment Advisors.

The first example is a straightforward round-trip firing and hiring decision in which the mandate size and type is the same, and the reason for the decision clearly delineated. The second contains two round-trip observations: (1) Denver Investment Advisors is terminated and replaced by Brazos and Royce. The mandates for the hired investment managers are different from the terminated investment manager and the allocation of the $14 million portfolio is not even. (2) Brinson Partners is terminated and replaced by Artisan Partners in the same mandate. Note that the Barclays Global Investors hiring does not create a round-trip observation since it is not the result of a termination but an allocation adjustment for an ongoing investment manager.

A. Sample Construction and Description

Because of the complexity of the process described above, we cannot mechanically associate hiring and firing decisions, and therefore build a sample using manual procedures. We start with our sample of firing decisions. For each firing decision, we match hiring decisions by the same plan sponsor up to one quarter after the firing date.[13] This produces 2,206 candidate firing–hiring decisions, which contain duplications, often because a hiring decision can be associated with more than one firing decision and vice versa. For each candidate observation, we then search for articles detailing the decisions in the following trade journals: *P&I*, *Investment Management Weekly*, *Money Management Letter*, and *Dow Jones Money Management Alert*. We mark each round-trip with an ID that allows us to track these decisions and eliminate duplications. This process identifies 663 round-trip firing/hiring decisions. We then match these round-trip decisions with our returns database, keeping only decisions for which we have some returns. As before, this eliminates decisions involving investments in hedge funds, venture capital funds, and private equity. Our final sample consists of 412 round-trip firing/hiring decisions between 1996 and 2003.

On average, each round-trip decision is associated with the firing and hiring of 1.1 investment managers, with a maximum of 11 investment managers hired or seven investment managers fired in a particular decision. The average mandate size for firing is $116 million while the average mandate size for hiring is $102 million.

B. Round-Trip Performance

If more than one firm is fired (or hired), we compute the excess return for that round-trip observation as the average across the fired (or hired) firms. In Example 2 described above, pre- and post-firing returns for Denver International Advisors would be compared to the average of the pre- and post-hiring returns of Brazos and Royce. Both hired and fired firms are required to have returns over a particular evaluation horizon.

Panel A of Exhibit 18.10 shows average pre- and post-event cumulative excess returns for fired and hired firms for the entire sample. Consistent with

EXHIBIT 18.10 Round-Trip Excess Returns for Investment Managers

Returns are cumulated separately for hired and fired firms. In Panel A, we show the separate returns for hired and fired investment managers, as well as the return differential for the entire sample of round-trips. In Panel B, we show only the return differential for various subsamples. Heteroskedasticity and serial correlation consistent standard errors are calculated using the procedure described in Jegadeesh and Karceski (2004) and appear in parentheses. Low and high cutoffs for the allocation index are based on the bottom and top quartiles. Similarly, small and large cutoffs for sponsor size are based on the bottom and top quartiles.

	Pre-Event Period			Post-Event Period		
	−3 to 0	−2 to 0	−1 to 0	0 to 1	0 to 2	0 to 3
Panel A: Cumulative Excess Returns						
Fired firms	2.03	−1.57	−0.11	1.83	3.14	4.26
	(1.56)	(1.51)	(0.83)	(0.82)	(1.47)	(1.45)
Hired firms	11.55	7.55	4.46	1.34	2.26	3.23
	(3.11)	(1.60)	(1.52)	(0.42)	(0.56)	(0.41)
Return differential (hired–fired)	9.52	9.12	4.56	−0.48	−0.88	−1.03
	(2.47)	(2.30)	(1.00)	(0.78)	(1.33)	(1.14)
Number of round-trips	331	389	412	412	389	331
Panel B: Return Differentials (Hired–Fired Returns) for Subsamples						
Performance	13.13	12.36	6.13	−0.66	−0.56	−0.79
	(2.67)	(2.94)	(1.27)	(1.34)	(1.73)	(1.79)
Nonperformance	7.89	7.58	3.80	−0.40	−1.04	−1.14
	(2.81)	(2.35)	(0.96)	(0.60)	(1.14)	(0.88)

(Continued)

EXHIBIT 18.10   (*Continued*)

	Pre-Event Period			Post-Event Period		
	−3 to 0	−2 to 0	−1 to 0	0 to 1	0 to 2	0 to 3
p-value for difference	0.06	0.10	0.02	0.81	0.56	0.73
Headline risk-sensitive	9.55	9.57	4.55	−0.26	−0.76	−0.68
	(2.33)	(2.48)	(0.70)	(0.66)	(1.41)	(1.29)
Headline risk-resistant	9.57	7.62	4.98	−1.46	−1.13	−2.18
	(2.51)	(2.51)	(2.72)	(1.45)	(1.85)	(2.29)
p-value for difference	0.99	0.58	0.87	0.30	0.73	0.38
Small plan sponsors	6.14	5.36	3.32	−0.54	−1.34	−1.39
	(1.91)	(1.62)	(1.02)	(1.14)	(1.37)	(1.33)
Large plan sponsors	13.21	11.68	4.80	−0.30	0.19	0.53
	(2.31)	(1.50)	(0.55)	(0.38)	(0.88)	(0.51)
p-value for difference	0.26	0.22	0.42	0.84	0.25	0.07
Low allocation index	11.59	10.73	4.39	−1.49	−1.79	−2.17
	(2.78)	(2.44)	(1.32)	(1.18)	(2.08)	(1.87)
High allocation index	10.61	9.87	5.33	0.06	−0.77	0.25
	(3.72)	(3.21)	(1.07)	(1.02)	(1.16)	(0.97)
p-value for difference	0.75	0.73	0.29	0.10	0.45	0.14
No consultant	3.24	2.08	2.00	−1.11	−1.04	−1.11
	(1.49)	(1.04)	(1.04)	(1.03)	(0.79)	(0.79)
Consultant	10.69	10.25	4.97	−0.39	−0.86	−1.02
	(2.27)	(2.19)	(1.01)	(0.92)	(1.67)	(1.53)
p-value for difference	0.10	0.05	0.03	0.57	0.85	0.92

earlier results, the pre-firing returns for the overall sample fired firms are statistically indistinguishable from zero because they mix different termination reasons. Post-firing returns are positive, and interestingly, statistically significant at all three horizons. Also mirroring results from earlier tables, pre-hiring excess returns are large and positive. In general, this pattern of returns is reassuring because it suggests that our round-trip sample is similar to the earlier (larger) hiring and firing samples. In addition to hired and fired firm's returns, we also report return differences (hired firm's excess returns minus fired firm's excess returns) with corresponding standard errors. Prior to the firing/hiring decision, the return differences are large, positive, and statistically significant. The three-year (one-year) cumulative excess return difference prior to the firing/hiring is 9.5 percent (4.6 percent) with a standard error of 2.5 percent (1.00 percent). After the hiring/firing decision, the performance of the fired firms exceeds that of the newly hired firms over all three horizons but with larger standard errors;

the three-year cumulative excess return difference is -1.03 percent but with a standard error of 1.1 percent.

We would like to understand the relation between the opportunity costs described above and plan sponsor attributes. Unfortunately, our cross-sectional analysis is hindered by small sample sizes; we cannot estimate cross-sectional regressions of the form reported in Exhibit 18.5. As a result, we report pre- and post-event return differentials for various categories of the data in Panel B of Exhibit 18.10.[14] The p-values for differences in returns between subcategories are also shown. Not surprisingly, pre-event return differences are significantly higher for performance-based terminations than nonperformance-based firings. Post-event return differentials are negative for both groups, but statistically indistinguishable from each other. Pre-event return differences are also larger for round-trips that use consultants but post-event return differentials are not statistically significant. In fact, for all the categories that we examine (headline risk, sponsor size, allocation index, and consultant use), the post-event return differentials across subcategories are not different from each other.

C. Discussion

How does one interpret the overall evidence from round-trips? The opportunity costs are positive but with high standard errors. If one adds transition costs discussed in the introduction (say, 1.0 percent to 2.0 percent) to these opportunity costs, the overall costs of firing and hiring investment managers rise further.[15] Moreover, if the costs associated with hiring and firing investment managers are important, then at the margin they should play a role in retention decisions. Typically, an investment management firm is hired for a given term, but then can be "rehired" for a subsequent term. If replacement costs are relevant, then the pre-rehiring performance that justifies retention should be lower than for brand new hiring. To determine if that is the case, we create a sample of retentions. We examine a random sample of 350 plan sponsors in Nelson's Directory of Plan Sponsors (2005). Nelson's reports the name of investment managers with mandates from each plan sponsor as of 2004, the year that investment manager was originally hired, and the investment mandate. We manually record this information for investment management firms that are in our returns database, where the mandate amount is recorded and where the original hiring year is before 2000. We then assume that a retention decision is made every three years. For example, if XYZ Asset Management was originally hired by ABC Plan Sponsor in 1996, we assume a retention decision is made in 1999 and 2002. In total, our sample consists of 1,867 retention decisions. We then compute pre-retention returns in the same manner as before and compare them to pre-hiring returns for the same plan sponsors. We find that the average one-year (three-year) cumulative excess return for retentions is 2.4 percent (6.1 percent), compared with 4.9 percent (14.7 percent) for hiring decisions by the same plan sponsors. This suggests that in making retention decisions, plan sponsors incorporate the costs associated with hiring and firing.

VI. CONCLUSIONS

To summarize, we find that plan sponsors hire investment managers after superior performance but on average, post-hiring excess returns are zero. Plan sponsors fire investment managers for many reasons, including but not exclusively for underperformance. But, post-firing excess returns are frequently positive and sometimes statistically significant. Our sample of round-trips shows that if plan sponsors had stayed with fired investment managers, their excess returns would be no different from those actually delivered by newly hired managers.

It could be the case that the costs documented and discussed above have compensating benefits that we are unable to measure. From an efficiency perspective, terminating investment managers could be critical to maintaining discipline among incumbents and maintaining a competitive marketplace. It is also possible that the agency relationships described by Lakonishok et al. (1992) create such high barriers to change so as to make it impossible to eliminate the costs. Some of our cross-sectional results are consistent with both of the above possibilities, especially since variation in the efficacy of hiring and firing appears to be related to the economic circumstances of plan sponsors. Although beyond the scope of this paper, there are several other analyses that could enhance our understanding of this form of delegated investment management. For instance, as pointed out by Hart (1992), it is useful to consider whether broad asset class allocations are efficient or reflect nonvalue maximizing behavior. Given the magnitude of assets under the jurisdiction of plan sponsors, correlated shifts in asset allocations could have important implications for asset pricing. We leave this to future research.

APPENDIX: STANDARD ERROR CALCULATION

The sample comprises N hiring/firing decisions of investment managers by plan sponsors ("events"). We wish to test whether the managers exhibit excess return performance from the event date through an H-quarter holding period. We define the H-quarter cumulative excess return (CER) for investment manager i that starts at the beginning of the event quarter t as the cumulative excess return:

$$CER_i(t, H) = \sum_{s=t}^{t+H-1} (R_{i,s} - R_{b,s}) \qquad (A.1)$$

where $R_{i,s}$ is the return on the mandate type by the investment manager i in quarter s, and $R_{b,s}$ is the return on the benchmark b in quarter s. We define:

$$\overline{CER}_{\text{sample}}(H) = \frac{1}{N} \sum_{i=1}^{N} CER_i(t, H) \qquad (A.2)$$

Let N_t equal the number of events in the sample in quarter t, and let N be the total number of events in the sample. Therefore $N = \sum_{t=1}^{T} N_t$. We define the average abnormal return for each event quarter t across all events in that quarter (we refer to this group of events as a quarterly cohort) as

$$\overline{CER}(t, H) = \begin{cases} \dfrac{1}{N_t} \sum_{i=1}^{N_t} CER_i(t, H), & \text{if } N_t > 0 \\ 0 & \text{otherwise} \end{cases} \qquad (A.3)$$

Let $\overline{CER}(H)$ be a $T \times 1$ column vector where the tth element equals $\overline{CER}(t, H)$. $\overline{CER}(H)$ is the average long-run excess return of each quarterly cohort. Define w as a $T \times 1$ column vector of weights where the tth element is the ratio of the number of events that occur in quarter t divided by N. Specifically, $w(t) = N_t/N$. Note that the sample average excess return is equal to the quarterly weight vector w times the average excess return of each quarterly cohort:

$$\overline{CER}_{\text{sample}}(H) = w'\overline{CER}(H) \qquad (A.4)$$

The variance of $CER_{\text{sample}}(H)$ is given by

$$\sigma^2\left(\overline{CER}_{\text{sample}}(H)\right) = w'Vw \qquad (A.5)$$

where V is the $T \times T$ variance covariance matrix of $CER(H)$.

Our estimator for V allows for heteroskedasticity as well as serial correlation and is denoted as HSC. The st^{th} element of HSC is

$$hsc_{st} = \begin{cases} \dfrac{(H-l)}{l} \overline{CER}(s, H)\overline{CER}(t, H), & \text{if } l = |s - t| < H \\ 0 & \text{otherwise} \end{cases} \qquad (A.6)$$

This estimator uses the Newey and West (1987) weighting scheme and ensures that HSC is positive definite.

EXHIBIT A.1 Investment Mandates and Indexes

Investment Mandate	Description	Index
Domestic Equity		
Largecap	Large-cap equity	S&P 500
Largecapcore	Large-cap—between growth & value	S&P 500
Largecapgrowth	Large-cap—growth	S&P 500/BARRA Growth
Largecapvalue	Large-cap—value	S&P 500/BARRA Value
Midcap	Mid-cap equity	S&P Midcap 400
Midcapcore	Mid-cap—between growth and value	S&P Midcap 400
Midcapgrowth	Mid-cap—growth	S&P/BARRA Mid Cap Growth
Midcapvalue	Mid-cap—value	S&P/BARRA Mid Cap Value
Smallcap	Small-cap equity	S&P Small Cap 600
Smallcapcore	Small-cap—between growth and value	S&P Small Cap 600
Smallcapgrowth	Small-cap—growth	S&P/BARRA Small Cap Growth
Smallcapmicro	Small-cap—value	S&P Small Cap 600
Smallcapvalue	Small-cap equity	S&P/BARRA Small Cap Value
Investment Mandate	*Description*	*Index*
Smid	Small to mid-cap equity	Russell 2500
Smidcapcore	Small to mid-cap—between growth and value	Russell 2500
Smidcapgrowth	Small to mid-cap—growth	Russell 2500 Growth
Smidcapvalue	Small to mid-cap—indexed	Russell 2500 Value
Equitygrowth	All equity–growth	Russell 3000 Growth
Equityvalue	All equity—value	Russell 3000 Value
Equitycombined	All equity	Russell 3000
International Equity		
Emergmkteq	Emerging market equity	MSCI Emerging Markets Free
Europeincuk	Europe incl. U.K.	MSCI Europe 15
Europeincuksm	Europe including U.K.—small-cap	MSCI Europe S/C
Globaleq	Global equity (incl. U.S.)	MSCI World Free
Intleq	International equity	MSCI EAFE Free

EXHIBIT A.1 (*Continued*)

Investment Mandate	Description	Index
Intleqsmall	International equity—small-cap	MSCI EAFE S/C
Pacbasinincj	Pacific basin incl. Japan	MSCI AC Pacific Free
Fixed income		
Convertibles	Convertibles	Merrill Lynch Inv Grade Convertible
Fixed1–3yrs	Duration between one and 3 years	Merrill Lynch Govt/Corp, 1–3 Years
Fixedcore	Inv. and non-inv. grade, duration 3–7 years	Lehman Aggregate
Fixedcoreinvest	Inv. grade, duration 3–7 years	Lehman Aggregate
Fixedcoreopportun	Non-inv. grade, duration 3–7 years	Lehman Aggregate
Fixedhighyield	High yield securities	Lehman High Yield Composite
Shortterm	Duration between 1 and 2.4 years	Citigroup 3-Month T-Bill
Fixedintermed	Duration between 2 and 4.6 years	Lehman International Aggregate
Fixedlongdura	Duration greater than 6 years	Lehman Long Govt/Credit
Mortgageb	Mortgage-backed securities	Lehman Mortgages
Fixedcombined	All fixed income	Lehman Aggregate
Emergmktdebt	Emerging market debt	JP Morgan ELMI+
Globalfixhedg	Global fixed income—hedged	Lehman Global Aggregate (Hedged)
Globalfixunhedg	Global fixed income—unhedged	Lehman Global Aggregate (Unhedged)
Intlfixedhedg	International fixed income—hedged	Citigroup Non-US WGBI (Hedged)
Intlfixedunhedg	International fixed income	Citigroup Non-US WGBI income—unhedged (Unhedged)
Others		
Realestate	Real estate	NCREIF Property
Realestateselect	Real estate select	NCREIF Property
REITs	REITs	NAREIT
TAA	Tactical asset allocation	Average of S&P 500 and Lehman
Balanced	Balanced	Average of S&P 500 and Lehman Aggregate

NOTES

1. Institutions are more likely to be marginal traders than individual investors in most markets; consequently, their impact on asset pricing could be substantial. This is eloquently described by Cornell and Roll (2005, p. 59) who argue ". . . consumption decisions, whether to buy a television or take a vacation are made by consumers. The decision to buy IBM or Intel is delegated," and develop a simple yet elegant delegated-agent asset-pricing model.

2. A partial list of contributions in the literature on performance and persistence includes Bollen and Busse (2005), Brown and Goetzmann (1995), Carhart (1997), Carhart et al. (2004), Daniel et al. (1997), Elton et al. (1992), Goetzmann and Ibbotson (1994), Grinblatt and Titman (1992), Grinblatt, Titman, and Wermers (1995), Hendricks, Patel, and Zeckhauser (1993), Ippolito (1989), Jensen (1968),Wermers (2000), and Zheng (1999). Fund flows and returns are studied by Chevalier and Ellison (1999), Gruber (1996), and Sirri and Tufano (1998). The third stream includes Barber and Odean (2000), Barber, Odean, and Zheng (2005), and Odean (1998, 1999). This list of citations is certainly not comprehensive. Omissions are not willful and we offer our apologies to authors not cited.

3. Although we frequently refer to "investment managers," our unit of analysis throughout the paper is the investment management firm, not individuals at these firms.

4. These results are similar to those of Odean (1998) for retail investors and Elton, Gruber, and Blake (2006) for 401(k) plans. Odean finds that the excess returns on winning stocks sold by individual investors are larger than the excess returns on loser stocks that could be, but are not, sold. Elton et al. (2006) find that administrators select funds that did well in the past but after the change, do no better than funds that were dropped.

5. If such frictions are important, then one would expect the return threshold for retention decisions (in which an incumbent manager is "rehired") to be lower than for brand new hiring decisions. Consistent with this, we find that pre-retention excess returns are positive but lower than pre-hiring excess returns.

6. A fourth possible explanation is that plan sponsors are simply unaware of these costs. We deem this explanation implausible.

7. Such plans are set up under Section 302(c)(5) of the Taft–Hartley Act, passed by Congress in 1947. Plan assets are jointly managed by a board of trustees representing labor and management. This is a sizeable market. Brull (2006) reports that 1,600 multiemployer plans had assets totaling $333 billion in 2002, and covered almost 10 million workers in 2005. He also reports that some 30,000 single-employer plans reported assets of $1.6 trillion in 2002 and covered 34.6 million workers.

8. Two well-known examples of this are David Swensen of the Yale University Endowment and Jack Meyer of the Harvard University Endowment.

9. Although this allocation index measures the strategic aspect of investment policy restrictions, to the extent that strategic and tactical restrictions are correlated, it is a proxy for both.

10. As a spot check, we check the value of this index for a handful of plan sponsors for which we obtain direct information on investment restrictions. We find that index values are indeed lower for plan sponsors that have quality and/or quantity restrictions on asset allocations.

11. Although the dependent variable is an excess return (say, raw return of a small-cap value manager minus the return on a small-cap value index), there may still be heterogeneity in investment manager returns within small-cap value asset class. For example, one manager might invest in micro-cap securities exclusively, even though its investment style is regarded as small-cap. These indicator variables account for such effects.

12. We also place some very low-frequency reasons in the above categories. Terminations because the consultant drops coverage of an investment manager (4 observations) or the plan sponsor is consolidating the number of managers to cut costs (22 observations), or the plan sponsor has funding needs (5 observations) are placed in the plan reorganization category. Three observations in which investment managers are terminated for style drift are included in the performance category.

13. We restrict our search for matching hiring decisions to one quarter after the firing to limit the amount of manual data collection required.

14. We only report results for subcategories with reasonable sample sizes. Also, we report return differentials, rather than separate firing and hiring returns to conserve space.

15. Subtracting a constant from the mean return obviously does not change the standard errors and will "make" the excess returns statistically significant.

REFERENCES

Allen, Franklin. 2001. Do financial institutions matter? *Journal of Finance* 56: 1165–1176.

Barber, Brad, and Terrance Odean. 2000. Trading is hazardous to your wealth: The common stock investment performance of individual investors. *Journal of Finance*, 773–806.

Barber, Brad, Terrance Odean, and Lu Zheng. 2005. Out of sight, out of mind: The effects of expenses on mutual fund flows. *Journal of Business* 78:2095–2120.

Barberis, Nicholas, and Andrei Shleifer. 2003. Style investing. *Journal of Financial Economics* 68:161–199.

Bollen, Brian. 2004. Lost in transition? *Financial News*, April 19.

Bollen, Nicholas, and Jeffrey Busse. 2005. Short-term persistence in mutual fund performance. *Review of Financial Studies* 18:569–597.

Brickley, James, Ronald Lease, and Clifford Smith. 1988. Ownership structure and voting on antitakeover amendments. *Journal of Financial Economics* 20: 267–291.

Brown, Keith, W. V. Harlow, and Laura Starks. 1996. Of tournaments and temptations: An analysis of managerial incentives in the mutual fund industry. *Journal of Finance* 51:85–110.

Brown, Stephen, and William Goetzmann. 1995. Performance persistence. *Journal of Finance* 50:679–698.

Brull, Steven. 2006. Rich plan, poor plan. *Institutional Investor* 40:30–35.

Busse, Jeffrey. 2001. Another look at mutual fund tournaments. *Journal of Financial and Quantitative Analysis* 36:53–73.

Busse, Jeffrey, Amit Goyal, and Sunil Wahal. 2007. Performance persistence in institutional investment management. Working Paper, Arizona State University.

Carhart, Mark. 1997. On persistence in mutual fund performance. *Journal of Finance* 52:57–82.

Carhart, Mark M., Jennifer N. Carpenter, Anthony W. Lynch, and David K. Musto. 2002. Mutual fund survivorship. *Review of Financial Studies* 5:1439–1463.

Chevalier, Judith, and Glen Ellison. 1999. Career concerns of mutual fund managers. *Quarterly Journal of Economics* 114:389–432.

Christopherson, Jon A., Wayne Ferson, and Debra Glassman. 1998. Conditioning manager alphas on economic information: Another look at the persistence of performance. *Review of Financial Studies* 11:111–142.

Coggin, T. Daniel, Frank Fabozzi, and Shafiqur Rahman. 1993. The investment performance of U.S. equity pension fund managers: An empirical investigation. *Journal of Finance* 48:1039–1055.

Cornell, Bradford, and Richard Roll. 2005. A delegated agent asset-pricing model. *Financial Analysts Journal* 61:57–69.

Daniel, Kent, Mark Grinblatt, Sheridan Titman, and Russ Wermers. 1997. Measuring mutual fund performance with characteristic-based benchmarks. *Journal of Finance* 52:1035–1058.

Del Guercio, Diane, and Paula Tkac. 2002. The determinants of the flow of funds of managed portfolios: Mutual funds versus pension funds. *Journal of Financial and Quantitative Analysis* 37:523–557.

Elton, Edwin, Martin Gruber, and Christopher Blake. 1996. The persistence of risk-adjusted mutual fund performance. *Journal of Business* 69:133–157.

Elton, Edwin, Martin Gruber, and Christopher Blake. 2006. Participant reaction and the performance of funds offered by 401(k) plans. Working Paper, New York University.

Elton, Edwin, Martin Gruber, Sanjiv Das, and Mathew Hlavka. 1992. Efficiency with costly information: A reinterpretation of the evidence for managed portfolios. *Review of Financial Studies* 6:1–22.

Fabozzi, Frank. 1997. *Pension fund investment management*. New Hope, PA: Frank J. Fabozzi Associates.

Fama, Eugene, and Kenneth French. 1993. Common risk factors in the returns on stocks and bonds. *Journal of Financial Economics* 33:3–56.

Franzoni, Francesco, and Jose M. Marín. 2006. Pension plan funding and stock market efficiency. *Journal of Finance* 61:921–956.

Gallo, J. G., and Larry Lockwood. 1997. Benefits of proper style classification of equity portfolio managers. *Journal of Portfolio Management* 23:47–55.

Goetzmann, William, and Roger Ibbotson. 1994. Do winners repeat? Patterns in mutual fund performance. *Journal of Portfolio Management* 20:9–18.

Grinblatt, Mark, and Sheridan Titman. 1992. The persistence of mutual fund performance. *Journal of Finance* 47:1977–1984.

Grinblatt, Mark, Sheridan Titman, and Russ Wermers. 1995. Momentum investing strategies, portfolio performance and herding: A study of mutual fund behavior. *American Economic Review* 85:1088–1105.

Gruber, Martin. 1996. Another puzzle: The growth in actively managed mutual funds. *Journal of Finance* 51:783–810.

Hart, Oliver. 1992. Comments on "The structure and performance of the money management industry." *Brookings Papers: Microeconomics*, 380–384.

Heisler, Jeffrey, Christopher R. Knittel, John J. Neumann, and Scott Stewart. 2007. Why do institutional plan sponsors fire their investment managers? *Journal of Business and Economic Studies* 13;88–115.

Hendricks, Darryll, Jayendu Patel, Richard Zeckhauser. 1993. Hot hands in mutual funds: Short-run persistence of performance, 1974–1988. *Journal of Finance* 48:93–130.

Investment Company Institute. 2004. Trends in mutual fund investing, www.ici.org/stats/index.html.

Ippolito, Richard. 1989. Efficiency with costly information: A study of mutual fund performance, 1965–1984. *Quarterly Journal of Economics* 104:1–23.

Jegadeesh, Narasimhan, and Jason Karceski. 2004. Long-run performance evaluation: Correlation and heteroskedasticity-consistent tests. Working Paper, Emory University.

Jensen, Michael. 1968. The performance of mutual funds in the period 1945–1964. *Journal of Finance* 48:389–416.

Lakonishok, Josef, Andrei Shleifer, and Robert Vishny. 1992. The structure and performance of the money management industry. *Brookings Papers: Micro-economics*, 339–379.

Logue, Dennis E., and Jack S. Rader. 1998. *Managing pension plans: A comprehensive guide to improving plan performance.* Boston: Harvard Business School Press.

Madalla, G. S. 1983. *Limited dependent variables and qualitative variables in econometrics.* Econometric Society Monographs, Number 3. Cambridge: Cambridge University Press.

Money market directory of investment managers and plan sponsors. 2004. Charlottesville, VA.

Nelson's directory of investment managers. 2002 and 2004. Port Chester, NY: Nelson Publications.

Nelson's directory of plan sponsors. 2005. Port Chester, NY: Nelson Publications.

Newey, Whitney, and Kenneth West. 1987. A simple, positive definite, heteroskedasticity, and autocorrelation consistent covariance matrix. *Econometrica* 55:703–708.

Odean, Terrance. 1998. Are investors reluctant to realize their losses? *Journal of Finance* 53:1775–1798.

Odean, Terrance. 1999. Do investors trade too much? *American Economic Review* 89:1279–1298.

Proszek, Stan. 2002. Transition management: Simple—but not easy. *Benefits and Pensions Monitor*, October 12.

Sirri, Erik, and Peter Tufano. 1998. Costly search and mutual fund flows. *Journal of Finance* 53:1589–1622.

Travers, Frank J. 2004. *Investment manager analysis: A comprehensive guide to portfolio selection, monitoring and optimization.* New York: John Wiley & Sons.

Wermers, Russ. 2000. Mutual fund performance: An empirical decomposition into stock-picking talent, style, transactions costs, and expenses. *Journal of Finance* 55:1655–1695.

Werner, Bob. 2001. The true costs and benefits of portfolio transition management, www.russell.com/AU/press room/Press Releases/PR20011004/AU/p.asp.

Zheng, Lu. 1999. Is money smart? A study of mutual fund investors' fund selection ability. *Journal of Finance* 54:901–933.

Five

The Execution
Challenges

CHAPTER **19**

The Market Price Challenge

Francis Gupta, PhD and
John A. Prestbo
Dow Jones Indexes

Are dark pools the sell side's tactic, or revenge? Do the benefits of dark pools' lower trading costs outweigh diminished transparency? Over the past 20 years, volume on Nasdaq has increased over 20,000 percent. Could one argue than innovation and adaptability have been achieved at reasonable costs to investors and beneficiaries?

From 1988 to 1998, the volume on the Nasdaq increased nearly sixfold, from an average 123.3 million shares a day to 700.3 million. A decade later, in 2008, average daily volume had jumped almost four times further, to 2.7 billion shares. But because the calendar didn't stretch, that increase translated to a growth in average daily trades from 46,273 in 1988 to 9.6 million in 2008—an increase of more than 20,000 percent. And because the official trading day remained fixed at 6.5 hours, the average number of trades per minute (tpm) ballooned from 119 tpm in 1988 to 24,607 tpm in 2008.

In other words, in 20 years, the Nasdaq went from two trades a second to 410. It's a story that has been repeated on every major exchange in the world, and is beginning to be duplicated on smaller exchanges in emerging and "frontier" markets. Apparently, the price-reporting challenge will not end as long as volume levels climb ever higher.

Date	Average Daily Trades	Number of Trades per Minute[*]	Average Daily Volume
1/1/1988	46,273	119	123,270,350
1/1/1998	468,891	1,202	700,347,950
1/1/2008	9,596,862	24,607	2,696,004,783

[*]Number of minutes in 6.5-hour trading day = 390.
Source: NASDAQ OMX Group.

Great leaps forward in technology enable the Nasdaq and all the other exchanges to accommodate the growing torrents of trading. But the technology leaps are never enough. "As soon as one market participant ratchets up the quickness of its trading environment, competitive forces dictate that others will play catch-up. Thus, the cycle . . . is never complete . . . ," says an April 2008 report by TABB Group, a Westborough, Massachusetts, research firm.

In addition to increased and widespread stock ownership, technology also is part of the problem. Those same advances also contribute to both the amount and the velocity of share volume. Algorithmic trading, for example, essentially uses computers to decide to initiate orders based on information that is received electronically, long before human traders are capable of being aware of the information, much less comprehending it. Dow Jones News Service sends out on its "algo" feed data-elementized versions of news such as the government's announcement of the un-employment number and the Consumer Price Index and Microsoft's earn-ings, among thousands of other hot statistics, and computers react with trade orders specifying price, size, and timing.

One consulting firm, Boston-based Aite Group, estimates that in 2008 more than a third of stock-exchange volume in the United States is gener-ated by algorithmically programmed computers. The firm forecasts that more than 50 percent of all equities trading will be done algorithmically by the end of 2010. "Most of this will still be driven by the sell side, but an increasing number of traditional asset managers and hedge funds are jump-ing into the algorithmic trading market, and they will ultimately lead the market into higher adoption rates," one Aite Group report says.

To be sure, the price-reporting challenge is broader than just the stock market. Commodities, currencies, and bonds are all traded vigorously. And there are some slower-trading markets—such as securities of financially distressed companies—that have different kinds of price problems. To more fully understand the price-reporting challenge, let's back up a few steps and review the role prices play in markets.

THE ROLE OF PRICES

The most obvious role of prices for a product (or service, for that matter) is in the creation of a market for that product and to assist in the continuing market-making for that product. By *market creation* we mean the rules under which buyers and sellers transact for a given good or service. Since price is defined as the amount of money to be paid by the buyer to the seller to acquire a given product, prices are the prerequisite to the creation of a market—though price alone will not necessarily create a market. For example, the existence of a price for a public good doesn't mean that buyers are willing to pay for it, and if they are not, the market will cease to exist.

Additionally, *price transparency*—meaning any buyer interested in purchasing a specific product can access the price of the product—assists in developing and making the market. If prices are not transparent, buyers who are unable to observe the price are excluded and efficient market-making is crippled. In some markets, transparency is intentionally diminished to give brokers and dealers a knowledge advantage over their customers. The brokers and dealers seek to make more money; they are not interested in fostering an efficient market, which tends to squeeze profit margins. Many parts of the bond market are examples of keeping prices out of sight of many customers.

Valuations

Valuing an asset, or a portfolio of assets, is important not only for accounting purposes but also for evaluating and making decisions regarding net worth, creditworthiness, insurance needs, and a multitude of day-to-day business transactions. Depending on the objective for the asset valuation, different types of prices may be called for. If the goal is estimating the liquidation value of a portfolio, for instance, the best proxy for valuation calls for prices at which the assets can be sold. If a market in the asset exists and is liquid (such as for publicly traded stocks and bonds), and market prices are readily available, valuation of the asset may be easy and relatively accurate.

However, if there is no market for the asset, or if the asset under consideration is not fungible (such as an artifact), methods other than market prices will have to be used to ascertain prices, which most likely will be approximate or best estimates. Approximations may not be very useful in many situations, such as assessing the liquidation value of a portfolio, but for some other purposes (such as estimating the value of a master painting for the reason of buying insurance) they can do as good a job as a cash equivalent valuation.

Asset Management

Most long-term (buy-and-hold) investment strategies—whether they are driven by quantitative models or fundamental objective analysis—rely on reasonably accurate security prices for implementation. The prices allow the manager of the portfolio to make "buy" decisions for the securities to include in the portfolio (those that are expected to grow in value) and to make "sell" decisions for the securities to remove from the portfolio (so as to lock in gains or to discard lemons). Though prices are crucial for portfolio management, it is important to note that a long-term investor still would be able to manage a portfolio if prices of component securities were determined only (say) once a day. Indeed, most mutual funds are priced daily. Since the objective of asset managers is to maximize returns, not through the timing of their buying and selling decisions, but through the buying and holding of securities that are expected to outperform the market, not much is gained or lost through real-time or "continuous" pricing of component securities. However, traders of securities for speculation rely to a great extent on accurate real-time and frequent prices.

Trading

Short-term speculative trading of securities and financial instruments, on a public or private exchange, in pursuit of short-run gains is a very specific type of market. Speculative trading can be defined as a bet on the price movement of a security. As long as there are buyers and sellers with opposing views on the short-term price movement of a security, then access to prices will create a speculative market. Therefore, these markets rely on quick access to the prices of securities and movements in prices due to changes in buyers' and sellers' short-term expectations, as a consequence of events believed to influence the prices.

In the case of speculative trading, price is seen less as a proxy of the asset's value and more as a signal that the current market for the asset can be exploited for a short-term gain. So, for instance, even if traders believe an asset is overpriced they may be willing to buy the asset if they believe that they will be able to sell it for an even higher price in the near future. Consequently, in addition to the availability of price, there are other factors that are equally important in the success of such a market. These include: changes (or volatility) in prices, momentum (or trends) in prices, spreads between the price being offered by a buyer (bid) and that being quoted by the seller (ask), and finally an outcome of all of this, the degree of exchange taking place (trading volume) in the asset. A lion's share of the daily trading volume can be attributed to speculative trading.

Basis of Arbitrage

For buyers and sellers to participate in arbitrage, prices of securities, commodities, or whatever must exist not only in one market but also in at least one other market. In addition, it must be priced using a common unit of value. If these conditions are satisfied, and the price for a commodity in one market differs from another market (including transaction costs), then buyers and sellers with access to both markets will buy in the market where the price is lower and sell in the market where the price is higher—thereby ensuring that the prices in the two markets move into equilibrium. Put differently, arbitrage ensures that the prices and therefore the markets for a commodity are "efficient." Real-time pricing is essential for this form of trading.

Risk Measurement and Management

All quantitative measures of risk require a time series of prices (to estimate the variance–covariance matrix) for the securities that make up the portfolio whose risk is being measured. The greater need in this instance is not real-time pricing—depending on what the risk estimate is being used for, once a day or even once a month can be adequate—but that the prices need to be consistently precise over the entire time series. Precise time series allow for a more accurate representation of the relationships among the component security prices, which is the key to the calculation of a better quantitative risk measure. Better risk measures are a prerequisite for better risk-management practices. Erroneous prices will lead to erroneous risk estimates that will lead to erroneous decisions, which can prove costly.

THE ATTRIBUTES OF PRICES

There are three key attributes of pricing, which together determine the information content within a given time series of prices.

Timeliness refers to the lapse between a transaction occurring and the price at which the transaction took place becoming public information. The more timely the price, the faster it is public information and therefore the more informative the price for certain kinds of investors. In general, all things being equal, the older (or more stale) that a security price is, the less informative it is regarding the future price of the security. But sometimes, for thinly traded securities or those old master paintings, a stale price is all that buyers and sellers have to go by.

The information technology (IT) folks call this time lapse *latency*. It is being attacked on two fronts: increasing the speed of computers and relocating computers. The fastest transaction processing currently is almost down to single-digit milliseconds (a millisecond is one-thousandth of a second). IT departments at the busiest exchanges now are working to boost that speed to microseconds (one-millionth of a second). Steve Rubinow, chief information officer of NYSE Euronext, which operates the New York

Stock Exchange, has been quoted as saying, "The core trading stuff has to be in the hundredths of microseconds." (Exchange feeds carry more information than prices. Other kinds of messages, such as time of trade, volume of trade, and corrections, also come through the pipe.) Multi-core processors have been important to increasing speed thus far. In the future, Mr. Rubinow expects to see high-speed optical, biochemical, molecular, and quantum chips accelerate speeds beyond what multicore chips can achieve.

The ceiling on speed is the speed of light. Light travels at the rate of one foot per nanosecond. With 5,280 feet in a mile and the NYSE's data centers being located about 10 miles from Wall Street, there are 105,600 nanoseconds, or 105 microseconds, of latency that faster computers can't overcome. But what really slows the data flow is the number of network "hops" that data makes along the way. So, the NYSE went into the collocation business, renting space in a NYSE data center for client firms' servers. That shortens the path data travels between the exchange and, say, a brokerage firm, which reduces latency. In 2007, Mr. Rubinow said, "[T]he biggest institution that collocates with us said they need 100 cabinets. Three months [later] another institution said they needed 300 cabinets. If we gave everybody 300 cabinets, we'd need a data center the size of New Jersey." Indeed, the NYSE is building a new data center that will have a "huge" amount of collocation space, he says. "Customers keep saying, make it bigger and faster. I don't know what the point of diminishing returns is. Infinity?"

Frequency is a function of the underlying market activity and the transparency of a marketplace. Most large blue-chip stocks are traded frequently on a fully transparent public exchange. Therefore, the frequency of price updates is high. By contrast, fixed-income securities are also traded frequently, but on a partially opaque private marketplace. Therefore, the frequency of price updates is limited. For other securities, such as distressed debt, the frequency of pricing may be low because the number of transactions is small.

Accuracy and precision refer to how good a job a given price of a security does at predicting the value of the security. Or, to put it another way, how closely a given price of a security predicts the price at which the next trade for that security happens. The smaller the difference between the most recent price and the price at which the next trade occurs, the more accurate the price. In cases where the security is highly liquid and the frequency of pricing is in real time (such as the large blue-chip stocks), the price at which the last transaction or trade occurred is the best predictor of the price of the next trade and therefore the most accurate price. The more illiquid the security, the less accurate the most recent price will be in predicting the next transaction price.

PRICE DETERMINATION

The most common form of quoting prices for publicly traded stocks is *mark to market*. When securities are traded in a liquid and transparent market-place (e.g., a blue-chip stock on a highly "efficient" public exchange with many buyers and sellers), the best indicator of value of a stock is the price at which the most recent trade took place. If you were an owner of that stock and were seeking to value the security for the purposes of accounting, or for a potential sale, then the best price to use would be the market price at which the most recent transaction took place.

Similarly, if you were seeking to buy this stock, the best indicator of how much you would be expected to pay would be the price at which the most recent transaction occurred. Clearly, the price at which the last transaction took place is the best indicator of the next transaction's price, but it is unlikely that the next transaction will take place at exactly that price. The market price (or the price at which the most recent trans-action took place), together with other factors, is used by the buyers and sellers to update their bids and asks, which in turn determines the evolu-tion of the market price.

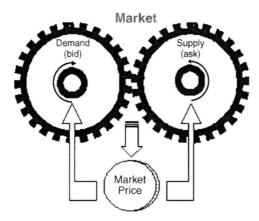

For thinly traded securities, the mark-to-market price may sometimes not exist. If it does exist, it is not timely and might not be the best indicator of the price (value) of the security. In the case of securities such as distressed debt, the market itself may not exist to mark the value to. Or if a market does exist, the price of the most recent transaction is so stale that it is no longer indicative of the value of the security. In such a case, the pricing agent may use a model to price or value the security.

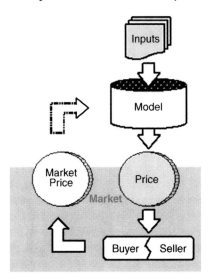

Typically, such a model will include characteristics of the security that are valued by buyers and sellers. Anyone who has used a *blue book* to assess the value of a used car is familiar with the *marked-to-model* concept. In the case of a used car, these characteristics could include make, model, year, miles, color, and so forth. With securities, if one were using a discounted cash flow model, these characteristics might include expected future cash flow and the discount rate as the inputs into the asset valuation model. As one might expect, prices for the same security will most likely differ depending on the model. One very large market using marked-to-model prices is the options market, where the Black-Scholes pricing model is well-entrenched.

Accuracy of the model does not necessarily increase with the more characteristics it has, however. Characteristics whose impact on price is poorly understood may be modeled incorrectly, thereby exacerbating the errors within the model-determined price. In any case, the marked-to-model price is used as a guide by the buyer and seller of the underlying security. The price at which the seller and buyer do business can differ significantly from that predicted by the model. As more esoteric securities and financial instruments are traded, good marked-to-model prices become a bigger and bigger challenge. The more esoteric the securities, the greater the risk of the mark-to-model price differing significantly from actual transaction prices.

In cases where a single security is traded through many private transactions (as in the case of bonds where the broker or market-maker is generally either a buyer or seller in the transaction), any given market-maker might share the transaction price with a third-party in return for, perhaps, an average price across all market-makers in that specific security. This system allows market-makers to gauge their specific transaction without learning the actual prices charged for the identical security by their competitors. The average price revealed by the third party to all contributing sellers is referred to as *marked to matrix* of observed prices for all buyers and sellers.

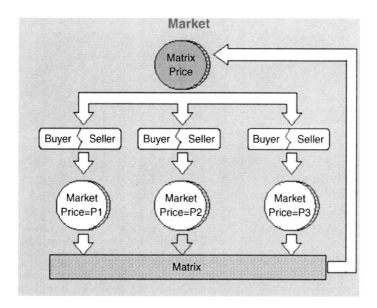

Together with a market-maker's own information set, the marked-to-matrix price for a specific security can be used to price the security for the next transaction. Sometimes, the marked-to-matrix price will be used in conjunction with the marked-to-model price together with a change in market conditions to determine the price that a market-maker will use for the next transaction. Again, depending on each party's bargaining power, the price at which a transaction actually occurs can differ significantly. But then that transaction price will be reported by the market-maker to the third party, which uses it to update the marked-to-matrix price and redistributes that to the market-makers.

PRICE-REPORTING CHALLENGES

The challenges in price reporting differ by the market. In the private-transaction markets (bonds being the biggest), the challenge is to bring more transparency into the reporting process. In the fixed-income arena, the market for U.S. Treasury securities is the most transparent, partly because it is the most actively traded segment and partly because the government wants it that way. Real-time pricing feeds have existed for a decade or so. Transparency for corporate bonds brightened with the launching in mid-2002 of the Trade Reporting and Compliance Engine (TRACE) by the National Association of Securities Dealers (which is now part of a larger organization called Financial Industry Regulatory Authority, Inc. (FINRA)). Since the launch, the minimum time for reporting corporate bond trades has fallen from within 75 minutes of the transaction to within 15 minutes, and the categories of corporate bonds eligible to be traded on TRACE have been broadened. Other parts of the bond market—including mortgage-backed securities, the centerpiece of the credit debacle of 2007–2008—remain stubbornly opaque, however. Maybe that will change a little because of the credit crisis, but as of this writing there is nothing but talk and relatively little of that.

What makes price transparency a "noble" challenge is that Wall Street dislikes it. Information is power, and pricing information is especially powerful—but not if everybody has it. There is an unavoidable trade-off: Widespread dissemination of price information increases trading volumes (and in turn Wall Street profits) but also makes markets more efficient (which eats into Wall Street profit margins). Those who now control price information are reluctant, to say the least, to share it—and they won't unless pushed, prodded, and provoked. Left to their own devices, the banks, hedge funds, and other investment professionals would reduce transparency to gain an edge over the other guy.

It's already happening in the stock market, now the most transparent of the securities-trading arenas. The new rage is *dark pools*, secretive electronic trading networks that match buyers and sellers anonymously. Large brokerage firms, trading boutiques, and even stock exchanges have designed or are designing these systems where shares can be bought and sold out of sight. As of mid-2008, there were 42 dark pools competing for U.S. stock trades, up from seven in 2003, according to the research firm Tabb Group. As a result, dark pools' market share zoomed to about 10 percent from less than 1 percent in those five years, Tabb estimates. By 2010, securities firms and their clients are expected to direct about 20 percent of their stock orders to dark pools, according to Aite Group, the Boston consultancy.

They are booming partly because big institutional investors are looking for ways to trade blocks of stock without affecting share prices, which can happen on traditional stock exchanges. Much of what portfolio managers call *trading costs* are the differences between the prices at which they decide to buy or sell 10,000 or more shares of stock and the transaction prices at which their orders are filled. Most of those differences are caused by their being visible market participants, signaling other traders to climb on the bandwagon and push prices in the wrong direction for somebody. Dark pools also are attractive to the rapid-fire algorithmic traders described at the beginning of this chapter. In addition to secrecy, they like the lower costs offered by these electronic systems, which have much less overhead than conventional exchanges.

But they aren't called *dark pools* for nothing. While they do have to report the price and share volume of each transaction after it occurs, they don't have to reveal bid/ask quotes or the order book. Naturally, investors and traders operating out in the light feel outraged at being deprived of this information, which provides additional guidance to what the price of the next transaction in a given security might be. It remains to be seen whether this reduced transparency in the expanding dark-pool segment will have any effect on the overall market. If one had to guess, the answer could be *no* for very liquid stocks, *maybe* for medium-liquid, and *probably* for low-liquidity shares. Ultimately, what determines whether this is working is whether investors—both the little guys and the big guys—are better off.

CHAPTER 20

The Sell-Side Challenge

Steve Wunsch
Wunch Auction Associates

Legislated order-handling rules and "shredded" algorithmic trading destroyed the longtime sell-side business model. Investments to enhance technological proficiency devour capital. And, buy-side firms have more venue options. Is beefing up proprietary trading the best way to survive? Is there any future for the smaller sell-side firms? A veteran innovator and successful exchange executive reflects on relationships, regulation, and the cost of doing business on both sides.

A NEW LIQUIDITY LINGUA FRANCA EMERGES AS ALGOS SMOOTH LUMPY FLOWS

Fragmentation, driven primarily by regulation (transparency, Reg NMS, decimals, etc.), has forced the computerized handling and algorithmic shredding of institutional blocks. Although this was not the intent of regulation—and it was at first a little scary to watch—one unintended consequence has been salutary. By spreading institutional orders out over time and space, their old "lumpiness" is ceasing to be the trading cost and liquidity problem it once was. The smoothing has already eliminated most of institutions' former trading costs and perhaps most of their alpha, too, which may have been more trading-process dependent than was generally recognized.[1]

Though salutary in some respects, this is bad news for the sell side, whose business model formed largely around the need to handle lumpy institutional order flow. The challenge to the sell side is exacerbated by the fact that their former protectors, the exchanges, have also been transformed by regulation into their adversaries. We'll come back to this one later.

But first, that lumpy flow.

The transformation that is unfolding is a market-structure sea change. The tipping point has already been reached and two strong positive feedback loops are driving those blocks that have not already succumbed to shredding to get with the program. The ease with which algorithms can get the job done increases as more and more traders adopt the strategy and it increasingly becomes the standard way that liquidity is sought, provided, and consumed.

In other words, the more that people adopt shredding, the easier, cheaper, and more convenient it will become and the more tempting it will be for others to adopt it. Conversely, but pushing in the same direction, is the fact that the more people who adopt shredding, the more those blocks left behind will stick out like sore thumbs. They will increasingly seem relatively difficult and inconvenient to execute—and at potentially embarrassing prices—when compared to the safe and smooth average of continuous prices that shredding naturally produces. So these two positive feedback loops are simultaneously pushing people away from blocks and toward algorithmic shredding.

The spreading out of institutional order flows is ongoing and may be less than half done. Various observers put the portion of institutional trading that is generated by algorithms (algos) now at about 20 percent. In one of the more visible consequences, average trade sizes have come down in a decade from a couple thousand shares to a couple hundred. Another consequence, message traffic—all that "transparency" of quotes and trades—has exploded over the same period from negligible to having the potential to reach a million messages per second by the end of this year.

Such markers of a fragmenting, deinstitutionalizing market will accelerate as most blocks disintegrate under algorithmic smoothing processes. This will, in the end, kill off all the block-handling systems, from traditional upstairs and floor block trading via spoken words to the anonymous crosses, whether operated by exchanges, ATSs, or broker-dealers—and whether run in call market format or via continuous negotiation. To remain prominent businesses, these systems will have to incorporate continuous, streaming, non-block adjuncts to their existing services, as the main ones are already doing. Ultimately, the adjuncts will have to become more important than the block services they are initially supplementing or the services themselves will cease to be relevant.

To get a better handle on why and how such dramatic future changes are possible, we'll need to take a brief look at the past.

THAT WAS THEN

Once upon a time, before trustbusters busted the practices by which exchanges held their membership networks together and became monopolies, the sell side was protected by their exchanges' ability to hold ticks wide and the competition at bay. Sell-side members were each able to develop their own unique mix of market making, trading, capital raising, and research, all based on the virtually guaranteed ability to make a trading profit off of wide ticks and spreads. The structure had its good side. New companies were sponsored by underwriters on the OTC market run by the National Association of Securities Dealers—NASD—where trading was done in quarter ticks. Once companies became seasoned, the more successful of them graduated to Big Board listings, where trading was done in eighths. The pipeline was thick with new technologies, for the potential underwriting and trading profits greatly rewarded sell-side members who beat the bushes looking for pioneering companies in need of capital. This structure and these incentives were undoubtedly responsible in large measure for creating what became known worldwide as the United States' high-tech advantage.

In terms of the sell side's business model, the environment gave rise to a heavy emphasis on block trading, an endeavor that provided each firm with opportunities to develop its own unique mix of agency trading, principal trading, research, and so forth. There was a positive feedback loop here, too: The more the institutions grew in size, the bigger their block trading needs became—and the bigger their customers became, the bigger the dealers became in order to handle their needs. So, the institutions grew because the dealers grew, and the dealers grew because the institutions grew—and blocks got bigger and bigger and bigger.

Then the reforms hit. The order-handling rules and related restrictions on member communication, which grew out of the antitrust investigations by the Securities and Exchange Commission (SEC) and the Justice Department in the mid-1990s, prevented Nasdaq (as it called itself at the time) from allowing its members to "tacitly" collude to hold ticks wide. Not surprisingly, ticks began to collapse, both on Nasdaq and on the NYSE. (Actually, they began to collapse almost from the moment that the Christie-Schultz study, which first pointed out the tacit collusion to avoid "odd eighths" on Nasdaq, was published in 1994.) Then decimalization delivered the coup de grace in 2001. Since then, these and similar reforms have forced the markets to become entirely electronic and anonymous, with narrow ticks and millions of tiny trades. This new environment is the diametric opposite in all major respects from that which prevailed before.

THIS IS NOW

A key effect of the antitrust reforms has been *demutualization*. Under demutualization, all of the exchanges, which once were not-for-profit organizers of profit opportunities for the benefit of their members, became for-profit competitors to their members. Where they once supported wide ticks, affording members the opportunity to create reputations for block trading based on intricate personal relationships with their institutional customers, now these same exchanges have gone electronic and anonymous, virtually eliminating the trading-relationship basis of their members' old businesses. Where the old positive feedback loop led to bigger and bigger blocks, the new one makes trades get smaller and smaller as everyone gets sucked into algorithmic shredding of those old blocks.

So, who wins and who loses? This is tricky. Although the rug was pulled out from under them, some of the big, old broker-dealers are beneficiaries of the new rules of engagement. There are two reasons for this. First, the reforms have forced vicious commoditizing competition upon the exchanges as even the biggest of them are headed toward becoming virtually indistinguishable electronic boxes, which drives down costs for members. Second, only the big brokers have the scale to survive and prosper in the new environment—their smaller competitors are being squeezed out of the game.

Both of these points need more explanation.

Reg NMS's prohibition against trading through better prices has given several new exchanges an opportunity to get started and it has also given a new lease on life to the old regionals—not to mention a chance for some new ECNs to form starter exchanges and new dark-pool ATSs to be sponsored by broker-dealers. The devoutly desired consolidation is nowhere to be seen: Even when two smaller regionals were absorbed by Nasdaq, their SRO medallions were kept alive, so the fragmentation they represent will survive.

In the face of all this fragmentation, institutions are rapidly adopting algorithms, provided by their sell-side brokers as part of their direct market access (DMA) offerings, which spread their trading out among many venues so as to achieve average market prices. The competition among venues for order flow translates into lower transaction fees when taking liquidity from the markets and higher rebates when providing liquidity to them. Even the bulk of the market data revenues that are earned by exchanges when they print trades or display quotes are making their way back to the members— either in the form of explicit sharing arrangements or in the form of lower fees and higher rebates. All in all, it is not a bad time to be a member of exchanges.

But the benefit is not evenly distributed. While the old environment was relatively supportive of all members, large and small, the new one is very unforgiving to all but the largest players. Connectivity costs to reach the proliferation of venues and data center operations costs have exploded.

Orders and trades are splitting into millions of little pieces. Quote-to-trade ratios are going through the roof. Regulations require the retention of massive amounts of all the markets' data to prove compliance with Reg NMS and "best execution" rules. Most important, the cost of reducing latency is soaring as firms scramble to shave milliseconds off the times required to send and receive trading-related messages.

Large firms that have the scale to fund such costs are far better able to stay in the game and benefit from the competition as exchanges vie for their business. Although the need for large amounts of dealer capital for block trading has shriveled, the size and scale of the big dealers have become even more important today, because they have enabled them to be connected to almost everywhere even as the fragmentation accelerates. Equally important, being connected everywhere has given them the additional big advantage of being able to test and offer a more complete menu of algorithms that take advantage of their wider range of venue connections.

Finally, while the big firms are not much different from each other in their DMA/algo offerings, they are all far preferable to any small firms that don't have the scale to connect everywhere and can't credibly provide advice on how to use all the algo-managed connections. The large firms market themselves as trading consultants, which, in the unfamiliar complexities of the new environment, is very appealing. Smaller firms, in contrast, are unable to fund the basic costs of connection and operation and therefore can make no credible claim to expertise. At best, their algos and expertise are white-labeled versions of the products of big brokers that their clients could use directly. Moreover, the impersonal metrics of direct access and algos leave little room for developing the unique styles on which all firms once had an opportunity to build brands when reputation-based customer relationships were the norm.

This doesn't necessarily mean that only the big, old bulge-bracket firms will win. Most of them are doing very well, particularly those that were early to convert their old relationship-based block businesses into algorithm-driven DMA offerings. But there are some newcomers, the most significant of which are the "high-frequency" marketmakers. A handful of these newcomers now dominate liquidity providing. They specialize in subsecond placement and revision of orders and do trades that are flipped in seconds or fractions of a second. Their normal trade size is a tiny 100 to 300 shares, like the shredded fragments of the former blocks they often trade with.

Interestingly, none of the leading newcomers were involved in the old marketmaking, whether as block dealers or as wholesalers to retail flows—and none of the old firms have successfully made the transition to the new marketmaking, except through a recent acquisition or two that have yet to prove themselves. It is an open question whether the new firms will be able to displace the old firms or whether the old firms will be able, through imitation or acquisition, to adopt the newcomers' methods and assimilate them. What is clear is that there is little place anymore for small sell-side firms of any description.

WHITHER CAPITAL?

What will the old block traders do? What will their firms do? And most important, what will their capital do? Notice that even those bulge-bracket firms that successfully made the transition from blocks to algos don't really need their capital for trading anymore. Sure, they need some to fund the larger scale of connectivity and data management in a fragmenting world. But DMA is primarily an agency business and, even if the oldsters manage to field a team of high-frequency computer jocks, those guys do tiny trades, turn them around quickly, and go home flat—they don't need much capital. So, what will that old block capital do? Given all the creativity on Wall Street, it's not likely to just fade away.

One possibility is that it will switch sides.

Much has been made of the fact that the trading reforms have made it possible for the buy side to take charge of their trading, as if they were sell side. Less has been made of movement in the other direction, but it has been happening, big time. Sell-side firms are increasingly behaving as if they were hedge funds; in fact, maybe they are. This could be dangerous. Without the institutional inducements to serving customers' block trading needs, the sell side has been pursuing *proprietary* trading with reckless abandon.

In the pre-reform days, sell-side prop trading was anchored by the fact that they had information advantages over their customers. Because institutions needed them for liquidity, sell-side block traders developed intricate trading relationships, supported by their firms' research products and by their investment banking divisions' ability to bestow IPO allocations on favored clients. While pairs trading, statistical arbitrage, and similar quantitative strategies were born on the sell side, these were departures from the basic business of knowing institutional flows sufficiently to keep a step ahead of the buy side's orders. While you might call this frontrunning, it was an essential and valuable component of processes as critical as liquidity provision for big institutions and capital flows to new businesses. More to my current point, making money by keeping ahead of institutional trading flows was a far smarter use of capital than taking potshots at subprime mortgages, for example.

Then two things happened. First, quant trading took off—everything from pairs trading and index arb to the newer high-frequency stuff. Second, the reforms killed the relationships with customers. Whether it was decimals, algos, and DMA; or Reg FD blocking analysts' information flows to best clients; or Chinese walls between investment banking and research; or bans on favoritism in IPO allocations—all the main bases for the old relationships were gone and individual customers dissolved into an anonymous cloud of counterparties. So, when the sell side woke up one morning in 2006 or 2007, they said to themselves, "I guess we really are just a bunch of hedge funds after all." From the perspective of the regulatory crusaders, of course, this was all to the good: democratization, level playing fields, and all that. But one wonders if there mightn't be a downside to the sell side's switching sides.

As several authors have noted, quantitative tools tend to generate interest by several or many firms in the same strategy simultaneously, resulting in destabilization of markets when everyone rushes for the exits simultaneously. Richard Bookstaber, in *A Demon of Our Own Design*,[2] describes how some now-infamous episodes unfolded, such as the portfolio insurance crash of 1987 and the LTCM debacle. As I was reading that book in the summer of 2007, I was astounded at how accurately it described the problems with stat arb piling-on that hit at the end of that summer when firms on both sides of the street got stuck and their frantic attempts to exit pushed bad stocks up and good ones down. That one was amusing and only cost a few billion and some jobs.

But I write these notes on the Ides of March in the midst of the subprime and credit crises of 2008, and the Wall Street cross-dressing is beginning to look ominous to me—not exactly sinister, but ominous. Maybe it's just part of a general fading of boundaries and traditional roles, but the fact that the Fed has to make a loan to Bear Stearns through J. P. Morgan Chase, because Bear isn't yet cleared to take a direct loan, seemed scary. And it's no less scary that they wouldn't have had to do it if it had happened two weeks later, when their just-pronounced new power to loan directly to the likes of Bear would have gone into effect, because both the new power and the selection of its effective date appeared entirely arbitrary to me. Without Glass-Steagall, of course, the distinction isn't as clear between investment banks and commercial banks anymore—but apparently the Fed's rules haven't caught up to that fact yet.

Why not, I wonder.

And I wonder if next they will be giving themselves power to make loans to hedge funds. I don't know whether that would be a good idea, but the uncertainty amid all these collapsing categories feels out of control to me. But what really feels out of control is that all these hedge funds that are starting to go bust are customers of the investment banks, or sometimes divisions of those investment banks, which are sometimes also owned by commercial banks—which have collateralized loans out to investment banks, which are prime brokers for hedge funds and loan them trading capital against collateral—and all of them have hidden credit default swaps with each other. So, all of their collateral is suddenly suspect.

It is unknown and unknowable, of course, whether the simultaneous exposure to the same type of suspect collateral that all of our investment banks now seem to have on their books would have occurred to this degree if they had stuck to their knitting—for example, remained dedicated to serving the block trading needs of their customers. By the time you read this, you will know whether I am just being paranoid or the worst really did happen. But right now, it sure seems to me that a little bit more order—even if accompanied by higher trading costs or even, God forbid, frontrunning—would be preferable to the systemic dangers that all this idle capital chasing the same phantom returns has produced.

NOTES

1. Plexus/ITG's Wayne Wagner presented statistics at a Best Execution conference in February 2008 that showed alpha and trading costs declining in recent years in tandem. (You can view this study in Chapter 21, "The Trading Challenge," by Wayne Wagner.) At first blush, one could be disappointed that, even after the great decline of trading costs under regulatory reforms, there was still no measurable alpha left anyway. But perhaps more importantly, what the parallel decline may be telling us is that alpha and trading costs were largely just two manifestations of the same process of trying to squeeze big orders into the market with tolerable impact.
2. Richard Bookstaber, *A Demon of Our Own Design* (Hoboken, NJ: John Wiley & Sons, 2007).

CHAPTER 21

The Trading Challenge

Wayne H. Wagner
Principal, OM◆NI

Our co-editor considers all the changes and reminds us that transactional basis points will always impact performance. And the clients know it.

Today's securities markets are evolving at the fastest pace ever, forcing significant changes on the investment management institutions that use them on an all-day/everyday basis. The impetus driving toward the new market structures is primarily attributable to technological change, mid-wifed by regulator dictates in the United States, the United Kingdom, the European Union, and Canada. As has happened in so many other industries, major functions formerly operated by "carbon-based" (people-centric) systems are being taken over by "silicon-based" systems of heavy computing power and advanced communications, leading to speeds faster than the human eye or brain can follow.

In the process, familiar landmarks of market structure are virtually obliterated, or transmogrified into something barely recognizable. Nowhere is this more starkly apparent than on the floor of the New York Stock Exchange (NYSE). Once a teeming mass of humanity, humming busily at the symbolic heart of capitalism, the floor is now depopulated to the point where rumor says it was necessary to throw fake traders onto the floor to create a proper television backdrop for President Bush's early 2007 visit.

The NYSE and other exchanges now need to prove themselves in a hotly competitive market for securities exchange services. Whereas eliminating unnecessary intermediaries has demonstrably benefited investors by significantly reducing trading costs, the parties being disintermediated are finding Schumpeter's *creative destruction* unpleasant, at least in the short term. However, investors find themselves needing new methodologies and communications to efficiently access the markets. Brokers, service providers, and exchanges that meet these communication needs are positioned to dominate the provision of exchange services. The pace of development is rapid, yet much room remains for further innovations.

Against this background, the world of the institutional trader has become seemingly simple—let the computer do it—but underlying this apparent simplicity are significant challenges: (1) the need for an entire new skill set emphasizing technological skills in addition to people skills; (2) a rapidly evolving set of trading methods whose quality and robustness are not yet deeply understood; (3) adjustment to a low-latency environment where what you see is not what you can get, and markets now operate faster than a human can think or even observe; resulting in: (4) a dilemma between the necessity of trusting trading robots while at the same time remaining aware that these preprogrammed responses are tuned to *foreseeable* scenarios that may behave unpredictably when confronted with unanticipated events.

Yet the questions haven't changed, only the answers. As Gavin Little-Gill of Linedata has said,

> *At the end of the day, whether I'm sending an order to the Goldman Sachs cash desk, to a Credit Suisse algorithm, or one of the block crossing networks is largely irrelevant. I still need to trade the order, I still need to pay attention to my broker list, and to allocate the executions back to the underlying accounts. The question then is how to access efficiently each of these components of the trading environment.*[1]

MUCH MORE ATTRACTIVE ALTERNATIVES

Little-Gill nicely summarizes the current and historic first question an institutional trader seeking size must ask: *Where* can I find the liquidity to complete this trade? Decades ago, the only available answer was "Call my broker, lay my sensitive parts on the table, hand him a rubber hammer, and hope he'll be gentle this time." In more recent years, the advent of the third market, Instinet and the crossing networks, and now dark pools and trading algorithms, have created more attractive alternatives to phoning the broker. Today's market is a free-for-all, divided into three main venues, as Little-Gill summarizes: (1) Call a broker as before, although the broker's options of how to handle the order have changed significantly—ironically, venues 2 and 3 might be broker options; (2) turn the execution over to an algorithm; or (3) turn to the dark pools to try to find block liquidity.

The word *or* in the above list isn't quite accurate: The operative conjunction in most institutional trading situations is *and*. Today's institutional traders must be prepared to search all venues at once to find the liquidity as fast as possible—that is, before other searchers get there first. In today's world of around-the-clock trading of internationally recognized securities, finding the liquidity is doubly difficult. Not only does the trader need to look everywhere, he or she needs to look everywhere *all the time*, wherever and whenever securities transactions can be completed.

INCREASES IN SPEED

Gandhi famously said, "There is more to life than increasing its speed." However, more than for most human endeavors, speed is valued in the exchange of securities: Recall how Baron Nathan Rothschild used pigeons to relay the victory news from Waterloo in 1815, a clear case of an information advantage attained through a (carbon-based!) system faster than anyone else's.

Exchange automation began with the stringing of the first Atlantic telegraph cable in 1863, which, coupled with the implementation of the ticker tape in 1865, reduced London/New York order-to-completion time cycles from six weeks to a matter of hours. Transaction latency was reduced by a ratio of roughly 500:1. Not that this sat well with later Rothschilds; as L. Gordon Crovitz points out:

> In the 1850s, James Rothschild complained that "it was a crying shame that the telegraph has been established" because suddenly anyone "can get the news."[2]

Recent years have produced increases in speed of the same 500:1 order of magnitude by switching from manual order submission to DOT, and similar speed enhancements with the move to fully electronic trading.

Some execution management systems can respond to price movements in less than 500 milliseconds. Compare that to the old familiar description for something being fast: the blink of an eye. A blink takes about a tenth of a second; 2,000 of these 500-millisecond responses could occur in that time span.

About Latency

These innovations have reduced time delay (latency) between decision and fulfillment of a trading order. Because the trading advantage accrues to the party that can react the fastest, buy-side traders need access to the latest high-speed technology and connectivity.

Latency is an engineering concept that describes a time delay between the moment something is initiated and the moment one of its effects begins to be or becomes detectable. With respect to markets, the common usage refers to the ability to quickly liquidate or convert an asset through buying or selling. In trading markets, the early bird always gets the price. Ten years ago, the term *latency* was virtually unknown. In the days of floor traders, latency was measured in minutes; in today's rapid-fire markets latency is measured in thousandths of a second.

Why So Fast?

The speed of today's advanced jet fighter planes outstrips human reaction time; so it is with today's rapid-fire securities markets. The speed of today's markets bestows an advantage on those who are able to trade and respond extremely fast. This speed far eclipses the speed of the human mind (or eye) and can be put to profitable use only through tightly connected computers executing preprogrammed trading tactics. At the extreme, some market participants locate a computer physically adjacent to the exchange to reduce the latency disadvantage attributable to the finite speed of light.

Why is it necessary to trade so fast? you might ask. Surely, there are securities that trade multiple times a second, but many securities are much more thinly traded, with minutes or even hours passing between trades. True enough; but when those occasional trading opportunities arise, the trader must be on-the-spot to be able to seize them. The trader must be as fast as all others who want to trade that security. This can be accomplished only with state-of-the-art technology and software.

The buy side today is trying to better coordinate strategy and execution to make the process more effective and efficient. Thus both buy side and sell side are driven to continual search for higher productivity and lower cost alternatives. Monitoring effectiveness before, during, and after the trade is becoming universal.

Nagging Questions

Still, nagging questions remain. Are the algorithms making decisions similar to those an intelligent human trader with sufficient time and intelligence would have made, both in process and in outcome? If not, are the shortcomings large enough to be of concern? Alternatively, do the advantages of speed and accuracy outweigh the costs of the occasional clumsy handling of a trade?

By way of analogy, do we sacrifice too much optimality when we substitute an automatic automobile transmission for a manual, or do we trade off better driving behavior in most situations for an occasional lag or miscue on the part of our automatic friend? To extend the analogy, most drivers overstate their ability to handle the manual control and optimize the shift points. Would we not be better off in safety, miles per gallon, and accident avoidance by evading the larger errors possible while wrestling with a manual transmission?

In large part, the whole debate is moot: As Thomas Friedman pointed out in *The World Is Flat*,[3] the distribution chains that served major connectivity functions, especially across time and geography, are becoming obsolete in many industries. The "middlemen" in the business of facilitating securities transactions are becoming unnecessary. The processes of connectivity are being simplified, and the costs are coming down. This technology-spawned increase in efficiency permeates and energizes today's securities markets.

SIGNIFICANT REDUCTIONS IN THE COST OF TRADING

According to the client trading data provided to Plexus Group's[4] investment manager universe, the cost of transacting in U.S. equity markets fell from 175 basis points in the fourth quarter of 2001 to 43 basis points in the first quarter of 2007, a remarkable 75 percent reduction.

Exhibit 21.1 shows the average costs for the years 1996 to 2007 (3 quarters) for large-cap and small-cap stocks. The chart shows that

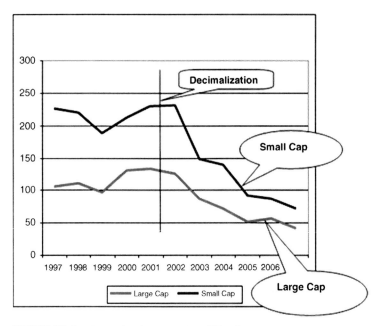

EXHIBIT 21.1 Cost of U.S. Institutional Trading

despite decimalization, total transaction costs remained high to the end of the frenzied Internet market. They began to decline steeply in 2003, and have continued downward in recent quarters, even as the market returns have recovered and volatility has increased. Clearly, investors benefited from the regulation-induced decimalization and changes to the order-handling rules.

Not all of the cost reduction may be attributable to the new market structure. Four major factors, I believe, combined to produce this unprecedented and downright startling reduction in costs. The first is supply driven, the second is driven by demand, the third represents a reformulation of the problem to incorporate new objectives, and the fourth is a possible sample bias:

- Efficient, low-cost trading mechanisms such as direct market access (DMA) platforms became widely available. This occurred just as regulatory zeal forced out higher-cost market structures through decimalization and changes to the order-handling rules.
- Simultaneously, money managers lowered the expected returns of their portfolios after the end of the market bubble, which also dampened volatility. High-cost trading became simply unjustifiable in a humdrum world of single-digit expectations. Portfolios with concentrations of highly volatile stocks were quietly replaced by stocks with greater predictability—the old-fashioned diversified large-cap stocks with heavy trading volume. These large cap stocks are simply less costly to trade.
- Increased scrutiny of portfolio operations, combined with a maturing of the cost-measurement industry, forced managers to more carefully consider the performance penalty incurred while implementing their decisions.
- The data for this study comes from a self-selected database of managers who have chosen to look carefully at transaction costs. Managers who did not avail themselves of this self-improvement may not have fully participated in the cost reductions. Thus, these results may not be representative of the universe as a whole.

How well have managers and traders responded to this opportunity to enhance performance through lower cost of trading and operations? The first thought is that we should see effects in the bottom line; specifically, we would expect that wised-up managers wasting fewer assets in transaction expenses would enhance their returns. Have we seen that happen? Consider Exhibit 21.2, which tracks trading decision returns and costs from 2000 to 2007:

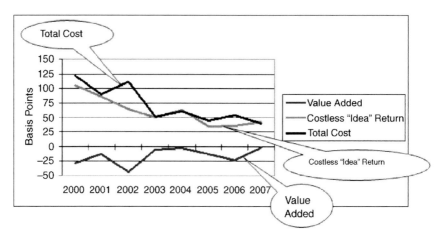

EXHIBIT 21.2 Gains from Trading versus Trading Cost

* Costs have improved, which shows as a lessening negative effect on portfolio performance.
* Decision portfolio alpha, defined as the value of trading decisions before acquisition costs are incurred, has declined from 2000 to current, as suggested above.
* Net value added—return on decisions less cost of implementing the decisions—has increased in recent years, indicating that some, though not all, of the reduction in transaction cost has been passed along to investors.

Note that the value-added series has touched zero in three recent quarters. Perhaps this is an indicator of market efficiency, in a "no-free-lunch" sense. Can the best that can be expected, in a hotly competitive contest to seek out and capture investment value, be that the search costs will on average be recovered?

Also note that portfolio returns come from the *held* portfolio, not the *transacted* portfolio shown in Exhibit 21.2. As turnover rates drop, the effect of portfolio changes on total portfolio return will be muted. According to the ICI, the average turnover rate fell from 73 percent in 2001 to 51 percent in 2004.[5] This drop is likely due to the lethargic performance of individual stocks in the mid-2000s. There have simply been fewer "story stocks" in the post–Internet frenzy period.

This topic deserves continuing observation going forward. Surely, more will be revealed.

PERPLEXING CHANGES IN THE WAY TRADERS ACCESS AND PROCESS MARKET INFORMATION

Many old-timers lament the passing of the rich traditions of the NYSE floor. The floor was quaint, it was fun, the relationships were rich and rewarding, the sense of being part of "the greatest market in the world" was intoxicating. The problem of the exchange floor may be that of the steam train: While peculiarly quaint and impressive, it was too noisy, too dirty, too slow, and, most importantly, technologically obsolete. To the institutional customers, the market was opaque, slow, uncontrollable, and prone to mischief. In a casino, the house always wins, and the nagging thought of institutional traders was that they were the patsies in this exchange/broker–orchestrated game.

Trading today is radically changed from the telephone-based systems used previously. Before decimalization and the changes in the order-handling rules, the buy-side trader would typically call a broker and give him trading instructions that included the ticker symbol for the security, whether the order was a buy or a sell, and the number of shares. If the total order was large relative to liquidity, which is often the case with institutional orders, only a portion of the order would be shown to the broker.[6] The broker would check the usual locations (such as other institutions known to have holdings or interest in this stock) for available liquidity. If none were available, he could send snapshot signals to potential sellers by adroitly offering to trade at slightly higher prices.

A Dark Side

However, this transparency has a dark side: Everyone in the market can observe or sense trading interest in the security and use that information *to their own advantage*. Proprietary trading desks, day traders, hedge funds, principal traders, momentum followers, and other market-signal readers (collectively, "prying eyes") all look for indications that an institution is buying or selling a security and has yet to completely fill its trading interest. Fred Federspiel of Pipeline has said that "there are billions of shares out in the market for the sole purpose of sniffing out institutional trading interests." Prying eyes can try to step in front of a buy order, knowing their risk is reasonably limited due to a failsafe fallback strategy of selling any acquired shares to the committed institutional trader. Traders try to avoid tipping off frontrunning buyers such as the prying eyes, but the transparency of the market makes that difficult. All of this has the potential to significantly affect the price of a security *without executing a significant portion of the order*. Thus, the traditional trading mechanism does not always work very well for institutional traders, whose order size tends to be large relative to available liquidity.

The question any trader needs to ask is: When I trade a few hundred shares in a liquid market, with whom am I trading? Is it a clueless retail trader, or someone posing as one? Could it be another buy-side algorithm? (This is less than likely, since most buy-side algorithms lift liquidity rather than post liquidity.) Or is it a posting from a different breed of algorithm, one designed to offer to provide liquidity while making a small statistical profit on a very large number of trades? In all likelihood, it is one of the latter, an algorithm designed to "sniff out institutional trading interests," in Federspiel's terminology. For these traders, posting a quote is offering an invitation to trade. Detecting a linked string of similarly sourced trades will create a disadvantageous situation for the institutional trader, whose presence has been detected and can be exploited.

A Dual Strategy

Information leakage makes it costly for investment managers to execute large trades on behalf of their clients. To avoid swamping liquidity and thus adversely impact the price of the security, institutional traders now use a dual strategy that combines tactics to capture smaller portions of the total order in the transparent markets through the use of traditional brokers, while simultaneously hunting for large blocks of liquidity. These strategies include (1) metering out shares into traditional auction markets at a pace the market can accommodate without upsetting market balance and (2) using *dark liquidity pools* to attempt to locate large sellers with whom they can negotiate discretely without adversely impacting the market price for the security.

Today's markets promptly display current quotes in ultra-low-latency timeframes. However, they can show only that which someone has chosen to reveal, and it is disadvantageous to an institutional manager to reveal his or her significant trading desires. Thus, the quotes show only a small portion of what the real trading interest is, and the buy-side trader needs other devices to discover significant liquidity.

COLOR

A common trader's lament these days is that it has become more difficult to get a feel for the market and to find the liquidity that's lurking out there in myriad possible locations—contextual information that commonly goes by the descriptor *color*.

When buyers and sellers are roughly in balance, there is no need for color, which has to do with the subtle signals and information. There are two ways to correct a buyer/seller imbalance: Advertise the imbalance through an easily read pattern of consistent price movement and wait until investors react, or stimulate interest on the other side by signaling parties that are (1) more neutral than the adversarial prying eyes; (2) likely to trade in significant size; and (3) likely to respond with an accommodation. Barclay, Hendershott, and Kotz[7] provide a definition of color for the Treasuries market that is perfectly applicable to equity markets:

> *Market color can best be described as non-payoff relevant information about short-lived variations in supply and demand that voice brokers collect from interactions with their customers.*
>
> *. . . when a dealer calls a voice broker, the voice broker may collect more information than just the price and quantity to which the dealer is willing to commit. This additional qualitative information, which often is referred to as "market color," can be valuable to the voice brokers' customers because it allows the broker to match natural counterparties that otherwise would have difficulty finding each other. The better matching of customer orders compensates the dealers for the higher commissions charged by the voice brokers.*

Electronic orders, in contrast, are monochromatic, anonymous, and indistinguishable. Written in the stiff, stilted language of high-speed messaging, they are individually black and white, without discernable personality. Correctly reading this torrent of carefully disguised electronic messages to interpret market conditions and reactions is difficult, although not impossible (or there would be no prying eyes in today's markets).

Shooting in the Dark

Electronic exchanges have tried to replicate the function of the voice broker with some success. For example, auto-refresh algorithms, reserve orders, and dark pools of liquidity are all attempts to add at least a tint of color to trader communication without granting or incurring a competitive disadvantage. Still, accessing dark liquidity is often referred to as *shooting in the dark*.

Another way to safely provide color is to polarize the messaging lines so that only selected individuals have access to it. Liquidnet and crossing networks like ITG's POSIT restrict membership to institutional traders. Pipeline sets a high threshold for minimum trade size.

Both systems filter out most prying eyes. The problem, as always, is that separate pools inhibit connectivity and impede the liquidity search. Since illiquidity is not without cost, the brokers are offering more ingenious solutions. Quoting Richard Balarkas of Credit Suisse, "Simply trying out each venue on a round robin basis is too slow. We build up a probability table . . . of where we think the liquidity is so we can target the hotter venues first."[8]

Color Is Knowledge

Color is not information, it is knowledge. Failure to distinguish the two leads to much confusion. For example, we speak loosely of "information technology," which is little more than switching technology for routing a stream of bits we call a message. The "information" passed makes no distinction between truth and falsehood, reality or fantasy. It's just bits; the technology has no means to assess the quality of the information being transferred. Using such a system requires *tacit* knowledge—understood without being openly expressed—and is subject to errors of interpretation. This is why we occasionally see a Corinthian College fiasco where the computer senses no difference between a 10-share trade and a 10-million-share trade.[9] The point is that the electronic provision of color, necessary to almost any market, has not been solved. There may be no electronic solution.

Color is valuable, but it is costly to provide. It requires the continuing maintenance of a worldwide network of information. Those who provide color expect to be compensated for their efforts. Color used to be provided on the exchange floor, but there never was a monopoly. Institutional block desks and third-market brokers provide similar services.

Progress and Robots

Meanwhile, progress is being made in the arcane areas of machine processing of news content and "smart" adaptive strategies. Increasingly, traders delegate the handling of orders to the machines while they focus on strategies to deal with difficult orders, deciding where and how to trade. Now the robots are beginning to decide *why* and *when* to trade.

THE CRAZY, OVERLAPPING WORLD OF INVESTORS, BROKERS, AND EXCHANGES

Tim Mahoney, then of Merrill Lynch, is quoted as saying, "It seems you can be a competitor, a client and a collaborator to everyone that you do business with."[10] Some examples:

- A buy-side trader uses direct market access (DMA), circumventing the execution capabilities of the broker.
- In the same example, the exchange is reducing the role of the broker by offering DMA.
- A broker sets up an internal ECN and crosses orders internally without sending them to the exchange for execution.

Certainly, the traditional structure of buy-side initiation, broker handling, exchange matching, and displaying and clearing the trade has become confused. Yet certain core competencies need to be in place. One doesn't have to be a defender of the old ways of conducting securities trades to recognize the exchange functions that are essential to an ability to trade. These functions include:

- Assuring anonymity of sensitive trading information
- Maintaining the trading queues; enforcing best price/best time priority[11]
- Facilitating signaling to draw out the other side of the trade
- Maintaining robust computer, data retention, and communications facilities to avoid system failure
- Providing adequate counterparty risk assessment and discipline to avoid systemic failure in a credit meltdown
- Clearing and settling the trades, and guaranteeing trade completion should any party default

Some organization must provide all of these essential services that were previously bundled together by the exchanges. The Securities and Exchange Commission and their non-U.S. equivalents worldwide need to keep a watchful eye that these critical functions are not compromised.

WHAT DOES TODAY'S TRADING DESK LOOK LIKE?

There's a joke going around that the trading desk of the future will consist of a computer, a human, and a dog. The computer will do the trading. The human's job is to monitor the computer. And the dog's job is to see that the human doesn't touch the computer!

Assuredly, the skill set to be a successful trader has changed and continues to change. Desk personnel these days are much more technically oriented. The problem for buy-side traders is less one of strategy in dealing with multiple liquidity venues and more a question of appropriate technology and software. This, of course, puts trading in a whole new technoworld, where statements such as the following can appear in a magazine that features itself as "working for the buy side":

> . . . *new micro architecture, quad cores, more on-chip cache memory and 45 nanometer technology. To exploit such capabilities, programmers now need to think parallel, using multi-threaded software and vector programming techniques.*[12]

In order to be effective in today's markets, a trading desk needs up-to-date (and constantly advancing) technology and a technologist who knows how to make it tick (and can understand the technospeak above!). An order management system (OMS) or execution management system (EMS) is mandatory. A well-equipped desk would also feature a transaction-cost module that provides pre-, post-, real-time, and periodic review capabilities, and feedback/warning systems to detect situations such as these:

- Is something happening in the real world that is affecting the price and liquidity of this stock? A rapidly spreading rumor would be an example.
- Is something happening in the electronic trading world that is affecting the price and liquidity of this stock? Sustaining interest from other buyers, sopping up all the liquidity, would be an example.
- Are my outstanding trades progressing as planned, neither too fast nor too slow, and exhibiting price patterns in line with what is happening elsewhere in the market? If not, perhaps it is time to retune or replace the current trading strategy.

All this technology can be quite expensive, which leads to considerations of whether it is better to (1) procure the needed facilities from a broker, (2) buy software packages from external suppliers, or (3) develop customized facilities internally. Smaller managers and less frequent traders may find that the cost and complexity rule out all but the first alternative.

Nor is it possible to solve this problem once and for all, since the field is mutating constantly. The buy side needs to continually reinvent its skills, facilities, and procedures. This imposes a continuing education and adaptation burden on the traders, compliance officers, and senior investment executives.

CONCLUSION

Much has changed, but traders are still subject to the laws of market microstructure—execution costs are a function of both finding liquidity (*opportunity/delays*) and capturing that trading liquidity (*impact*). Traders do not deal in stocks and bonds; they deal in trust and information. Controlling the trust and information in a rapidly evolving market is the true challenge.

Trust and *information*: Those words sound good, but what do they really mean? They mean what they always did: *Trust* means having confidence that your agents are putting your interests first while making a fair return on their investment and activity. *Information* means being fully tuned into what is going on in the company, the stock, and the market, and the ebb and flow of trading in the stock under consideration.

Trust used to mean having confidence in an organization and an individual. Today, the market is opaque enough and fast enough that trust defined as an intuitive conviction in a human relationship is not adequate. In today's complicated world, trust must come from evaluation, which means recording data, analyzing the results, evaluating the outcomes, and retuning for the future. "Trust, but verify" takes on a whole new context.

Information in today's markets also requires a technology base to keep up with the fire-hose flow of data being directed at a trader. A whole sub-industry has sprung up to provide traders with facilities such as ultrafast processors, signal interpreters, data visualizations, and rapid responses.

Thus trust and information are the same as they've always been, but we can no longer rely on our intuition to process the information and come to the correct conclusion.

We have moved from a high-touch world to one where high tech dominates. We've merely begun to appreciate what technology can do. The applicability of high-tech solutions appears much broader than we had anticipated. Yet there will always be room for high-touch solutions: Technology—at least so far—works only when trading interest is exposed or readily exposable.

The power that the exchanges once held has moved to the brokers and the institutions, and it's not going back, despite the continuing need for the exchange functions listed earlier. Of course, there are winners and losers in this Schumpeterian "creative destruction." Survival has become a game of staying one step ahead of everyone else in a portion of the market where a firm can deliver services that are important to a clientele base.

It is important not to lose sight of the benefits of operating in this new world. Bottom line, the real winners in this upheaval are the investing public. The increased efficiency of the markets has been *very good* for investors. And that is a very good thing.

NOTES

1. Gavin Little-Gill, Senior Vice President, Linedata. Quoted in *The Trade*, October/December 2007, p. 58.

2. L. Gordon Crovitz, "Optimism and the Digital World," *Wall Street Journal*, April 21, 2008, p. A15.
3. Thomas F. Friedman, *The World Is Flat* (New York: Farrar, Straus & Giroux, 2005).
4. Plexus Group was acquired by ITG, Inc. in December 2005.
5. Brian Reid, and Kimberly Millar. "ICI Research Commentary: Mutual Funds and Turnover," November 17, 2004 (http://www.ici.org/pdf/rc_v1n2.pdf). Please note that the turnover rates expressed here are required by the SEC to be measured as the *minimum* of purchases and sales, while transaction costs are paid on the *sum* of purchases and sales. Thus these numbers are understated by a minimum of 100 percent.
6. According to the New York Stock Exchange's website (www.NYSE.com), the average retail trade is under 400 shares. In contrast, the average institutional trade based on the Plexus dataset is 13,000 shares, an approximately 30-fold multiple of a retail trade.
7. Michael J. Barclay, Terrence Hendershott, and Kenneth Kotz, "Automation versus Intermediation: Evidence from Treasuries Going Off the Run" (http://opim-sun.wharton.upenn.edu/wise2004/sat311.pdf).
8. Quoted in Bob Giffords, "Ever Faster, Ever Smarter," *The Trade*, October/December 2007, p. 139.
9. On December 5, 2003, the Nasdaq Stock Market (NASDAQ) halted trading in Corinthian Colleges Inc. (COCO) from 10:58 A.M. to 11:55 A.M. due to extraordinary market activity that resulted from multiple orders being caught in a systemic loop and routed to multiple market centers and electronic communications networks (ECNs) by a single customer of a market participant. Nasdaq also determined that all trades reported to Nasdaq in COCO that were executed from 10:46 A.M. to 10:58 A.M. would be canceled as clearly erroneous. Other markets also canceled trades in COCO that occurred during this period. See Nasdaq Head Trader Alert #2003-164 (December 5, 2003). Referenced in ww.cnmv.es/cnmvdia/decetes/IOSCOPD190.pdf.
10. Pierre Paulden, "Trading: Daggers, Dark Pools and Disintermediation," *Institutional Investor*, April 2007.
11. Jay Peake points out correctly that time priority is not guaranteed across today's multiple venues. No trader can be assured of being "first served" unless he or she is at the top of the line in *every* feasible exchange/network.
12. Nigel Woodward, director of global financial services, Intel. Quoted in *The Trade*, October/December 2007, p. 140.

CHAPTER 22

The Settlement Challenge

Steve Webb and
Simon Bennett
CAPCO

The globalization of asset allocation is just one of several pressures compli-
cating clearing and settlement processes. The pressures are significant fac-
tors in the buy-side search for frictionless trades and low transaction costs.
Two acknowledged experts discuss these factors in the context of driving
down the costs "to the end investor."

For those who toil in the engine room of the world's capital markets—the operations departments that manage clearing and settlement—the idea that they are involved in a Noble Challenge may at first appear alien. On reflection, however, the critical value provided by those professionals who deliver timely, accurate clearing and settlement services is undeniable. The impact of their efforts on global liquidity, the efficient allocation of investment capital, and the management of risk could indeed be described as "noble." At the same time, a variety of factors ensure that continuing to deliver these services to the quality required in a dynamic and changing environment is highly challenging.

The clearing and settlement functions within the global capital markets are vital both in finalizing billions of dollars of transactions daily and in managing critical risks within the market. While operations professionals may not receive as much publicity as their trading and investment management counterparts, their contribution to meeting the challenge of servicing the investment community, both safely and cost-effectively, is vital to the health of the global economy.

The clearing and settlement arena faces significant pressures today with a number of change initiatives demanding attention. Looking out over the horizon, there is a steady stream of additional market and regulatory change lined up in the coming years that will continue to place demands on management focus and capital investment.

Among the challenges that we will discuss in this chapter are:

- Globalization of asset allocation with rise of emerging economies
- Volatility and volume driven by a variety of factors including automated trading
- Regulatory and political pressures, in particular, those in Europe as the European Community (EC) strives for a single European capital market
- Competition and fragmentation, in particular, of trading venues, and consolidation change and competition among the clearing and settlement venues
- Different operating models within operations

While many of these challenges may, at first, gain the most discussion with the sell-side brokers, they all have an impact on buy-side operations. The need to support the use of an ever-broader range of execution venues and range of assets, to adjust to regulatory change, and at the same time to manage costs aggressively, places a significant burden on buy-side operations managers. This burden comes at the same time as an increase in scrutiny on operations costs driven by the need to improve total returns, especially in a time when markets are turbulent.

For each of these challenges, we will draw some conclusions as to how participants in the global clearing and settlement ecosystem can respond. Overall, we hope to highlight what we believe some of the main issues are that will be the focus for operations professionals over the coming years.

GLOBALIZATION

The huge increase in cross-border investment activity is evidenced in a number of statistics:

- Between 1980 and 2001, U.S. activity in foreign securities grew from $53 billion to $58,000 billion.[1]
- In 2006, net private capital flow to Emerging Asia amounted to $197 billion.[2]
- In January 2008, EPFR (Emerging Portfolio Fund Research) reported that net inflows to global emerging markets and Latin American equity funds were 261 percent and 205 percent higher than 2006 totals.[3]

Aside from the dry statistical evidence for the shift in investment patterns, many will have personal experience of investing in overseas businesses, either directly or through investment funds. Many of these funds attract the interest of more adventurous investors because they offer exposure to higher-growth economies. Many of the highest-growth economies are in countries that are considered *emerging economies* (Brazil, Russia, India, and China and the Asian tigers).

The buy-side community is therefore obliged to provide access into these markets in order to offer attractive products to increasingly sophisticated investors.

Time-Zone Differences

The difference between the U.S. and Asian time zones presents a particular challenge to clearing and settlement organizations. A New York institution settling with an Asian bank effectively loses a day from the settlement cycle due to time differences. In order to settle on $T + 3$, for example, instructions must leave the U.S.-based bank by close of day $T + 2$.

In isolation, the reduced settlement window does not represent a major issue for the clearing and settlement cycle. When issues arise with the trade, however, the delay to settlement can quickly spiral. The extremely limited overlap between working days in the two regions contributes a delay to each interaction between the two banks (or between the U.S. bank and its agent) as they try to resolve an issue. This has the potential to result in a lengthy resolution process. This not only results in increased cost, but by increasing the period between trade date and actual settlement date, the overlap contributes to significantly greater operational risk and a reduction in liquidity.

The extent to which this becomes an issue for the buy-side firm will be determined by its operating model and the extent to which it manages its broker and agent relationships directly. Even where the investment firm utilizes a global custodian relationship, however, such delay and additional effort will cause impact, not least in the form of higher charges.

Cross-Currency Settlement Risk

The global flow of investment across the world's financial markets drives a significant flow of FX transactions that occur from inter-currency trading and are driven as a result of a trade in other instruments that require FX to settle (e.g., a Japanese institution needing to obtain U.S. dollars in order to buy U.S. Treasury bonds).

Because of the differences of settlement timing between time zones, banks are exposed to counterparty risk from the moment the counterpart local market FX trade is finalized until they receive funds in their own market. This risk is often known as *Herstatt risk*, after Bankhaus Herstatt, which failed in June 1974, defaulting on payments owed to U.S.-based counterparts for FX trades.

For many of the world's most liquid currencies, this risk is eliminated by the introduction of the CLS (Continuous Linked Settlement) system, a real-time system that enables simultaneous settlement globally—irrespective of time zones. Although CLS eliminates Herstatt risk for major currencies, it does not address the issue for many emerging economies. Russia, China, and India, for example, are not supported by CLS, and it will be some years before those countries are included in the system. Cross-currency risk will remain an issue for banks trading in emerging markets for some time to come. An Asian Development Bank (ADB) survey found that some 57 percent of institutions questioned were concerned or very concerned about this.[4] It is important to note that CLS eliminates Herstatt risk for FX trades but not for cross-currency securities trades—the foreign currency delivery is *not* linked (dvp) to the securities delivery leg.

Fragmented Market Environment

Two factors influence a more consistent environment in the United States and Europe when compared to emerging economies, in particular those in Asia:

1. *Regulation:* In both cases, the regulatory regime and underlying legal situation are either wholly consistent (the United States) or being driven toward consistency (EC). Asia, with multiple independent states and no pan-regional legislative body, suffers with a fragmented and inconsistent regulatory environment. The significant differences in the regulatory and legal framework propagate differences in market practice across the region that require specific "local" knowledge.
2. *Regional intermediary:* The DTCC provides the unified point of clearing and settlement in the United States and is expanding globally. This central utility came into being after the certificate logjam of 1968, and, post-1973, became the dominant national infrastructure by virtue of SEC pressure—and because it was user driven (industry-owned and not-for-profit).

   Euroclear and Clearstream in Europe provide international central securities depository (ICSD) facilities and interconnection that provides a focus for clearing and settlement across their regions. In particular, Euroclear has developed its pan-European business model. This harmonization program is one of the key forces behind European infrastructure rationalization.

Across other markets no such commercial organization drives regional consolidation. The Asian Development Bank has raised the possibility that a Regional Settlement Intermediary (RSI) may have a role to play in helping to develop the region. At the time of writing, however, no firm plans exist to deliver this.

Reacting to the Globalization Challenge

The risk and complexity of working with the emerging markets can be addressed by the actions of different players within the clearing and settlement landscape.

Legislators and regulators should strive to create an environment within which the industry can develop more effective practice and closer ties globally. In Europe, the political will to drive for a unified capital market has resulted in a number of significant initiatives. In other regions, notably Asia, similar efforts are required to help eliminate barriers. The ADB has mooted the idea of an Asian version of the Giovannini report,[5] which identifies barriers to a more effective consolidated market and the actions required to remove them.

Global banks should maximize effectiveness and minimize risk by adopting rational operating models based on regional hubs. Such a model will bring together "street-facing" operational functions in regional processing centers that take responsibility for managing clearing and settlement within a specific region. In that way, expertise in local market practice is concentrated in one place, which undertakes all the activity for the region on behalf of the whole bank. This also has the benefit of placing the local clearing and settlement activity in the appropriate time zone, allowing the bank to manage liquidity and risk globally and to manage queries and issues in the local working day.

Buy-side investment firms should consider the regional capabilities of their broker and custodian providers, as well as their own operational capabilities. This capability should be reviewed against the business needs of their investment portfolios. For the largest and most sophisticated firms, this means that consideration should be given to best-of-breed regional providers for different funds. A custodian bank that has its own multidirect links into Asian markets, for example, can potentially offer both cost and service benefits to investment firms. An example of service differentiation could be offering later cutoff times for corporate action instructions, which can be critical in more sophisticated investment strategies.

Global infrastructure providers can expand their service offerings and open up services that will allow both inter- and intraregional settlement to become more effective. Whether this is through opening multilateral links to local providers entering the region directly, or through alliances with local firms, only time will tell. Looking at the statements of the firms, the intent is clear. For example, DTCC states:

> *Our purpose is to help grow the world economy by furthering the development of low-cost, efficient capital. . . . Our mission is, by 2010, to be the acknowledged world-class provider of servicing solutions to financial markets through leadership, innovation, technology, risk management and strategic alliances.*[6]

In this section, we have focused on the impacts of the emerging economies as a factor in globalization. As we will see, globalization is a recurring theme that influences most of the other topics within this chapter as we look at European legislation, competition, and fragmentation, and operating model differences.

Investing in emerging markets remains challenging for buy-side firms, not only due to information scarcity, but also for operational reasons, which include, *inter alia*, repatriation of proceeds, qualified foreign investor restrictions, and liquidity. Investment managers may choose to leverage global service providers as a route to managing complexity, while others will need to leverage the services of local agent banks and clearing providers. In all cases, the complexity of the market and local differences impact cost, and thus the absolute returns available, making these a key consideration for portfolio managers.

VOLUME AND VOLATILITY

One of the factors that has increased the *volume* of transactions in the market is the increased use of algorithmic trading tools by firms. (For more information on algorithmic trading, see Chapter 20, "The Sell Side Challenge," by Steve Wunsch.) These tools offer firms the opportunity to pursue multiple trading strategies and achieve specific risk and price objectives by having technology monitoring prices, identifying opportunities, and creating bursts of orders to achieve a particular trading strategy measured against a benchmark price such as VWAP (volume-weighted average price) or TWAP (time-weighted average price).

The pressure on brokers to deliver algo trading and direct market access (DMA) to buy-side firms has been driven by the desire to drive down cost and the need to be highly reactive to market changes (especially in hedge funds and firms adopting hedge-fund-like strategies).

With a computer placing orders automatically, the volume of orders can increase dramatically as a trader entering trades is no longer a constraining factor on market volumes. In 2005, the New York Stock Exchange estimated that 50 percent of their volumes were now resulting from automated trading systems. Automated trading volume will continue to increase. Algo-driven trades are typically of a lower average value, and hence the number of transactions rises while market turnover growth runs at a lower rate. Sell-side institutions offer their algorithms to the buy side both as a means of effective execution of specific trading strategies and as a way of reducing cost.

From an operations perspective, the challenge is that each (smaller) transaction still needs to be confirmed, instructed, settled, reconciled, and allocated to the correct fund. Operations functions have therefore needed to become more scalable in an environment where cost pressure and headcount freezes are set against the context of material volume growth. Broker-dealers who were processing about 50,000 securities trades per day globally in 1998, are handling around 1.5 million trades per day in 2008—typically at similar headcount levels. In order to achieve this change, firms are obliged to invest in efficient processes via automation. With continued pressure on margins, and the need to invest continually in technology, firms need to achieve maximum economies of scale to justify the cost of information technology (IT) platforms.

For buy-side firms, investing in their own technology is only part of the picture, as seamless linkage to both broker and custodian settlement providers is critical if genuine end-to-end STP (straight-through processing) is to be achieved.

The increase in volume places strains on processes and controls while at the same time aggravating the impact of any failure of process. Those that continue to deliver global operations in a high-volume world must be sure of their ability to maintain the integrity of books and records. Any breakdown in procedures or systems that leads to control breaks and an increase in the aging of the reconciliation backlog will swiftly become a major incident in a high-volume world. The resilience required in the high-volume processing factories now has parallels in many of the *nonstop* attributes of retail banking infrastructures—one of the few areas where retail financial services lead the wholesale markets.

Another aspect of the markets to consider is *volatility* (wide swings in prices and indices). Volatility in the market is influenced by external market conditions, as it always has been. In addition, the size and power of the hedge fund segment has an influence. Hedge funds are not afraid to take large directional positions and drive both upward and downward price movement (through short selling) in reacting to event risk.

Volatility assumptions create a headache for risk managers. For operations professionals, volatility coupled with high volumes simply increases the probability of realizing significant operations losses. Increase in volume leads to a higher incidence of operational errors, and the cost of such operational errors is impacted by volatile price movement since the cost of most operational mistakes depends largely on price movement between event and discovery.

Reacting to the Volume and Volatility Challenge

Volume and volatility, coupled with downward pressure on the investment returns available, put enormous pressure on the settlement operations of all firms.

In reaction, firms can:

- Invest in high-volume, large-scale infrastructure (and the process efficiency required to process high volumes at low unit costs, via technology). The firms that invest in these systems must then ensure that they attract sufficient volume to achieve economies of scale.
- Selectively outsource functions to service providers that have the scale and technology to reduce cost. As discussed earlier, the trend toward outsourcing operational functions for buy-side firms needs to be tempered against the ability of provider firms to support agile and more sophisticated investment strategies. The major service providers remain more effective around their cash securities services in established markets than they do when handling more complex derivatives or emerging economies.
- Where a reasonable technical or sourcing solution cannot be found, firms without scale need to consider selectively exiting from markets and products to focus on niche business areas where there is still sufficient value for them to make money as specialists (market specialization or complex products).

EUROPEAN MARKET AND REGULATORY CHANGE

Within Europe, the pace of, and pressure for, regulatory change is driven by the political will of EC member states that are committed to creating a more effective and integrated financial services market that will deliver "the most competitive and dynamic knowledge-based economy in the world capable of sustainable economic growth with more and better jobs and greater social cohesion."[7]

The benefits sought by European regulators and legislators can be summarized in the following objectives:

- Allow European retail customers to have access to a wider range of cost-effective services and financial products.
- Give firms the opportunity to access markets in other member states within a common framework and to carry out cross-border business effectively and on a level competitive playing field.
- Reduce the costs of doing cross-border financial services business within Europe.
- Improve the accessibility of capital and enhance the allocation of capital across the whole of the European Union.

On the face of it, the objectives for all this change are laudable; however, the reality of change generates its own specific set of issues:

Summary of Key European Market and Regulatory Changes

FSAP. The ambition to create an integrated market has been embodied in the Financial Services Action Plan (FSAP), which was endorsed by the European Council in Lisbon in March 2000. The FSAP sets the overall direction and is effectively a framework for other legislation. The FSAP is not focused specifically on clearing and settlement.

Giovannini. The Giovannini report (named after Alberto Giovannini, chair of the group) was published in 2001 and identified 15 specific barriers to achieving consolidation in the European capital markets. The group followed up in 2003 with specific recommendations on activities that were required to eliminate the barriers and improve the post-trade environment.[8]

MiFID. The Markets in Financial Instruments Directive[9] is focused primarily on transparency and consumer protection. It came into force in November 2007, replacing the Investment Services Directive (ISD). While it does not directly impact clearing and settlement, it creates the potential for increased competition between trading venues that is already driving fragmentation in European markets with the corresponding increase in complexity around potential settlement venues (e.g., the Turquoise alternative trading initiative, a new multilateral pan-European equity trading platform owned by a consortium of leading investment banks).

Code of conduct. The EC has developed a code of conduct that European stock exchanges have endorsed. There are three main elements to the code (the third of which has the most significant impact on clearing and settlement):

- Price transparency, where the exchanges reveal all trading tariffs
- Access and interoperability, opening up access to exchanges and firms around Europe
- Unbundling and accounting separation, splitting clearing and settlement services from execution so that firms will have freedom of choice to achieve best cost

Euroclear Single-Settlement Platform

Euroclear—which initially provided depositary and settlement services for European bonds—has aggressively expanded its European business model. Euroclear has acquired control of the national CSDs (central securities depositories) of the UK, France, Netherlands, and Belgium. It has plans in place to make cross-border settlement cheaper and more efficient through the introduction of its *single platform*, which will replace the current group CSD core settlement and custody applications. Over 2008–2010, Euroclear plans to roll out new releases of the platform that will be the foundation for the full consolidation of all IT systems within the group.

T2S

The introduction of Target 2 allows banks to settle euro transactions in any central bank within the euro zone from a single Target 2 account. The ability to settle the cash leg of a transaction has led to pressure for similar capability in the settlement of the securities leg. T2S[10] (Target 2 for Securities) is the initiative of the ECB (European Central Bank), through which it proposes to deliver real-time settlement through a single platform. At a high level, the model would see national CSDs "deliver" their positions to the T2S platform daily so that intraday settlement occurs on a real-time basis.

Challenges Posed by Change

One of the major challenges facing firms in accommodating all of the potential changes that arise from the initiatives outlined is being able to clearly define the likely target state of Europe's markets. The differences between the stakeholders in the different initiatives means that they will impact the market environment in different ways and, as a package of measures, make it difficult for participants to quickly establish certainty of the target state.

- EC-directed initiatives such as FSAP and MiFID define the regulatory environment. This causes a certain amount of mandatory change in process but also creates an environment that is intended to evolve through market forces (e.g., MiFIDs desire to create trading venue efficiency). Projecting whether and how fast the market will react to changes in regulation is not easy.

- The Giovannini group recommendations require a combination of industry behavioral change, national legislative change, and commitment by commercial organizations (e.g., SWIFT) to help drive change.

- The ECB T2S initiative will require a significant investment, and, given the nature of the project organization, will take a number of years to develop. The size of the undertaking and the time it will take to deliver make it highly likely that the market model will change during the life of the project.

- Major commercial players such as Euroclear (and DTCC with EuroCCP) may deliver change at a pace that further impacts the direction of EC- and government-led initiatives. For example, if Euroclear and Clearstream combined their operations, it is debatable whether the ECB would need to continue with its own T2S plans, or would instead leverage the combined organization as a catalyst for change.

Reacting to European Regulatory and Market Challenge

Given an uncertain target state, European investment firms have to develop their own investment plans and technology architectures with a high degree of agility. This flexibility requires both a rational and pragmatic approach to understanding the market changes and a technology architecture that isolates the internal processes of the company from changes in the external environment (to the extent that this is possible).

Firms should also look to proactively cooperate with national and European regulators, with suppliers (such as the ICSDs), and with peer firms to help shape the changes that will occur. In this way, firms are able to seek benefit from change rather than constantly being reactive in responding to imposed mandatory change.

Given the likely impact in terms of mandatory spending, we would expect that smaller firms will want to examine their operational strategy and determine to what extent managing their own clearing and settlement activities is a core competence. For many, the answer will be that it is not a differentiating service, and they will therefore look to buy more services from the biggest players in Europe.

Conversely the largest firms, and those for which settlement is a core business, will seek to develop their services to both deepen (in terms of richness) and broaden (in terms of geographic and instrument scope) their services, picking up the demand for service from smaller players and driving more volume through their infrastructure.

For buy-side firms, there are two categories of change to consider: direct impact of their own compliance with regulatory change and indirect impact as suppliers pass through their own investment costs.

COMPETITION AND FRAGMENTATION

Traditional national markets have experienced competition for a number of years with the emergence of *alternative trading systems (ATSs)*. The number of ATSs identified by CESR rose from 29 to 48 between 2000 and 2004 in Europe alone.[11] The change in the trading venue environment looks set to accelerate, with Europe's MiFID rules encouraging activity from a number of players (e.g., Turquoise, NYFIX, Chi-X, Equiduct) and different technical trading models (such as dark pools) bringing technically led innovation.

Fragmentation of business across trading venues presents Operations with specific challenges in managing the reference data associated with instrument and trading venue.

At the clearing level, the European landscape is changing in two ways. First, cash securities are moving to a CCP clearing model (requiring collateral and margin management for these vanilla products). Second, the European Commission Code of Conduct is pushing clearing houses and their GCMs to implement a competitive clearing model whereby users have a choice of clearing venue for cash equities and potentially other products. The potential operations benefits (collateral pooling, interface simplification) may well be outweighed by the high degree of operational complexity required inside the clearing houses, which results in new IT costs that will be passed on to their users: the operations cost center.

At the settlement layer, Europe has seen significant consolidation, notably driven by Euroclear's activity. However, the operational benefits will not be visible or leveraged by the user community until their massive single-platform IT investment is rolled out—a process that is very much a work in progress. Equally, the Clearstream organization retains separate platforms (and hence operations process complexity) for its ICSD business and its German domestic business.

We do not expect to see further material consolidation in Europe or Emerging Europe at the CSD level; we do, however, expect a stronger degree of transatlantic cooperation and hence operations service offerings, which will underpin new and improved multimarket securities services offerings from top-tier providers.

From a buy-side perspective, both the regulatory- and competition-driven changes present opportunities as well as challenges. There may be opportunity to reduce costs by directly benefiting from new service models, or to engage with those firms that benefit the most from the changed competitive environment and are able to reduce their costs of supply.

Reacting to the Competition and Fragmentation Challenge

What opportunities and challenges result from this market landscape change? Perhaps the most important is to align long-term operations technology investments with expected market offerings, and thereby avoid investing in functionality that will quickly become redundant as market gateways and market protocols shift.

Another opportunity is to open a dialogue with the central market infrastructure providers, either bilaterally or via a trade association, to lobby and influence how things will work in the future—and ideally to force standardization and additional functionality into the center.

Finally, the increased level of competition at all three levels of market operations is expected to reduce external transaction costs, and so tariffs can be renegotiated and refined.

DIFFERENCES IN OPERATING MODEL

The key choice of operating model, both for operations and for technology functions within firms, involves how to strike an optimum balance between the vertical model (product silo, front-to-back) and the horizontal (utility or factory) approach.

The vertical model has the attraction of close business alignment, which simplifies decision making, reporting, and cost allocation.

The horizontal model implies sharing as much of the operations function as possible across multiple business lines and geographies. It is attractive from the perspective of reducing cost as technology and processes are shared rather than duplicated.

In most complex organizations, something of a hybrid model will be utilized either by accident or design. The need to reduce cost and maximize the benefit of investment by sharing operational processes drives firms toward the shared-service horizontal model. At the same time, the pressure to innovate and support new specialist products and markets drives demand for agile product-aligned operational support. Managing the tension between these two competing demands is complex and at worst leads to wasted investment in failed shared-service initiatives.

Achieving clarity around the balance of the vertical and horizontal operating model is a major benefit with regard to further operational strategy decisions:

- Big decisions on the outsourcing of operational services (placing responsibility for part of the business process in the hands of a third party) are more readily justified across the organization rather than in individual product or geographic silos.
- Moving functions or processes to a low-cost location, whether near-shore or offshore, will again have more impact in the horizontally aligned organizational model

Reacting to the Operating Model Challenge

Part of the problem facing the operations departments of banks and investment firms when they are attempting to settle on a model that best meets the needs of the organization is the need to accommodate constantly changing demands.

Striking the balance between "industrialized" operations factories and the need to react to client-led demand is difficult. We believe that there are lessons to be learned from other industries (notably manufacturing) in how to make operations both industrial scale and agile:

- *Customer demand orientation:* Rather than employing a supply-push approach to operations, where processes are designed and executed in the best interest of the operations environment itself, agile operations orient their activities and outputs around customer requirements. Customers can be either internal or external, but the important notion is that it is customers that dictate production content and levels.
- *Supplier mentality:* Operational departments need to adopt supplier mentality and practices toward their internal and external customers. Formally agreed interaction and performance measures as documented in service-level agreements (SLAs) helps to drive transparency within an organization and allows the identification of issues in an end-to-end process. Such formal definition of how operational departments interact with the wider organization also provides clarity to sourcing decisions.
- *Unbundled and disaggregated value chains:* Manufacturers have become flexible and agile in their operations by unbundling the traditionally integrated value chains through process decomposition and

splitting operations into "self-sufficient" components aggregated by capability, rather than by business line. Typical functions that banking and investment firms' operations managers may look to leverage across the organization include reconciliations, reference data management, pricing, and depot management.

■ *Information orientation:* Looking outside of pure functional analysis, firms need to review the ability of the organization model to service information needs effectively. Elements of the horizontal model have the key added advantage of more readily allowing data consolidation across multiple business and product lines. This is important for a number of reasons:

  ■ Client reporting across products is more readily achieved. This is critical to investment firms and to their service providers, such as prime brokers and global custodians.
  ■ Utilization of capital and credit. The firm can more readily monitor and pool liquidity and collateral across the firm.
  ■ Risk reporting and measurement are more readily achieved across the firm.

CONCLUSIONS

We started this chapter by discussing the impacts of globalization, specifically focusing on emerging market issues.

After exploring areas such as European legislation, fragmentation, and competition and even volume and volatility, it is possible to conclude that much of the pressure we see is driven by the need for investors to allocate their capital in the most attractive market, and for the investment firms to expand their operations across borders. In turn, buy-side firms need to react to and develop operating models that support this. As discussed at some length, the approach needs to consider both internal capability and the capabilities of broker, custodian, and other providers.

The opportunity not just to invest but to attract customers more easily across borders allows the largest and most successful investment firms to optimize their models and drive down cost for the end investor. This requires sharp focus on the need for efficiency, both in managing operations and in the use of investment spend.

The sub-prime crisis and the credit crunch at the end of 2007 have increased regulatory scrutiny and that is likely to result in yet more regulatory burden for the industry to manage.

With the buy side being underinvested in terms of in-house technology, the pressure to generate alpha via global securities markets creates cost, control, and capacity pressures, which in turn require a strategic response if profitability is to be maintained or improved. Investment firms that leverage suppliers and market infrastructures intelligently, and in alignment to their internal capability, will shift their cost/income ratios onto a different plane from their competitors.

With the ever-increasing desire to innovate and introduce new products, adding complexity to the massive flows of capital around the markets of the globe, the burden on the professionals who carry out clearing and settlement operations is already significant. As if the "day job" of accurately settling and allocating each day's business were not already challenging enough, the need to accommodate mandatory change and take advantage of opportunities to drive down the cost to the end investor presents a noble challenge, indeed.

NOTES

1. "G30 Global Clearing & Settlement:A Plan of Action," January 2003.
2. Haruhiko Kurodo, "Challenges and Opportunities for Central Securities Depositories Supporting Deeper Regional Financial Market Development in Asia," ADB, April 2007.
3. "FT Report: Emerging Market Fund Gains," FT.com, January 7, 2008.
4. "Minimizing Foreign Exchange Settlement Risk in the ASEAN+3 Market," *Asia Bond Clearing and Settlement Conference*, 2007.
5. "The Giovannini Report," sponsored by the EU Commission and produced by the Giovannini group of financial experts, laid out a three-year plan for the removal of 15 barriers hindering the creation of an integrated clearing and settlement system for European securities trades. The report was first published in 2001 and updated in 2003.
6. http://www.dtcc.com.
7. European Parliament Lisbon Treaty, March 2000.
8. "Cross-Border Clearing and Settlement Arrangements in the European Union," Giovannini Group, November 2001.
9. Markets in Financial Instruments Directive 2004/39/EC of the European Parliament and of the Council.
10. "T2S Consultation Paper," ECB, April 2007.
11. Marion Mühlberger, "Alternative Trading Systems: A Catalyst of Change in Securities Trading," Deutsche Bank Research, 2005.

The Challenges to Management

Investment Belief Systems

A Cultural Perspective

John R. Minahan, CFA
Senior Investment Strategist, NEPC

Beliefs permeate the investment business. They shape our decisions and our institutions. Beliefs themselves are shaped by culture, by experience, and by deliberate attempts to clarify ambiguity and reduce uncertainty. Beliefs are never perfect representations of reality, and therefore benefit from ongoing assessment and refinement. In rapidly changing times, it is especially valuable to examine one's beliefs in light of theory, evidence, and alternative points of view.

Investment management is a judgment-rich endeavor. The major components of managing an investment program—determining objectives, finding and exploiting opportunities, and evaluating the extent to which objectives have been achieved—all involve judgment as much as data. Judgments in turn are framed by one's system of beliefs about how the investment world works. Given this, it seems worthwhile to ponder where our beliefs come from, to assess their validity, and to attempt to improve them as opportunities exist to do so.

Not all beliefs are conscious. Some beliefs are taken for granted and have receded into the back of our minds until something draws our attention to them. Unconscious beliefs can have a significant impact on our decisions because they are unexamined. While I doubt we can ever become fully conscious of our beliefs, there are things we can do to become more conscious of them and to refine them over time. My goal in writing this chapter is to draw attention to the importance of beliefs in investment management and to suggest that active management of one's belief system can make one a better investor.

Specifically, I:

- Illustrate by example that beliefs can be a determining factor in investment decisions and strategy.
- Discuss the unconscious aspect of beliefs, especially the role of culture in determining unconscious beliefs.
- Show how a cultural perspective on beliefs can illuminate investment behavior that otherwise seems puzzling.
- Offer some suggestions on how to make beliefs more conscious and deliberate.
- Argue that a key part of evaluating an investment manager is assessing the manager's belief system.

Section I begins with some basic concepts and definitions. Section II illustrates the centrality of beliefs and culture using two examples drawn from my consulting experience: liability-driven investing and equity-style analysis. Section III addresses the management of belief systems, including how beliefs can be made more conscious and deliberate. Section IV addresses the role of belief systems in evaluating active investment managers. Section V summarizes the chapter.

I. BELIEFS, BELIEF SYSTEMS, AND CULTURE

A *belief* is a hypothesis one holds to be true. A *belief system* is an accumulated set of beliefs and the process by which this set changes in response to new information and ideas. Beliefs and belief systems are *cognitive* phenomena, and, as such, reside within the minds of individuals. However, because beliefs tend to cluster within groups—such as organizations, occupations, or societies—they can also be understood as *cultural* phenomena.[1,2,3]

Beliefs differ from each other in the extent to which they are supported by evidence. Some beliefs are in obvious conflict with evidence (e.g., housing prices only go up), and others are solidly supported by evidence (e.g., bubbles eventually pop). In the middle is a vast array of potential beliefs that have varying degrees of plausibility (e.g., the expected equity risk premium is 3 percent, standard deviation is a good measure of risk, active management is more likely to succeed in inefficient asset classes, etc.). Investment management primarily operates within this "broad middle," where facts do not unambiguously lead to one conclusion or another, and where one must make judgments that are framed by a belief system.

Beliefs also differ in the process by which they are acquired. Our experiences growing up, our professional training and organizational affiliations, our mentors and role models, and our successes and failures all influence our beliefs. Indeed, the whole sum of our accumulated experience contributes to our beliefs and the process by which our beliefs change in response to new experiences.

Culture is a particularly important determinant of beliefs. Culture can be understood as a shared set of not fully conscious assumptions that shape the behavior, attitudes, and beliefs of a group of people, including beliefs about what to pay attention to, what is "real," and what "works." Culture is a property of any group that has had a sufficient history, including organizations, occupations, societies, ethnic groups, and subunits of these groups.

A particular culture emerges in a group because it serves a function for that group. Once established, culture tends to recede into the background—assumptions that are shared are not challenged—and becomes change-resistant. The stability of culture can be an asset if the environment is stable, but may become dysfunctional if the environment is rapidly changing. In such an environment, a key challenge of leadership is to find the right balance between preservation and adaptation. In an investment context, the challenge is to find the right balance between longstanding, taken-for-granted practices and new approaches based on insights into the rapidly changing environment. This is the Noble Challenge, and belief systems are front and center.

II. INVESTMENT BELIEF SYSTEMS IN ACTION

This section illustrates the power of culture and belief systems in investment management using two examples from my consulting experience, *liability-driven investing (LDI)* and *equity-style analysis*.[4]

Economic and Accounting Views of Liability-Driven Investing

When I talk about LDI[5] with my fellow economists, we take it as given that the accounting rules[6] for valuing pension liabilities are largely irrelevant to assessing the merits of LDI. We have all been trained to have a keen eye for the potential of *accounting illusion*—situations where accounting fails to adequately reflect the economics one is analyzing. In such situations, our professional conditioning calls for decisions to be based on the best assessment one can make of the economics, and not on distortions introduced by poor measures of those economics. An implication of this perspective is that the attractiveness of LDI does not hinge on its accounting treatment. Accounting may make the benefits of LDI more or less transparent, but the benefits are still there even when the accounting treatment masks them. The fact that some plan sponsor types (public and Taft-Hartley in the United States) do not mark liabilities to market has little to no bearing on the potential benefits of LDI for those plans, in an economist's view.

A different perspective emerges if one talks to people responsible for administering public or Taft-Hartley funds. Numerous times I have heard such plan sponsors express frustration with money managers and consultants (presumably trained as economists) who want to talk to them about LDI. "Don't they know we are a public fund?" they scoff, or "Don't they know public funds don't mark liabilities to market?" The context of these questions is typically one where the plan sponsor is citing the LDI overture as an example of how clueless some money managers and consultants are about the objectives and problems of public or Taft-Hartley fund management.

Whether to hedge liabilities is one of the most significant decisions an investor makes. Yet here we have two diametrically opposed views, not because of any dispute about facts, but seemingly because of *beliefs* about the relative importance of economic and accounting frames of reference—beliefs of which the holders may not even be aware.

Here's what we can learn from this:

- *Beliefs matter.* The outcome of major investment decisions can hinge on beliefs as much as on facts.
- *Beliefs are not always conscious.* The beliefs that determine decisions may be so ingrained that the holder of the beliefs isn't aware that he or she is acting on a belief.
- *Beliefs tend to cluster in groups* (such as occupations) where they are reinforced by the social validation of others in the group holding the same beliefs.
- *The behavior and points of view of people in a different group with different beliefs can be quite puzzling.*

The LDI example is fairly straightforward. In some situations, the role culture plays in determining beliefs is more nuanced, and can involve not just different cultures, but multiple subcultures in a single organization, multiple cultural identities in a single individual (e.g., an individual can be a member of a profession, an organization, and a society, all of which have different cultures), and a changing mix of these things over time. The following example attempts to capture some of these complexities.

A Cultural Interpretation of the Relationship between Investment Managers and Consultants: The Case of Style Boxes

Many times, I have evaluated value managers whose strategy might be summarized as follows: Purchase stocks of companies that are fundamentally troubled, but where the manager believes a catalyst is present that will turn the situation around and that catalyst is not yet priced into the stock. Then hold such stocks until either the thesis has played itself out, or it becomes apparent that the thesis is unlikely to play out.

I was new to the industry the first time I encountered such a manager. The manager came to my attention because she showed up in a holdings-based style analysis having migrated from value to growth, and this set off alarms regarding *style discipline*. The manager had very good performance, and this happened during a period of time when growth was outperforming value, so on the surface it looked like the manager had broken her value discipline because growth was where the returns were.

A closer examination of the portfolio revealed that the manager had very little turnover during this period, and that the stocks that were now plotting as growth had plotted as value when the manager bought them. All that had really happened was that the manager was correct with many of these stocks: Earnings were up and price even more, and the stocks starting plotting as growth stocks. She was able to explain the original investment thesis for any stock I asked about, and for those she still held, justify that the thesis was still intact. This led me to suspect that the style-box program I was using just wasn't subtle enough to accurately capture the manager's style, and that the style was in fact consistent through this period.

When I discussed my concerns with the more senior consultant with whom I worked on this account, he dismissed my interpretation. He claimed the style analyzer was "objective," whereas the manager's explanation was "spin." He told me that when I get a little more experience I will learn to be more skeptical of charming managers who will "say whatever it takes" to win or keep the business.

I have seen variants of this scenario play out many times, from both sides of the consultant–manager divide. The situation looks somewhat different from the manager's perspective. Not only are these situations very frustrating, but ironically, they can lead managers to make difficult decisions between staying true to their investment style or changing their style to conform to a consultant's notion of style discipline. I know of several cases where managers' product development efforts reverse-engineered consultants' evaluation criteria, and effectively said, "Who are we to question what the market wants? If the market wants style boxes instead of superior returns, we can do that."

Some comments on and lessons from this example are:

- *Consultants and managers can have very different beliefs about what is important, about what information is valid, and about what kinds of information define a manager's style.* Consultants are concerned with classification of managers so that performance can be assessed relative to a benchmark or peer group and multimanager portfolios can be constructed to ensure a certain spectrum of market coverage. *Style consistency* for the consultant means having stable measures for those financial ratios that define style boxes. Managers are primarily concerned with exploiting their skill to find undervalued securities, and the intersection of skill and opportunity does not necessarily produce stable financial ratios through time. To many managers, it is puzzling why that should be important.

- *A key mechanism by which culturally based belief systems sustain themselves is the socialization and sorting of new members of the cultural group.* An important part of this can be the "stripping down" of new members who, often inadvertently, violate the norms of the culture. Such new members will usually either adapt to the norms or exit the group, so that surviving members of the group share the norms, and validate them for each other. This sorting and subsequent social validation is a key reason why cultures resist change.

- *Social validation of a culture's beliefs does not necessarily mean that such beliefs contribute to the economic competitiveness of the culture.* In the case of style boxes, a key dysfunction derives from the fact that they encourage uneconomic buying and selling of securities. For example, our value manager may feel pressed to sell a stock before the thesis has fully played out to insure that she still plots in her style box. This creates an incentive for managers not constrained by style boxes (e.g., hedge funds) to pick up the money left on the table by style-box managers. Although there are presumably many reasons for the rise of hedge funds in recent years, one reason may be the opportunity for flexible, skill-based investing left unexploited by managers constrained by style boxes. The poor performance of tightly constrained portfolios also puts pressure on the business model of consultants advocating such approaches. Interestingly, many consultants formerly constrained by the style-box framework have now embraced "alternatives" due to their superior risk/return characteristics.[7]

- *Holdings-based style analysis is extremely useful, but the rigid use of it can be a crutch.* I probably would never have come to understand the value manager described above as well as I did if holdings-based analysis didn't raise some questions for me. However, one has to wonder if the prevalence of rigidly defined style boxes is due to their giving consultants a sense of purpose, a "substitute problem" if you will, which diverts attention from the fact that the real problem—finding talented investment managers and building sensible portfolios of them—is in some cases beyond the consultant's reach.[8]

- *The balance of cultures in a money management firm can be influenced by consultants and clients.* It has often been noted that some investment management firms have an investing culture and others have an asset-gathering culture. I think this is an accurate observation, but I would add that some investment firms have both an investing subculture and an asset-gathering subculture existing in tension with each other. While one will likely dominate at any point in time given the direction from the top, as a firm's environment changes, there may be opportunities for the latent subculture to assert itself. Consultants and clients, as key elements of a manager's environment, are in position to influence the balance between subcultures. I believe that a rigid adherence to the style-box framework on the part of consultants tips the balance of money-manager cultures toward asset gathering.

III. MANAGING BELIEF SYSTEMS

As time proceeds, beliefs are continuously put to the test. We are constantly immersed in new data and ideas. And, if we are fortunate, we encounter people who challenge our views. These situations present us with opportunities to reevaluate and perhaps refine our beliefs. Different belief systems respond in different ways to these opportunities, and we can classify them accordingly:[9]

- A *fixed belief system* is one that does not consider new ideas and data, either because it is blind to them or because it responds defensively to them.
- An *adaptive belief system* is one that is aware of new ideas and data and is open to learning from them.
- A *proactive belief system* is one that explicitly seeks out new ideas and data with the purpose of improving beliefs over time.

Because investment management is judgment-rich and rapidly changing, there would seem to be little place for fixed belief systems among investment professionals. Not that stable core beliefs aren't an asset—they most certainly are—but even core beliefs should be open to examination and should sometimes be refined. Also, the process of building stable core beliefs may benefit from periods of experimentation.

Below I discuss three aspects investment belief system management: self-awareness of one's beliefs, the relationship between investment theory and investment beliefs, and the role of evidence in managing beliefs.

Enhancing Self-Awareness of One's Beliefs

Because our beliefs are in part unconscious, management of them first involves becoming more aware of them. Three ways of doing this are:

1. *Attempt to write down your beliefs.*[10] Ambachtscheer (2007) encourages investment professionals to write an "Investment Belief Statement" and to have as a centerpiece of the statement one's views on the determination of expected returns; for example, do you believe the equity risk premium changes over time and are these changes predictable? I would add that any belief that shapes your decisions should be included. For example, do you believe there exists an economic reality distinct from accounting measurements? Do you believe style boxes are a useful way of organizing an investment program? Do you believing in active management? If so, under what circumstances?

2. *Become introspective when you are surprised.* Our expectations are generated by our belief systems. Every time we are surprised by the outcome of an investment, or by what happens in the markets even if it didn't effect our investments, it means our belief system missed something, and this provides us with an opportunity to reflect on and perhaps refine our beliefs.

3. *Expose yourself to different cultures.* Because people in the same culture have similar unconscious beliefs, they are less likely to challenge each other's most fundamental beliefs than are people of a different culture, especially if the different culture has its own well-developed views on a topic you care about. For example, as a financial economist I find my beliefs about liability valuation are challenged and refined by my discussions with actuaries, even though I continue to disagree with them on some points.

Cross-referencing one's beliefs with investment theory is another useful device for enhancing self-awareness. This is a big enough topic to warrant its own subheading.

Using Investment Theory to Refine
Your Belief System

Investment theory is part of the professional toolkit. Not that one should automatically "believe" theory, but a professional should be aware of what it can and cannot do, and use it effectively in those situations where it is applicable.

It is useful to distinguish two types of theory. Some theory is what one might call *bedrock theory*—theory that it would take an earthquake to move. Most bedrock theory is not open to interpretation by a belief system. For example, the idea that diversification reduces risk has a status close to that of fact, as do many similar principles. Bedrock theory is very useful, but it does not tell us specifically what to do. It can be thought of as a set of guardrails that keep us from going off the road should our thinking go astray. The big decisions—where to drive, if you will—are still strongly influenced by judgment, judgment that derives from our belief system and the interpretation of all that we deem to be relevant.

A different type of theory is the conceptual framework. These theories help professionals think a problem through, help us focus the issues needing judging, and help us identify data that would be useful to gather. Of particular interest for investment professionals are what economists call *irrelevance propositions*. These are theories that take the form: "If a certain set of conditions are satisfied, then X doesn't matter." For example:

- The theory of perfect competition specifies conditions under which economic profits for the producers in an industry are zero.
- Efficient market theory specifies conditions under which excess returns from active management are expected to be zero.
- The Modigliani-Miller theorems specify conditions under which a firm's capital structure and dividend policy don't matter.

At first blush these theories may not seem useful for the businessperson or investor since they all seem to imply that the items of interest—profits, excess returns, financial policy—either don't exist or don't matter. Yet all of these theories are extremely valuable as *inversions*—if you have a list of conditions under which something is irrelevant, the inverses of these conditions constitute the reasons the item matters. For example, Porter's (1980) *five competitive forces* are a restatement of the list of conditions that imply zero profits. This inversion of competitive market theory takes an unstructured problem—how to formulate a strategy for a business—and narrows the focus to five key questions that must be explored and judged. Efficient market theory can play a similar role in investment management, as I will discuss in Section IV. The takeaway at this point is that a theory doesn't have to be "true" to be useful. Often the mere logical structure of a theory brings focus to the issues one must judge, and using theory in this manner is a key tool of belief system management for investment professionals.

The Role of Evidence in Managing Belief Systems

The whole reason investment decisions must rely on beliefs is that we don't have enough information to determine the best course of action unambiguously. So we rely on our beliefs to fill in the gaps. Every time we experience the results of actions that were guided by beliefs, we get feedback that enables us to judge how well our beliefs filled in those gaps. An adaptive belief system pays attention to this data, and modifies beliefs as appropriate. For example, I suspect that in the past year many investment professionals have refined their beliefs about the potential for forced de-levering to damage the economy and investment returns.

While learning from experience (i.e., having an adaptive belief system) is an essential aspect of belief system management, proactive data gathering on those issues we have identified as needing judging and using that data to narrow the range of uncertainty—a proactive belief system—allows for even more powerful belief system management. Since this is the kind of belief system management one likes to see in an active investment manager, I discuss this further in the next section in the context of evaluating belief systems.

IV. EVALUATING BELIEF SYSTEMS[11]

When I evaluate an active investment manager, I usually try to uncover what I can about the manager's belief system, for two reasons. First, an active investment process is designed to exploit a manager's beliefs about how superior performance is generated, so understanding the manager's beliefs is central to judging the manager's investment process. Second, I want to know how proactive the manager is about using the available tools to self-assess his investment process and beliefs. At the very least, I want to see managers with adaptive belief systems, and if they are proactive, all the better. While I don't have any hard evidence that adaptive or proactive belief systems affect performance—perhaps some data gathering is appropriate here—I have more confidence in managers that actively wrestle with learning and improving using whatever tools they can get their hands on, formal or improvised.

Talking about beliefs is difficult. Most managers are not accustomed to doing it in a substantive way. Consequently, approaching the topic directly ("So, what are your investment beliefs?") will likely generate superficial responses. It is better to let the manager tell his story on his own terms, and then seek opportunities to ask follow-up questions that flow from the manager's story, but that also serve the purpose of shedding light on the manager's belief system. Often, simple questions such as "Why do you think that?" or "Why do you expect that to continue?" can go a long way to uncovering a manager's beliefs. Other times, using concepts from capital market theory to frame one's questions increases the mileage of the inquiry.

However the conversation goes, in the end I would like to have a sense for the content of the manager's beliefs and for the process by which the manager manages his beliefs. Let me discuss each.

Evaluating Belief Content

Every now and then I meet a manager whose beliefs seem to violate bedrock theory. For example, some managers pursuing a high dividend yield strategy cite the "compounding power of reinvested dividends" as a reason for expecting them to generate superior performance, as if dividends somehow compounded more effectively than capital gains. As Alfred Rappaport (2006) has so eloquently pointed out, as a purely mathematical matter, it is total returns that compound; the division of returns between capital gains and dividends, all other things equal, has no impact on how returns compound over time.[12]

So when I listen to a manager making his case, one of the questions I am alert to is, Does the manager's case seem to rest on any violations of bedrock theory? If it does, after making sure I haven't misunderstood the manager, I usually dismiss these managers without a second thought. Of course there is always the possibility that it is merely the marketing pitch that violates the bedrock, and that I may reject a good manager because of poor marketing. But I am not worried about this. Having a marketing strategy that is at odds with what the manager actually does is itself a sign that something is wrong with the organization. No point in wasting time—on to the next manager.

With managers who get past the "no-bedrock violations" screen, I would like to have a sense of the managers' beliefs on the following:

- Where do superior opportunities come from? What is it about the workings of capital markets that cause some opportunities to be available for less than they are worth?

- What is it about the manager that allows him to pick up these opportunities before someone else bids the price up?
- How does the opportunity set change over time? What are the underlying causes of opportunities changing over time? What is the manager's view on his own possible need to change in response to a changing opportunity set?

I find efficient market theory extremely helpful in guiding an interview so as to uncover answers to these questions (assuming the manager has answers). More specifically, I find *inverted* efficient market theory helpful.

Although there are several variants of efficient market theory, the basic idea is that the process of trading on information or a point of view causes that information or view to be reflected in asset prices, and once reflected in prices, the information can no longer be used to generate superior returns. The inverse of this statement is this: "If a manager is to generate superior returns, he must be able to trade on value-relevant information or perspectives before that information becomes reflected in price." This is the value of efficient market theory as a logical construct. It simplifies all the possible reasons for superior performance into one focused question: How does the manager trade before his perspective or information is reflected in prices?

Ultimately, every coherent belief about how to generate superior returns ought to be able to be translated into a reason why the manager can trade before his information or perspective is reflected in price.[13] If the manager cannot make this translation, I am inclined to assume the manager doesn't have a coherent belief system.[14,15]

Sadly, most traditional managers I interview are unable to credibly explain how they trade before their perspective gets into prices. Many managers appear to not even think in these terms, but instead focus on exploiting past patterns (e.g., "low price–book always works in the long-run") or buying "Mom-and-apple-pie" stocks (e.g., "we only buy the highest-quality companies, the companies that made America great"). There is nothing necessarily wrong with attempting to exploit past patterns or with buying quality companies, but unless a manager can explain why his perspective is not reflected in the prices of what he buys and sells, there is no reason to expect he will outperform.[16,17]

Evaluating Belief Management

The key questions I have regarding a manager's belief management are:

- How does the manager self-evaluate his investment process? What evidence does the manager look at to do this?

▓ Does the firm's culture support or retard greater awareness of potentially unconscious beliefs?

I will discuss each in turn.

How Does the Manager Self-Evaluate? The fundamental problem of performance evaluation is that returns have a substantial random element. This makes it difficult for an evaluator to conclude that good performance derives from successful execution of a sound investment strategy. This is obviously true for an external evaluator such as myself, but an internal evaluator faces the same problem.

Some managers don't put much thought into self-evaluation. If performance relative to a benchmark or peer universe is good, they stop there. If performance is poor, they may put more effort into analysis so as to craft a favorable spin on the situation. These are not the managers I want to hire.

I prefer to hire a manager who is driven to make honest and careful assessments of his investment process in good times and bad, and who understands that good performance can occur for reasons other than successful execution of the investment strategy. That is, I prefer a manager with a proactive belief system with respect to self-evaluation of his investment process. There are two things such a manager can do to partially mitigate the fundamental problem of performance evaluation:

1. *Get the benchmark right.*[18] This ought to go without saying. Yet the overwhelming majority of managers I review use a benchmark that is not meaningfully connected to either the investment process or a reasonably specified passive alternative. The simplest example of this is a manager who selects securities from a universe materially different from the index to which the manager is compared. Externally, managers may have no choice about their benchmark. Internally, they can use whatever they find most useful. If they are not careful about this choice, that tells me they are not serious about self-assessment.
2. *Supplement performance data with nonperformance indicators of process success.* A manager with a proactive belief system wants to know if her process is working, and recognizes that good performance (even relative to a good benchmark) is not sufficient to come to that conclusion. Therefore, such managers seek additional indicators that the process is working. For example:
   ▓ A manager who predicts earnings can track the accuracy of these predictions.
   ▓ A manager who predicts bond upgrades and downgrades can track those predictions.

■ A manager who develops a fundamental view of the future can confirm whether the future actually plays out as predicted.

The key is that a manager recognizes that there is a wide variety of data that can bear on self-evaluation, and proactively seeks out and uses the available data. If a manager does not do this, it seems fair to conclude that it is not important to the manager to improve over time.

Does the Firm Culture Support or Retard Greater Awareness of Beliefs? A strong culture is usually viewed as a good thing. However, since all the members of a culture by definition share a set of unconscious assumptions, a risk of a strong culture is a weak capability for surfacing beliefs. Here I give you two examples of how firms have dealt with this, one where culture is used to enhance awareness and one where it seemed to reduce awareness:

1. *Using subcultures to enhance awareness.* I once reviewed a manager whose investment process had two independent subprocesses, one quantitative and one fundamental. Each subprocess was run separately, but then each group critiqued the other's stock picks, and where they disagreed, each had to explain what they thought the other was missing. These debates were used to identify blind spots in both subprocesses, and to improve them over time.
2. *Hiring practices and culture.* Another manager I once reviewed emphasized that the firm always hired inexperienced analysts and then trained them in their way of doing things. All of the senior investment people in the firm started as junior analysts. They considered this to be a positive thing, as it ensured consistency in their approach. However, it raised concerns in me about inbreeding. So I asked for clarification: Did they *never* hire experienced analysts or was it just uncommon? They responded that a few times they hired experienced analysts but they never worked out. The analysts' thinking had been too "contaminated" by the outside world and could not adjust to the culture of this firm. So the firm "learned" from this experience that they shouldn't hire experienced analysts. I came to a different conclusion.

SUMMARY

1. *Beliefs permeate the investment business.* All investment decisions are framed by beliefs about appropriate objectives, about how to assess opportunities, and about how to organize an investment program. Our

beliefs can determine what we pay attention to and what we consider
important.

2. *Beliefs matter.* Important decisions can hinge on beliefs as much as
on facts. Beliefs may shape what options we even consider. We illustrated this using the example of liability-driven investing, where we
saw that attitudes toward whether to consider LDI hinged on seemingly
unconscious beliefs about the comparative relevance of accounting and
economic frames of reference.

3. *Beliefs are cognitive phenomena, but also have a cultural aspect.* We
illustrated how differing beliefs about LDI seem to be determined by
professional or occupational culture. We also showed how different beliefs about style discipline contributed to the cultural dynamics both
within and between money management and consulting firms.

4. *When different cultures interact, there is potential both for great
misunderstanding and for great learning.* The LDI and style analysis
examples illustrated the potential for misunderstanding and bewilder-
ment when observing the behavior of someone with different beliefs.
Multicultural interaction also provides a vehicle for surfacing the unexamined assumptions of a culture, and is consequently a powerful tool
of belief system management.

5. *Culturally based belief systems resist change.* The cultural dynamics of
organizations leads to social validation of conforming beliefs and ostra-
cizing of deviant beliefs. This makes it difficult for beliefs to change.
This can be a good thing if the organization is in a stable environment
and the belief system "works" in that environment.

6. *Sometimes, belief systems must change.* In a rapidly changing world,
adapting to and even anticipating change is necessary. This means that
some beliefs that previously helped an organization to excel may become dysfunctional. A key task of belief system management and of
leadership more generally is balancing the value of cultural stability
with the need to change.

7. *The first step to proactively managing beliefs is to become more aware
of them.* Writing down your beliefs, reflecting on situations that surprise you, and exposing yourself to different cultures are all useful techniques for surfacing and clarifying beliefs.

8. *Cross-referencing beliefs with investment theory is also a useful belief
management tool.* Theory can bring focus to the issues that must be
judged and can identify data that, if gathered, would narrow the range
of uncertainty in those judgments. Of particular help in investment management is "inverted" efficient market theory, which simplifies all the
possible reasons for superior performance into a focused question: How
does a manager trade before his point of view is reflected in prices?

9. *Evaluating belief systems is a key part of assessing active managers.* All attempts to generate superior performance are based on a belief system regarding how the capital markets work. If evaluators really want to know what drives an investment process, they need to understand the belief system behind its design.

10. *A manager who is serious about generating superior performance ought to be serious about self-assessment.* Such managers should be *driven* to find tools and data that will enable objective self-assessment. At the very least, they should benchmark themselves right. If they don't, it is hard to take seriously any claims they make about how they generate superior performance.

ACKNOWLEDGMENTS

I thank Michael Antony, Barclay Douglas, Michael Mauboussin, Larry Pohlman, Rodney Sullivan, Satish Thosar, Barton Waring, Jarrod Wilcox, and seminar participants at Boston QWAFAFEW, NEPC, Northfield Information Services Summer Seminar, and UMass–Boston for helpful comments and discussion. All opinions expressed are mine.

NOTES

1. The concepts of beliefs and belief systems used in the chapter are strongly influenced by Dennett (2006) and James (1896).

2. The treatment of culture is adapted from Schein (2004). Schein's concept of culture is similar to that of Ware (2004). For both Schein and Ware, the less visible aspects of culture (shared assumptions, beliefs, and values) determine the more visible aspects (behavior and artifacts), making it hard to change visible culture without surfacing the less visible elements. Schein is especially focused on shared unconscious assumptions as the most fundamental aspect of culture, but both agree that surfacing the less visible is necessary to manage the visible.

3. Several times, I have been asked how this chapter relates to the behavioral finance literature. I don't have a very complete answer at this point, but I do think that the cognitive concepts I use resemble those of Kahneman (2003), and could probably be reframed to more closely resemble Kahneman. I am not aware, however, of any strand of the behavioral finance literature that uses the cultural framework of Schein as I do. Nor am I aware of any strand of behavioral finance that is guided by the clinical methodological perspective as this paper is (see note 4). Ware, et al. (2004, 2006) probably come closest on both the cultural perspective and the clinical methodology. Ware's work is not, to my knowledge, considered part of the mainstream behavioral finance literature,

though perhaps it should be. I think the behavioral finance enterprise has much to gain by incorporating the cultural and clinical perspectives into its toolkit, and I hope this paper and Ware's work spark some interest in doing that.

4. For the methodologically minded: The development of these descriptions was strongly influenced by the clinical perspective in fieldwork articulated by Schein (1987). The *clinical perspective* is defined in counterpoint to the *ethnographic perspective*. An ethnographer enters a human system as a *participant-observer* and tries very hard to not change the system being studied—the idea being that if you change it you are no longer getting clean data on the system. A clinician, on the other hand, enters a human system specifically in order to help members of the system solve problems. Schein argues that clinicians are often in a better position to gather cultural data than are ethnographers—the idea being that you can never really understand how a human system works until you try to change it. Schein also points out that many real-world work situations provide opportunities to act as a clinician even when one's role is not explicitly so defined. In my 15 years experience in the pension consulting industry, I have often found this to be true.

5. The phrase *liability-driven investing* means different things to different people. I use it to mean investing that treats a liability-mimicking asset portfolio as the risk-free benchmark against which all risk exposures are measured. LDI does not necessarily involve selecting the liability-mimicking portfolio, but it can. The commonly held view that LDI means holding a long-duration bond portfolio identifies the term with a particular way of implementing LDI rather than with the approach broadly defined.

6. I use the term *accounting rules* broadly to include valuation rules for funding purposes.

7. Unconstrained investing has its own challenges, not the least of which is the risk that managers and consultants will operate outside their skill set. Another challenge is determining the appropriate benchmarks for evaluating performance.

8. A possible middle ground between rigid style boxes and unconstrained investing is discussed by Surz (2008).

9. This classification is influenced by Senge (1990) and Argyris and Schon (1978).

10. It is important to distinguish between an individual writing down beliefs for the sake of clarifying them and an organization publishing a statement of beliefs. As noted earlier, beliefs are cognitive phenomena residing in the minds of individuals. The members of an organization may share beliefs or may not. Even if we assume they share beliefs—or act as if they do because of strong leadership—what is written in a statement for external consumption may or may not reflect the actual beliefs of the organization. Often these statements reflect aspirations of the organization and/or how it would like to be perceived, which can be different from the beliefs that actually exist within the minds of the members of the organization. While creating external statements is a very worthwhile exercise, as is the study of them (Slager and Koedijk, 2007), such statements serve a different purpose from that of an individual writing down beliefs as part of a process of self-discovery.

11. Some of the material in this section first appeared in Minahan (2006).
12. There may indeed be reasons to like stocks with a high dividend yield, but compounding power is not one of them.
13. Most reasons for being able to trade before price reflects one's perspective fall into one or more of three categories: The manager has an information-gathering advantage; the manager is able to make more accurate predictions with the same information; or the manager is able to react more quickly when circumstances are changing rapidly and prices have not yet found an equilibrium.
14. I am often challenged on this point. Critics say that it is not uncommon for talented managers to be inarticulate, so one doesn't know what to conclude if a manager can't explain himself. I think there is merit to this point of view if one is talking about an individual. However, investment management firms put enormous effort and expense into articulating their stories. If, despite this, the firm can't explain something as basic as how it views and exploits the opportunity set, I don't see how one can come to any conclusion other than that the firm doesn't have a coherent view of how it generates value for its clients.
15. Another challenge I receive is that some managers don't wish to reveal how they generate superior returns. I think this is a legitimate issue, but it doesn't really come up that much in practice. Most managers want to provide consultants with whatever it will take for the consultant to get comfortable with their process.
16. It is important to note that not all managers fail this test. Some managers understand that trading ahead of price is *the* central issue, and are very good at explaining how the opportunity arises and how they exploit it. I have had somewhat better experience with alternatives managers than traditional managers in this regard, but in both camps there are managers who do this very well.
17. Even when a manager can offer a *plausible* reason for superior performance, there remains the question as to whether there is any evidence that the plausible reason is the actual reason. It can be very difficult to generate such evidence, but as an evaluator I want to see that the manager has tried. Any manager that is seriously attempting to outperform realizes that he has as much at stake as anyone in understanding whether good performance has actually derived from the manager's strategy or just good fortune.
18. Benchmarks are essential. As Waring and Siegel (2006) have argued, the universal goal of all active management is to add value over a benchmark. *Benchmark-free* investing is more a matter of not being clear about what the benchmark should be than it is an actual style of investing.

REFERENCES

Ambachtsheer, Keith P. 2007. *Pension revolution: A solution to the pensions crisis.* Hoboken: John Wiley & Sons.
Argyris, Chris, and Donald Schon. 1978. *Organizational learning.* Reading, MA: Addison-Wesley.

Dennett, Daniel C. 2006. *Breaking the spell: Religion as a natural phenomenon.* New York: Viking Penguin.

James, William. 1896. The will to believe. *New World.* Reprinted in *Essays in Pragmatism*, Alburey Castell, ed. New York: Hafner Publishing, 1966.

Kahneman, Daniel. 2003. Maps of bounded rationality: Psychology for behavioral economics. *American Economic Review*, December.

Minahan, John R. 2006. The role of investment philosophy in evaluating investment managers: A consultant's perspective on distinguishing alpha from noise. *Journal of Investing*, Summer.

Porter, Michael. 1980. *Competitive strategy: Techniques for analyzing industries and competitors.* New York: Free Press.

Rappaport, Alfred. 2006. Dividend reinvestment, price appreciation, and capital accumulation. *Journal of Portfolio Management*, Spring.

Schein, Edgar. 1987. *The Clinical Perspective in Fieldwork.* Newbury Park, CA: Sage Publishers.

Schein, Edgar. 2004. *Organization culture and leadership, 3rd edition.* San Francisco: Jossey-Bass.

Senge, Peter. 1990. *The fifth discipline: The art and practice of the learning organization.* New York: Doubleday.

Slager, Alfred, and Kees Koedijk. 2007. Investment beliefs. *Journal of Portfolio Management*, Spring.

Surz, Ron. 2008. The attribution challenge. Chapter 26 of *Investment management: The noble challenges of global stewardship*, Ralph Rieves and Wayne Wagner, eds.

Ware, Jim, Beth Michaels, and Dale Primer. 2004. *Investment leadership: Building a winning culture for long-term success.* Hoboken: John Wiley & Sons.

Ware, Jim, Jim Dethmer, Jamie Ziegler, and Fran Skinner. 2006. *High performing investment teams.* Hoboken: John Wiley & Sons.

Waring, M. Barton, and Laurence B. Siegel. 2006. The myth of the absolute-return investor. *Financial Analysts Journal*, March/April.

CHAPTER 24

Ethical Leadership in the Investment Firm

Jim Ware, CFA, and Jim Dethmer, ThM
Focus Consulting Group

The authors build this chapter by developing the concept of energetic integrity, which they describe as the preventive medicine against legal and ethical breaches. They conclude with a description of the key elements necessary for energetic integrity.

Ethical leadership in the investment world is challenging. Several times a year, the financial press reports on the latest lapses in ethical behavior. When you consider the competitive nature of the business, the pressures to succeed, and the accompanying rewards, these results shouldn't surprise us. Consider the number of penalties that occur on Sundays in NFL football games. Even with 80,000 fans and six referees looking on, pro football players routinely break the rules—say, by furtively holding the opponent—in an effort to gain an advantage.

Similar competitive pressures drive investment people to churn accounts or fudge pitch books to win a new client. For example, a client whom we've worked with admitted that the firm's investment process was broken (an assessment with which we would agree). And yet this firm's marketing department aggressively continued to win over consultants and new clients. Behind the scenes, we worked with the investment team to fix the process while the marketing team presented a dishonest front: "Everything is fine; our investment process has never been stronger." Would you have done anything differently? How would you handle the situation in an ethical manner? How do you preserve your integrity—or can you?

Investment professionals routinely face the following nine ethical challenges:

1. *Presentation of performance in finals and client meetings:* Often the worst-performing time period of a fund is omitted in presentations in favor of the time period over which its performance looks the strongest (usually 3 years, 5 years, or the previous quarter). The manager does this to prevent the client from seeing all the facts. This is why *every* manager has a graph or table in which his fund's performance looks muscular and robust.

2. *Putting the best spin on personnel changes:* Employees "no longer with the company" are often portrayed as "non-team players" instead of the key contributors they actually were. This is also true when a manager describes personnel changes that have occurred over time, especially when competitors acquire her top performers.

3. *Hiding the salient features of a product:* Actively managed, high-turn-over strategies have no place in taxable accounts because the gains are short-term. This is true of mutual funds and wrap accounts. Regardless, these accounts are often sold to those who have taxable funds (as opposed to retirement accounts). This feature is often not discussed. Even when asked, the salesperson will often say something like, "These strategies may work best in tax-exempt accounts, but I'm certain this will work well for you."

4. *Portraying someone as the "portfolio manager":* This misrepresentation often occurs when an employee is merely working in a client-service role.

5. *Selling load funds:* This happens when the load exceeds the long-run alpha of the strategy. Managers justify this strategy by rationalizing that the client needs to be "educated."

6. *Pitch books:* Pitch books often create a tension between how a particular analysis is conducted, and the need to make the analysis seem unique and different. When this happens, the investment team will often wince when they hear the marketer interpret the product or process.

7. *Sponsored conferences:* Trade organizations run conferences where plan sponsors attend for "free." However, conferences are sponsored by investment managers. In exchange, managers get access to the plan sponsors. All this does is give plan sponsors a nice mini-vacation, not that much different from a timeshare!

8. *Capacity versus fees:* More assets equal higher fees, but higher assets often translate into poor performance. Few managers are willing to set hard targets on their capacity.

9. *Performance reviews in times of poor performance:* A manager may not know what is causing the poor performance of a fund, or when things may turn around. Admitting this might get him fired, so the manager focuses on convincing the client that things will soon

return to normal, even though he does not have the data to back up his assertions.

Given the pressures and track record of the industry, perhaps you can appreciate why investment ethics is a tricky challenge. Perhaps a bigger problem is the unwillingness of many investment leaders to take the challenge seriously. Every investment firm we've ever worked with has agreed that *integrity* is one of their core values.[1] However, when we asked them to define *integrity*, we get a standard answer: "doing the right thing." Deeper thought than this is required to create and maintain ethical business practices.

This chapter examines the issues that confront the leader who wants to establish an ethical culture in his or her firm. We will first define the terms and then address three levels of integrity:

1. *Legal* (obeying the relevant laws and professional codes)
2. *Ethical* (identifying and resolving legitimate ethical dilemmas)
3. *Energetic* (establishing and practicing a set of personal behaviors that strengthen and maintain moral intelligence)

CONTEXT AND DEFINITIONS

Ethics can be defined as the study of what is morally right or wrong. By definition, it is a study of *shoulds*. In other words, people *should* do certain things and they *should not* do others. There are usually no final, definitive answers to most ethical questions. There are, however, certain moral principles which are commonly accepted. Generally speaking, these rules shape most ethical decisions.

In their book, *Moral Intelligence* (Wharton School Publishing), authors Lennick and Kiel conclude that most cultures and religions around the world recognize four principles that are vital to personal and organizational success:

1. Integrity
2. Responsibility
3. Compassion
4. Forgiveness

Here is how they define these terms:

- *Integrity* is the hallmark of the morally intelligent person. When we act with integrity, we harmonize our behavior to conform to universal human principles. We *do* what we know is right; we *act* in line with our principles and beliefs. Generally speaking, our behavior matches our beliefs. If we lack integrity, by definition, we lack a sense of moral intelligence.

- *Responsibility* is another characteristic of moral intelligence. Only a person willing to take responsibility for his or her actions—and the consequences of those actions—will guarantee that those actions conform to universal human principles.
- *Compassion* not only communicates care and respect for others, but increases the odds that others will be compassionate toward us when we need it most.
- *Forgiveness* completes the set of moral principles. When we refuse to let go of mistakes and slights, we are likely to become rigid, inflexible, and unable to engage with others in ways that promote our mutual good.[2]

In "How Good People Make Tough Choices," author Rushworth Kidder summarizes 24 interviews with experts in 16 countries, where he asked each person, "If you could formulate a global code of ethics for the twenty-first century, what would you include?"

They said:

- Love
- Truth
- Fairness
- Freedom
- Unity
- Tolerance
- Responsibility
- Respect for life

Kidder goes on to say that in his ethics seminar work with business professionals, "I have yet to find a group that did not include on its list some word for love, truth, tolerance, responsibility, or fairness."[3]

Ken Wilber argues that ethics have a hierarchy to them, much like Maslow's hierarchy of needs. The stages or levels are as follows:

1. *Egocentric:* morality centered on "me"
2. *Ethnocentric:* moral development centered on "us" (the family, clan, or nation)
3. *Worldcentric:* a moral consideration for all of humanity that applies to men and women everywhere, regardless of ethnicity or beliefs.

Wilber calls these states hierarchical because "each stage has a higher capacity for care and compassion."[4] He argues that men and women progress through these stages, but with different "yin and yang" emphases. Males tend to focus on autonomy, justice, and human rights, whereas women focus on relationships, care, and responsibility. Men follow rules; women follow connections. Men tend toward individualism, women toward relationships. Wilber uses a story to illustrate his point: A little boy and a little girl are playing. The boy says, "Let's play pirates!" The girl says, "Let's play like we live next door to each other." Boy: "No, I want to play pirates!" Girl: "Okay, you play the pirate who lives next door."[5]

In all of the above, there is a strong emphasis against *moral relativism*, or the notion that "anything goes." Each of these experts would argue that there are common areas of agreement that shape the ethical code.

ETHICS AND INTEGRITY IN THE INVESTMENT WORLD

In our surveys of investment firms, they rank "Ethics/Integrity" and "Accountability/Responsibility" in their top-five moral values. You can see the cumulative results for the firms we've worked with below. The employees of these firms were shown a list of 67 common values and behaviors for investment agencies and asked to name their top picks. The first list is the "Actual Values" (meaning what is currently true) and the second list is the "Aspirational Values" (what needs to be true if the firm is to become a top-performer):

Actual

1—Client Satisfaction
2—Ethics/Integrity
3—Collaboration/Teamwork
4—Accountability/Responsibility
5—Balance (home/work)

Aspirational

1—Collaboration/Teamwork
2—Accountability/Responsibility
3—Ethics/Integrity
4—Client Satisfaction
5—Balance (home/work)

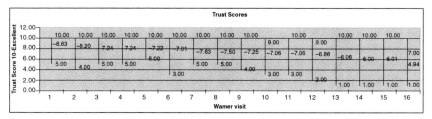

EXHIBIT 24.1 Trust Scores

As you can see, "Ethics/Integrity" is a top-five choice for all firms. So, why do firms that clearly esteem ethics and integrity have so much trouble implementing these values? You might ask, "Well, why do you think it *is* a problem? Just because a few infamous people make the headlines doesn't mean the profession is riddled with unethical people."

True enough; to their credit, many investment firms have maintained highly ethical cultures. Nevertheless, many more have created cultures in which trust (among co-workers and clients) is very low. Consider the trust scores from a team of investors who manages more than $6 billion. Each member of this team rated his or her co-workers (anonymously) on a scale from 1 (poor) to 10 (excellent) on this question: "Based on this person's behavior over the past 6 months, how much do you trust him or her?" Exhibit 24.1 shows the results (each team member has high, mean, and low ratings).

Note that eight of the co-workers received ratings of 4 or less from their teammates! This was one of the organizations that agreed, "We value ethics and integrity as a core value for our firm"—and yet they are not able to operationalize it, at least based on these trust scores. To use an *efficient market* analogy, a purely rational thinker might look at these results and say, "Impossible! Intelligent people who are committed to living ethically would not generate these scores!" But they do—in firms all over the world. (As a point of interest, high trust scores generally correlate with superior fund performance.) How is it, then, that intelligent and well-intentioned people make such poor ethical choices—and apparently do so consistently?

BEHAVIORAL FINANCE AND ETHICAL DECISION MAKING

In our opinion, it's useful to view ethical behavior via the same lens through which behavioral finance views the markets. The neoclassical theory of investing holds that markets should be efficient. Moreover, rational decision makers make rational choices that accurately price securities. Hence, no one can earn excess returns.

However, behavioral finance—and the performance records of people like Warren Buffett and Bill Miller—tell us that there are gaps between theory and practice. People do earn excess returns. *Markets are not perfectly efficient.*

Likewise, leaders of investment firms tell us that they value and *practice* ethics and integrity in their firms. They reason that since the CFA Institute and others have laid out guidelines for ethical behavior, rational and well-intentioned professionals will follow those rules and thus be free of ethical violations. Further, they believe that intelligent agents will realize that good ethics and good business go hand-in-hand. Look what happened to the fortunes of Janus or Putnam after some dubious actions were discovered; compare these to the fortunes of a firm like Vanguard, which has a squeaky-clean reputation. Given that investment professionals generally *know* "the right thing to do" (the standard definition of integrity put forth by most investment firm CEOs), and see the benefit of doing it, one would surmise there would be no ethical shortcuts.

One would be wrong to so surmise. The problem, as we see it, is that professionals in the investment world have ignored the behavioral (or psychological) aspects of the problem. Most professional investors are strong at abstract thinking, but weaker in a messier world of practical thinking. Robert Prentice, professor of business law, writes:[6]

> *The unethical actions of the infamous wrongdoers who have recently populated the crime sections of the financial papers do not prove that they are evil people. Rather, they simply illustrate one of the most fundamental lessons of psychology research in the past century: The circumstances in which we find ourselves often (not always) have more to do with the decisions we make and actions we take than do our basic character traits.*

ETHICS AS A LEADERSHIP AND CULTURAL ISSUE

We agree with Prentice. We view the creation of an ethical firm as a leadership and cultural issue. Leaders must articulate, embrace, and practice strong ethics if they are to maintain an ethical culture. Herein lies the gap between theory and practice. We have yet to meet an investment leader who says, "I've tried to be ethical and maintain my integrity, but I can't seem to do it. My nature is to be sleazy and dishonest. So, our firm is going to reject 'ethics and integrity' as core values. We are going to be authentic and just practice sleazy and dishonest behavior." That's never going happen or be acknowledged. Every investment leader we have worked with (and we've worked with dozens of them, from at least 10 different countries) has stated that integrity is a core value. Professionals within these firms have reinforced this notion in our surveys (as shown earlier).

Some Advice

What advice, then, would we offer to investment leaders who want to narrow the gap between ethical theory and practice?

First, the terms must be defined. It is not enough to say, "Ethics and integrity simply means to do the right thing." This definition is insufficient for two reasons:

1. People don't often know what the "right thing" is. (Imagine saying, "Do the right thing" to a pro-choice person and then to a pro-life person. You would get widely different and passionately expressed views of what the "right thing" is. How would a gay couple and a fundamentalist differ in their opinions about doing the "right thing" in regard to homosexual marriage? This list of possible examples is endless. People need clear guidance as to what *right thing* means in the context of their business transactions. The CFA Code of Conduct is an excellent example of a document that provides just such guidance. Furthermore, the CFA test presents situations in which candidates are asked to evaluate and apply the Code in practice.
2. Even when people think they know the right thing to do, they often don't do it. In the Prentice article mentioned earlier, the author states that the same biases affecting an investment decision will also affect our ethical decisions. For example, a merely self-serving bias will cause people to "gather information, process information, and even remember information in such a manner as to advance their perceived self-interest and to support their preexisting views."[7] The ability of human beings to minimize the impact of their unethical behavior cannot be underestimated. Rationalization covers a multitude of sins.

Defining the terms means that investment leaders must shake off denial, jettison the bias of overconfidence, and realize that creating an ethical firm requires careful thought and vigilance. Good intentions won't get it done. Defining the terms means that leaders must allocate the time to discuss and agree on what is meant by *ethics and integrity* and—more importantly—how these principles and guiding actions will be operationalized.

Mark the Boundaries

An analogy may be useful here. When playing touch football, people often just use rocks to mark the four corners of the playing field. This process is inexact, but works well enough for a pickup game on Sunday afternoon.

Imagine what would happen if the NFL marked the boundaries of their game fields with small rocks! No paint; just pebbles. Given the stakes, chaos would ensue. In our view, a leader saying, "Do the right thing" is similar to the rock-approach to defining boundaries. The stakes are way too high in professional money management to have blurry lines on the field. Leaders must take the time to carefully and thoughtfully mark the boundaries of the playing field.

GUIDING PRINCIPLES FOR RIGHT VERSUS WRONG ETHICAL DECISIONS

One of the most practical guidelines for ethical behavior comes from none other than superstar investor Warren Buffett. After the Salomon scandal, when Buffett was asked to take over the helm, he gave these instructions to the staff: "I want employees to ask themselves whether they are willing to have any contemplated act appear the next day on the front page of their local paper—to be read by their spouses, children and friends—with the reporting done by an informed and critical reporter."[8]

This guideline does a good job of bringing any double standards to the surface. It is a strong practical test for individuals who are faced with any ethical dilemma. However, one could imagine issues for which Buffett's test would not provide an answer. I might be fine with the newspaper covering any aspect of my decisions and behavior and still not know whether it was the right thing to do.

For ethical dilemmas that present more than one "right path," Kidder's book summarizes the three of the most common ethical tests developed over the centuries:

1. Do what's best for the greatest number of people. (This is called *ends-based thinking*, or *pragmatism*.)
2. Follow your highest sense of principle. (This is called *rule-based thinking*, or Kant's *categorical imperative*.)
3. Do what you want others to do to you. (This is *care-based thinking*, or the *Golden Rule*.)

These three methods of resolving ethical dilemmas are hardwired into our brains. Based on personality type, one can reliably predict which method a particular person will favor. Pragmatists ("gut types") tend to follow a very practical approach, namely (1) the greatest good for the greatest number of people. Rationalists ("head types") tend to choose (2), the rule-based approach. Feelers ("heart types") tend to rely on (3) the Golden Rule, often asking themselves, "How would I feel in that person's shoes?"

ETHICAL CHOICES: FOUR PARADIGMS FOR RIGHT VERSUS RIGHT

Kidder goes on to say that the truly difficult ethical questions are often between positive values. For example, if you are a tax accountant and you prepare tax returns for a friend who employs an "illegal" nanny (and does not report her), do you let the matter slide or do you confront it? The value of "truth" would argue that you say what is true; that is, report it. In contrast, the value of "loyalty" would argue that you side with your friend; in other words, let it slide. Kidder argues that there are four paradigms that capture most ethical dilemmas:

1. *Truth versus loyalty.* Example: illustrated in the story above.
2. *Self versus community.* Example: A newspaper reporter is about to release a story that will cause widespread panic and chaos in a major city. Do the authorities detain him and prevent him from publishing his story, or do they allow him to publish and create chaos?
3. *Short term versus long term.* Example: Do I manage for quarterly results and satisfy Wall Street analysts, or do I take short-term hits to satisfy long-term goals?
4. *Justice versus mercy.* Example: You're grading a set of final exams, and one ordinarily good student gets a 59 and fails the course. He pleads extenuating circumstances, and you are sure he's telling the truth. Do you round him up to a passing grade of 60, or do you stick by your system?

These four paradigms provide a useful way to think through ethical issues. Consider the dilemma at hand and then see which of the paradigms of "right versus right" values it fits into. The act of carefully defining the problem is essential to prudent ethical thinking.

Too often we frame ethics as a simple decision between right and wrong. Marianne Jennings, a law professor at Arizona State University and expert on professional ethics, writes, "I am convinced that everyone knows the difference between right and wrong. Everyone knows when they have crossed the line with a client, not disclosed enough information, or not allocated fees properly. Everyone knows the answers."[9] Jennings goes on to write about rationalizations and how people often act unethically because they are unwilling to face the reality. Here are some examples:[10]

- Everybody else does it, so it must be okay.
- That is the way they do it at such-and-such firm, so it must be okay.
- If we do not do it, someone else will.
- This is the way it has always been done.
- It does not really hurt anyone.
- It's just a tiny breach of integrity.

Real Dilemmas

Challenging ethical dilemmas truly exist. They are not easily rationalized away with pat answers behind a smokescreen. For example, a firm that we worked with was faced with the decision of whether to fire the COO. The person in question was a female in her mid-50s, a long-time employee, and—most importantly—had always received high marks for job performance. However, the firm had grown rapidly and needed a "more sophisticated, global person" to run the business side of the firm. The CEO and the president of this firm had long discussions and often used the language: "What is the right thing to do?" If there was an easy answer to this situation, they didn't see it. In the end, they fired the COO, who to this day would say, "All their talk about valuing employees is just talk; in the end they chose money over the employee." Would it have been fairer to keep her on? Fairer to the other employees and shareholders?

We could identify a legitimate ethical dilemma for every firm with whom we've worked closely. A common challenge for investment professionals is the tension between work and family. Most investment professionals state that their number-one priority in life is *family*—and yet most of them work long hours and spend more time with their colleagues than with their family members. Many of them openly express guilt about it, too. Are they being honest when they state their priorities? Would it be more honest (and therefore ethical) to state that their top priority is professional success?

What's true at your firm?

PROCESS FOR RESOLVING ETHICAL DILEMMAS

Here is a nine-step process that will help you resolve difficult ethical dilemmas:

1. *Acknowledge that there is an ethical issue.* This is where self-awareness plays an important role. As mentioned earlier, humans have a

tremendous ability to rationalize. Self-awareness and reliable feedback from colleagues allow us to see past our own blind spots and recognize legitimate issues.

2. *Determine who is faced with—and owns—the problem.* There is a difference between being involved and being the one responsible. The question is not whether I am involved but whether I am responsible— whether I am morally obligated and empowered to do anything in the face of the moral issue raised.

3. *Gather the relevant data.* Carefully separate the facts from the stories (opinions, judgments, beliefs, etc.). Ethical decision making does not take place in a theoretical void, but in the messy world of real experience. Getting all the relevant facts on the table helps you to fully understand the dilemma, and may suggest a possible "third" way that could resolve the issue.

4. *Test the "right-versus-wrong" parameters.* Does the issue involve wrongdoing? The first test here is legal. Was the law broken? If so, then the issue is a legal one, not a moral one. If the answer to the legal test is not clear, then Buffett's headline test is useful: Would I feel comfortable reading about this in the newspaper? If the issue fails the newspaper test—then you have resolved the moral dilemma: Don't do it.

5. *Test for "right-versus-right" paradigms.* If the action passes the newspaper test, but you still feel conflicted about what to do, then you are faced with a right-versus-right question. Two positive values are clashing. Figure out which paradigm you are dealing with:
   a. Truth vs. loyalty
   b. Self vs. community
   c. Short term vs. long term
   d. Justice vs. mercy
   Identifying the paradigm will bring clarity to a dilemma that pits two deeply held core values against each other.

6. *Apply the resolution principles.* Once you have determined that the issue is a genuine dilemma and have identified the two opposing values, bring to bear the resolution principles mentioned earlier:
   a. Do what's best for the greatest number of people.
   b. Follow your highest sense of principle.
   c. Do what you want others to do to you.
   The goal is not to arrive at a 3–0 or 2–1 victory using these principles, but rather to locate the line of reasoning that seems most relevant and persuasive regarding the issue at hand.

7. *Investigate the "third way" options.* At any point during this process, you may see that there is a creative "third option" to solving the dilemma. Sometimes this way will be a compromise, requiring each

side to loosen up its position a bit. Sometimes the third way will be a genuinely creative choice that requires no compromise.

8. *Make a decision.* After appropriate reflection, a choice is required. Sometimes this requires a good deal of courage. We will cover this topic later: How can people increase their moral courage?

9. *Reflect on what you can learn from the decision.* Go back over the issue and the resolution you chose, soliciting feedback and clarifying what you learned. Record the insights so that they can be used to teach future team members about the process.

In our view, a rigorous process like the one outlined in these nine steps will develop your ethics and integrity muscles. Like physical fitness, moral health requires exercise and practice. Good intentions are not enough. People need to continually practice reasoning and feeling their way through a variety of ethical dilemmas in order to develop this skill set.

THE FINAL PIECE: ENERGETIC INTEGRITY

So far, we've talked about legal and ethical integrity, but there is also a third, all-important piece to developing ethical leadership and culture. We call this final piece *energetic integrity*. This level of integrity goes beyond the common definition of integrity—"consistently acting in line with our principles and beliefs"—to include a secondary definition: "the quality or state of being complete; unbroken; whole; integrated."

The importance of this secondary definition is that it demands a way of life that strengthens moral character. Living in a state of wholeness and completion will prevent legal or ethical breaches. We are convinced that if a person practices energetic integrity, he or she will safely stay miles from the edge of the slippery slope of unethical behavior, and even further from illegal behavior. Practicing energetic integrity is the best way we know to safeguard against the ethical breaches that Prentice wrote about in his behavioral finance piece on ethical decision making.

The Key Elements of Energetic Integrity

1. Emotional intelligence (EI, à la Dan Goleman). EI is characterized by these four skills:
   a. Identifying my own thoughts and emotions (emotional "literacy").
   b. Managing my own thoughts and emotions, so that I am in charge of how I feel. I have many feelings over the course of a day; they don't have me.

   c. Anticipating the thoughts and emotions of others (the capacity for empathy, putting myself in someone else's shoes).

   d. Managing my relationships (building trust and respect with colleagues, addressing and resolving conflict with others).

2. Taking 100 percent responsibility for what occurs in my life (not blaming others; not becoming a victim).
3. Making and keeping clear agreements (including knowing how to clean up broken agreements and make amends).
4. Skillful communication (practicing candor—honest and open discussion that does not create defensiveness—along with active listening that demonstrates respect and genuine curiosity).

Important Defenses against Breaches

Individuals who commit to living these behaviors will experience high levels of energy and clarity of thought. Most importantly, they will be developing three important defenses against legal or ethical breaches:

1. Heightened self-awareness, and increased openness to examining their own behavior; greater access to the "still, small voice" of conscience.
2. More feedback from colleagues to help discover possible blind spots and creative rationalizations.
3. Greater moral courage—a willingness to do the right thing even when the cost is significant.

Self-Awareness

The first factor—self-awareness and openness—allows individuals to recognize, in a nondefensive way, that they are facing an ethical dilemma. For many people, they simply don't know how to flag an ethical issue, so it never makes it onto their radar screen. Often this results from operating on "automatic pilot," and not reflecting on decisions and actions that they have taken. Energetic integrity encourages people to become more conscious about their thoughts and behavior, so that there is a greater likelihood of noticing and acting on ethical issues before they become destructive. Thomas Aquinas once said, "If faced with a choice between ethical doctrine and my conscience, I would choose my conscience." This is the notion of trusting the "still, small voice" inside.

More Feedback

There is a second factor that is essential to high-performing, high-integrity organizations. Feedback is necessary for all of us because we simply don't

3

see what's in our blind spots. That's how they got their name. Because of the human tendency to be overconfident, we tend to believe that there isn't much outside of our peripheral vision. A powerful defense against any ethical or legal breaches is to create and maintain a feedback-rich environment in which all employees are encouraged to state their opinions and call attention to issues that concern them—without any fear of consequences.

Greater Moral Courage

This leads us to the third factor, which gets at the heart of what causes so much illegal and unethical behavior: primal fear. Why aren't there more whistleblowers in corporate America? The answer is simple: fear of retribution. Energetic integrity addresses this issue head-on by providing reliable tools for reducing trepidation. When people learn to manage their emotions, they can honestly say, "I am in charge of how I feel and not the other way around." When they have this skill, people can learn to release their fears by fully acknowledging them and then identifying which one of three "hotspots" has been threatened:

1. Fear of losing control
2. Fear of losing approval
3. Fear of losing security/safety

Hale Dwoskin, author of *The Sedona Method*,[11] has been researching and teaching these release methods for more than 30 years. We have tested them at Focus Consulting and found them to be very effective in managing emotions. As people reduce their fear levels, they become increasingly skilled in addressing ethical and legal issues.

ACHIEVING THE PEACEFUL STATE OF MIND

Another tool we use to reduce fear and manage emotions is meditation. We have written on this topic for investors[12] and recommend the tools provided by Centerpointe Research. Lennick and Kiel also recommend meditation to manage emotions: "Many people find deep breathing and meditation to be effective in calming their minds and bodies."[13] They go on to recommend Dr. Herbert Benson's best-selling book, *The Relaxation Response*, which "provides an easy and efficient method for achieving a relaxed state."[14]

Tools and techniques for achieving a peaceful state of mind abound. Regardless of the tools we use, energetic integrity demands that we find an effective method of managing our emotions so that we can do the right thing, even when it is difficult.

This is the path to moral courage.

SUMMARY

Investment leaders around the world agree that establishing an ethical culture is crucial to long-term success of their organizations. Given the numerous lapses in ethics, we believe this goal is much harder than most leaders appreciate. Many of the ethical slips can be explained by concepts from behavioral finance, such as the bias of overconfidence. More than 99 percent of people surveyed believed that their ethical standards were higher than those of the people with whom they worked.[15]

Most of us tend to think it's always the *other* guy who is unethical. Therein lies the danger.

The solution involves time and effort on the part of leaders to define the terms *ethics* and *integrity*. It requires a deep commitment to creating an ethical culture. It also involves a personal commitment to practicing what we call *energetic integrity*. This concept, and the life that energetic integrity engenders, involves personal skills such as emotional intelligence, communication, and moral courage.

NOTES

1. Some firms might use different language—*accountability* or *ethics* or *morality*—but each agrees that the firm must operate by some set of guiding principles that represent a moral compass.
2. Doug Lennick and Fred Kiel, *Moral Intelligence* (Upper Saddle River, NJ: Wharton School Publishing, 2005), p. 7.
3. Rushworth Kidder, *How Good People Make Tough Choices* (New York: HarperCollins, 1995), p. 92.
4. Ken Wilber, *The Integral Vision* (Boston: Shambala, 2005), p. 48.
5. Ibid., p. 47.
6. Robert Prentice, "Ethical Decision Making: More Needed Than Good Intentions," *Financial Analysts Journal*, November/December 2007, p. 17.
7. Ibid., p. 21.
8. From an interview with an ex-Salomon employee.
9. Marianne Jennings, "Professional Responsibilities, Ethics, and the Law," *CFA Conference Proceedings*, December 7, 1999, Charlottesville, VA, p. 9.

10. Ibid.

11. Hale Dwoskin, *The Sedona Method* (Sedona, AZ: Sedona Press, 2003); or visit the website www.sedona.com.

12. See whitepaper from Jim Ware, CFA, Focus Consulting Group, "Why Every Investor Should Meditate" (www.focuscgroup.com).

13. Lennick and Kiel, *Moral Intelligence*, p. 127.

14. Ibid., p. 128.

15. Jennings, "Professional Responsibilities, Ethics, and the Law," p. 7.

CHAPTER 25

The Adaptive Leader

Jim Ware, CFA
Focus Consulting Group

The author suggests asking 14 questions to ascertain the effectiveness of a firm's leaders. Investment management is a talent business. Bad bosses will drive out good talent.

Three smart people start a firm, rack up early successes, gain momentum, and before long find themselves managing $5 billion with a team of 40 people. One of the three founders becomes the CEO and is put in charge of—*gulp*—leading and managing the firm. Rarely is the founding CEO excited about this prospect. He loves markets and success, but not the actual job of leading the firm.

Joe is a terrific individual contributor in the fixed-income department of a large firm. His skills are spotted early, so the department head names him the heir apparent. Eventually, Joe is promoted to run the department. Surprise! He has no interest in or talent for managing people. His love is investing. *How did this happen?* he wonders. Everyone congratulates him, but inside he feels like he's sinking.

These hypothetical cases are reality in the investment world. Talented investment professionals are routinely promoted out of their areas of expertise and into jobs that have totally different requirements, and use entirely different abilities/skill sets. Before we get into the scorecard that we use for measuring management excellence in the investment world, our first important point is this: Don't get seduced into taking on a management role if your real gift—what we call "genius"—is running money, or analysis, or trading, or any of the specialty jobs that are so vital to investment success. *Stick to your area of excellence.* Everyone will benefit, and you'll be a lot happier.

FEEDBACK

The most important predictor of success is your relationship to *feedback*. The adaptive leader is genuinely open to feedback from the environment. Adaptive leaders are willing to hear the tough feedback because they realize that only in this way do we learn and grow. The typical response to reading the previous sentence is: "Well, of course I'm open to feedback, assuming it's *good* feedback!" The problem with this reasoning is that "good" feedback invariably means "feedback that agrees with my position"!

Human beings have an amazing capacity for denial. We instinctively avoid hearing things that upset us or deflate our egos. In the face of tough feedback, many of us get defensive. We close down our learning faculties and fire up the fight-or-flight response. In contrast, adaptive leaders have learned to recognize when they are getting defensive and know how to shift back to an open and curious attitude.

Curiosity

So, skill number one for an investment leader is this: Cultivate an attitude of *curiosity* toward feedback. Create a feedback-rich environment in your team or firm. Make it clear that you are approachable and really want to hear people's opinions. Manage your behavior carefully, so as not to create the impression (or the reality) that you punish people who give you direct, honest feedback. If you haven't received any "tough" feedback in the past two weeks, ask yourself *why not?* The best leaders solicit feedback. Warren Buffett asks first for the bad news in his executive meetings—and he always makes it clear that the news is welcome.

Adaptability

Why the emphasis on feedback? Because if you are not responsive to feedback, you won't manage well. Darwin was right when he said that survival of a species goes not to the strongest, or the fastest, but to the most adaptable. It may take a while, but if you are not responsive to feedback, you'll die out as an investment species.

THE SCORECARD

The scorecard we introduce in this chapter is a form of feedback. It's a way to score yourself on the basics of management. If you don't take the feedback seriously, though, the scorecard is pointless. You won't make any changes. We've seen investment leaders receive horrible scores on this assessment and rationalize away the entire experience. Of course, these folks go their merry way without making any changes. As I said earlier, people's ability to deny reality is remarkable. This is especially true of intelligent people, because their powers of rationalization are extraordinary. (For more on this important topic, read Chris Argyris on why smart people don't learn.[1])

The assessment described here is a feedback tool. We recommend it for measuring the effectiveness of your firm's leaders. It is based on a great deal of research,[2] and yet it is very practical in nature. Each of the 14 statements relates to an important aspect of the employee's work experience—and each of the 14 items implies specific remedies for a low score. The statements are ordered in a manner similar to Abraham Maslow's hierarchy of needs. Abraham Maslow was a twentieth-century psychologist who posited that some human needs take precedence over others based on survival criteria, the most critical of which is physiological. That need is followed in order by security, belonging, esteem, and self-actualization. Our parallel hierarchy does not include a safety concern. Physical safety is not an issue in the context of this chapter. (Safety with respect to managing the risk against market loss is assumed in our survival category.)

Basic Survival

Statements 1–4: If a manager does not score well on these first four items, the odds are that the team is seriously dysfunctional. These questions involve the very basics of a team's formation.

1—What are we trying to do? (What is our purpose?)
2—What is my role?
3—Do I have the necessary resources?
4—Do I have the right team members?

Belonging Needs

Statements 5–8: Once you understand the basics of who we are as a team and what we are aiming for, then naturally the attention turns personal, to discern whether you belong on that team.

5—Am I appreciated? Do I feel valued?
6—Do I trust and respect my fellow team members?
7—Can I be candid and open?
8—Do my opinions matter?

Self-Esteem Needs

Statements 9–11: When survival and belonging needs are satisfied, people naturally move up to self-esteem.

   9—Am I respected?
  10—Do I feel proud of what I'm a part of?
  11—Is this a high-performing team?

Self-Actualizing Needs

Statements 12–14: Finally, people want to perform at their highest level.

  12—Am I challenged?
  13—Am I given opportunities to grow and develop?
  14—Am I using my unique talents and gifts?

COHESION AND SLUDGE

Before going into more detail concerning these 14 diagnostic statements, let me briefly explain the relationship between this leadership scorecard and our firm's work on culture in the investment firm. Exhibit 25.1 shows a firm's managers as circles inside the larger circle of the firm's culture.

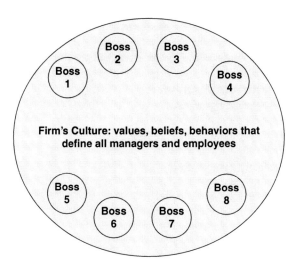

EXHIBIT 25.1 Managers and Culture

The senior leadership team, and especially the CEO, is the caretaker of the firm's culture. The leadership team members determine and articulate the values, beliefs, and behaviors that they want all employees to embrace and practice. This is the *macro* piece of the culture concept. It's measured with a tool that determines:

Cohesion: What percent of the firm's employees are embracing the top-10 values and behaviors? The investment industry, on average, scores around 45 percent (on a scale of 100 percent). Employees at cohesive firms are all on the same page and score around 80 percent.

Sludge: What percent of the culture is slowed down by "sludge" behaviors (such as blaming, gossiping, etc.)? The investment industry in general scores around 17 percent. The best firms are under 5 percent.

YOUR FIRM'S CULTURE

The culture issue is important for investment leaders. As David Fisher at Capital Group says, "Culture is our only competitive advantage." A key job for investment leaders, then, is to have a clear understanding of their firm's culture and to practice it themselves, thereby modeling it for staff. In our experience, the most important factor in having a strong culture is whether the senior team is aligned around it. If the senior team really practices the values and behaviors, those values and behaviors invariably cascade down to all the staff. Conversely, if the staff perceives that senior team members continually violate the standards of the articulated culture, then they assume it is okay to do the same.

Let's return now to the 14 diagnostic statements. The role of this tool is not to measure a culture, but to measure the *bosses* within that culture. This could be viewed as the *micro* piece of leadership. The big picture is culture (macro); the smaller picture is individual workgroups (micro).

THE CRITICAL FACT

Here's the critical fact for investment managers: *People join companies, but leave bosses.* In a business that is all about talent, it is hugely important to keep this idea front and center. Bad bosses will drive out great talent. No matter how good Joe was as a bond trader, if he becomes a bad boss, he'll cost the firm millions by driving out the other talented professionals. Hence, the importance of the 14 items: They are the best gauge we know of for measuring employee loyalty and commitment. High scores on these 14 items translate into high retention rates.

So, here are the 14 statements, presented in their "Maslow" groups, with some commentary. (Scoring goes from 1 = strongly disagree to 5 = strongly agree.)

Survival
1. We have a clear purpose. I know what our team is trying to achieve.
2. I know my role on the team and what is expected of me.
3. I have the resources to do my work well.
4. We have the right team members to accomplish our goals.

Strange as it may seem, lots of teams score poorly on statement 1. Obviously, managers need to clearly indicate what the team is trying to achieve and how that purpose fits into the larger picture of the firm overall. Without clarity of purpose, employees feel lost and frustrated. They disengage.

Likewise for statement 2: I need to know what my role is and what is expected of me. Roles and responsibilities should be discussed with each team member and descriptions of each should be written out, along with criteria for performance reviews.

Statement 3 is clearly a survival issue. I have to have the right tools, equipment, and other resources to perform my job at the highest level. In the case of investment professionals, this item often draws low scores because travel budgets for company visits or conferences have been cut.

Finally, we consider the right team membership to be a survival issue. This criterion is straight from Jim Collins.[3] He clearly states that having the right people on the bus, in the right seats, is the first—and most important—management decision. Nothing kills morale on a team like having one or two nonperformers. Investment professionals are competitive by nature, and take great pride in being on a top team. Add in the factor that nonperformers often are getting paid nearly the same as top performers, and you *really* have a morale problem.

If your average score on one or more of these statements is lower than 3, chances are your team is suffering. The leader is responsible for choosing a strong team, creating a clear purpose, defining each person's role, and giving people the resources to do their jobs.

Belonging
5. I feel valued and appreciated for my work.
6. I trust and respect the people on our team.

7. I experience a high level of candor and openness on our team.
8. My opinions matter on this team.

Statement 5 is so important that we devoted an entire chapter of *High-Performing Investment Teams*[4] to this one topic: appreciation—the basic human need to feel valued. However, the concept of appreciation is more profound than simply backslapping and issuing "well-dones." In our view, appreciation is the antidote to entitlement. The latter is fueled by expectations: "I should get a raise. I should get a bonus. I should get stock options." Entitlement is all about expectations. As one pundit said, "Expectations are premeditated resentments."[5] Wise managers learn to be appreciative of the little things in life, starting each day fresh. They develop an appreciative attitude toward themselves and their staff. The alternative is an entitlement attitude, which is fueled by ever-greater expectations.

Statement 6 measures trust and respect on a team. Investment teams will never function at a high level if trust and respect are lacking. We define trust in this way:

1. *Character*
   - Integrity: aligning words and actions
   - Intention: showing concern for others; creating win–win scenarios
2. *Competence*
   - Capabilities: talents and skills
   - Results: delivering on promised results

We've measured trust in this way for dozens of investment teams and found that trust correlates with fund performance. Quite simply, the higher the trust, the better the performance.

Why is trust so critical? As master investor Buffett has stated many times, the high level of trust at Berkshire Hathaway allows them to function with "less overhead and faster decision-making than any other place of our size in the world." Buffett's approach to choosing business partners is simple: "I only do business with people whom I like, trust, and admire." His trust and admiration for his partner is so high that he boasts, "Charlie Munger and I can handle a four-page memo over the phone in three grunts." Buffett doesn't waste any mental energy wondering, "Can I trust what he just said?" or "Will he remember that he made this agreement?" or "Is he telling me the whole story?" In fact, Buffett says just the opposite of his business partner: "Charlie never 'grabs' for himself and can be trusted without reservation. He has an absolute commitment to honesty, ethics, and integrity."

It is possible to develop extraordinarily high levels of trust on an investment team. The Delaware Growth team in San Francisco has nine members, all of whom averaged higher than 9 (on a 10-point scale) when rated by their colleagues.

Statement 7 is a logical follow-on to item 6. When trust exists on a team, people feel safe enough to be candid. We define *candor* as having three important elements:

1. *Honesty:* I say what is true for me. My words and thoughts align.
2. *Openness:* I say all that is relevant, and do not withhold important information.
3. *Awareness:* I make it a point to be well-informed, and I avoid being naïve. This includes the awareness that *none* of us is fully informed; there is always more to learn on any subject. (Overconfidence is well documented in behavioral finance literature.)

Without candor, a team cannot fully vet investment ideas and cannot operate at a world-class level.

Finally, statement 8 gets at the heart of the issue: Does my opinion matter on this team? When I belong—that is, when I am a valued member of a team—my voice counts. We use the term *key opinion leaders* to designate people in firms who are listened to. Similarly, each team member wants to be heard and valued for his or her contributions. When this is not the case, team members tend to disengage.

Self-Esteem

9. I have clear performance goals that measure my success on this team.
10. In the past three months, I have received performance feedback from my manager.
11. We make and keep clear agreements on this team.

These three statements address the issue of excellence and pride. Once my basic needs for survival and belonging have been met, I then move up to self-esteem issues. I want to feel a sense of mastery. I want to be excellent at what I do.

Statement 9 measures whether the manager has established clear performance goals for each individual. A low score here indicates that team members don't know whether they are succeeding. We recommend very clear, written performance goals based on thoughtful discussions between the manager and each employee. Statements 9 and 10 relate to the content of Ken Blanchard's famous little book, *The One Minute Manager*.[6] Each manager must negotiate a written performance contract with each staff member; then the manager must provide constant feedback (item 10) to indicate whether the employee is on-track or off-course.

Statement 11 is the basic proposition of accountability. In high-performing teams, individual team members pride themselves on making and keeping clear agreements. The team's efficiency and pride grow as the team builds a reputation for accountability. High marks on these three items tend to indicate a high-performance team, one that thrives on being the best.

Self-Actualization
12. My work allows me to use my talents and abilities.
13. Leadership encourages my development and growth.
14. I feel that my work is important to reaching our firm's goals.

At the top of the Maslow pyramid is self-actualization. Skillful managers who score well on statements 1 through 11 are mindful that team members still have another level of aspirations. Individuals want to play the game at their highest level. This involves discovering and leveraging their natural strengths. Again, this notion is so important that we devote an entire chapter to it in *High-Performing Investment Teams*. We call it *genius*. We don't mean genius as in Mozart, Shakespeare, or Einstein. Rather, we use the term as a name for the natural abilities that allow an individual to perform at an extraordinary level. Some may call it simply *talent*. Whatever you call it, genius goes beyond learned abilities to tap into the energies of our true passions. Smart managers encourage their staff members to find their genius areas, so that they will be intrinsically motivated. They will love their work. Capital Group practices this concept. They have a program called TAP (The Associates Program), which allows new employees to try various positions within the firm until they find something that really turns them on.

Statement 13 dovetails with statement 12. Individuals may be in their area of genius, but feel like management has put a lid on their growth. Smart managers understand that investment professionals are naturally ambitious and curious and love to challenge themselves. Hence, a good manager will continually challenge the team members and give them opportunities to grow to higher levels in the areas they love.

Finally, statement 14 gets at the all-important issue of *meaning*. Do I feel that my work is meaningful? Does it contribute to the firm's success? Can I see the direct impact of my work on the firm's overall mission? When the answer is no, chances are that the employee's commitment will suffer and sag. At some level, the employee will wonder, "Why am I doing this? What difference does it make?" Astute managers make sure that employees see the direct connection between their day-to-day tasks and the firm's overall mission.

SUMMARY

These 14 statements provide a comprehensive tool for measuring the effectiveness of managers. They are great feedback for identifying and honing management skill. If managers are committed to their own improvement, they will embrace a tool like this. Leaders of investment firms realize that they are in the talent business. As with professional sports teams, you can't win without a certain minimum level of talent—and bad bosses drive out top talent. Hence, there is a double-incentive for investment firm leaders to measure the skill of their managers:

1. Bad bosses will drive out good talent.
2. Mediocre bosses will not get full commitment and effort from their teams.

The good news is that these 14 "pressure points" are not illusory or cryptic. They are readily identifiable and, if necessary, fixable.

It all depends on the first and most important skill: Is the leader adaptive? What is the leader's relationship to feedback? Will the leaders take the results of this assessment and use them to improve team performance? Or will they rev up their powers of rationalization and dispute the facts?

As the old saying goes, when people are confronted with the choice of changing or proving that there is no need to change, most people get busy with the proof. In our experience, top leaders have mastered the ability to adapt.

NOTES

1. Chris Argyris, "Teaching Smart People How to Learn," *Harvard Business Review*, May/June 1991.
2. Our deep appreciation goes out to a number of thinkers who have influenced our work, including Jim Collins, Marcus Buckingham (Gallup Organization), Gay Hendricks, Robert Bruce Shaw, Steven Covey, Richard Barrett, and Kate Ludeman/Eddie Erlandson.
3. Jim Collins, *Good to Great* (New York: HarperCollins, 2001).
4. Jim Ware, Jim Dethmer, Jamie Ziegler, and Fran Skinner, *High-Performing Investment Teams* (New York: John Wiley & Sons, 2006).
5. Familiar saying at AA meetings.
6. Ken Blanchard, *The One Minute Manager* (London: HarperCollins, 1983).

CHAPTER 26

The Staffing Challenge

Monika Müller
FCM Finanz Coaching

The whole is reflected in the detail.
—Chinese proverb

The author identifies seven traits of successful portfolio managers. She describes a matrix composed of these characteristics, and explains how its use can enhance the recruitment and retention of consistently high performers. First, however, one should reflect on some research.

Business strategy, hardware, and software are important—but only people can make the difference. Finding, cultivating, and committing to the right people is considered today's most important factor of success in the investment industry. This type of well-honed corporate expertise will become even more important in the future.

Global markets are changing at an ever-increasing pace and there is no slowdown in sight. A constantly expanding and increasingly confusing amount of information is available to us every day, leading to increased complexity in decision making. What separates the winners from the losers are those managers who glean the best of the information, evaluate it properly, and act on it.

How have asset managers confronted this information challenge up to now? They've done it by focusing on specialized training and by updating their information technology (IT) resources. Despite these efforts, new statistics appear every year indicating that more than half of funds perform worse than their benchmarks. It seems particularly difficult for portfolio managers to make consistently successful decisions. Managers who deliver outstanding performance over time are rare. Obviously, it's not enough to beef up one's IT processes.

In addition, the industry is increasingly faced with questions of ethical norms. Customers and employees prefer to buy from, and work for, companies whose values are similar to theirs. Values give orientation and security in a fast-moving, risky environment. Thus, the formula for success consists of *both* performance and appropriate values.

WHAT SHOULD TODAY'S INVESTMENT MANAGERS BRING WITH THEM FOR THE FUTURE?

The successful investment management firm inspires its staff with sound business processes, perceptive pattern recognition, and a degree of continuity. Only a strong corporate culture that supports these three characteristics will guarantee that the company stays on track. In addition, a flexible work environment is essential. Even the newest developments in strategy and control show that strict budgeting and adherence to rigid goals have a debilitating effect—especially when innovation and growth are needed the most.[1] Asset management companies require intelligent, flexible people who are capable of making decisions and acting at the right moment with a certain amount of detachment. In addition, portfolio managers require composure in the face of sudden and unexpected market events.

Many asset management companies follow the motto: "The best talent will bring out the best in us." Can you rely on this simple formula? No. *Talent alone is not enough. Studies show that more than two-thirds of a fund's success is not due to the performance of individual fund managers, but to the health of the organization as a whole.*

The first part of this chapter discusses the psychological characteristics of most successful portfolio managers. Next, we talk about the dilemma that many investment companies face when they rely solely on talent searches. We have learned that it is an advantage to merge talent management (selection, training, and coaching) with organizational development. The final part of the chapter focuses on implementing this approach in your company.

SEVEN CHARACTERISTICS OF SUCCESSFUL PORTFOLIO MANAGERS

What differentiates winners from losers? What makes a portfolio manager an experienced master? Investment decisions result from the interplay of rationality, intuition, and feeling. To be at the top of his game, a portfolio manager needs a wide range of abilities and resources. The following characteristics emerged from hundreds of training and coaching sessions with traders and portfolio managers:

1. Wisdom, intuition, and patience
2. Knowledge, determination, and willingness to learn
3. An ability to manage stress and a sense of inner clarity
4. An intuitive sense of important changes on the horizon
5. Self-assurance and the courage to admit ignorance
6. Self-awareness
7. An ability to manage personal impact

Wisdom, Intuition, and Patience

Portfolio managers and traders are often exposed to complex decision-making situations. These are best dealt with subconsciously because conscious thought is usually not fast enough to cope with the unmanageable amount of data a manager faces every minute. Excellent results are achieved, not through deliberation alone, but also through intuitive pattern recognition. This is usually based on long-term observation and experience.[2]

Intuition is an inner confidence that cannot be explained with words or rational arguments. Reliable intuition cannot be hurried; it needs *patience* to develop over time. Nevertheless, the need for accuracy and effectiveness when making intuitive decisions cannot be underestimated. *Most portfolio managers have an intuitive sense, but only a few can consistently tap into it.* Like a muscle that can be trained, intuition can be strengthened over time. *Wisdom* is the natural result of the regular use of intuition over a period of time.

How would you rank your intuitive sense?

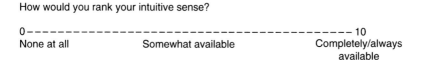

0 – 10
None at all   Somewhat available   Completely/always
available

Knowledge, Determination, and Willingness to Learn

Skilled selection is necessary to filter out irrelevant information. Managers often use processes that are supported by specially designed software applications. Investment processes must also be tested for clarity, conclusiveness, and stability. Conscious, rational thinking and constant monitoring on the basis of a limited number of decision-making criteria are of supreme importance.

The course of the decision-making process is often characterized by several phases. During the initial phase, the way information is gathered is crucial. It is the manager's innate curiosity and willingness to learn that opens him up to new ideas during this phase, allowing the constant flow of innovative thinking. The subsequent decision/action phase[3] is clearly different from the first step. During the transfer between phases, hurdles are cleared. The first phase of information gathering is brought to a close, and a new phase of processing the information is set in motion. *The challenge for the portfolio manager lies in controlling his or her emotions during the transition to the second phase.* Fear of mistakes or ambiguous objectives can extend the information-gathering stage unnecessarily, and cost the firm time and money. Using too many information sources in an effort to minimize risk reduces potential success.

During the application phase, the manager directs his attention to a selected target (e.g., equities, currencies, etc). Secondary targets (e.g., other securities) should be kept in the background; they will merely prove to be a source of distraction. The manager must shield against new information, or the influence of others (e.g., brokers), until trading is completed. Managers must maintain distance, discipline, and patience, even when new information surfaces. The will to succeed and disciplined, continuous improvement are essential. Indeed these are characteristics often mentioned by experts in other disciplines as essential components of success.[4]

The biggest difference between the novice and the expert is that the expert knows when to close the information-gathering phase. When he closes that door, he uses the knowledge gained to make effective and successful decisions leading to profitable action.

How would you rank your level of knowledge, determination, and willingness to learn?

```
0 - - - - - - - - - - - - - - - - - - - - - - - - - - - - - - - - - - - - - - - - - - - 10
Zero                        Medium                        Extensive
```

An Ability to Manage Stress and a Sense of Inner Clarity

The power to make effective decisions grows out of inner clarity. In highly dynamic environments, such as the market's turmoil in 2008, creative stress management techniques can be used to maintain inner clarity.

An individual's relative performance during the 2008 "meltdown" demonstrates whether that investment manager is prepared for *situations outside his or her comfort zone.*

0— —10
Not at all   Fairly well   Very well

When the tides are against you, how well can you maintain calm, reduce physical stress, and keep control of yourself with constructive internal dialog?

An Intuitive Sense of Important Changes on the Horizon

Important strategic decisions (involving product development, restructured departments, and new customer segments) require imagination and freedom of thought. If experience is the basis, then curiosity is the most essential ingredient. However, concentrating too much on the past and future sometimes prevents us from seeing what is right in front of us.

This is what distinguishes visionary leaders: those who act astutely, openly, and from a state of neutrality, with eyes and ears open and not fixed on popular opinions.

0— —10
None   Some   More than I could
                                                             ever imagine

How much innovative power do you develop in your everyday working life?

Self-Assurance and the Courage to Admit Ignorance

How a manager handles risk is of key importance. *Risk* means deviating from your own comfortable expectations. In portfolio management, managers face the challenge of shouldering and managing risks every day. This requires inner independence and discretion. Only those with enough self-assurance can deal with the uncertainty.

The discipline to stick with decisions once made also requires self-assurance. Fear of making mistakes and clinging to the wrong guidelines, anchors, or benchmarks can reduce success.

I know what I know, and what I don't —and when I act, I do so with confidence:

0— —10
Never   Sometimes   Always

Self-Awareness

Awareness of one's own thoughts and actions is prerequisite for careful preparation of decisions and profitable analysis. This ability to reflect allows scenarios to be developed and solutions to be formed and then discarded or changed if need be. High-performance teams in sports (e.g., Formula 1 racing) or in extreme vocations (e.g., trauma surgeons, paramedics) also use a consistent system of analysis for their missions.[5] This allows them to quickly integrate new situations, which can appear from out of nowhere.

When it comes to investment decisions, pay attention to the irrational need for control and to overconfidence. The ability to keep these in check is often the factor that separates winners from losers. This has been demonstrated by a number of empirical studies on behavioral finance.[6] The culture of investment firms flows directly into the portfolio manager's process[7]: one more good reason to be aware of your own thoughts and feelings when making decisions.

How good is your self-awareness?

0--10
Not at all good   Medium   Very strong

An Ability to Manage Personal Impact Using Communication and Presentation Skills

In a multimedia world, a successful external image and personal impact—including the ability to communicate a firm's investment processes—is just as important as the internal communication that happens in meetings and committees. Both demand clarity, courage, and candor.[8]

Even introverted portfolio managers are able to achieve success in this area. Everything has changed dramatically because of media focus, the growing star-hype, and most customers' desire for a hands-on manager. Today, external image counts just as much as internal communication. Both are fundamental to the success of a portfolio manager and his or her firm. Anyone can improve his or her charisma and impact on others and learn to use them more effectively.

I communicate clearly, openly, and courageously:

0--10
Seldom   Sometimes   Totally and completely

I am conscious of my impact with customers, the media, and in meetings:

0---10
Not at all								Somewhat							Totally and completely

ASSESSING YOUR FIRM

What follows is an initial strengths and weaknesses analysis. Note any questions you may have and items you would like to examine more closely.

The Seven Characteristics of Successful Portfolio Managers[C] (Exhibit 26.1) illustrate why the selection of employees is a major challenge for asset management firms. Even if a portfolio manager candidate has top marks in all the areas, it does not necessarily indicate that that person will be successful in your company. The degree of individuality and that person's values will most likely change the dynamic of your firm. Searching for talent is expensive, just like searching for undervalued shares. The expense of the search can be limited if you employ some deliberate strategy.

Before crafting a strategy, however, one should ask: "How much is any investment firm's success likely to be attributed to a few highly talented portfolio managers?"

There are several challenges when searching for and working with talent: How do we find the star—but avoid the prima donna? What usually

EXHIBIT 26.1   The Seven Characteristics of Successful Portfolio Managers[C]

	Myself	My Team	My Board	My Company	Average
Wisdom, intuition, and patience					
Knowledge, determination, willingness to learn					
Stress management and inner clarity					
Feel for important changes and the future					
Self-assurance and admitting ignorance					
Self-awareness					
Communication and presentation skills					
Average					

happens to the "average" portfolio managers? When should you pay above-market value for talent?

There are only a limited amount of truly talented managers available and the price to obtain them is usually high. Even when you have a star portfolio manager, the threat of an implosion is still significant if arrogance catches up with a lack of self-awareness.

A CHANGE OF PERSPECTIVE

How much of a fund's success can be attributed to a single manager? How does the performance of a team change when the manager is replaced? These are fascinating questions, which U.S. university professor Klaas Baks[9] pursued in a major study in 2003 with astoundingly clear results.

The study at Emory University in Atlanta, Georgia, compared the performance of one manager with the performance of the organization where he worked. The performance of more than 2,000 managers over a span of seven years served as a database. In evaluating the results, one fact in particular made clear the respective contribution to the performance of a managed fund: 20 percent of the fund managers being followed changed companies during the study period. By means of variance analysis, the study was able to clarify what contributed to a fund's total performance and the degree of that contribution.

The 70 Percent Formula of Fund Success

The Emory study showed that more than two-thirds of the performance is produced by the organization as a whole. In other words: *70 percent* of a fund's total performance is delivered by the company itself, and only *30 percent* of the performance rests in the hands of an *individual manager*.

Are you surprised by the results? One thing in particular must be considered when interpreting this empirical study: The exception proves the rule. On one hand, it is very likely that a single manager significantly influences the success of a fund. On the other hand, this success can be generated only through the quality of the company. The fund manager himself is replaceable.

What Can We Learn?

The study shows a company's *success* does not depend only on a few talented people. It is always *the interplay of the culture, structure, and organization of a firm* that is crucial to lasting positive results. Therefore, employee recruitment should focus not only on talent and early career success, but on the more important integration aspects of *willingness, commitment, and values.* Does the future employee have the will to apply herself in the interests of the firm? Is the candidate prepared to integrate herself into the established team? What barriers does she bring with her in this regard? Do her values and motives fit those of the company? Is the candidate's investment philosophy and risk tolerance compatible with that of the firm?

Investment talent evolves best in a successful company—but only if the values match! This poses the question: Has the company defined its values well before trying to find the pearls of the industry? The first step is to ask, out loud, the most critical of all questions: "With which values do we want to lead our company into the future?"

THE FCM MATRIX FOR SUCCESS© IN INVESTMENT MANAGEMENT

The FCM[10] Matrix for Success© (Exhibit 26.2) was created through years of practical experience with hundreds of traders and portfolio managers in asset management. The nine-field diagram facilitates the rapid understanding of a company's identity.

The FCM Matrix for Success© is a coaching tool. It does not dictate a direction or solution, but instead shows essential dependencies and crosslinks within a company or team. Visualization of the matrix gives valuable insight into whether the interplay, from the business plan level through to the investment process—all the way to the actual daily schedules of individual portfolio managers or teams—shows promise.

The spaces are filled with important criteria of the value chain. Each company identifies these criteria before implementing them in a customized design for success. Take, for example, company culture. The company determines for itself which culture and which investment philosophy is appropriate. The resulting coaching design is determined by the goals set by the customer and the coachee.

The matrix allows companies to quickly recognize where strengths and weaknesses lie.

Collecting information from the viewpoint of various participants is also useful. In accordance with good coaching practices, observations are collected on a neutral basis and facts are arranged. The evaluation and classification is carried out by the group or committee that requested the change. Self-perception is required and encouraged. Possible solutions can be played out in case scenarios[11] and changes in the company simulated.

EXHIBIT 26.2 FCM Matrix for Success© in Investment Management

	Company	Department/Team/Committee	Individual Portfolio Manager
Business Plan	*Strong Culture:* values, visions, goals, and the appropriate . . .	*Strong Composition:* heterogeneity or homogeneity and the appropriate . . .	*Strong People:* character above expertise and the appropriate . . .
	▪ Organizational structure ▪ Clear task definition ▪ Structured management ▪ Understanding of People ▪ Leadership concept ▪ Quality management ▪ Reward system ▪ Risk tolerance ▪ Early warning system/risk control ▪ . . .	▪ Responsibility- and task-delegation ▪ Clear distribution of roles in the decision-making process ▪ Bonus/salary ▪ . . .	▪ Scientifically-based personnel-selection model (e.g., Hogan Assessment) ▪ Bonus/salary ▪ . . .
Investment Plan	*Investment philosophy*	Pragmatic model for cooperation (e.g., team role model by Meredith Belbin; see note 14)	Clever investment ideas
	▪ Transparent investment process ▪ Benchmark and performance measurement	▪ Clear rules of cooperation	▪ Effective information processing ▪ Clear presentation of information

	Personnel/technical application	Knowledge about the psychodynamics of financial decisions in the team	Simple rules for investment decisions
	Crisis management	Ways to control it	Knowledge about the psychodynamics (rationality, intuition, emotion) of financial decisions in the internal team
	…	…	…
Daily Schedule	**Back office**	**Thinking and acting from a single team mindset**	**Self-reflection**
	Transparent communication of current decisions	Clear, task-oriented communications processes	Application discipline
	…	Meta-communication for reflecting on the daily pitfalls of decision making (behavioral finance)	Self-management
		Conflict management	Mental techniques (e.g., for stress management)
		…	…

This is comparable to the application of new algorithms in the programming of a trading system.

Everyone on Board

Again, when working with the matrix in your company, remember the approach must also fit your in-house culture. This means that the more hierarchical your company, the more likely it will depend on top management to make room for change on its own terms.

The process is different with more open and lean companies. These offer the opportunity to build a heterogeneous group for conducting a current analysis. Hierarchy, expertise, and personality are some of the factors to consider when forming these groups.

In any case, trust within the company will be the gauge and impulse for success. A lack of trust will require moving forward in small steps! But never fear; your goals are still attainable. However, it will be important to bring individual elements together. *Detail is reflected in the whole!*

Managing Talent

Now let us transfer the procedure to the core theme of this chapter: talent management.

Working with the matrix shows that only organizations with a strong culture and a clear, transparent business and investment processes can derive customized concepts for:

- The selection of talented people suited to the company
- The building and integration of individual portfolio managers through mentoring, training, and coaching
- The development of effective teamwork through team coaching, and as a special assignment
- Suitable leadership development program for portfolio manager teams

The optimal interplay of many small process steps accounts for a major part of the shared success. If these process steps are adhered to, then a high level of performance is created in which ordinary people are able to work together in an extraordinary way.

The picture resulting from the matrix is a point of departure for the change process and serves to help find the most valuable application points (i.e., the best point of leverage). Initial discussions often deal with the reasons for which coaching was requested in the first place. But sometimes, as dialogue progresses, a completely different subject emerges as being important.

UTILIZE CRISIS AS OPPORTUNITY

The following are a few possible symptoms of crisis to remember when beginning an analysis with the FCM Matrix for Success$^{©}$:

- Performance breakdown
- Employee turnover
- Customer loss and mistrust
- Ethical infringements (e.g., insider trading, corruption)
- Stagnation
- Decrease in profits and turnover

The FCM Matrix can identify potential consequences of these symptoms. Here a few examples:

- A once-successful culture slackens because company growth leads to employee turnover.
- The introduction of different payment systems following a company merger leads to differing risk-tolerance behavior among portfolio managers.
- Entrepreneurial risk increases alienation in employees with lower risk tolerance (or the opposite).
- Investment processes become convoluted and are no longer easily communicable to new employees. They in turn feel overwhelmed and suffer performance setbacks or quickly leave the company.
- Innovation capabilities are lacking; customers switch to competitors.
- A lack of employee stress management leads to irrational traps/errors (herding, splitting-effect[12]) and performance suffers.
- Bonus system encourages risk-averse behavior (or the opposite), resulting in a tendency toward home bias in portfolio investment, leading to subpar performance.
- Successful portfolio managers leave the company when significantly differing opinions within the team or asset allocation committee are not confronted; this is usually because self-reflection within the organization is discouraged.

You may have already noticed similar situations in your company. The analysis can yield clues to application points in your firm with the greatest leverage potential. But before you begin, consider the following:

Instead of spending huge amounts of time and money changing management again and again, a firm chooses instead to invest in the development of a well-defined leadership culture. But which concept is right for the company and its employees? For any sustainable solution, a firm cannot avoid reviewing a variety of potential management concepts.

Basically, there are people-oriented and task-oriented management styles. Which one is right for your company? Let us assume that your executives tend to be introverted, lack emotional intelligence, and prefer talking about numbers more than communicating with people. In this case, it might be better to invest in well-structured processes with clear rules and a clearly defined division of tasks, while simultaneously distributing leadership among team members.[13] The task-oriented hierarchy will lose some of its impact, but this approach demands more self-management from team members. The advantage is there is no need to create a personnel-oriented leadership strategy focusing on interpersonal relationships (which in this case would be complicated and hold little prospect for success). Instead training and coaching can concentrate on the communication of information within the team.

Companies that put a priority on individuals, and where recognition of executives and employees is of great importance, invest more time and money in people-oriented leadership training.

FOCUSED QUERIES

In light of the FCM Matrix for Investment Success©, consider the following issues and how the foregoing can be applied to addressing them:

- *Continuous improvement in investment management:* Successful companies develop a culture of continuous improvement (consider Toyota). Even if no crisis exists, or the talent search has been solved, an FCM Matrix analysis can serve to increase success by helping a company deal with ongoing issues through self-coaching.
- *Company culture:* What is our culture? What are the company's values, visions, goals? How clear are these to us? How strong is the culture anchored within our company? How consistently do we live it on a daily basis? Are there differences between the formal (business plan) and the informal (daily cooperation)—between what is supposed to happen and what actually prevails in the company? Would it help to close the gap?
- *Team composition and decision responsibility:* What about our teams? How are they formed? Do we have a method that goes beyond the

evaluation of mere technical qualifications? What scientific findings are available for helping create successful teams and teamwork (e.g., the team role model by Meredith Belbin[14])? Do we utilize these already? If teams do not communicate well, it means valuable information is lost and decisions are error-prone. Ironically, the problem of a lack of information exists, even though large amounts of money are spent on research. How is responsibility for decisions divided among individual fund managers? Are roles and tasks clear for everyone? In addition, what role does research play in the preparation of decisions? Have we adjusted work processes optimally? Are rules for teamwork already in place? How do we measure contributions by team members during a meeting?

▪ *Manager selection as leadership task:* What does being a good portfolio manager mean to us? Can the question be answered that easily? There are a number of things to consider: The stronger the company culture (at the corporate level) and the more effectively cooperation is regulated (at the team level) the more likely competent employees will reach their potential. That is why it pays to ensure that any prospective employees fit into a company's culture. In addition, candidates should have the type of personality that allows them to react well under stress. In this manner, the company maximizes resources at all levels. How does it look at your company?

▪ *Unifying decision-responsibility and reward:* Which reward systems are best suited for working with fund managers? A good answer is impossible without considering the previously discussed aspects of culture, team, and investment process. A study at a German university showed that pay programs designed to motivate employees do not always produce the desired effects. They are successful only if they are suited to the company's organization and strategy.[15] Pay programs work well when objectives are clear. If you want to encourage teamwork and team decisions, you will utilize group-oriented bonuses, which in turn motivate fund managers to create first-class communication and decision-making systems.

THE INVESTMENT PROCESS

An investment process's effectiveness is clearly reflected in risk management and the discipline applied to its daily application. With successful asset managers, every investment process is a reflection of the company's processes. Furthermore, good processes allow for the unique psychodynamics of financial decision making. For all process phases (information processing, decision, action, profit-and-loss management) as well as challenges (control illusion, overconfidence, perception distortion, etc.), appropriate rules are in place concerning the tasks of individuals and teams. Ask yourself how your portfolio managers would react in a crisis. The answer immediately shows process strengths and weaknesses. An intelligent reward system supports process rules and facilitates courage and independence in decisions under uncertainty. A strong culture enhances trust in the total system—and hence that of the individual manager—in the investment process.

EARLY WARNING SYSTEM

Early warning systems in companies work only as well as the roles defined for executives, teams, and portfolio managers in normal everyday decision-making situations. Something that is not lived on a daily basis cannot be used in a crisis situation. For that reason, knowledge about how portfolio managers react under pressure is necessary. If the majority of a team's members tend to react emotionally and aggressively, then ways must be found to bring adrenalin levels under control. In contrast, if the tendency is to remain silent while losses accumulate, then individuals and teams must become proactive in requesting support to get communication flowing again. Both cases demand self-assessment and self-management. The interconnections within the matrix show that without clear, bold communication processes, requirements for successful crisis management are lacking. In other words: The effectiveness of the respective system will make itself apparent in crisis situations.

COACHING AND TRAINING: CUSTOM-MADE LEARNING PROCESSES

The company itself can take on many of the necessary developmental steps. But just like people, firms also have their blind spots. A fresh, unbiased view from the outside, coupled with intelligent questioning by the coach, will put the company on the fast-track toward effective solutions. A good coach should take your company well beyond its initial goals.

Here are some valuable questions for the coaching process (these questions should be answered before a portfolio-manager selection assessment, combined with coaching and training, can be reasonably implemented):

1. Which values are used to lead your enterprise? Without clear values there is no orientation on a daily basis.

2. Which management concept has the company chosen (more people oriented or task oriented)? Without a clear leadership concept, useful dynamics will be lacking in the company, teams, and individuals.
3. What degree of investment risk tolerance exists in your company on a scale from 0 to 10? Good decisions are not possible without being conscious of risk tolerance.

CONCLUSION

People are often hired for their "expertise" and because they are "nice." But why do people get fired? Employees are let go because of reactions that occurred under stress, or because the new person did not fit into the company culture and did not feel or behave like part of the company. Either can be avoided through appropriate selection of personnel and by employing coaching and training measures early on.

Assessments can be used for leadership development and the selection of the managers. A scientifically based instrument used around the world is the Hogan Personality Assessment (HPA). The HPA works on a three-dimensional level, delivering extensive reports and forecasts for the following areas:

- Strengths—the profile of the person in everyday life
- The "stress person"—how the person behaves under pressure
- The "driver"—a person's motives, values, and preferences

Special attention should be paid to the *driver*, a person's motives, values, and preferences, which should match company objectives. This often determines whether a portfolio manager's performance will increase or decrease once she enters the company. Since this is often observed in the field, the HPA offers the option of customizing assessments to the individual needs of the enterprise.[16]

An assessment will also help to uncover a candidate's individual strengths. It may become apparent that a rather mediocre portfolio manager is actually an undiscovered sales talent or an even better consultant! Or it may show that poorly performing employees are just in the wrong company, the wrong workplace, or the wrong team. An assessment-supported change brings out their true potential. Have you ever thought about checking whether the culture at your workplace is appropriate for bringing out the best in you?

If a portfolio manager's or a team's reaction under pressure becomes apparent early enough, coaching can help to develop the required employee resources. Recognizing inner dialog at an early stage is a good first stress indicator, which can help portfolio managers develop timely countermeasures. In asset management, where a cool head and willingness to act on intuition can determine success, dealing with emotions in a professional manner is a most important criterion for lasting success.

Talent management is an exciting challenge when a firm's culture, management strategy, and investment process harmonize well together. That makes selecting new people easy; work-in phases go quickly, and employees feel like part of the company. The Seven Characteristics of Successful Portfolio Managers©, the FCM Matrix for Success©, and a sound procedure for personality assessment are tools that can significantly influence strategic organizational development as well as personnel development in an asset management company.

Whether your aim is to fundamentally change an existing company, establish a new asset management firm, or create a new department, the Matrix should be a valuable aid.

NOTES

1. Niels Pfläging, *Führen mit flexiblen Zielen* (Frankfurt a.M.: Campus Verlag, 2006; http://www.metamanagementgroup.com/).
2. G. Gigerenzer, *Simple Heuristics That Make Us Smart* (Oxford University Press, 2006); G. Gigerenzer, *Gut Feelings* (New York: Penguin, 2007); Gavin de Becker, *The Gift of Fear: Survival Signals That Protect Us from Violence* (New York: Dell Publishing, 1998).
3. H. Heckhausen, P. M. Gollwitzer, and F. E. Weinert (eds.), *Jenseits des Rubikon: Der Wille in den Humanwissenschaften* (Berlin: Springer, 1987).
4. George Leonard, "The 5 Keys to Mastery" (DVD), 2001 (www.itp-life/products/index.html).
5. G. Klein, *Sources of Power. How People Make Decisions* (Cambridge: The MIT Press, 1998).
6. de Bondt, Werner. *The Psychology of World Equity Markets* (Cheltenham, UK: Edward Elgar Publishing, 2005).
7. H. Shefrin, *Beyond Greed and Fear: Understanding Behavioral Finance and the Psychology of Investing* (New York: Oxford University Press 2007); Biais, Bruno & Hilton, Denis & Pouget, Sébastien, 2002. "Psychological Traits and Trading Strategies," CEPR Discussion Papers 3195 in W. M. O'Barr and J. M. Conley, *Fortune and Folly: The Wealth and Power of Institutional Investment* (Homewood IL: Business One Irwin, 1992).
8. J. Ware and J. Dethmer, *High Performing Investment Teams: How to Achieve Best Practices of Top Firms* (Hoboken, NJ: John Wiley & Sons, 2006).
9. K. P. Baks, "On the Performance of Mutual Fund Managers," 2003 (http://www.bus.emory.edu/kbaks/research.htm).

10. FCM is the name of the author's company (FCM Finanz Coaching).
11. A. de Geus, *The Living Company* (Boston: Harvard Business School Press, 1997).
12. H. Shefrin, *Beyond Greed and Fear: Understanding Behavioral Finance and the Psychology of Investing* (New York: Oxford University Press 2007);
13. http://www.quatuorannesci.com.
14. http://www.belbin.com.
15. C. Antoni and A. Berger, "Entgelt-Variabilisierung: ideologisch verklärt, oder empirisch bewährt? In *Wirtschaftspsychologie aktuell* (Heidelberg: Economica Verlag, 2/2005), pp. 39–42.
16. http://www.hoganassessment.com/ and http://www.hoganassessment.com/products_services/hpi.aspx.

CHAPTER 27

The "Same Page" Challenge: Communicating Effectively

Jamie Goodrich Ziegler
Principal, Focus Consulting Group

The single biggest problem in communication is the illusion that it has been accomplished.

—George Bernard Shaw, Irish playwright

A veteran industry executive addresses the necessity of clear communications among all the players: consultants, trustees, sell-siders, and portfolio managers with some practical suggestions on overcoming barriers and misconceptions.

Last summer, the chief investment officer of a midsized value manager called us to discuss his concerns about the firm's culture. "Don't get me wrong," he said, "I think it's great that we've tripled our assets under management over the past three years. But we've added so many new people to support that growth—our staff size has more than doubled and we've opened new offices on both coasts—that I don't know everyone individually any longer. I'm worried about how well the new people understand our culture, and whether they really know where we are going. Our culture has always been a competitive advantage for us . . . but now I'm not so sure."

I listened as he told me about the firm's founding 10 years earlier, with four partners and six staff members, and how they operated in an office so small that communication was never an issue. "We just stood up and yelled over the sides of our cubicles," he laughed. "Talk about having no privacy.

But we all knew everything about every client, and we operated as a tightly knit group. We were more like a family than a company, in those days. Now, however, we have more than 200 employees, and I barely know all their names, let alone anything about them as individuals."

We hear this story frequently from our investment clients. A firm is founded by a handful of intelligent investment professionals who like and trust one another. With a well-thought-out investment process (or sometimes just by sheer luck), they produce good results, and they're off to the races. Investment success attracts clients, which leads to growth, which in turn supports additional resources. If they adhere to their processes (or the stars align) and investment success continues, they attract more clients, which leads to more growth . . . and before you know it, the tight-knit family with one superior product has turned into a midsized (or even larger) business with more than 100 people, organized into several divisions, with multiple products and services for a spectrum of markets, working from regional (or international) locations. Suddenly they're dealing with communications issues they never dreamed of during their cubicle days.

What is the common response to these issues? Well, join me in our subsequent meeting with the CIO, his CEO, and the other senior leaders of this firm, and you'll see firsthand why communications can be the Achilles' heel—or a competitive edge—for investment firms.

We started our conversation as we typically do, by asking the CEO about his vision of success.

"My vision is simple," the CEO stated. "It's to reach $20 billion in AUM by 2010, increase our market share in the institutional business by 25 percent, and grow our high-net-worth business at the rate we've been achieving over the past three years. We will continue our U.S. expansion in the wealth market by opening five more regional offices, and we will begin our international expansion by establishing a London presence. Throughout all of this, we will adhere to our investment style, no matter what the market conditions are, which will contribute to maintaining our top-decile ranking for three-year performance for our cornerstone products."

That seemed pretty clear to us. But was it clear to all the staff members? So we asked the CEO whether he thought all the employees understood this vision. He responded with a frown, "Of course they understand my vision. I talk about it all the time." Then he looked around at his senior staff, and said, "Yes, I'm sure they all know where we're going."

The other leaders said nothing. There was a knock on the door, and the CEO was called away to take a pressing client call. After the door closed, the rest of the leaders looked at each other uncomfortably. Finally, the CIO cleared his throat, leaned toward us and said, "No, they don't. They don't understand his vision at all. Particularly the new people. He thinks he talks about it all the time, but he's really only talking to himself and a few of us about it. But he blows up if we point that out, so we don't say anything about it to him anymore. And *that's* the problem." The other senior leaders nodded in agreement.

This example aptly illustrates the various levels on which communications issues can be found within an investment firm. The first level identified by the CIO—that the ranks didn't understand the vision—indicated a weakness in the communication loop between the leadership team and the rest of the staff. We see that fairly often with rapidly growing firms, because senior management efforts are typically focused more on managing the investment process or on building client relationships than on managing—and communicating with—a growing staff.

However, the larger a firm grows, the *more* time the senior leaders need to spend with their teams, across all functions, to ensure that everyone is pulling in the same direction. David Fisher, chairman of Capital Group, knows this well. With more than 9,000 employees in 19 locations in seven countries, Capital Group has cultivated a culture that focuses heavily on the team members. "After all," Fisher points out, "this is a people business. We want to attract, retain, and motivate talented people so we can provide our clients with the best experience possible." Implicit in this people-oriented culture is world-class communication. Fisher stays in touch with his large group by spending a significant amount of his own time—roughly 75 percent—internally. He and his senior team travel to their different locations regularly, using in-person meetings, retreats, and other face-to-face forums to keep communication flowing freely. They supplement in-person meetings with technology tools that include videoconferencing, daily conference calls, and, of course, e-mail—though Fisher is quick to point out that e-mail is never used as the primary tool for conveying sensitive information. "Key messages need to be discussed in person," he explains.

So if one of the largest investment firms in the world has a handle on the communication challenge, why do so many smaller firms struggle? We believe it often has more to do with *mindset* than *method*, though both are important. This brings us to the second, and more troubling, communication issue we observed for our midsize value firm—the interaction of the senior leaders with one another. First, the refusal by the CEO to listen to the feedback from his leadership team about whether his vision was understood by everyone indicated that, on this issue at least, his mind was closed, rather than open and curious. This was a red flag for us, because the ability to listen openly and nondefensively is critical, especially for the person at the top. Good listening is the *receiving* half of the communications equation. Without it, even the most accurately sent message will wind up as an incomplete pass.

On the *sending* side of the equation, we noted weaknesses there as well, as illustrated by the lack of candor among the senior leaders. Their unwillingness to directly challenge the CEO about whether his vision was understood was also contributing to the problem. The other leaders appeared to be more willing to talk *about* the CEO after he left the room than *with* him while he was in it.

We find that, unfortunately, this type of unhealthy dynamic feeds on itself if it's not addressed, as poor listening by the leader typically breeds a lack of candor among the rest of the staff—which breeds more poor listening and more lack of candor. The result can be a passive-aggressive environment where trust levels are low and communication is transmitted among the troops informally via gossip rather than by direct and healthy dialog. In this type of environment, the leader is often cut off from the true communication, thus losing some of the most important sources of feedback and information. Without accurate information, the leader may end up making decisions that are suboptimal—or even downright disastrous, like the emperor in his "new clothes." (Trust me on this one. If you haven't seen it happen, I can tell you that it's not pretty.)

THE ART OF CLEAR COMMUNICATION

Our previous example focused on common issues that we see in internal communications for investment firms. But the same issues often surface in external communications—with clients, consultants, third-party distributors, and the media—as well. That's not surprising, since the same skill set is involved in the art of clear communication, regardless of the audience.

What are those skills? We touched on two of them in our example—*openness* and *candor*—which, along with *relationship orientation, awareness*, and *appreciation*, are the building blocks of clear communication.

Messaging and *method* are also important, because how the message is framed and the manner in which it is delivered will also have an impact on how well it is received.

Let's look at the role each of these skills plays in addressing the communications challenge.

Relationship Orientation

The first and most important competency of world-class communication is having a positive and genuine relationship orientation. Jon Hunt, chief operating officer of Convergent Capital Management, LLC, has a good perspective on this, given his role in working with the leaders of eight investment management affiliates in 14 offices across the country—preceded by nearly 25 years in a variety of leadership roles at Northern Trust. Hunt points out, "Communications improve significantly when the players are approachable, have empathy, and show the ability to really listen." Ginger Lapid-Bogda, Ph.D., author of *Bringing Out the Best in Yourself at Work* (New York: McGraw-Hill, 2004) agrees, ranking the ability to create positive relationships as one of the top competency components to becoming an excellent communicator. She defines this competency as "being approachable, making time for people, and putting others at ease; being warm, gracious, open and non-judgmental; showing empathy, having personal credibility and integrity based on congruence between action and words; demonstrating respect for diversity of thought, style, culture, skill sets, and perspectives, relating comfortably with people from diverse demographic groups and various levels; and generating trust by honoring confidences and being honest."

Now, does this sound like your typical investment professional? Perhaps some of these characteristics do. But the aspects of "being approachable, showing empathy, and putting others at ease" are not usually part of an investment professional's DNA. In fact, many investment professionals would see such a relationship orientation as a sign of weakness. However, in the best-performing firms, we actually do find that on display—and most often modeled by the people at the top. In terms of world-class communication, a relationship orientation literally opens the door to the natural flow of information that is the lifeblood of any human organization, and thus represents a competitive advantage to those who decide to master it.

Openness

Once the door is open, being curious about the new information that comes in—particularly if it is at odds with what one believes—is another important requirement to becoming a world-class communicator. It's also the number-one predictor of success for leaders, according to the Center for Creative Leadership in Greensboro, North Carolina. Openness is the listening—or *receiving*—half of the communications equation, and it is another skill we often find overlooked by investment professionals. As Jon Hunt points out, "Listening is the most important—yet most underappreciated—aspect of communications. Most people are busy doing one-way communicating, and few people stop to really listen."

We see this often when we first begin our work with investment teams, particularly if the topic at hand is controversial and emotionally charged, or if the stakes are high. While one team member is sharing his or her point of view, the others are comparing what's being said with their own beliefs about the matter. If these opinions don't align, they begin planning their responses before the first team member has even finished saying all he or she has to say. (My partner, Jim Dethmer, refers to this as *reloading*.) When this happens, the true meaning of the original message is often missed.

One antidote to this problem is *active* listening. As Mellody Hobson, president of Ariel Capital Management and *Good Morning America's* financial contributor, notes, "It's critical to be an active listener, with the goal of *truly* understanding the other person." Active listening means suspending your own beliefs and judgments, and focusing all your attention on the speaker, to improve your understanding. An important step in active listening is checking back with the speaker to ensure that you really *got* the message. "When we have our teammates practice this with one another, they are often surprised at how often they 'miss' the intended message," Hobson says. "They sometimes need to hear it several times before getting it right."

Openness may not come naturally to many investment types, yet it can be learned, practiced, and mastered. One of the most useful related skills is learning to seek and listen to feedback. Along with that, it's important to learn how to recognize whether the feedback triggers defensiveness (because some of it will), and then shifting from defensiveness to openness quickly. This is a skill that is not gained overnight, but with ongoing practice, we've found that even the thickest-skinned investment types can learn to be better listeners. The payoff for doing so can be significant. As Warren Buffett, chairman and CEO of Berkshire Hathaway, advises, "Continually challenge and be willing to amend your best-loved ideas." The only way to do this is by hearing—and really listening to—different points of view.

Candor

Candor is the *sending* half of the communications equation. Having a candor mindset means being willing to tell the whole truth—without withholding. It also means knowing the difference between opinion and fact, and holding on to your opinions lightly. A third dimension of candor—and the one most frequently misunderstood—is being aware that there is always more to the picture than meets the eye. Thus, when you have mastered candor, you are committed to sharing what you know openly and nondefensively, in the belief that what you have is only one part of the story. By combining everyone's story, you'll have the most complete picture of reality. Michelle Seitz, head of investment management at William Blair & Company, is well-regarded by her team for her commitment to candor. She understands the importance of getting the complete story, remarking, "The power and nuance of communication can be vastly underestimated, especially in an intellectual capital business like investments. As a leader, it's critical to keep your communications open and clear, and that your team members do the same, so you can assess reality clearly."

Awareness

Awareness is important to world-class communications at several levels. Daniel Goleman, author of *Emotional Intelligence* (Bantam, 1997), describes awareness in an *emotional competence* framework, which includes both personal and social awareness. These skills determine how well we manage ourselves, and how well we handle relationships, and thus are critical components of a communications mindset. Specifically, *self-awareness* means knowing one's internal states, preferences, resources, and intuitions. *Social awareness* means understanding others' feelings, needs, and concerns. In the world of investments, where facts are typically valued more highly than feelings, awareness is often a missing ingredient that can add significantly to a team's ability to communicate well and thus improve their chances of winning in the game.

However, that is beginning to change at some investment firms, where leadership teams see the value in understanding what motivates people to do what they do. By using tools like the *Enneagram personality system* and the *Myers-Briggs Type Indicator*, team members can learn to understand their own personal operating systems better, as well as how to optimize working with others.

We find the Enneagram system particularly helpful when it comes to identifying communication strengths and areas for improvement. The nine-point Enneagram system dates back more than 2,000 years and suggests that there are nine basic worldviews, with related patterns for feeling, thinking, and communicating associated with each one. These types are known as the Perfectionist, the Helper, the Achiever, the Individualist, the Investigator, the Loyal Skeptic, the Enthusiast, the Controller, and the Peacemaker. By identifying and understanding your own type, you can become more effective as a communicator.[1]

Appreciation

Having a mindset of appreciation means finding the positive in other people and in oneself. However, like openness, appreciation is among the most poorly developed skills among investment professionals. That's not a surprise, given the critical and analytical mindset that helps in the investment process. Yet by adopting a mindset of appreciation, it's much easier to build trust. The greater the trust among the team, the faster the decision making.

Mark Anson, president of Nuveen Investments, shows appreciation and respect for his team in a number of ways that include—and extend beyond—one-on-one expressions of gratitude. First, consider how he describes his role at the $162 billion firm: "My job is to work *for* the employees, not vice versa. I focus on making sure they have the resources, the support, and the structure they need in order to perform at their best." Anson spends time visiting the teams "where they live," so they know he is accessible. "I get bored sitting at my desk," he adds. (In fact, Anson spent the morning of our interview meeting—which took place in the midst of the market turmoil in March 2008—sitting with the traders, to stay in close touch and lend support. Contrast that with the executives in some organizations who never leave the executive suite.) Along the same lines, after joining the senior team at Nuveen in 2007, he and the recently promoted CEO, John Amboian, moved to reconfigure their executive suite into smaller offices, turning much of the private area (with some of the most spectacular views of the city of Chicago) into conference rooms and other common space. This action of literally "tearing down the walls" between themselves and the rest of the team sent a strong message of connection and respect.

Appreciation is important in groups of all sizes, but is particularly key for teams that are growing rapidly, such as Michelle Seitz's investment team at William Blair & Company, which has more than tripled in size over the past five years. With a team of 350 people, Seitz says that she now delegates more decision making to her senior leaders, and so, trust—and communication—are more critical than ever. "When you're growing as rapidly as we are," Seitz says, "you have to develop trust quickly, and mutual respect is essential to that."

Jon Hunt also recognizes the value of connection in world-class communication. He says, "When you communicate, you should engage your head *and* your heart, and show that you really care. If people feel genuinely appreciated, they'll go to the ends of the earth for you."

We believe that having these building blocks in place—openness, candor, a relationship orientation, awareness, and appreciation—provides the foundation for world-class communications. But obviously, that's not all it takes. Next comes the actual implementation, which has two elements: messaging and method. Messaging answers the *what* question, and method answers the *how*.

THE WORLD-CLASS DISCUSSION MODEL

The relationship between candor (sending) and openness (receiving) is an important determining factor in the quality of a team's overall communications, as well as a good indicator of the type of culture that has been created. The model shown in Exhibit 27.1, developed by my partner, Jim Ware, illustrates the four basic communication cultures we find most often among investment firms—as well as a fifth culture, which we consider to be world-class, and have found in only a handful of firms. In this model, the *x*-axis is openness, or receiving, and the *y*-axis is candor, or sending. The five resulting communication cultures are:

1. *Fear-based:* Groups with low levels of candor and low levels of openness tend to experience high levels of fear, so we call this the fear-based culture. Here, we find a concentration of people with "victim" mentalities, where they believe themselves to be helpless and unable to speak up for what they want, because of the low level of openness in the culture. People operating in fear-based cultures tend to become cynical and closed, even to new ideas that could improve the situation. As a result, they often exhibit passive-aggressive behavior, which clearly undermines decision making and productivity. In our survey work, we find that firms in this quadrant tend to have the highest overall levels of sludge (nonconstructive values and behaviors), with specific sludge values that include gossip, defensiveness, and blame. This group also

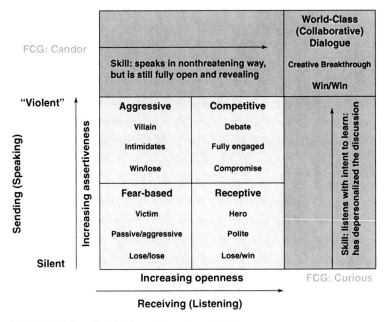

EXHIBIT 27.1 World-Class Discussion Model

exhibits the lowest levels of trust of all types. Fear-based firms also, unfortunately, are the least likely to succeed over the long term (and even the near term, in some cases), unless direct and focused changes are made to improve the unhealthy dynamic.

2. *Aggressive:* In an aggressive culture, openness is as low as in a fear-based culture, but candor is higher. That means that although people are willing to send their messages out, they are not willing to really listen to one another. When a sender isn't being heard, it's human nature to turn up the volume, which results in more aggressive behavior. Here we often find intimidation used as a tool to persuade, thus producing the "villain" persona. The result is a win–lose mentality, where the sender appears to seek to win at the expense of the others. Firms that are identified as having this type of culture tend to exhibit above-average sludge values, with *blame* surfacing as the number-one nonconstructive value. Unlike fear-based cultures, aggressive cultures have a better chance of longer-term survival, but the cost is often higher levels of staff turnover due to higher levels of job-related stress.

3. *Receptive:* In a receptive culture, candor (sending) is low, but openness (listening) is high. That implies that people are willing to listen to other points of view openly and curiously, but are not willing to share their own opinions completely. Here we typically find polite and well-mannered exchanges that don't really address the true issues because of high levels of withholding. We often find receptive cultures in large organizations, including banks and insurance companies, where it may be more important (from a political standpoint) to be supportive of senior management decision making than to challenge it. In our survey work with receptive firms, the most common sludge factors we find are gossip, reactive, bureaucratic/territorial, and slow-moving. These cultures sometimes exhibit above-average levels of loyalty to—and among—long-term staff members (sometimes unrelated to their perceived relative contributions), which can, unfortunately, serve to demotivate other staff members. Thus, receptive organizations sometimes have lower overall staff turnover, but also suffer from lower levels of creativity and energy, and greater difficulty attracting top investment talent.

4. *Competitive:* When candor and openness are present but not fully mastered, we find cultures that are higher-functioning than the first three, with a debate orientation and full engagement among team members. Sludge levels tend to be lower, trust scores tend to be higher, and decision making is usually faster, thus improving the chances for superior performance. However, because the highest levels of candor (speaking in a nonthreatening way, yet still open and revealing) and openness

(listening with the intent to learn, and depersonalizing the discussion) have not yet been reached, the tone of the discussions is more competitive than collaborative. Many investment professionals are highly comfortable in this type of environment, and teams that operate here tend to have below-average staff turnover and a solid ability to attract top talent.

5. *World-class (collaborative):* If you have the good fortune to work in what we define as a world-class culture (or have had the opportunity to visit one), you will find an environment that is distinctly different from the previous four. These elite firms experience very little sludge, enjoy high levels of trust, have speedy decision making, and not surprisingly, often have superior long-term track records. Turnover is very low, and talent attraction is a non-issue. As employers-of-choice, these firms have their pick of the talent pool, and tend to be very selective about finding individuals who not only are skilled in their roles, but also display good cultural fit. Their team members typically have high levels of energy and creativity and, with a win–win mindset, tend to have lower-than-average levels of stress. (In fact, if you walk through the hallways of these firms, you'll often hear a lot of good-natured laughter coming through open doors, in sharp contrast to the fear-based environments where the only laughter is usually sarcastic and done behind closed doors.)

MESSAGING WITH IMPACT

Good messaging means crafting your message in a way that makes it clear and understandable. Remember, you're competing for shelf-space in the mind of your audience, whether that's another teammate, a client, a consultant, or a reporter, so it's important to frame your message so it can be easily heard and understood.

First, consider your audience, and how their "receiver" is set. This is where your skill of social awareness comes into play. Do you understand your audience's feelings, needs, and concerns? Try putting yourself in their shoes as you craft your message—it will help in making the connection stronger.

Next, keep in mind that words have real power. The right words can clarify, motivate, and empower. Poorly chosen words can create confusion or defensiveness. In the sending/receiving analogy, think of the words as the ball that's being tossed. If the ball is easy to see and easy to catch, then the sender has a greater chance of success in having the message "caught." However, if the ball has sharp edges or is hard to see, then the receiver will have a hard time catching it (or even wanting to!).

Ariel's Mellody Hobson know this well. She says, "World-class communicating means keeping the message clear and simple, and staying focused on one key theme. I'm amazed at the jargon-laden investment world. It's far behind the rest of the consumer products industry in terms of good communication." Hobson credits her well-honed communication skills to her eight years as the financial spokesperson on *Good Morning, America.* "I learned to speak in headlines," she explains. "I identify the most important concept, and then I say it in as few words as possible. If you can't keep it simple, you'll lose your audience."

The words you choose will also depend on the type of communication at hand. Three common types of communications in business are *information-based, feedback-based,* and *motivational.*

Information-based

Sharing information quickly and accurately is critical in the investment world, and here, clarity and precision are key. A clear message is one that uses precise words that leave no room for misinterpretation.

Compare:

I'll try to get the quarter-end report out to you as soon as I can.

with

I will send you the quarterly report via overnight mail so that you receive it on April 6.

Which message has greater clarity? Which one gives you greater confidence in the sender of the report?

Precise words don't leave wiggle-room for another outcome. Imprecise words (such as *trying to, maybe,* and *hopefully*), however, are all just indirect ways of not agreeing to an action. Precision inspires confidence, while lack of precision creates doubt.

Information-based communication often revolves around agreements—making them and clarifying them. Remember that all agreements have three parts: *who, what,* and *when.* When you make an agreement, it's important to ensure that the other person understands it, and also agrees to it, and that you record it so you don't forget it. And then, of course, you keep it! And if you see that you won't be able to keep it, you renegotiate it with the other person as soon as possible. While all this sounds straightforward, we find that many investment professionals are actually sloppy around their agreements, which can lead to communication breakdowns, excessive drama, and stress.

Feedback-Based

If you are giving feedback, especially if it's constructive criticism, it's important to select words that are neutral and factual, rather than subjective or judgmental. Compare the following two statements:

> *You are undependable and clearly don't care about your work.*
>
> *I've noticed that you have been a half-hour late every day this month and have missed your deadlines on the last three projects you did. I'm wondering about why that is happening.*

Which one would be more likely to land constructively? On high-performing teams, ongoing feedback is a way of life, and when handled well, can provide a real opportunity to clear up misunderstandings and improve relationships. We use the following clarification model with our clients to help them learn how to give and receive feedback effectively:

1. Start with your *intention*: "I want to clear up some misunderstanding so as to have a better working relationship with you."
2. Assume *100 percent responsibility* for the outcome (with no finger pointing or blaming).
3. State the *facts* (what you saw, heard, etc.).
4. Identify your *feeling*. (Choose one of these three basic ones: mad, sad, afraid.)
5. Make your *request*. (What do you want? You may not get it, but ask for it directly.)

If the feedback receiver is a skilled active listener, he or she will listen carefully and nondefensively to all that is said, with the goal of gaining a better understanding of the situation and the feedback provider's perspective. That is easier said than done! Becoming proficient at this give-and-take process is something that requires a lifetime of practice for most people. We have yet to see anyone do this perfectly all the time. The key is to keep working at it, knowing that sometimes it will come more easily than at other times.

Motivational

Investment leaders at all levels have the opportunity to use their communication skills as a way to motivate and inspire their teams. This is particularly critical when the markets are difficult and stress levels are high. As Mark Anson pointed out in the spring of 2008, "It's been a tough time in the market over the past few months, and no one's having much fun. So I felt it was important to get a message out to the team that despite the market turmoil, we are the right part of the industry, and while other firms are cutting back (or worse), we are continuing to build. That way, we'll be in an even stronger position when the markets turn around." Anson believes that one of his key roles as a leader is to find the silver lining and send an upbeat message to the team, while still addressing the straight facts. He adds, "That's a skill you have to learn and practice, because it's not taught in business school."

CHOOSING THE RIGHT METHOD (*HINT:* IT'S PROBABLY *NOT* E-MAIL)

Now that you have the right foundation, the right mindset, and just the right words for the occasion, you should be in good shape to get that message out, right? Wrong; the next question you need to ask yourself is, "What's the best method?" Is it face-to-face, or via phone, memo, or e-mail, in a meeting, in voice mail, or on a posting in Linkd In, MySpace, or Facebook?

The right method isn't always the most convenient method, on the surface, but using the right method will almost always save you time in the long run. For example, if you want to give one of your teammates some constructive feedback, the best way to do so is privately, and in an unrushed manner. The worst ways to give that kind of feedback would be in a public forum or in a one-way delivery method (via e-mail or voice mail.)

As a rule of thumb, the more sensitive the information, the more the need for an in-person, private meeting. The less sensitive the information, the more appropriate to use group forums or e-mail distributions.

At Ariel Capital Management, Mellody Hobson uses a variety of forums and methods to share information with her teammates, including:

- Weekly Status Reports from each department, distributed to everyone in the firm. ("By avoiding surprises," Hobson says, "We stay on the same page.")
- Staff meetings after every board meeting, to provide a complete debrief to the entire team.
- Open "office hour" every day where Hobson is available to her direct reports, for discussions that are less than 10 minutes long. (Longer discussions are scheduled as separate meetings at another time.)
- Open staff meetings every Friday, where direct reports attend and present, and all team members are welcome.

■ Direct-reports-only meetings for one half-hour per week.

■ Posted agendas for Hobson and CEO John Rogers, accessible by all staff members.

■ Judicious use of e-mail, and the Rule of Three (if an e-mail goes back and forth more than three times, then an in-person discussion takes place).

At William Blair, Michelle Seitz is also sensitive about which communication methods are appropriate for various situations. "E-mail can cause more harm than good," she points out. "It should never be used to communicate sensitive information." In fact, most of the leaders we speak with have the same view about e-mail. It can be extraordinarily useful in its speed and its scope. But for the same reasons, it can be just as harmful. E-mail guidelines can help a team avoid common e-mail pitfalls. For example, Convergent's Jon Hunt saves his nonroutine e-mails as drafts so he can review them again before sending them to ensure that their tone is what he intended. "Measure twice, cut once," he says. He also picks up the phone and calls the other person if he believes there's been a misunderstanding, rather than starting an e-mail volleyball series.

So, given the focus on the trials and tribulations of using e-mail, we're pleased to share here a compilation of the best advice we've heard. (Feel free to copy this and e-mail it to everyone on your team, with our compliments!)

Before You Hit *Send*, You Should CYA

■ *Consider Your Audience:* Who are they? What do they know already, and what do they need to know now? How can they be expected to react, and what questions might they have? Based on that, include as much relevant information in the message as possible.

■ *Check Your Attitude:* Are you in the right frame of mind to send an effective e-mail? If you're upset, annoyed, or even rushed, take a breath and wait. Better to *draft* the e-mail, and then come back to it later to review before you send. And if it's a sensitive situation, don't use e-mail at all. Schedule a meeting!

■ *Clarify Your Assumptions:* Know the difference between fact and story, and let the reader know that your assumptions are simply that. This helps to reduce defensiveness from your readers.

■ *Check Your Attachments:* That's right—after you attach them, click on each one to open it, and read it through. Be sure you have the right version of the document and that the "track changes" function is turned off, with changes accepted (unless you really want your readers to see the path of changes made). We've seen many instances where the wrong attachment was sent, which can be embarrassing in the best case, and disastrous in the worst.

COMMUNICATING WITH THREE KEY AUDIENCES: CLIENTS, CONSULTANTS, AND REPORTERS

We've focused most of our comments in this chapter on general communication skills and specific advice for internal communications. Much of that advice also applies to your external audiences, including clients, consultants, and reporters. After all, as you've seen here, the biggest key to communicating well is establishing and maintaining personal rapport, no matter who the audience may be. But for your key external audiences, we think it's helpful to list some additional thoughts and suggestions.

Clients and Consultants: Six Rules for Successful Communication

There are six key areas that are most important in client and consultant communications, according to Kris Ford, senior consultant with Ennis Knupp + Associates. These include flexibility, recognition of "reportable events," frequency of contact, meetings with key personnel, availability for inquiries, and sharing research.

1. *Flexibility:* Ford says, "Depending on client preference, we find that e-mail, phone, mailings, webcasts, and in-person visits are all important and used to varying degrees at different times." Multiple tools are critical for getting important issues communicated to consultants, as well, in a timely, direct manner, and help to accommodate consultant travel and meeting demands.
2. *Recognition of "reportable events":* "Recognizing the important events that should trigger immediate contact is absolutely critical to both clients and consultant audiences," says Ford. Consultant callers should be aware of shared clients and the kinds of events that clients and consultants want to hear about directly from the investment manager. That means really knowing what is and what is not important to your client. Changes in ownership and key personnel are two issues that should be communicated as soon as possible (hence the need for multiple tools). Performance that falls short of expectations as well as difficult markets are also issues that should be high on the reportable event list. New products are not a "reportable event." "Know your consultant; know your client."

3. *Frequency of contact:* Unless there is a change underway, unusual market conditions, or an event requiring ongoing communication, the need for quarterly contact other than written hardcopy or e-mail is low. Annual in-person meetings are important for staying in touch and keeping up to date with the growth of the firm. But overkill is not attractive. "Think dating," Ford advises.

4. *Meetings with key personnel:* Firms that use their meeting time with consultants to allow interaction with key investment personnel are using meeting time to their best advantage. Generally, consultants will make those meetings known outside of the specific research group assigned to the firm in order to take advantage of and learn more about the investment manager's expertise, which translates into a higher profile with the consulting firm.

5. *Availability for inquiries:* From time to time, consulting firms have the need to quickly update current client data or positions, gather data for search work, or simply get another opinion. Investment firms that have dependable, knowledgeable staff available for these kinds of fire drills have an edge. Unresponsive firms leave the impression—especially during search activity—that the future will not be better and if there is a serious need for information, it will be unavailable. Competitive firms respond quickly.

6. *Research:* Sharing relevant research is helpful to differentiate firms, add to the general discussion about investments, and develop a deeper relationship with a consulting firm. Good research is useful to clients as an educational tool as well.

Reporters: Build Rapport and Respect the Deadlines

There are many benefits to establishing good relationships with reporters, and by following these guidelines, you can increase your effectiveness with this important group. First, however, be aware that not all publications— nor all reporters—are created equal. Some publications have reputations for excellent journalism and professionalism, while others . . . well, don't. (During my years as chief marketing officer at Northern Trust Global Investments, I received many calls from reporters looking for industry gossip, and promising me that anything I shared would be "off the record." Needless to say, we always politely declined those calls, believing it was more important to say whatever we were comfortable saying "on the record.")

Just as it's important to know your client and consultant, it's also important to know your reporter contacts. The best way to get to know them is in person, over breakfast or lunch. Once you've established some rapport with them as individuals, you can manage your relationship just as you would any other key relationship—by staying in touch and being available.

Joel Chernoff, executive editor for *Pensions & Investments*, has been covering the investment management industry since 1982, and has talked to hundreds of investment firms over the past 26 years. He offers this advice: "The best relationships in my view are with senior people willing to have a healthy exchange of information, a true back and forth, where we develop a high level of trust for each other." Developing good relations with a news outlet also means being willing to spend time educating junior reporters, being willing to provide background information, and being accessible.

The *accessibility* point cannot be overemphasized here. It's critical to understand that reporters work under tight deadlines, so a quick response to a call (even if it's "no comment") is very much appreciated. Also, offering accessibility to the right people is important. While professional media relations people play a key role in coordinating meetings, reporters want to talk to the subject-matter experts when working on a story. And reporters have keen noses for smelling a sales pitch versus true information. It's best to be candid and authentic—your message will have a much better chance of being heard. (Does this ring a bell?)

"It's irksome to have firms come to us to pitch their stories, but then refuse to talk to us later when they feel their story is not so glowing," Chernoff says. "It's so much better to have longstanding relationships with people I trust." It's clear that staying in touch through thick and thin goes a long way with reporters.

Relationships Matter

No matter who your audience is, world-class communicating really comes back to good relationship building, which can be done using the skills we covered in the beginning of this chapter: openness, candor, relationship orientation, awareness, and appreciation.[2]

NOTES

1. For more information on the Enneagram, you can refer to Jim Ware's April 2008 column, "What Type of Investor Are You?" on the CFA Institute website (http://www.cfainstitute.org/memresources/communications/warecolumn/april08.html).
2. For more information on developing and refining these skills, see *High Performing Investment Teams* by Jim Ware, Jim Dethmer, Jamie Ziegler, and Fran Skinner (New York: John Wiley & Sons, 2006).

CHAPTER 28

The Data Management Challenge

Don DeLoach
Aleri, Inc.

There always will be challenges to the interdependency and efficiency of information systems. Here are some recommended approaches to designing, utilizing, and monitoring the "lifeblood" of the firm.

When I think of investment managers in the context of history, an image of "Charles," a conservative gentleman in a wool suit with a leather satchel containing a ledger of data, comes to mind. The register contains what was bought and sold and how the assets were allocated to those who had entrusted their investments to this gentleman.

OLD-SYSTEMS THINKING ISN'T GOOD ENOUGH ANYMORE

The image of Charles is now counterfactual. The capital markets are moving at a frenetic pace. They are now defined by worldwide expansion, the growth and combination of traded asset classes, and an increasing reliance on electronic trading. These changes require an increased number of quotes and trades executed in smaller values, but in higher volumes. A decade ago, this pace was unimaginable. To Charles's detriment, the data to run his business has become far too vast to keep in a mere ledger.

What Has Changed?

Today's markets are drastically different from what they were in Charles's day. With the emergence of electronic trading, fragmentation in market venues, proliferation of cross-asset trading, and corresponding trends such as penny pricing for options, exploding volumes of quotes and trading converge to a different world of high-velocity trading activity.

For an investment management firm to operate effectively in today's speed-of-light market, each team member must understand the key elements of the firm's operating policy:

- What are we trading?
- How do we trade as efficiently as possible?
- How do we service our investors efficiently and effectively?
- How do we balance multiple informational needs when data may be scattered across multiple systems, trading silos, times zones, currencies, and structures?

In keeping with this book's intention, this chapter is not intended to be a prescription of what should be done to meet constantly changing data-management challenges. Rather, it will help identify what those challenges are, and how to anticipate them within today's turbulent and ever-changing markets.

Changes in the markets have created a massive increase in the demands on underlying systems. It's as if the transportation infrastructure designed for Chicago's eight million people were forced to accommodate, almost overnight, the 26 million people in Mexico City. The trains that now run on time, the highways that flow reasonably well, and the subways that normally sustain the load would all be crippled, rendering the city incapable of functioning. This is analogous to the load that is being placed on trading operations today.

Where and How Does This Problem Surface?

The quick answer is *everywhere*. As too much data flows too fast for the underlying systems to handle, problems emerge everywhere, and in a variety of ways and locations, including the front office, middle office, and back office. We see client services issues, performance problems stemming from trading, problems with trade execution, and increased firm risk as evidenced by firms blowing up in extremely high-profile ways. These quickly translate into problems with operational and technological complexity and escalating costs. While some of these problems affect many types of firms, some are more problematic in high-velocity operations, while others affect large asset managers and mutual fund complexes.

Issues of data consistency, accuracy, and timeliness are all critical. For example, a manager engaged in multi-asset-class trading might be able to record a new instrument into the OMS, but what happens when the OMS communicates with the portfolio accounting system? How hard or time consuming will it be to reflect such a change? How are the instruments valued, and will those valuations be consistent across systems? When data is transmitted to the middle and back offices, how is the data analyzed and what do the downstream systems need to understand?

As the pace of the market increases, the volume and complexity expand. If the middle and back offices fall behind on end-of-day processing, every function in the firm will be impacted. Many hedging tactics are exceptionally complex, and most systems are not designed to accommodate what's needed. Manual intervention is needed to reconcile the data, which throws off all the systems, calculations, and fundamentally, the effectiveness and efficiency of the firm's operations.

The Need to Manage Risk

Risk and reporting are areas confronted with data-management challenges. In order to accurately analyze risk, a firm must operate with clean, accurate, and timely information, yet still be able to report this information in a flexible manner.

How much of the firm's ability to manage risk comes down to data-management challenges? As the rate of the market innovation increases, product innovation may be outstripping many firms' ability to manage risk. Credit derivatives in particular are prone to significant reference data problems, while the burden to "get it right" becomes increasingly heavier. Exposure to abrupt changes in pricing and the evaporation of liquidity creates a critical need to manage risk in an automated fashion. Yet today, a great deal of analysis, valuation, and projection are still done in the middle or back office on standalone spreadsheets. That is not adequate either for regulatory requirements or for risk management in a firm with high volumes or any level of complexity. A senior manager concerned about the firm's risk exposure will be blinded by insufficient, stale information.

Regulatory and Compliance Requirements

Regulatory and compliance requirements make record and data systems critical to survival. We have recently seen new regulations in the markets—Reg NMS in North America and MiFID in Europe—that significantly impact the buy side and the sell side alike.

Reg NMS and MiFID accelerate the migration to electronic trading. The data issues revolve around the need to facilitate clean trade execution and to store and recall the appropriate information. Storage considerations for SEC and FSA compliance are forcing firms to reengineer information processing and storage. From a buy-side perspective, this means the ability to effectively monitor trade execution and understand when and where there may be vulnerabilities in the process.

HOW DID ALL THIS HAPPEN?

In a nutshell, computing made this happen. Looking back at the role of computing in almost any industry, it first impacted back-office record-keeping systems, and over time moved more and more to the front office, where the event, service, or key business was conducted. Moreover, only technically sophisticated "programmers" could operate these early computers; over time computing has become more and more accessible to the point that the Internet is now second nature for kids.

Technology has invaded almost every dimension of every conceivable business, and nowhere is this more obvious that in capital markets. The trading pits of the Chicago Board of Trade and the floor of the NYSE have seen the order flow change to where the vast majority of trades are executed by computer. As a result, markets are more accessible by more people in more locations and across more asset classes. Again, the vast majority of trading is now done electronically. With that evolution has come increased volume, velocity, and complexity in the markets, leading to a massive increase in demands on the underlying infrastructure to support the increased workload. These systems must be accurate and consistent, and facilitate timely access to the information.

A Closer Look at the Data and Related Imperatives

While everyone would agree that consistent and accurate data is a requirement, they might not agree on what that means, how it looks, and how to go about meeting the required functionality. From a buy-side perspective, a firm needs to spot "fails" as they occur and cancel and correct as quickly as possible. When trading a multi-asset strategy, however, a firm has to deal with expanding classifications, higher volumes, global venues, and new and evolving instruments. Keeping up with these requirements is essential to the ability to monitor operations, process trades, manage risk, and report accurately.

In the past, the need for "enterprise data" may have taken the form of a traditional *data warehouse*. However, these have proven too limiting in terms of accessibility, timeliness of the data, and integration with the constituent applications.

The goal of consistency facilitated by a *golden copy* security master file used to be a luxury limited to high-end operations that could afford the additional capability. Now, data consistency and the integration across business silos is an absolute necessity for every operation. Along with this are the associated issues of controlling multiple versions of the security master file, employing standards for describing assets, and applying controls over how data is inputted, updated, utilized, and distributed. Reference data management has grown into *enterprise data management (EDM)*, which facilitates data accuracy and consistency across the firm's domain.

WHERE ARE THINGS HEADED?

Symphonic Technology

We have become a world of codependent *specialists*. For example, determining the right mix of futures investments might require the services of a metals specialist who understands the minutia of the metals markets. That specialist might flush out considerations lost to others and positively impact performance.

Now more than ever, however, there is a need to coordinate a rich, well-understood macroscopic view of the things that define an investment strategy. To call that coordinator a *generalist*, however, would be a misnomer. It's more like being an orchestra conductor. The conductor might be able to play any one or all of the parts, but would seldom be able to play any single part *better* than one of the musicians. However, this masterful manager has the "big picture" understanding that can get all the parts to play better *together*—resulting in the symphony.

A buy-side firm is a symphony—or rather, the buy-side technology must come together to form a symphonic synthesis. The end result will seldom be optimal if all the parts cannot play well together. This is the data management challenge. The issues of a misaligned technology and data strategy have far-reaching implications. Firms must confront questions such as: "How does the timeliness of information constrain data management choices, and where do those issues arise?," or "To what degree is scalability of the infrastructure an issue? Will the firm need to deal with infrastructure scalability issues in the coming years?"

It seems that buy-side firms are constantly playing catchup to the innovation in financial markets, which creates competitive disadvantages as well as operational risk. As new instruments are created, the underlying technology may not be updated to be able to process those instruments. Even where a basic system is designed to deal with an esoteric instrument, the linkages of the corresponding systems may still fail. The ever-increasing pace of the markets means that all this happens at higher frequency, placing ever-increasing demands on the infrastructure. Getting the pieces to play together at the right speed and scale on an enterprise level is a huge challenge.

The Blueprint: The Value of Establishing a Technology Architecture

The *technology architecture* is the fundamental blueprint for the deployed technology within the firm. Just as the architectural blueprint for a house defines the flow between the rooms, the materials, the plumbing, the wiring, and so on, the technology architecture defines the building blocks for receiving and storing data, processing the data in different applications, coordinating how those applications will work together, and resolving how the resulting data is communicated, reported, and distributed.

A modern architecture for managing data for a buy-side firm will have two critical pieces: A *golden model* that establishes a baseline for the data structure itself, and an *event-driven architecture (EDA)* that provides the template for how the various pieces of technology inside the firm interact.

The golden model is really an extension of the *golden-copy* approach to maintaining a *security master file*. These are usually supplied by a reference data vendor like Asset-Control, Golden Source, AIM, Eagle, and others. There are other EDM firms also supplying solutions, such as CAPCO, Reuters, and more. At the heart of this is the need to establish a blueprint of what data (mainly but not exclusively security data) will reside in the firm and how that data is related. This will allow the various systems in the firm to deal with consistent data, vastly improving the accuracy of the information. For example, this will provide a mechanism for reconciling symbology, for understanding corporate actions, and for myriad other facilities to keep information aligned and accessible.

An event-driven architecture is that technology blueprint that allows for producing, detecting, consuming, and reacting to events. It is basically an extension of a *service-oriented-architecture (SOA)*, which groups business processes as interoperable services. One of the main benefits of SOA is the ability for applications to exchange data with one another. A service-oriented architecture is loosely coupled, where the understanding and interaction between silos are minimal. An EDA, however, goes further. Its architecture is *decoupled*, where an application silo will deliver information without regard to where it is being consumed, and it may also consume information without the knowledge of the data producer. This approach mainly takes advantage of a *publish–subscribe* model, where an application will publish data out or subscribe to data that is consumed by the application. While there are many technologies that have been used in association with an SOA, or more recently, an EDA, one very compelling technology ideally suited for an EDA is *complex event processing (CEP)*. This is a new modality in computing, much like relational databases in the early 1990s. CEP is designed to absorb extremely large amounts of fast-moving data and then normalize, possibly aggregate, and analyze the information.

CEP with a golden-model approach to managing data for the buy side is a powerful combination indeed. The model can provide the definition of what the data should look like, and the event-driven architecture, made possible using CEP, can the take data from external sources such as market feeds, as well as internal sources like trading systems, accounting systems, and so forth, and transform that data by *mapping* it into the golden-model version, where it can then be analyzed or propagated to other systems as needed.

HOW TO PROCEED

At the beginning of this chapter I suggested that I would mainly pose questions, not supply answers. I am convinced that many of the data management problems faced by buy-side organizations result from not asking the right questions of the right people, soon enough. In fact, the answers themselves may be less important than the questions, and those answers will surely vary from firm to firm. Yet, there are a few key considerations worth noting as we close out this discussion:

1. Pursue a service-oriented, event-driven architecture (SOA/EDA).
2. Pursue an enterprise data management strategy (EDM) and work with a vendor that specializes in this.
3. Seek outside ideas.
4. Make organizational considerations a critical part of this, not a mere afterthought.

> *Employ SOA/EDA.* We have discussed the role of architecture. The right architecture provides flexibility, connectivity, and a framework through which the firm can operate effectively. If done correctly, this will allow the firm to lower costs and maximize the effective use of information, increasing its competitive advantage. Complex event processor technology (CEP) is surely an enabling technology for such architecture, and should absolutely be a key technology employed in the firm. I expect this will be true for all larger or more sophisticated firms in the not-too-distant future.

Pursue an EDM strategy. If you don't already have one, consider putting a firm-wide EDM initiative in place. This does not require you to touch every point in the firm at the same time: It would be better to start small and iterate. This may seem counterintuitive, but it isn't. I suggest you start with a small-scale, Phase I, EDM project of limited reach, and expand with the benefit of experience gained by each iteration. An SOA/EDA approach is perfectly suited for such an implementation style.

Vendors can be your friends, so seek outside ideas. Vendors have a great deal of exposure to common problems and solutions. Whether they are technology suppliers, application suppliers, consultants, or other related services companies, all are likely to have ideas worthy of your consideration. While the views of any one of them may not be dominant, the combination of ideas from the larger community is likely to be helpful. To that end, getting the financial industry analysts involved can provide great benefit. These would be firms like Financial Insights, The Tower Group, The Aite Group, The Tabb Group, Celent, and more. These firms study the market and the players, and will often have a good grip on considerations worthy of attention when dealing with the data challenges.

Address the people issues. Organizational structure is really an issue of governance. Who owns the data? Who can use the data? Various parts of the firm need to operate with commonality to embed utility value into the data. Then you need to achieve buy-in across departments, each of which will have its own agenda, internal needs, budget, and personalities. As a result, many technology issues evolve bottom-up, from the needs apparent at a workstation level. This is even true with any set of reference data and CEP. And again, while the argument can be made that these are enterprise capabilities, they still tend to start locally.

Training is seldom given the proper level of consideration. One of the universal truths is that most people on the buy side, along with much of the sell side, are certain that they are the smartest human beings in the world. They may very well be. However, as training increases, "problems with the system" almost always diminish. The data challenges contribute a great deal to these comprehension problems.

Getting everyone on the same page, with the same set of goals, ideals, and underlying belief systems, unfortunately never happens. It's easy to see why an industry would have to reconcile divergent needs and goals, but the same problems arise within an individual firm. Conflicts often appear to lie in technological challenges, even though the technology to resolve these problems actually exists. Most often, the real issues are about people's conflicting needs and not about technology.

The best architecture for the enterprise will never work if people don't work together. Senior leadership in the firm must embrace the approach and ensure that disconnects among the departments are avoided or at least kept to a minimum. This also means investing in the people, the processes, and especially the training to capitalize on the effort. To that end, I would underscore the value of soliciting input from those with broad exposure, including the vendors. The best-run financial services operations all view vendors as true partners in their efforts.

HOW DO YOU CONTROL THESE PROJECTS?

In a word, *carefully*; enterprise software projects are often problematic. Too many people get involved, too much feature-function is prescribed, and in the end, the projects often run overbudget and behind schedule, only to underdeliver in the end. Projects like this need ownership, agreed-on timelines and objectives, and careful and ongoing scrutiny by a limited number of people. The only magic formula is to keep it as simple as possible, ensure accountability, endow those responsible with the appropriate resources, and plan to be flexible, to learn, and to adjust along the way.

How Do You Keep It from Interfering with Day-to-Day Needs?

This is the beauty of an event-driven architecture and a well-run project. A well-run project will have someone who lays out the various considerations associated with the project and accommodates them. This requires understanding exactly the day-to-day business needs, and where it is appropriate to apply a top-down approach where reconfigured processes can be more efficient and less error prone. Finding that path with minimal static is the job of the project manager. This is where the elegance of an event-driven architecture comes into play.

Most traditional technologies are invasive. To implement enterprise software would require a fair amount of tinkering with the underlying participating systems. As a result, day-to-day operations are impacted. For an event-driven architecture, the EDM capabilities can be introduced alongside the existing systems without interference. When they are ready, they can be "plugged in and turned on." While the promise of this technology was elusive just a few years back, it is very real and proven today, especially in the context of complex event processing (CEP) solutions and enabling technology.

Securing Buy-In

Because these projects can span across so many people, systems, and areas of a firm, it is critical to get buy-in across the board. But how can that be done?

All involved personnel have to believe the project serves their best interests, as well as the interests of the firm. By definition, a holistic initiative like an EDM strategy must be endorsed from the top down. The best interests of all in the firm must be addressed in the context of the project. Understanding the impact on specific areas of the firm and communicating those expected results is a critical step. This is also a good portion of the upfront definition and design work. The executive team, largely facilitated by those who will be the project owners, must first assess and then communicate the potential gains in terms of reduced problems and added capabilities. Specifically, this should yield an increase in STP (straight-through processing) rates, increasing the quality of trades and lowering cost of execution. Risk strategies should be better informed, understood, and executed. Overall operational costs should go down, and client-servicing capabilities should be significantly enhanced. To the extent the executive team can quantify some of these objectives in terms of both time and value, all the better.

END GAME: A BRAVE NEW WORLD WITH WELL-MANAGED DATA

Chip, Charles's grandson, comes into work every day. Like most of those around him, he is more narrowly focused than his grandfather. Chip is a quant trader. He trades across multiple asset classes, and multiple geographies, and relies heavily on computing. In the seven seconds that Chip's grandfather, Charles, took to convey an order to buy a cash equity and write it down in his book, Chip and his trusty computers are in and out of 200 positions. The information that results from Chip's efforts ripples through the firm's systems from the accounting systems to the risk systems to the client-services systems. Chip and his firm are keeping pace with the market today and remaining competitive in the face of more and smarter competition.

Moreover, they are able to service the needs of their investors well with the flexibility gained by their technology. The flexibility, speed, and consistency achieved through the event-driven architecture approach to EDM has allowed them to prosper. The firm does well. Their clients are happy. The government stays off their back because the reporting is done on time and correctly. They are able to achieve great performance and then do stellar performance benchmarking. And through all of this, they are able to scale the operation with their costs in check.

One of their biggest clients, Charles, is pleased. He gets performance updates on his iPhone.

But Life Marches On

Getting it right is more of a process than an outcome. You have to *keep* getting it right. The need to iterate and to continue to improve will be constantly present. Technology will certainly continue to evolve. Today, an event-driven architecture provides a great path, but who knows what that path will look like in 2015? The path today is drastically different from what it was in 1995.

We live and work in a fast-moving world that is only speeding up and getting more complex. The local reach of yesterday is dwarfed by the global reach of today. We see advances in the trading ecosystem that include hardware-assisted network processing and co-located services—because the speed of light has become a limitation. Today, electronic trading is being extended to BlackBerries integrated with order-management systems. Client servicing includes customized Web-based reporting delivered intraday instead of end-of-month.

Even so, there is no end to the increase in the pace, the volume, and the complexity of the capital markets. Managing the data against this backdrop has become a challenge that must be dealt with in a manner that addresses the questions we have explored. It is impossible to understate the importance of managing the data challenge in the years to come.

ACKNOWLEDGMENTS

This work draws from a multitude of meetings and interactions with various funds, banks, and other participants in the ecosystem involving the buy side. In addition, and certainly noteworthy, this chapter has been largely influenced by papers dealing with reference data and enterprise data management by Financial Insights (an IDC Company), The Tower Group, and The Aite Group, along with personal interaction with analysts from each of these firms, whose insight was invaluable.

About the Editors

Wayne H. Wagner is the principal of OM◆NI, an investment management consultancy. He is co-founder and former chairman of Plexus Group, Inc. and was co-founder of Wilshire Associates. Mr. Wagner serves on the board of directors of the Institute for Quantitative Research in Finance and on the editorial board of the *Journal of Trading* and the *Financial Analysts Journal*. He has taught MBA courses at UCLA and the University of Southern California.

Ralph A. Rieves is editor-in-chief and managing director of Farragut, Jones & Lawrence, Inc. *FJL* develops reference sources for institutional investing professionals and fiduciaries. Mr. Rieves was executive editor for capital markets books for Dow Jones–Irwin and Irwin Professional Publications, and founding managing editor of *The Journal of Investment Consulting*. He is a recipient of the book industry's Bowker LMP Award for Excellence in Book Publishing.

About the Contributors

Keith Ambachtsheer, CFA is director of the Rotman International Centre for Pension Management at the University of Toronto, and is an adjunct professor of finance at the Rotman School of Management. He is the founder and president of KPA Advisory Services in Toronto, which provides strategic advice on governance, finance, and investment matters to governments, industry associations, pension plan sponsors, foundations, and other institutional investors around the world. He is also co-founder of CEM Benchmarking Inc., which monitors the organizational performance of pension plans around the world. He is the author of three books about pension funds, and is a frequent contributor to the *Financial Analysts Journal,* for which four of his articles were awarded the Graham and Dodd Award for excellence in investment writing.

Simon Bennett is a partner at CAPCO, focusing on delivering transformational change to capital markets clients. With over 20 years' experience primarily at UBS Investment Bank and J. P. Morgan (Fleming) Investment Management, Simon has successfully delivered a variety of large-scale change programs on a global basis. He earned an MBA from Henley and is ACIB qualified.

Peter L. Bernstein is president of Peter L. Bernstein, Inc., an advisor to institutional investors worldwide. He is *the* acknowledged leader in sustaining the academic and practical integrity of investment management. He was founder of the *Journal of Portfolio Management* and is the author of several books on economics and finance, the most recent of which is the best-selling *Capital Ideas Evolving* (Hoboken: Wiley, 2007).

Richard Bookstaber, PhD is an acknowledged authority on global risk management and quantitative research. He was director of risk management at Ziff Brothers Investments and at Moore Capital Management. He has also held senior management positions at Salomon Brothers and Morgan Stanley. He writes frequently about investment risks. His most recent book is the widely praised *A Demon of Our Own Design* (Hoboken: Wiley, 2007). He earned a PhD in economics from the Massachusetts Institute of Technology.

Jacqueline L. Charnley is co-founder of Charnley & Rostvold, Inc. in San Juan Capistrano, CA, a 31-year-old firm focused on helping investment management and pension consulting firms retain clients, grow assets, and build successful, well-diversified businesses. She speaks and writes frequently about the challenges confronting the industry. She is a member of the Association of Investment Management Sales Executives (AIMSE) and a founding board member of the Professional Association of Investment Communications Resources (PAICR). She earned a BA from the University of California at Irvine.

Kathleen T. DeRose, CFA is a senior managing partner at Hagin Investment Management, where she supervises all portfolio management and research. Starting her career as an analyst at Chase, she has successfully managed multi-billion-dollar equity portfolios while overseeing equity departments at Scudder Stevens & Clark and at Bessemer Trust. She was the subject of a *Barron's* cover story and has been quoted in many publications and on television. She earned a BA from Princeton University.

Jim Dethmer, a principal with Focus Consulting Group, is a world-class coach, speaker, and team builder. He has lectured before more than 250,000 people worldwide. He has worked with teams and executives from leading investment organizations, strengthening their effectiveness through customized coaching and consulting interventions. He has been featured on webcasts for the CFA Institute, addressing topics of world-class decision making and the essential behavior of high-performing investment teams.

Donald DeLoach is president and chief executive officer of *Aleri*, a global leader in supporting mission-critical applications for financial institutions. Before joining *Aleri,* he was president and CEO of YOUcentric, a leading provider of customer relationship management software. He has also had management positions with Sybase, Prime Computer, Bull Information Systems, and Hitachi Data Systems. He earned a BS degree in industrial and systems engineering from Georgia Tech.

Fi360 promotes a culture of fiduciary responsibility through training and resources based on the Defined Practices for Investment Fiduciaries. Fi360's education and training programs promote a culture of fiduciary responsibility. It awards the professional designations: Accredited Investment Fiduciary (AIF) and Accredited Investment Fiduciary Analyst (AIFA). Fi360 also develops sophisticated Web-based toolkits, as well as the innovative Fiduciary Score and the Fund Family Fiduciary Rankings.

Ron Gold is president of Gold Consulting, Inc., a firm he launched in 2006 that helps investment managers improve the effectiveness of their communications in three key areas: sales, client servicing, and consultant relations. Previously, he was a senior consultant with Callan Associates, a founding partner of Ennis, Krupp & Gold, a pension consultant with A. G.

Becker, and a trust officer with American National Bank & Trust in Chicago. He earned a BS in mathematics from the University of Illinois and an MBA from the University of Chicago.

Amity Goyal, PhD is an associate professor of finance at the Gozueta Business School at Emory University. His research interests include pension funds, predictability of stock returns, behavior of volatility, and portfolio optimization. He earned his PhD from the UCLA Anderson School. He holds an MBA from the Indian Institute of Management, Ahmedabad, and a B.Tech in computer science from the Indian Institute of Technology New Delhi.

Francis Gupta, PhD is director of research and product design at Dow Jones Indexes. His team is actively involved in the research of index ideas, the design of index methodologies, and the testing of index concepts leading to the creation of new indexes for benchmarking purposes and as the basis of investment products. Prior to joining Dow Jones Indexes, Mr. Gupta worked for J. P. Morgan Asset Management and Credit Suisse Asset Management, where he performed research in the areas of asset allocation and implementation, benchmarking, manager selection, and market risk monitoring and management. Mr. Gupta earned his doctorate in economics from New York University.

Robert L. Hagin is CEO of Hagin Investment Management in New York, which provides quantitative asset management to institutional clients and qualified individual investors. He is a 35-year veteran of the industry, and pioneered the use of computers in investments and finance. He is the author of five books about portfolio management, the most recent of which was *Investment Management: Portfolio Diversification, Risk and Timing* (Hoboken: Wiley). He has led investment and research teams at Kidder Peabody, Miller Anderson, and Sherrerd, and was an executive director at Morgan Stanley Investment Management. He has been an editorial advisor to the CFA Institute and to IMCA. He is a founding member of Q-Group, past president of the New York Society of Quantitative Analysts, and a former professor at the Wharton School. He earned his PhD from UCLA.

Robert A. Jaeger, PhD is senior marketing strategist for BNY Mellon Asset Management, advising institutional clients on investment policy and asset allocation. Previously, he was vice chairman and chief investment officer of ECAM Advisors, LLC, a BNY Mellon Asset Management subsidiary that acts as a manager of managers for institutional clients in the United States and around the world. He is the author of *All About Hedge Funds* (McGraw-Hill, 2002). He has been a member of the faculties of Yale University and the University of Massachusetts at Amherst. He earned a BA from Princeton and graduate degrees from Oxford and Cornell.

Harry Liem, CFA is a principal with Mercer in Sydney and has 15 years of investment management experience as a portfolio manager and as a strategist for companies in Europe, Asia, and Australia. He is a frequent speaker and writer about the global challenges the industry faces. He is the author of *2020 Vision: Investment Wisdom for Tomorrow* (Mercer, 2007). He earned a B.Sc and an M.Sc in Computing Science from Delft University of Technology, as well as an MBA from Stirling University.

John Minahan, CFA, PhD is a senior investment strategist in the Asset Allocation Group at NEPC, an investment consulting firm. He serves as president of the Boston Security Analysts Society. He is the author of several insightful and provocative articles about investment management and manager selection. He earned a BS from Boston College and a PhD from the Sloan School of Massachusetts Institute of Technology.

Monika Müller is founder and managing director of FCM Finanz Coaching in Wiesbaden, Germany. She specializes in investment firm organizational development, the coaching of high-performance investment teams, and mental coaching for traders and portfolio managers. She holds an MCC (Master Certified Coach; ICF) and a master's degree in psychology.

John Prestbo is editor and executive director of Dow Jones Indexes. He has responsibility for marketing, public relations, benchmark indexes, and developing new index concepts. He also is chairman of the Dow Jones Index Oversight Committee. For 30 years prior to the establishment of Dow Jones Indexes as a business unit within Dow Jones & Company, he was a reporter and editor for the *Wall Street Journal*. Mr. Prestbo has co-authored or edited several books over the past 30 years. The most recent was *The Market's Measure: An Illustrated History of America Told Through the Dow Jones Industrial Average*, published by Dow Jones Indexes in 1999. He earned his bachelor's and master's degrees from Northwestern University in Evanston, IL.

Christine M. Røstvold is the other co-founder of Charnley and Røstvold, Inc. Prior to founding that firm, she was with Collins Associates, a consulting firm specializing in investment management searches and in research on alternative investment services. She is a member of AIMSE and of PAICR. She currently serves on PAICR's advisory board. She speaks and writes frequently about the challenges confronting the industry, and has conducted classes at the University of California, Irvine and at Santa Ana Community College. She earned a BA from the University of California at Irvine.

Ted Siedle, JD is the founder of Benchmark Financial Services and publisher of *Benchmarkalert.com*. Benchmark specializes in investigations of pension fraud, money management abuses, and wrongdoing involving securities brokerages and pension investment companies. He has been called "the nation's most vocal critic of abuses in the money management industry." He began his career with the SEC's Divisions of Investment Management. He earned his JD from Boston College Law School.

Ronald Surz is president of PPCA, Inc. in San Clemente, CA. PPCA provides investment management due-diligence software. He is a principal of Target Date Analytics (TDA) LLC, which provides management, benchmarks, and research on target date lifecycle funds. He is also a principal of Risk Controlled Growth LLP (RCG), a fund of hedge fund managers. He earned an MS in mathematics from the University of Illinois and an MBA from the University of Chicago.

David Tittsworth, JD is executive director and executive vice president of the Investment Adviser Association. He manages all of the Association's activities, including its involvement in a wide variety of advocacy, regulatory, educational, and business issues that affect the investment advisory profession. He has held a number of federal government positions, including serving as Counsel of the House Committee on Energy and Commerce. He earned a BA and a JD from the University of Kansas.

Sunil Wahal, PhD is Jack D. Furst Professor of Finance at Arizona State University in the W. P. Carey School of Business. He held previous faculty positions at Emory University and at Purdue University. His areas of interest are market microstructure, portfolio management, and trading strategies. He is a recipient of the Q Group Research Award. He earned a PhD from the University of North Carolina at Chapel Hill.

James W. Ware, CFA is the managing partner of Focus Consulting Group. Focus Consulting Group helps financial leaders understand and leverage their firm's culture for competitive advantage. He is the author of several books on leadership, the most recent of which is *Key Behaviors of High Performing Investment Teams* (Hoboken: Wiley). He is on the advisory staffs of *Institutional Investor* and the CFA Board of Regents. He has taught at Northwestern University's Keller Graduate School of Management. He writes a quarterly column for the CFA website: "Firm Success: Leading the Investment Firm." He earned an MBA from the University of Chicago.

Steve Webb is a partner at CAPCO and leads the capital markets practice. He has worked with many banks, including Security Pacific Bank in California and in Europe. His experience has provided him with an extensive knowledge of banking operations with BPM, architecture, and planning. He earned a B.Sc in physics from the University of South Hampton.

Arnold S. Wood, CFA is president and chief executive officer of Martingale Asset Management. Prior to founding Martingale, he was senior vice president of Batterymarch Financial Management. He is a trustee of the Research Foundation of the CFA Institute. He is the recipient of numerous awards, including the Daniel J. Forrestal Leadership Award for Professional

Ethics and Standards of Practice. He is a faculty advisor at Harvard University's John F. Kennedy School of Government. He is a graduate of Trinity College and attended Amos Tuck School at Dartmouth.

Steve Wunsch consults on market structure issues at Wunsch Auction Associates, LLC. His commentaries on volatility have been relevant and prescient for over two decades. He is widely acknowledged as an innovator of both dark pools and transparent auctions. He is the principal inventor of the Arizona Stock Exchange and the ISE Stock Exchange.

Jamie Ziegler, CFA is a principal with Focus Consulting Group. She speaks, writes, and consults on teamwork, leadership, and culture for investment management firms around the world. Previously she served as senior vice president of marketing for Northern Trust Global Investments, and also has been marketing director for Stein Roe and Farnham. She earned a BA from the University of Notre Dame and an MBA from DePaul University.

Index

A. G. Becker, 223
Abbot, Edwin, 126
Accounting, 87–88, 205–206, 335–336
Active listening, 403
Active management, 111, 114–115,
    141–142, 171, 173
Activism, 8, 203–210
Adaptive leadership, 369–378
Adaptive market hypothesis, 132–133,
    160
Administration, 17–18
Aesop, 58
*Against the Gods: The Remarkable
    Story of Risk* (Bernstein), 81
Agency costs, 46, 48
Agency issues, 55
Aggressive culture, 406
AIG (American Insurance Group), 1
Aite Group, The, 282, 290, 426
Algorithmic trading, 282, 292–293,
    295–296, 320–321
Allen, Franklin, 227
Alpha:
    beta separation from, 10–11, 126
    decline of, 299n1, 306
    introduction of, 121
    portable, 113–114
    skill reflected in, 172–173
Alternative trading systems/alternative
    investments, 163, 326
Amaranth Advisors, 155
Ambachtsheer, Keith P., 340
Ambiguity aversion, 90–91
Amboian, John, 405
American Bankers Association, 65–66
American Insurance Group (AIG), 1
Anson, Mark, 405, 410–411
Antitrust investigations, 294

Apodaca-Johnston Capital
    Management, 234–235
Appreciation, 375, 404–405
Aquinas, Thomas, 365
Arbitrage, 284–285
Arbitrage Pricing Theory, 140
Argyris, Chris, 371
Asian Development Bank, 318,
    319
Asset allocation:
    globalization impacting, 12–13,
        316–320
    investor skill impacting, 9–12
    for plan sponsors, 237, 243–246
    restructuring of, 3–9
    to styles, 146–147
Asset management, 283–284
Asymmetry factor, 49, 56, 84
Attribution. *See* Performance/
    performance attribution
Audit committees, 204

Backfill biases, 148
Baks, Klaas, 386
Balarkas, Richard, 310
Barberis, Nicholas, 247
Barclays Global Investors, 234
Bear Stearns, 1, 298
Behavior:
    behavioral finance research on, 155,
        157, 159–161, 167, 348–349n3,
        357–358
    belief systems impacting,
        333–348
    causes of irrational, 100–107
    efficient market hypothesis impacted
        by, 131–133
    ethics impacting, 352–367

Behavior: (*Continued*)
patterns of, in decision making,
81–93, 103, 131–133, 177–178
unpredictability of, 176–178
Belbin, Meredith, 393
Beliefs/belief systems:
evaluating, 342–346
illustrations of, 335–339
managing, 339–342
role of, 333–335, 346–348
Benchmarks, 112–116, 140–144, 146,
150–152, 198–199, 345
Benson, Herbert, 366
Berman, Gregg, 38
Bernoulli, Nicholas, 85–86, 92
Bernstein, Peter, 81, 115–116, 129–130
Beta, 10–11, 121, 126, 140
Biases:
backfill, 148
classification, 147–148
composition, 148
ethical/unethical behavior reflecting,
359
hindsight, 135–136
personal, 133
survivorship, 148, 238
Black, Fischer, 122, 133
Black swans, Taleb's, 31–33, 41, 45,
135–136
Blake, Christopher, 240
Blanchard, Ken, 376
Blindness, willful, 37–38
Bloom, Allan, 29
Board of directors. *See* Trustees
Bohr, Niels, 154
Bollen, Brian, 230
Bonds, 114, 290
Boneparth, John, 213
Boness, James, 157
Bonuses, 205
Book-smart *vs.* street-smart, 157–158
Bookstaber, Richard, *A Demon of Our
Own Design,* 108, 298
Bounded rationality, 34–35, 102–103,
133

Boycotts, 208
Brainerd, Irving, 120
Brewster, Kingman, 162
Brickley, James, 241
Broker-dealers:
marketing to, 216
overlapping roles of, 310–311
regulation of, 59–60, 72–75
sell-side challenges of, 294–299
trading by (*see* Trading)
Brown, Keith, 263
Brown, Stephen J., 154–168
Bubbles, 174–175
Buffett, Warren, 173, 360, 370, 375,
403
Bull market, 112–113
Business leadership, 14
Busse, Jeffrey, 228, 230, 254, 263

*CA Inc. v. AFSCME Employees Pension
Plan,* 211
Callan Associates, 223
Candor, 375–376, 403–404, 405–408
Capital:
investment of, 297–299
liquidity of, 110, 301–302, 308–310
structure, 206–207
Capital Asset Pricing Model (CAPM),
140
Carhart, Mark, 240
Casey, Quirk & Associates, 13
Center for Creative Leadership, 402
Centerpoint Research, 366
Centre for Fiduciary Excellence
(CEFEX), 188
CFA Institute, 238, 358, 359
Chernoff, Joel, 415
Chesterton, G. K., 159, 177
Chevalier, Judith, 263
Chicago Board of Trade, 419
Christopherson, Jon A., 228, 230, 254
Classification biases, 147–148
Clearing and settlement functions. *See*
Settlement functions
Clearstream, 318, 325, 326

Client service/satisfaction, 14–15, 222–223, 413–414
Cliffwater, 224
CLS (Continuous Linked Settlement) system, 318
Codes of conduct, 323–324, 326, 355, 359. *See also* Ethics
Coffee, John, 74
Coggin, T. Daniel, 228
Collaborative culture, 407–408
Collective action, 46, 49, 51, 56
Collins, Jim, 374
Color, market, 308–310
Communication:
  with clients and consultants, 413–414
  during crisis management, 394
  cultures, 398–399, 406–408
  of distinguishing characteristics, 220–223
  effective, 384, 398–415
  feedback-based, 410
  information-based, 409
  integrity of, 365
  of investment philosophy, 218
  by leadership, 398–401
  marketing and, 13, 16–17, 214–215, 218, 220–223
  messaging through, 408–411
  methods of, 411–413
  motivational, 410–411
  relationship building through, 214–215
  with reporters, 414–415
  skills for clear, 401–405
  technology improving, 18–19
Compensation:
  consultant, 224
  executive, 205–206
  performanced-based, 47, 49, 139, 149–152
Competition, 7, 326–327
Competitive culture, 407
Compliance, 15, 203, 418–419
Composition biases, 148

Computers, 120–123, 282, 285–286, 300–301, 303, 419–426. *See also* Technology
Confidence, 104–105
Consultants:
  communicating with, 413–414
  consultant specialists, 16
  investment professional relationships with, 16, 20–21, 223–225, 337–339
  marketing to, 223–225
  plan sponsors using, 229, 234, 246–247, 250, 252, 261
  proliferation of, 20–21
  role of, 223–224
  style boxes of, 112, 337–339
  as trustee advisers, 186–187, 188
Continuous Linked Settlement (CLS) system, 318
Corinthian Colleges, Inc., 310, 314n9
Corporate governance, 8, 54–56, 203–207
Costs. *See also* Prices
  agency, 46, 48
  awareness of, 8
  of consultants, 188
  of ESG funds, 209–210
  operational, 321, 326–327
  opportunity, 268–269
  research, 209–210
  returns impacted by, 196–197, 306
  trading, 291, 295–296, 299n1, 304–306
  transition, 230–231, 269
Counterparty risk, 317–318
Credentials, 63–64
Crisis management, 394
Cross-currency settlement risk, 317–318
Crovitz, L. Gordon, 302
Culture:
  aggressive, 406
  belief systems and, 335, 336, 339, 340, 346, 348n2
  collaborative, 407–408
  communicating, 398–399, 406–408

Culture: (*Continued*)
  competitive, 407
  ethics and, 358–360
  fear-based, 406
  leadership driving, 358–360, 372–373
  receptive, 406–407
  staff reflecting, 386–390, 392–393
  world-class, 407–408
Currencies, 317–318

Dark pools, 290–291, 308, 309–310
Data. *See* Information
Databases, 235–238
Data management, 416–426
DeBondt, William, 132
Decision making:
  behavior patterns in, 81–93, 103, 131–133, 177–178
  belief systems impacting, 333–348
  ethics impacting, 352–367
  factors influencing, 34–38, 100–107
  failure of invariance in, 86–89, 195–196
  inverted reasoning in, 95–99
  in normal (non-crisis) times, 29–31
  quantitative *vs.* fundamental analysis in, 121–128, 163
  rationality of, 81–93, 100–107
  role of prices in, 282–285
  skill reflected in (*see* Skills)
  staff authorization for, 393
  staff characteristics impacting, 380–385
  Taleb's Black Swan method of, 31–33, 41, 45, 135–136
  under uncertainty, 46, 48, 51–55, 81–93
  unpredictability of, 176–178
  weaknesses in, 54–55
Defined-benefit plans, 3–6, 54, 216, 232
Defined-contribution plans, 3–6, 54, 55, 216, 232
Del Guercio, Diane, 228, 263
de Moivre, Abraham, 92

Demon of Our Own Design, A (Bookstaber), 108, 298
Demutualization, 294–295
Department of Labor, U.S., 5, 186
Derivatives strategies, 204
Dethmer, Jim, 403
Dimson, Elroy, 36, 134
Disclosure, 164, 166. *See also* Transparency
Discolor, Robert, 10
Discontinuities:
  decision making in normal times *vs.* during, 29–31
  factors influencing to, 33–38
  frequency of, 27–29
  methods of addressing, 38–42
  sources of, 29
  Taleb's Black swans as, 31–33, 41, 45, 135–136
Disposition effect, 132
Distribution (of services), 21–22
Distribution (statistical):
  probability, 32–34, 241–247, 255–261
  of selection decisions, 241–247
  of termination decisions, 255–261
  of winners and losers, 49, 56
Dow, Charles, 159
Dow Jones News Service, 282
Dow theory, 159
DTCC, 318, 320
Dwoskin, Hale, 366

Economy:
  discontinuities in, 27–42, 45, 135–136
  emerging, 317–320
  financial crises in (*see* Financial crises)
  politics impacting, 29, 41–42
Education, 8–12, 41, 63–64, 387, 394–395
Efficient market hypothesis/theory, 121–122, 129–137, 156–159, 171–176, 178–179, 344
Einstein, Albert, 50

Electrical Numerical Integrator and
    Calculator (ENIAC), 120
Eley, Randall R., 148
Ellison, Glen, 263
Ellsberg, Daniel, 90
Elton, Edwin, 240
E-mail, 412–413
Emerging economies, 317–320
Emerson, Ralph Waldo, 38
Emotional intelligence, 364–365
Employee Retirement Security Income
    Act (ERISA), 166, 186
Endogenous risk, 108, 110
Endowments, 5–6, 162–163, 185–186,
    202, 233, 241–242
Energetic integrity, 364–366
ENIAC (Electrical Numerical Integrator
    and Calculator), 120
Enneagram personality system, 404
Ennis Knupp + Associates, 218–219, 224
Enterprise data management, 420–426
Environmental, social and governance
    (ESG) investing:
    activism impacting, 203–210
    competitive advantage from, 7
    corporate governance and, 203–207
    demand for, 201–202
    intangible valuations of, 212
    proxy access in, 210–211
ERISA (Employee Retirement Security
    Income Act), 166, 186
Ethics:
    challenges to, 352–354
    context of, 354–356
    definition of, 354–355
    energetic integrity and, 364–366
    guiding principles of, 360–361
    in investment firms, 356–357
    leadership based on, 358–360
    peaceful state of mind and, 366–367
    process for resolving ethical
        dilemmas, 362–364
    right-*versus*-right paradigms in,
        361–362
Euroclear, 318, 324–326

European Central Bank, 324, 325
European Community, 322–326
Excess returns:
    expected *vs.* required, 54
    measuring, 47
    selection/termination of investment
        professionals reflecting, 226–227,
        229–230, 239–241, 247–254,
        261–265, 267–271
Exuberance, 35–37

Fabozzi, Frank, 228, 231
Fads and fashions, 111–116
Failure of invariance, 86–89, 195–196
Fama, Eugene, 121, 156, 251
FCM Matrix for Success, 387–393
Fear-based culture, 406
Federal Reserve Bank, 50, 176
Federspiel, Fred, 307
Feedback, 178, 365–366, 370–372, 378,
    402–403, 410
Fees. *See* Costs
Ferson, Wayne, 228
FFS (Foundation for Fiduciary Studies),
    188–189
Fiduciary duty, 69–70, 72–73, 74,
    165–166, 208, 216
Financial Accounting Standards Board,
    205–206
Financial crises:
    bubbles and panics in, 174–175
    discontinuities and, 27–42, 45,
        135–136
    methods of preventing, 47–56
    recession as, 176
    sub-prime crisis as, 44–56, 59–60,
        248
Financial Insights, 426
Financial Planning Association, 65
Financial Services Action Plan (FSAP),
    323, 325
Financial Services Institute, 66
FINRA (Financial Industry Regulatory
    Authority), 59, 74–75, 290
Fisher, David, 373, 400

Ford, Kris, 413–414
Forecasting, 103–104
Foreign exchange transactions, 317–318
Foundation for Fiduciary Studies (FFS),
    188–189
Foundations, 5–6, 162–163, 185–186,
    233, 241–242
    401(k) plans, 4, 216–217, 223
Fox, Craig, 90–91
Fragmentation, 293, 295, 318–319,
    326–327
Frank Russell Company, 223
Franzoni, Francesco, 236, 242
French, Kenneth, 241, 251
Friedman, Thomas, 304
FSAP (Financial Services Action Plan),
    323, 325
Fundamental analysis, 121–128, 163

Gallo, J. G., 263
Galton, Francis, 82, 92
Gandhi, Mohandas (Mahatma), 302
Gilbert, Daniel T., 132
Gilovich, T., 180
Giovannini report (Alberto Giovannini),
    323, 325, 330n5
Glassman, Debra, 228
Global Investment Performance
    Standards, 139
Globalization, 12–13, 316–320
Goetzmann, W. N., 161
Goleman, Daniel, 364, 404
Goyal, Amit, 228
Gracie, Carlos, 108–109
Gracie, Gastao, 108
Gracie, Helio, 108–109
Gracie, Renzo, 109
Gracie, Rorion, 109
Gracie, Royce, 109
Graham, Benjamin, 121
Gruber, Martin, 240

Hamilton, William Peter, 159
Hanachi, Shervin, 147
Hansell, Saul, 37

Harlow, W. V., 263
Hart, Oliver, 229, 232, 254, 270
HBSA (holdings-based style analysis),
    142–144
Headline risk, 241–242, 246–247,
    252, 261
Hedge funds:
    challenges of, 114
    diversification through, 155, 163–164
    growth of, 10
    investment strategies involving, 111,
        114–115
    investor skill in, 172
    risk associated with, 155, 163–165,
        166, 167–168
    sell-side block traders as, 297, 298
Heisler, Jeffrey, 228
Herding, 47, 54
Herstatt risk, 318
Hewitt Associates, 217
Hewlett-Packard, 3–4
Hindsight biases, 135–136
Hiring practices, 234–235, 346. *See also*
    Selection of investment
    professionals
Historical data, 127, 174, 179,
    197–198
Hobson, Mellody, 403, 409, 411–412
Hogan Personality Assessment, 395
Holdings-based style analysis (HBSA),
    142–144
Hot hand phenomenon, 180
Hubris, 36
Hunt, Jon, 401–402, 405, 412

IBM, 3
iisearches, 234, 235–236
Incentive compensation, 47, 49, 139,
    149–152
Independence, 67
Index funds, 112–113, 141–143
Individual retirement accounts (IRAs),
    3–5
Information:
    databases of, 235–238

historical, 127, 174, 179, 197–198
information-based communication, 409
latency of, 285–286, 296, 302–303
management of, 416–426
operational models impacting access to, 329
overload, 34–35, 102–103, 122, 127
on plan sponsors, 236–237
price reflecting, 121–122, 129–137, 156–159, 171–176, 178–179, 344
selection/termination data analysis of, 235–241, 255
trader access to and processing of, 307–310, 313
Institutionalization, 112, 215–218
Insurance, portfolio, 168
Intangibles, 212
Integrity, 354–355, 356–357, 364–366. *See also* Ethics
Integrity Research Associates, 209
Interest rates, 47
Intuition, 381, 383
Invariance, failure of, 86–89, 195–196
Inverted efficient market theory, 136–137, 344
Inverted reasoning, 95–99
Investment Adviser Association, 65, 70, 74
Investment Advisers Act, 60, 64, 69, 71–75
Investment belief systems. *See* Beliefs/belief systems
Investment Company Institute, 65
Investment consultants. *See* Consultants
Investment funds. *See specific types of investment funds by name*
Investment philosophy, 218. *See also* Theories
Investment plans. *See also specific types of investment plans by name*
globalization impacting, 12–13
institutionalization of, 112, 215–218
investor skill impacting, 9–12, 133, 171–181

restructuring of, 3–9
Investment professionals/firms:
academics as, 156–158
active management by, 111, 114–115, 141–142, 171, 173
adaptive leadership of, 369–378
associations/organizations representing, 65–67, 70, 74
belief systems of, 333–348
business leadership of, 14
causes of irrational behavior by, 100–107
client service of, 14–15, 222–223, 413–414
communication by (*see* Communication)
compensation of, 47, 49, 139, 149–152
compliance of, 15, 203, 418–419
consultant relationships with, 16, 20–21, 223–225, 337–339
core characteristics/values of, 68–70
corporate governance of, 8, 54–56, 203–207
credentials of, 63–64
culture of (*see* Culture)
data management by, 416–426
decision making by (*see* Decision making)
distribution opportunities for, 21–22
diversity of, 61–62
ethics of, 352–367
fads and fashions of, 111–116
fiduciary duty of, 69–70, 72–73, 74, 165–166, 208, 216
hiring practices of, 234–235, 346 (*see also* Selection of investment professionals)
independence/self-reliance of, 67
industry size of, 61
inverted reasoning of, 95–99
investment philosophy of, 218 (*see also* Theories)
leadership in, 14, 189–194, 204–205, 352–367, 369–378, 379–396, 398–401

Investment professionals/firms:
(*Continued*)
marketing of (*see* Marketing)
measures of success for, 221–223
operations and administration of,
17–18, 315–316 (*see also*
Settlement functions)
organizational stability of, 222
overlapping roles of, 310–311
performance of (*see* Performance/
performance attribution)
publicity aversion of, 68
quantitative analysis by, 41, 119–128,
155–156, 163
regulation of, 58–60, 70–77 (*see also*
Investment Advisers Act)
regulatory involvement of, 68,
76–77
relationship building by, 214–215,
295–296, 401–402, 415
responsibility of, 150, 355, 365
sales management by, 15–16
selection of, 226–231, 234–255,
265–270, 346, 379–396
self-awareness of, 340, 362–363, 365,
384, 404
self-evaluation of, 345–346
sell-side challenges of, 294–299
size of, 295–296
skill of (*see* Performance/performance
attribution; Skills)
solidarity of (*see* Solidarity)
specialization of, 13–18
staffing challenges in, 379–396
style analysis of, 138–139, 140–143,
146–149, 247–250, 337–339
style drift of, 116
technology impacting (*see*
Technology)
termination of, 226–231, 234–235,
255–270
terminology describing, 62–64
trading by (*see* Trading)
as trustee advisers, 186–188
Investment theories. *See* Theories

Investors:
behavior of (*see* Behavior)
collective action by, 46, 49,
51, 56
decision making by (*see* Decision
making)
loss aversion of, 85, 87, 103,
131–132, 161
regulations protecting (*see*
Regulation)
skills of, 9–12, 133, 171–181
(*see also* Performance/performance
attribution)
technology impacting (*see*
Technology)
IRAs (individual retirement accounts),
3–5
Irrational exuberance, 35–36
Ivkovic, Zoran, 155

J. P. Morgan Chase, 298
Janus, 358
Jaynes, E. T., 179
Jegadeesh, Narasimhan, 240, 248, 251,
262, 264
Jennings, Marianne, 361–362
Justice Department, U.S., 294

Kahneman, Daniel, 82–93, 131–132
Karceski, Jason, 240, 248, 251, 262,
264
Keith, Chris, 37
Keynes, John Maynard, 175
Khandani, Amir E., 134
Kidder, Rushworth, 355, 360–361
Kiel, Fred, 354, 366

Lakonishok, Josef, 132, 156, 227, 229,
231, 232, 247, 270
Lanier, Jason, 39–40
Lapid-Bogda, Ginger, 402
Latency, 285–286, 296, 302–303
Laws of probability, 102
LDI (liability-driven investments), 11,
115, 335–336, 349n5

Leadership:
  adaptive, 369–378
  business, 14
  communication by, 398–401
  ethical, 352–367
  staffing challenges of, 379–396
  of trustees, 189–194, 204–205
Lease, Ronald, 241
Leeson, Nick, 37
Lehman Brothers, 1
Leibowitz, Martin, 34
Lennick, Doug, 354, 366
Lettau, Martin, 155
Leverage, 110
Levitt, Arthur, 71
Liability-driven investments (LDI), 11,
  115, 335–336, 349n5
Liability-hedging portfolios, 53
Lifestyle/lifecycle funds, 5
Liquidity, 110, 301–302, 308–310
Liquidity risk, 40, 134, 164
Listening, 402–403. *See also* Openness
Little-Gill, Gavin, 301
Lo, Andrew W., 130–131, 132, 134,
  160
Lockheed-Martin, 3–4
Lockwood, Larry, 263
Logue, Dennis E., 231
Long Term Capital Management,
  123–124, 156
Loss aversion, 85, 87, 103, 131–132,
  161
Lowenstein, Roger, 156
Luck, 135–136, 138, 179, 180
Ludvigson, Sydney, 155

Mackell, Thomas, *When Good Pensions
  Go Away,* 8
Madalla, G. S., 249
Madoff, Bernard, 1, 15, 59, 74
Maeda, Mitsuyo, 108
Mahathir bin Mohamad, 165
Mahoney, Tim, 310
Malkiel, Burton, 157, 201
Managed Funds Association, 65

Management:
  active, 111, 114–115, 141–142, 171,
    173
  asset, 283–284
  of belief systems, 339–342
  crisis, 394
  data, 416–426
  leadership providing (*see* Leadership;
    Trustees)
  risk (*see* Risk management)
  sales, 15–16
Managers, investment. *See* Investment
  professionals/firms
Marín, Jose M., 236, 242
Marked-to-matrix prices, 289
Marked-to-model prices, 288–289
Marketing:
  challenges of, 213–214
  communication as key to, 13, 16–17,
    214–215, 218, 220–221
  to consultants, 223–225
  elements of effective campaign, 217
  ethical considerations of, 353
  globalization impacting, 13
  identifying strengths in, 218–220
  of improbable products, 197–198
  institutionalization of retail sales
    impacting, 215–218
  investment professionals providing,
    16–17
  measures of success promoted
    through, 221–223
  multi-year campaigns, 217–218
  outsourcing, 215
  relationship building as, 214–215
Markets:
  bull, 112–113
  contrariness of, 96–99
  creation of, 282–283, 296
  discontinuities in (*see* Discontinuities)
  efficient, 121–122, 129–137,
    156–159, 171–176, 178–179,
    344
  endogenous risks of, 108, 110
  European, 322–326

Markets: (*Continued*)
 fragmentation of, 293, 295, 318–319,
  326–327
 globalization of, 12–13, 316–320
 institutional, 232–233
 market color, 308–310
 role of prices in, 282–285
 trading in (*see* Trading)
 unpredictability of, 174–176
 volatility of, 164–165, 321–322
Markets in Financial Instruments
  Directive, The (MiFID), 323,
  325, 418
Markowitz, Harry, 121, 133
Marks, Howard, 40
Mark-to-market prices, 287–288
Martin, William McChesney, 50
Maslow, Abraham, 371
McKenzie, Obie, 214
Media, 414–415
Meditation, 366–367
Mencken, H. L., 29
Mental accounting, 87–88
Mercer Investment Consulting, 234,
  235, 237–238
Merger and acquisition strategies, 206
Merrill Lynch, 1
Merton, Robert, 122, 133
Messaging, 408–411
MiFID (Markets in Financial
  Instruments Directive, The), 323,
  325, 418
Miller, Edward, 86
Modern Portfolio Theory, 140
*Money Market Directory of Investment
  Managers and Plan Sponsors*, 236,
  238
Monte Carlo simulations, 149, 150–152
Moore, Gordon, 120–121
Moral courage, 366–367
Morgenstern, Oskar, 86, 92
Morningstar, 143
Motivational communication, 410–411
Multicollinearity, 142–143
Munger, Charlie, 375

Myers-Briggs Type Indicator, 404

Narrow framing, 131–132
National Association of Personal
  Financial Planners, 66
National Association of Securities
  Dealers (NASD), 294
National Australia Bank, 162
Negative feedback loops, 178
Nelson's Directories, 234, 236, 237,
  238, 269
Network for Sustainable Financial
  Markets, 56
Newey, Whitney, 271
News, 99, 414–415
New York Stock Exchange, 286, 300,
  307, 321, 419
Normal portfolios, 141, 142

Occam's Razor, 102
Odean, Terrance, 132
Openness, 375–376, 402–403, 405–408
Operational costs, 321, 326–327
Operational models, 327–329
Operational risk, 164, 166
Operations, 17–18, 315–316. *See also*
  Settlement functions
Opportunity costs, 268–269
Organizational stability, 222
Outperformance, 195–200
Outsourcing, 9, 20, 215, 322, 328
Overconfidence, 104
Overexuberance, 36–37

PAICR (Professional Association for
  Investment Communications
  Resources), 17
Panics, 174–175
Peer groups, 150, 152
Pension Benefit Guarantee Corporation,
  U.S., 163, 232–233
Pension funds. *See* Retirement funds
Pension Protection Act, 5, 186
Pensions and Investments, 235, 236,
  237

Penzias, Arno, 158
Performance/performance attribution:
  accurate benchmarking for, 140–144
  behavior impacting, 100–101,
    106–107
  challenges of, 138–140
  evolution in, 144–149
  for incentive compensation, 47, 49,
    139, 149–152
  measures of success, 221–223
  outperformance myths and, 195–200
  plan sponsor selection/termination
    impacted by, 234, 239–241,
    247–254, 261–265, 267–270
  returns reflecting, 150, 195–200
  self-evaluation of, 345–346
  skill vs., 133, 179–181
Personal biases, 133
Personnel. See Staff
Picasso, Pablo, 119
Picerno, James, 143
Plan sponsors:
  asset allocation for, 237, 243–246
  consultant use by, 229, 234, 246–247,
    250, 252, 261
  data analysis by, 235–241, 255
  distribution of hiring/firing decisions
    by, 241–247, 255–261
  headline risk of, 241–242, 246–247,
    252, 261
  information on, 236–237
  investment mandates and indices for,
    272–273
  investment process of, 231–235
  liability-driven investments by, 336
  post-hiring performance analysis by,
    250–254
  pre- and post-firing performance
    analysis by, 261–265
  pre-hiring performance analysis by,
    247–250
  reasons for termination by, 255–261
  role of, 226–228
  selection of investment managers by,
    228–231, 234–255, 265–270
  termination of investment managers
    by, 228–231, 234–235, 255–270
Politics, 29, 41–42, 241–242
Ponzi scheme, 15, 59. See also Madoff,
    Bernard
Portable alpha, 113–114
Porter, Michael, 341
Portfolios:
  bond, 114
  ESG-constructed, 208–209
  liability-hedging, 53
  normal, 141, 142
  portfolio insurance, 168
  portfolio simulations on, 149,
    150–152
  quantitative vs. fundamental
    construction of, 126
  returns on, 306
  risk-optimizing, 53
  synthetic, 113
  valuation of, 283
Predictability:
  barriers to, 46
  of black swans, 31, 45, 135–136
  efficient market hypothesis impacted
    by unpredictable events, 134,
    135–136, 174–176
  of investor behavior, 176–178
  of market changes, 174
  random walk vs., 175–176
  of sub-prime crisis, 44–47
Prentice, Robert, 358, 359, 364
Prices:
  attributes of, 285–287
  determination of, 287–289
  information reflected in, 121–122,
    129–137, 156–159, 171–176,
    178–179, 344
  marked-to-matrix, 289
  marked-to-model, 288–289
  mark-to-market, 287–288
  price transparency of, 283, 290–291,
    307–308, 324
  reporting, 290–291
  role of, 282–285

Prince, Charles, 30–31, 36, 44
Princeton endowment, 202
Principles for Responsible Investment
(PRI), 7, 56
Probability, 32–34, 102, 241–247,
255–261. *See also* Statistical
analysis
Procedural prudence, 186, 202
Professional Association for Investment
Communications Resources
(PAICR), 17
Professional organizations, 65–67, 70,
74. *See also specific organizations
by name*
Prospect Theory, 82–93, 131
Proszek, Stan, 230
Proxy access, 210–211
Prudent Investor Law, 166
Psychology of the Stock Market, The
(Seldon), 95
Public opinion, 95–99
Public plans, 5, 55, 232, 237, 241–246
Purchasing boycotts, 208
Putnam, 358

Qualified default investment alternatives
(QDIAs), 5
Quandt, Richard, 157
Quantitative analysis/investing, 41,
119–128, 155–156, 163

Rader, Jack S., 231
Rahman, Shafiqur, 228
Rajan, Raghuram, 44, 46–47, 50
Random walk, 175–176
Rappaport, Alfred, 343
Raptures, self-delusional, 37
Rationality:
of behavior, 100–107
bounded, 34–35, 102–103, 133
of decision making, 81–93, 100–107
RBSA (returns-based style analysis),
142–144
Receptive culture, 406–407
Recession, 176. *See also* Financial crises

Redelmeier, Donald, 89, 90
Regression analysis, 142–143, 148–149,
249–250, 252–254
Regression to the mean, 82–83, 92
Regulation:
of broker-dealers, 59–60, 72–75
compliance with, 15, 203, 418–419
on corporate governance, 203–204
data management challenges from,
418–419
in emerging economies, 318
in European Community, 322–326
of investment advisers, 58–60, 70–77
(*see also* Investment Advisers Act)
of past performance figures, 197–198
Reg NMS, 295–296, 418
of retirement funds, 166, 186
solidarity of investment profession
regarding (*see* Solidarity)
sub-prime crisis prompting changes
in, 59–60, 298
of trustees, 186
Relationship building, 214–215,
295–296, 401–402, 415
Reporters, 414–415
Research costs, 209–210
Responsibility, 150, 355, 365
Retirement funds:
agency issues in, 55
alternative investments by, 163
collective action by, 51
consultant role in, 223
decision making under uncertainty by,
51–55
fluctuations in, 1–2
marketing to, 216–217
outsourcing management of, 9
plan sponsors of (*see* Plan sponsors)
redistribution of, 3–9
regulation of, 166, 186
risk management by, 53–54
trustees of (*see* Trustees)
Returns:
costs impacting, 196–197, 306
databases on, 237–238

excess, 47, 54, 226–227, 229–230,
  239–241, 247–250, 261–265,
  267–271
as performance measurement, 150,
  195–200
portfolio, 306
risk-adjusted, 121–123
risk-reward ratio of, 173–174
Returns-based style analysis (RBSA),
  142–144
Risk:
concealing, 37–38, 47
counterparty, 317–318
cross-currency settlement, 317–318
efficient market hypothesis impacted
  by, 134
endogenous, of markets, 108, 110
factors influencing, 34–38
headline, 241–242, 246–247, 252,
  261
hedge funds and, 155, 163–165, 166,
  167–168
Herstatt, 318
identifying, 32
liquidity, 40, 134, 164
operational, 164, 166
prices impacting, 285
probability distribution of, 32–34
quantitative analysis of, 121–123
research on, 154–155
returns and, 121–123, 173–174
staff handling of, 383
systemic, 163–164
tail, 168
tolerance for, 54
understanding, 39
Risk-adjusted returns, 121–123
Risk management:
behavior patterns in, 82–93, 103,
  131–132
conflict with management supervision, 161–162
data management challenges of, 418
failure of invariance in, 86–89,
  195–196

hedge funds as tool in, 155, 163–164
manipulation of systems measuring,
  37–38
prices impacting, 285
by retirement funds, 53–54
shareholder activism impacting, 8
sub-prime crisis impacted by, 47–48
RiskMetrics Group, 8
Risk-optimizing portfolios, 53
Rogers, John, 412
Rogers, Will, 58
Roh, Richard, 156
Ross, Stephen, 156, 160
Roth, Alvin, 92
Rothschild, Nathan, 302
Rotman International Centre for
  Pension Management, 56
Rubinow, Steve, 285–286
Russell Investment Group, 11

Sales management, 15–16
Sarbanes-Oxley Act, 203
Schapiro, Mary, 59
Scholes, Myron, 122, 133, 134
Schwed, Fred, 36, 121
Securities:
bonds as, 114, 290
prices of (*see* Prices)
trading of (*see* Trading)
Securities and Exchange Commission
  (SEC):
antitrust investigations by, 294
on audit committees, 204
on broker-dealer regulations, 73–74
on chief compliance officers, 15
on hedge fund disclosure, 164, 166
on investment adviser regulations,
  59–60, 71
on past performance figures, 197
Securities Exchange Act, 72
Securities Industry and Financial
  Markets Association, 65
Seitz, Michelle, 403, 405, 412
Seldon, G. C., *The Psychology of the
  Stock Market*, 95

Selection of investment professionals:
  data analysis for, 235–241
  hiring practices for, 234–235, 346
  post-hiring performance analysis in,
    250–254
  pre-hiring performance analysis in,
    247–250
  research on, 226–231
  round-trip, 265–270
  sample distribution in, 241–247
  staffing challenges in, 379–396
Self-awareness, 340, 362–363, 365,
  384, 404
Self-delusional raptures, 37
Self-evaluation, 345–346
Self-reliance, 67
Settlement functions:
  challenges of, 315–329
  competition and fragmentation
    impacting, 326–327
  European regulation impacting,
    322–326
  globalization impacting, 316–320
  operational models of, 327–329
  volume and volatility impacting,
    320–322
Shafir, Edlar, 89
Shareholder activism, 8, 203–207
Sharpe, William (Bill), 39, 121, 133,
  142–143
Sharpe ratios, 167–168
Shaw, George Bernard, 398
Shefrin, Hersh, 132
Shleifer, Andrei, 227, 229, 247
Signons, Jim, 157
Silos, 54–55, 421
Simon, Herbert, 34, 102, 133
Simons, Jim, 156
Simulations, Monte Carlo, 149, 150–152
Skills:
  communication, 401–405
  elusiveness of, 171–181
  investor, 9–12, 133, 171–181
  marketing, 218–220
  matrix identifying necessary, 387–393

measurement of (*see* Performance/
  performance attribution)
performance *vs.*, 133, 179–181
self-actualization of, 377
Smith, Clifford, 241
Social activism, 207–210
Social awareness, 404
Socially responsible investing. *See*
  Environmental, social and
  governance (ESG) investing
Solidarity:
  challenges to, 61–68
  core characteristics/values impacting,
    68–70
  reasons for, 69, 70–72, 75–77
  regulatory changes necessitating,
    58–60, 70–77
Soros, George, 164–165, 173, 174
Sovereign wealth funds, 5, 12
Speculative trading, 284
Staff. *See also* Investment professionals/
  firms
  characteristics of successful, 380–385
  coaching, 387, 394–395
  communicating with, 398–401
  corporate culture impacting, 386–390
  crisis consequences in, 391–392
  crisis management by, 394
  employment strategy for, 385–386
  hiring practices for, 234–235, 346
  (*see also* Selection of investment
    professionals)
  importance of skilled, 379–380
  investment process of, 393–394
  matrix for identifying needed,
    387–393
Starks, Laura, 263
State Street Global Advisors, 234
Statistical analysis:
  discontinuity impact on, 30
  probability distribution in, 32–34,
    241–247, 255–261
  regression analysis as, 142–143,
    148–149, 249–250, 252–254
  regression to the mean in, 82–83, 92

of risk management, 37–38
of selection decisions, 241–254, 265–271
standard error calculations in, 270–271
style analysis using, 142–143, 148–149, 247–250
Taleb's Black Swan approach to, 32–33
of termination decisions, 255–271
Statman, Meir, 132
Stein, Herb, 113
Stock exchanges, 293–297, 300–301, 311. *See also* New York Stock Exchange
Stock options, 205–206
Street-smart *vs.* book-smart, 157–158
Style analysis/effect, 138–139, 140–144, 146–149, 247–250, 337–339
Style boxes, 112, 139, 337–339
Style drift, 116
Style palette, 142–144
Sub-prime crisis:
    barriers to preventing, 46
    methods of preventing, 47–56
    predictability of, 44–47
    regulatory changes as response to, 59–60, 298
Surowiecki, James, 35
Survivorship biases, 148, 238
Surz, 143
Surz, Ronald J., 147
Sustainable investing. *See* Environmental, social and governance (ESG) investing
Swensen, David, 162
Synthetic portfolios, 113
Systemic risk, 163–164

T2S (Target 2 for Securities) initiative, 324–325
Tail risk, 168
Taleb, Nassim Nicholas:
    Black Swans of, 31–33, 41, 45, 135–136

on luck, 135–136
on probability distributions, 32–34
Target-date funds, 5
Target-risk funds, 5
Taxes, 166
Teamwork, 392–393
Technology:
    advances in, 18–19, 119
    algorithmic trading using, 282, 292–293, 295–296, 320–321
    data management impacted by, 419–426
    future investing altered by, 166–167, 300–301, 311–313
    investment in, 321
    operational models of, 327–329
    performance attribution using, 144
    quantitative investing using, 119–128
    relationship building using, 214
    speed of, 285–286, 300–301, 303
    trading volume impacted by, 282
Termination of investment professionals:
    data analysis for, 235–241
    firing process, 234–235
    pre- and post-firing performance, 261–265
    reasons for, 255–261
    research on, 226–231
    round-trip, 265–270
Thaler, Richard, 86, 88, 91–92, 132
Theories:
    adaptive market hypothesis, 132–133, 160
    Arbitrage Pricing Theory, 140
    belief system refined using, 341–342, 347
    Dow theory, 159
    efficient market theory, 121–122, 129–137, 156–159, 171–176, 178–179, 344
    Modern Portfolio Theory, 140
    Prospect Theory, 82–93, 131
    "Thrive and survive" strategy, 38–41
Time delays. *See* Latency

Time-zone differences, 317
Tkac, Paula, 228, 263
Tower Group, The, 426
Townsend Company, The, 224
Tracker database, 235–236
Tractability, 134
Trade Reporting and Compliance
    Engine (TRACE), 290
Trading:
    algorithmic, 282, 292–293, 295–296,
        320–321
    alternative trading systems, 326
    challenges of, 294–313, 315–329
    costs, 291, 295–296, 299n1, 304–306
    desks, future, 311–312
    information access and processing in,
        307–310, 313
    market color impacting, 308–310
    overlapping roles in, 310–311
    sell-side challenges of, 294–299
    settlement challenges of, 315–329
    speculative, 284
    speed of, 285–286, 300–304
    volume, 281–282, 320–322
Transition costs, 230–231, 269
Transparency:
    downside of, 307–308
    European regulation on, 323–324
    hedge fund disclosure providing, 164,
        166
    price, 283, 290–291, 307–308, 324
Travers, Frank J., 231, 234
Treasury Department, U.S., 60, 72–74
Trends, 175–176
Triguboff, Michael, 157
Trilling, Lionel, 138
Trust, 313, 374–376, 404–405
Trustees:
    headline risk of, 241–242
    investment professionals as advisers
        to, 186–188
    leadership of, 189–194, 204–205
    plan sponsors as (see Plan sponsors)
    procedural prudence of, 186, 202
    proxy access impacting, 210–211
    qualifications of, 204–205
    regulation of, 186
    role of, 185–186
Tversky, Amos, 82–93, 131–132,
    180

Uncertainty, 46, 48, 51–55, 81–93.
    See also Predictability
Union plans, 5, 232, 241–242, 243–244,
    246
Unpredictability. See Predictability
U.S. Departments. See specific
    departments by name
    (e.g., Treasury Department)
U.S. Pension Benefit Guarantee
    Corporation, 163, 232–233

Vallone, R., 180
Valuation, 212, 283. See also Prices
Values, 68–70. See also Ethics
Vanguard, 358
Verizon Communications, 3–4
Vishny, Robert, 227, 229
Volatility, 164–165, 321–322
Volume, trading, 281–282, 320–322
von Neumann, John, 86, 87, 92

Wahal, Sunil, 228
Walter, Elisse, 59
Ware, Jim, 406
Watkins, Michael, 45–46, 48–49, 50
Website effectiveness, 19
Werner, Bob, 230
West, Kenneth, 271
When Good Pensions Go Away
    (Mackell), 8
Wilber, Ken, 355–356
Willful blindness, 37–38
World-class culture, 407–408

Yale endowment, 162–163

Lightning Source UK Ltd.
Milton Keynes UK
UKOW04n1558130715

255097UK00001B/35/P